Adobe®
Analytics

by Eric Matisoff and David Karlins

for
dummies®
A Wiley Brand

Adobe® Analytics For Dummies®

Published by: **John Wiley & Sons, Inc.,** 111 River Street, Hoboken, NJ 07030-5774, www.wiley.com

Copyright © 2019 by John Wiley & Sons, Inc., Hoboken, New Jersey

Published simultaneously in Canada

Contents at a Glance

Table of Contents

Introduction

Adobe Analytics For Dummies is a comprehensive survey of creating and managing analysis projects with Adobe Analytics. We've endeavored to make the bulk of the content accessible to those of you new to Adobe Analytics, while providing plenty of depth and substance to carry data analysts through advanced and complex challenges. We had a blast writing this book, and appreciate your coming along with us on a journey of discovery to wield the state-of-the-art application for data analytics.

About This Book

Adobe Analytics For Dummies provides an in-depth exploration of how to use Adobe Analytics. As an analyst, you face unique challenges analyzing and leveraging data from users who engage your company's or institution's web presence. With that in mind, throughout this book we show you how to accomplish essential and complex tasks, and we bring these processes to life by using a range of real-life examples. We've also drawn on experiences in the trenches to share globally applicable tips and techniques that you can use throughout Adobe Analytics — especially in Analysis Workspace, Adobe's most-used analytics product.

In organizing and presenting the material, we embrace and adhere to the easy-to-access structure of Dummies books: Although you can read the chapters sequentially, they also stand alone as explorations of specific functionalities in Adobe Analytics.

Here are some conventions we use throughout the book:

>> Text that you're meant to type just as it appears in the book is **bold**.

>> There is little coding in this book, but where appropriate, web addresses and programming code appear in monofont. If you're reading a digital version of this book on a device connected to the Internet, note that you can click web addresses to visit websites, like this: www.dummies.com.

>> As you're familiar with in other Dummies books, we use the command arrow to identify sequential steps. For example, to share a file, choose Share ➪ Send File Now.

Foolish Assumptions

This book aims to fill the needs of two audiences (and those of you who fall in between). One audience consists of folks who are new to Adobe Analytics and have only some acquaintance working with data in general. The second audience consists of people who have substantial expertise in data analysis but are adopting or transitioning to Adobe Analytics (including from Google Analytics). This book combines specific techniques to take advantage of the full power of Adobe Analytics, with frequent excursions into *why* you would want to use the rich toolset you get with this industry-leading application.

Other than that, we have no assumptions. Come as you are. Welcome. And get ready to discover how to wield Adobe Analytics to enhance the success rate of your enterprise, whatever it is.

Icons Used in This Book

If you've read other *For Dummies* books, you might have noted that they use icons in the margin to call attention to particularly important or useful ideas in the text. In this book, we use four such icons.

The Tip icon marks tips (duh!) and shortcuts that you can use to make working with Adobe Analytics easier.

Remember icons mark information that's especially important to know. To siphon off the most important information in each chapter, just skim through these icons.

The Technical Stuff icon marks information of a highly technical nature that you can normally skip over.

The Warning icon tells you to watch out! It marks important information that may save you headaches and avoid potentially costly mistakes.

Beyond the Book

Throughout this book, we provide links to detailed reference material from Adobe (and in some cases other sources) that will support your Adobe Analytics journey.

In addition, we have two handy cheat sheet articles that will help you instantly get more value from Adobe Analytics. The topics focus on getting around Analysis Workspace and building two useful calculated metrics. To get to the cheat sheet, go to www.dummies.com/cheatsheet/adobeanalyticsfd. Or go to www.dummies.com and type **Adobe Analytics For Dummies cheat sheet** in the search bar.

Where to Go from Here

This book isn't linear. That is to say, you can flip to the material you need, get help with any particular aspect of Adobe Analytics, and come back for more when you're ready. That said, if you're new to Adobe Analytics, we suggest starting with Part 1 for a basic foundational introduction.

1

Getting Started with Adobe Analytics

Chapter **1**

Why Adobe Analytics?

I n this chapter, you begin your journey into analytics powered by Adobe. In the remainder of this book, we dive deeply into specific features of Adobe Analytics, enabling you to perform in minutes analyses that would take days with other tools. But here at the beginning, it's important to be able to identify *why* you're analyzing data as well as how the data is populated and configured.

Adobe Analytics has been a premier web, mobile, and customer-focused analysis tool for well over a decade. If you're new to Adobe Analytics or reading this book to beef up your ability to wield this powerful set of tools, experience with similar tools, such as Google Analytics, Webtrends, or Microsoft Excel, is valuable. But whether you're reading this with substantial background in data analytics or the concept is new to you — or anywhere in between — we first pull the lens back to understand the history of web data so you can better understand the role it plays today.

In this chapter, we give you a chance to expand your horizons in terms of how you think about why you're analyzing data using Adobe in the first place. Next, we answer that age-old question: "Where does my data come from?" That is, we dig into how data gets pushed onto the Adobe platform. Finally, we present an overview of what's involved in sifting and squeezing valuable insights out of all the data you have access to in Adobe Analytics. So, buckle up your seat belts and let's begin!

Understanding Why You're Using Adobe Analytics

People have been attempting to analyze data generated by interactions with the World Wide Web since Tim Berners-Lee invented it. Yes, that process has become exponentially more developed and complex, but we're pretty sure one of the first questions asked after the first website went live was: "So, is anyone going to it?"

If we fast-forward a few decades, you'll be hard-pressed to walk through an international airport today without seeing ads for cloud technology, data security, and digital transformation. The business of data analysis has exploded, and there is no sign of it slowing down. According to a 2018 Forbes study, "Over the last two years alone, 90 percent of the data in the world was generated" (`www.forbes.com/sites/bernardmarr/2018/05/21/how-much-data-do-we-create-every-day-the-mind-blowing-stats-everyone-should-read/ - 7ceaab1460ba`). That equates to 2.5 quintillion (18 zeros) bytes of data captured every day. And most of it is coming from the web, mobile phones, and the Internet of Things (IoT), meaning the universe of devices that connect to the Internet, each other, or both, ranging from wearable devices to refrigerators.

Now that you have a feel for this ever-expanding amount of data, it's time to think about what to do with it. You might remember a time when you couldn't go into a meeting without hearing the words "big data." The thinking was, "Let's collect all the data we can and figure out what to do with it later." However, as made clear by the consistent decline in searches of that term on Google Trends (`https://trends.google.com/trends/explore?date=all&geo=US&q=big%20data`), a new sheriff is in town. And that new sheriff is driven by analysis. Collecting data is a start, but analysis is required to derive meaningful insights, form hypotheses, and take action.

Avoiding HiPPO!

Data analysis is what helps people avoid HiPPO. Zoo animals? Have Eric and David gone crazy in the first chapter? No, we're talking about *highest paid person's opinion*. The HiPPO acronym has come to describe the phenomenon of people in any grouping in an organization deferring to the opinion of the person highest in that group (generally the highest paid), resulting in unscientific and often harmful analysis and conclusions not supported by data. Table 1-1 provides a scenario of how this plays out.

TABLE 1-1

Business Decisions Not Based on Data

Employee	Comment
HiPPO	We need to sell more widgets!
Marketer	A lot of our new customers tell us they like our new TV ad.
HiPPO	I don't like the jingle; it gets stuck in my head.
Marketer	I really think we should try expanding it to more markets.
HiPPO	Here's the budget for additional ads in the local newspaper.
Marketer	[Sheds a tear while heading back to desk to look for a new gig]

Don't let your organization's decision-making process be driven by HiPPO. Imagine how much better that conversation could have gone if it was based on actual data, as shown in Table 1-2.

TABLE 1-2

Business Decisions Based on Data

Employee	Comment
CEO	We need to sell more widgets!
Marketer	A lot of our new customers tell us they like our new TV ad.
CEO	That jingle really gets stuck in my head; how can we learn whether it's positively affecting sales?
Marketer	Let's run some online preroll video tests (short audio or video ads that run before a user's selected audio or video) and judge the ad's effectiveness.
CEO	Sounds great. Can you use segmentation to make sure the results are not skewed by the fact that I've viewed the video a thousand times? (Segmentation is a marketer's ability to filter analysis or action to a specific set of users based on behavior, demographics, or other factors. Chapter 2 dives into segments.)
Marketer	Of course. We'll test, learn, and even save some money!

See how much better that went? It's all due to the decision-making process based on analyzing data that has been segmented (filtered) to avoid distorting the results. HiPPO shouldn't drive decisions when data can provide context and insight.

Now that we've used a hyperbolic (but revealing) example to illustrate why data needs to be the basis for decision-making in marketing, it's time to think about how else we can use data. We've seen data used to help make decisions on brand logos, campaign headlines, button colors, navigational menu hierarchy, internal and external search optimization, article titles, product bundle options, checkout steps, page layout, and more! And we've seen data used to measure not just sales but the effectiveness of customer support tools, educational resources, and branding campaigns. In essence, data analysis can inform the quality of any part of a website, mobile app, digital screen, desktop application, or even voice skill.

Knowing when you need Adobe Analytics

We hope you agree that data analysis needs to be ingrained in your everyday work life, but you may be asking yourself, "How do I know when it's time to use Adobe Analytics?" The Adobe Analytics sales team has been trying to answer this question since the product was first sold as SuperStats by the Omniture team in 1996. Before that, most web masters (remember that term?) like us were using basic server-log analysis tools just to figure out if anyone was even visiting the site!

Analyzing the effectiveness of websites has become even more complicated as the analytics industry has matured. In 2005, Google purchased Urchin — an early pioneer in the business of analyzing web traffic — and quickly made it available for free. Today, that product is known as Google Analytics, and it paves the way for tens of millions of people to take their first steps into the world of web analytics. Adobe purchased Omniture in 2009 to kick-start a slew of acquisitions that became the Adobe vision for an integrated enterprise marketing cloud, now called Adobe Experience Cloud.

Adobe has succeeded with this vision of an enterprise marketing cloud vision in large part because of the success of Adobe Analytics. It is the foundation that sits as the data hub in Adobe Experience Cloud. Adobe Analytics has been successful for plenty more reasons than this. Forrester, a market research firm that tests and compares developments in technology, reported that Adobe was the clear leader in its current offering. Forrester writes that Adobe "has concentrated on making the UI more intuitive and building on capabilities that allow the exploration of data breakdowns, relationships, and comparisons."

Knowing the difference between reporting and analysis

When it comes to data, we believe it's important to distinguish *reporting* from *analysis*. These terms are often used interchangeably outside the analytics industry but certainly not within it.

Reporting is a process used to organize data into static summaries. When you think of a report, do the words *interactive* and *flexible* come to mind? Or does the word *report* take you back to school, where you were asked to provide a summary of a book you just read? *Analysis* is the process of exploring data to derive meaningful insights and optimization opportunities. A report will often force its end users to ask questions; an analysis answers questions. A report will tell you that something is happening, such as the following:

> "Page views are increasing month over month by 3.5%. We have added 500 new keywords to our paid search campaign."

An analysis provides the context that explains why something is happening and what can be done, for example:

> "Page views have increased significantly this month due to new paid search keywords added to our campaign, but bounce rate has skyrocketed and conversion rate has dropped across the nation. Attached is a list of keywords that are driving the majority of this unqualified traffic and that should be removed from the campaign."

See the difference? The analysis does more than simply describe what happened. The analyst performing this analysis dug further into the data by answering questions about the who, where, when, and why. That, my fellow analyst, is where you come in.

Adobe Analytics may have some of the most advanced data science features powered by one of the most innovative web analytics engines available for the enterprise, but it takes an inquisitive analyst to apply these features to their dataset to derive insights. Good analysts know so much more than just the data at their fingertips and the tool providing it to them. Good analysts are curious and creative, and they sweat the details. To become one of the best analysts, you must have conversations with teams you've never spoken to before and join meetings you didn't know existed. And we hope you'll prove, once and for all, that HiPPO is useless without data to back it up.

Identifying Where Adobe Analytics Data Comes From

You may not know this, but Adobe Analytics users analyze much more than data from their websites. Adobe also captures data on behalf of their customers in mobile apps, tablet apps, and more. Plus, Adobe has built significant flexibility into their product to handle a more digitally connected consumer world that seamlessly switches from voice assistant to phone to laptop.

Perceptions of the nature of data analysis were defined in the realm of popular culture by the Jonah Hill character in the movie adaptation of the book *Moneyball*. In that true story, a small-market baseball team (the Oakland A's) managed to dramatically outperform teams with much larger payrolls by innovatively identifying and acting to acquire underpriced players based on statistical measures of a player's effectiveness beyond and in many ways going against traditional metrics, such as batting averages, home runs per season, and RBIs (runs batted in).

Since that movie came out, new and ever more complex challenges in collecting data have emerged. For example, users of online devices have been conditioned to quickly navigate from one place to another, requiring more nuanced and detailed metrics to accurately track user activity. And users are increasingly conscious of privacy considerations and making more informed decisions about how they want to manage the relationship between the convenience provided by having their activity tracked versus maintaining confidentiality in their online activity.

On the other side of the coin, vastly more sources of user data exist than just a few years ago. Today, Adobe has a number of mechanisms to import data from digitally disconnected sources such as call centers, customer relationship management (CRM) systems, and in-store commerce engines.

REMEMBER

Before diving into the details of how data is collected, we want to emphasize that capturing data and pumping it into Adobe Analytics is *not* normally the domain of *data analysts*. Your job as an analyst is to, well, *analyze* the data captured from user activity. But the following basic overview of *how* data is collected is important to analysts for two reasons. One, it's good to know where data comes from when you want to assess its validity; and two, having a basic grasp of the process of mining and sending data into Adobe Analytics allows you to have more productive interactions with the folks who set up the tools that extract data. At the end of this chapter, we discuss how to forge this relationship.

Capturing data from websites

Let's start with the most common Adobe Analytics data source: websites. Web data was originally analyzed based on server logs. Server-log data is automatically generated by servers that host websites and provide a count and timestamp of every request and download of every file on the site. Unfortunately, the data is highly unreliable because server logs don't have the capability to distinguish bots from humans.

Bots are automated computers that scan websites. These bots are often friendly and used to rank websites for search engines or product aggregator websites. Some bots, however, are unfriendly and used for competitive intel or worse.

Because server logs can't tell a human from a bot, the industry quickly migrated to tags, which are now the industry standard. Generally, *tags* are JavaScript-based lines of code that append an invisible image to every page and action on your website. These images act as a beacon to analytics tools, where several things happen in just a few milliseconds:

1. JavaScript code runs to identify browser and device information as well as the timestamp of the page view.

2. More JavaScript code runs to look for the existence of a *cookie,* which is a piece of text saved on a browser. Cookies can be accessed only by the domains that set them and often have an expiration date.

3. If it exists, a visitor ID is extracted from the cookie to identify the user across visits and pages. If a visitor ID doesn't exist, a unique ID is created and set in a new cookie. These IDs are unique for each visitor but are not connected to a user's personal data, thus providing a measure of privacy for users.

4. More JavaScript is used to capture information about the page: the URL, the referrer, and a slew of custom dimensions that identify the action and behavior of the visitor.

After all that JavaScript logic runs, the image beacon is generated to send data into the collection and processing engine in Adobe's analytics.

Intimidating isn't it? Well, that's how web developers felt. When we first started working in web analytics, our toughest job was teaching developers how to write and test all this JavaScript to ensure that our tags fired accurately. Teaching developers to develop — not a fun job.

Lucky for us, an even smarter developer came up with an idea to move all that JavaScript into a single UI (user interface). Web developers only had to add one or two lines of code to every page of the site, and the marketer could then manage their tags in this new platform named a *tag management system,* or *TMS.* It wasn't long before the tag management industry exploded, leading to dozens of vendors, and then acquisitions, mergers, and technology pivots.

The good news is that the tag management system industry has become commoditized and is available for free from Adobe in the form of Dynamic Tag Manager (DTM) and Adobe Launch. You may already be familiar with Google's TMS, Google Tag Manager, or one of the independent TMS players such as Tealium, Ensighten, or Signal. Chances are your company is already using one of these technologies to deploy marketing tags on your website. All of them can deploy Adobe Analytics, although Adobe's recommendation for best practice is to use Adobe Launch.

Capturing data from mobile devices

If standard websites delivered to a laptop are the natural place to start with our data collection discussion, moving to a smaller mobile screen is the logical next step.

You may already know that at this stage of the evolution of web design, mobile websites are fully functioning web pages, not afterthought appendages to laptop, desktop, or large monitor sites. These smaller-scale websites are created by using an approach to web development called *responsive design*, in which the code used to create website content is the same regardless of the size of the web visitor's screen and browser. Your company is most likely already leveraging responsive design.

When responsive design is applied, the same tags that fire on the desktop site should work on mobile- and tablet-optimized websites because they're essentially the same thing, which is good news in the tag management world. However, the world of responsive-design-based mobile apps is completely different than that of native apps.

Mining data from native apps

Native apps present particular challenges for data collection. These mobile and tablet applications are programmed in a different way than responsive websites. In general, *native apps* don't run in browsers, don't use HTML, and can't run JavaScript. In fact, applications built for iOS are built in a different programming language (Objective C) than Android apps (Java). We mention these technical programming languages for one important reason: A tag management system is not going to work on your mobile and tablet applications.

Some tag management system vendors have hacked the capability to incorporate JavaScript into apps, but the result has limited capabilities and is far from a best practice. The most complete, accurate, and scalable way to deploy Adobe tools is to use the Adobe mobile software development kit (SDK). The Adobe mobile SDK is built to work as a data collection system, like a tag management system, but uses the app's native programming language (Objective C for iOS or Java for Android).

The Adobe SDK is important because it has deeper access into the code that runs the app and therefore can be used for more than just data collection. In addition to sending data to Adobe Analytics, the Adobe SDK is required to do the following:

>> Capture geographic location data based on GPS.

>> Utilize geofences based on that GPS data for analysis or action.

>> Send push notifications to users.

>> Update content in the app via in-app messaging, personalization, and testing.

TIP

Access to these capabilities may be limited to the SKU, or version, that your company has purchased from Adobe. Work with your Adobe Account Manager to understand which of these capabilities is included with your contract.

Data from IoT and beyond

Now that we've discussed data collection standards for the two biggest use cases (web and mobile), it's time to branch out to a more generic set of the Internet of Things (IoT). Everyone who asks questions about data needs to be thinking about digital kiosks, smart watches, connected cars, interactive screens, and whatever other new devices our tech overlords have announced since this sentence was written.

Vendors such as Adobe find it difficult to stay on top of every new device because building SDKs takes time, money, research, engineers, code, quality assurance, and more. But don't worry: Devices that don't have native-built SDKs can still send data to Adobe Analytics.

The best practice for sending data from one of these devices is through an *application programming interface (API)*. In short, this means the developers of the IoT application can write their own code to create a connection to your Adobe Analytics account and then send data to it. APIs have become the default way in which data is sent from any device connected to the Internet either full time or part time. Adobe has some recommendations to share too, especially for some of their big bets when it comes to these new devices, such as voice and connected car. At the time of this writing, SDKs are not available for voice-activated devices or connected car applications. However, Adobe does have best practices for data customizations, variable settings, and code options for both of these technologies.

REMEMBER

Enterprise software — software licensed to institutions — is updated regularly, and Adobe releases best practices for tracking data associated with new digital mediums such as voice and the connected car.

You've now explored all types of data generated by devices that have part-time or full-time access to the web: computers, phones, tablets, and IoT.

People's digital experiences and interactions on those devices are captured by some combination of TMS, SDK, and API. According to marketers and analysts, that list is missing something: data that isn't based on behavior. Perhaps the best example of nonbehavioral data comes from your customer relationship management (CRM) tool. *CRM tools* are used to organize, categorize, and manage your prospects and customers. Other examples of nonbehavioral data that marketers and analysts would be interested in include the following:

>> Call center

>> Offline or in-store purchases

>> Returns or cancellations

>> Product cost of goods sold

>> Ad campaign

>> Customer satisfaction

Adobe Analytics can import any of these data types along with plenty of others. In general, this data is imported into Adobe Analytics via either File Transfer Protocol (FTP) or API. In Chapter 16, we describe some of the options for connecting data into Adobe Analytics.

Configuring and Analyzing Data

Can you imagine a chef who didn't know the source of the food she cooked? The chances of getting that coveted Michelin star would be significantly worse. The same concept applies to becoming a rock star analyst.

That's why we dug as deeply as we did into where data comes from. As an analyst, you'll be working with that data, and you need to know its source. And you need to be able to communicate in a meaningful and productive way with the team that harvests that data.

Preparing to slice and dice data

With so many options for collecting and customizing Adobe Analytics data, an analyst needs to understand the details of how data is collected in his or her organization. The more you know about the intricacies of your implementation, the faster you'll be able to slice and dice your data and think creatively to solve problems. In fact, that creative thinking is some of the most fun you'll have as an analyst. One particularly creative portion of the Adobe Analytics process is tied to the decisions associated with your data configuration and implementation.

It's possible that your Adobe Analytics version has upwards of 1,500 possible custom variables and therefore a virtually unlimited number of ways to collect data. The decision-making associated with how to populate those variables needs to be a combination of left and right brain. That is to say, you should start with specific data you need to track, and then trip out a bit on other variables that might shed light on the effectiveness of your website, app, or other digital interactions.

Optimizing your raw data

Throughout this chapter, we point to the importance of a dynamic relationship between analysts and the folks who set up the scripts and other tools used to collect data from websites, apps, and other digital engagement with users. Let's dig into *how* that interaction works.

If you've recently had or are planning a site or app re-platform, this is the perfect time to integrate data collection into the process. If it's been awhile, it's time to dust off your documentation, commonly referred to as a solution design reference (SDR), and immerse yourself into the details. Think of your SDR as a data dictionary that your company uses to keep all of the data in your Adobe Analytics instance organized and accessible.

REMEMBER

First, it's important to know *who* in your organization is responsible for data collection. At least one person is responsible for the data collection strategy at your company, and you should find that person, introduce yourself, and begin to forge a relationship. It's hard to think of a peer at your company who will influence your life as an analyst more than the person making decisions about how data flows into Adobe Analytics.

Being a data collection detective

We'd like to provide you with a few tips to help you find this magical implementation master at your company. Many companies outsource analytics tagging projects because it's a specialized skill and outsourcing keeps the implementation specification and deployment processes out of the hands of developers who have much bigger fish to fry.

If your company is working with an agency, they are most likely driving your implementation decisions or can at least point you to the person who is. If you weren't successful finding an agency that helps with your analytics deployment, it probably makes sense to think about the digital channels that Adobe Analytics is deployed on and the team responsible for adding code to them. For example, if Adobe Analytics is collecting data from your website, you'll want to check and see whether you have a tag management system.

TIP

One of the best free ways to discover marketing technologies on your website is Ghostery, a browser plug-in. After you install it, you'll be able to see a list of all marketing and advertising technologies deployed on any page you visit on the web. It's a great way to discover what, if any, tag management system is in use on your website. Ghostery can be used to block tracking and marketing, but it can also be used as a tool for surveying and understanding how tracking and marketing work, as shown in Figure 1-1.

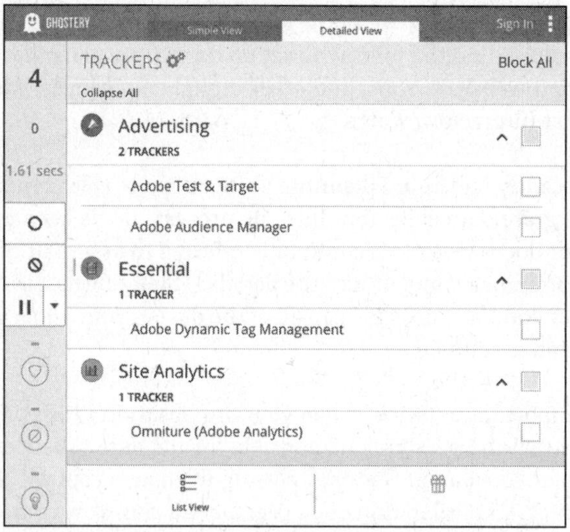

FIGURE 1-1:
Using Ghostery to identify tracking technologies associated with the Adobe.com site.

As you identify and learn about tracking associated with any site (including your own!), the next step is to find the owner of that technology. A tag management system is generally owned by one of three groups: marketing, IT, or analytics/business intelligence. Start asking people on those teams about your tag management system and you're bound to come up with the name of your next new friend.

TIP

If you don't have a tag management system, your tags are almost definitely managed by IT or your engineering/development organization, so start there. Marketing technology teams are another great place to look if your company has such a team. If you're instead trying to track down the implementation associated with your mobile, tablet, or IoT apps, your path is less clear. The same team that manages your website tagging is the right place to start, but some companies outsource their mobile applications to developers who specialize in apps.

Situating Adobe Analytics in the Universe of Data Analysis

Now that we've identified and begun to explore key elements in how Adobe Analytics works, why it works, and how it fits into successfully accomplishing an organization's goals and mission, let's address the elephant in the room: What's the relationship between Adobe Analytics and Google Analytics?

We've had countless customers and friends in the industry ask us which analytics solution we like best. Instead of answering that question, we provide an answer to a more objective one: What are the strengths and limitations of each analytics solution?

This focus has helped prospective buyers of an analytics solution quickly map features and integrations to their requirements. And by comparing and contrasting the two, you will understand why your organization made the call to implement Adobe Analytics. Or, if you are part of the team making that call, this section will help you evaluate the relative strengths and limitations of different data analytics options.

Surveying how Adobe Analytics stacks up

We start this comparison by focusing on Adobe Analytics because that's the topic of this book. Adobe's analytics solution is often thought of as the Ferrari in the industry — impressively powerful but costly. That analogy has some truth to it. But let's break down some of the features unique to Adobe Analytics.

Peeking at Analysis Workspace

In terms of power, nary an analytics solution can top the Adobe capabilities that you'll be walking through in this book. The first key differentiator for Adobe is *Analysis Workspace,* the default engine in Adobe Analytics for analysis, visualization, curation, and sharing. Built with both the marketer and the analyst in mind, Analysis Workspace provides unlimited breakdowns, on-the-fly segmentation and calculated metrics, a slew of data visualization capabilities, and four key built-in, data-science-powered features. To take just one example, Adobe Analytics employs Anomaly Detection algorithms to identify anomalies such as hard-to-find drops in average order value, spikes in orders with low revenue, statistically significant increases in trial registrations, and drops in landing page views.

We describe how Adobe Analytics marshals data science in Chapter 16. For now, you can get a sense of what we're talking about by looking at Figure 1-2, which shows Analysis Workspace.

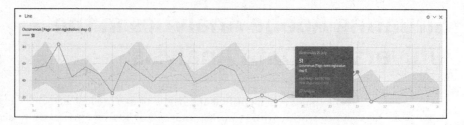

FIGURE 1-2:
Using Analysis
Workspace in
Adobe Analytics
to identify
anomalies.

Adobe has recently added to Analysis Workspace a much-needed component for attribution that allows almost all metrics to have one of ten attribution models that you can apply to almost any dimension in the platform. You explore the significance of accurate attribution in Chapter 12, but in short, marketing attribution helps you understand how your customers and clients are interacting with your online presence and what they want in a way that makes possible highly focused and accurate marketing or service decisions. Attribution IQ in Analysis Workspace, for example, lets you add many new types of attribution models to freeform tables, visualizations, and calculated metrics. Attribution IQ is shown in Figure 1-3.

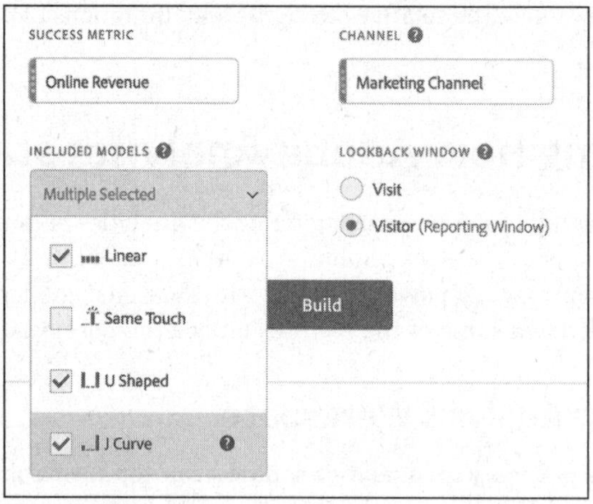

FIGURE 1-3:
Using the
Attribution IQ
panel in Analysis
Workspace.

As of this writing, algorithmic and data-driven models require an upgrade to Adobe's Data Workbench solution at significant cost.

Visualizing flow and fallout

Two huge differentiators for Adobe are tied to their customer journey visualizations: flow and fallout. Other vendors seem to fail to get the flexibility and ease of use right for these types of analyses, In addition, Adobe is primed to release

Customer Journey Analytics, a feature focused on stitching visits and devices across devices based on logins or Adobe's Device Co-op. (For an exploration of flow and fallout, see Chapter 14. For an explanation of Adobe's Device Co-op, see Chapter 16.) Figure 1-4 illustrates visualizing flow in Adobe Analytics.

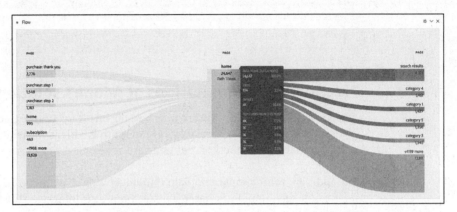

FIGURE 1-4:
Visualizing flow in
Adobe Analytics.

Adobe also has built-in data connectors with dozens of partners that allow for relatively seamless and often bidirectional integrations of datasets across email, search engine optimization (SEO), commerce, advertising platforms, and more. If these pre-built integrations aren't good enough, Adobe recommends a custom integration via a number of options including the recently released Adobe Experience Platform.

The other big selling point of Adobe's integrations comes from deep within their own Experience Cloud — integrations with other Adobe solutions. Adobe was the first (and, as of this writing, only) company to have a bidirectional integration with an Analytics and Data Management Platform (DMP). DMPs are used for merging data from multiple datasets, building audiences from that merged data, and activating those audiences in advertising platforms. Don't worry. If that topic is too advanced, you should just know that marketers can define segments in Analytics that are then enriched by additional data sources in Audience Manager (Adobe's DMP), and then share those segments back into Analytics for further analysis. Adobe also has quality integrations with Target (testing and personalization), Campaign (1:1 marketing campaign management), Experience Manager (content and asset management), and Ad Cloud (advertising bid optimization). For more information on how Adobe uses data across products, review Chapter 16.

PAY-FOR-WHAT-YOU-NEED MODEL

Like a Ferrari, the biggest complaints about Adobe are often tied to price. Adobe has put serious thought towards this problem by offering a set of SKUs at multiple price points based on the features and functionality that your company can access. Some advanced features, such as Contribution Analysis (see Chapter 15 for details), are limited in the lower-cost tiers.

Identifying the limitations of Adobe's solution

Adobe's biggest missing feature may be a big one for you: integration with Google Ads. Adobe does have several ways of integrating with advertising data from their biggest analytics competitor, but none are as seamless or as complete as Google's.

In addition, some people complain that Adobe's solution is too difficult to use, but we think this opinion is based on the Omniture interface (the program Adobe acquired that evolved into Adobe Analytics), which was, frankly, daunting. Analysis Workspace has removed these limitations and created unique ways to empower new users. And we're confident that this book will put those tools well within your reach!

Understanding how Google Analytics fits into the picture

If you've never used Adobe Analytics but have used an analytics solution, odds are that you've used Google Analytics. Let's take a step back and look at how Google Analytics fits into the world of analytics.

First, it's important to note the difference between Google's free tool, Google Analytics, and the enterprise (and not free) level, Google Analytics 360.

Distinguishing between Google Analytics and Google Analytics 360

Google has cornered the free analytics solution market, doing the entire industry a service by helping to drive a huge wave of businesspeople to start asking questions about their data. The free version of Google Analytics is a valuable and accessible tool for generating *reports* on who is coming to a website and how they are interacting with that site. It is not an enterprise-level tool for data *analysis*. (See "Knowing the Difference between Reporting and Analysis" in this chapter.)

Our focus here is on Google Analytics 360. Google released this for-pay solution several years ago. A significant differentiator and advantage of Google Analytics is its native integration with Google Ads. If advertising is your analytics raison d'être, you're probably spending more of your budget and time in Google's ad tools than any other tool and therefore will find Google's ad integrations valuable. Figure 1-5 shows the process of configuring Google Analytics with a Google Ads account.

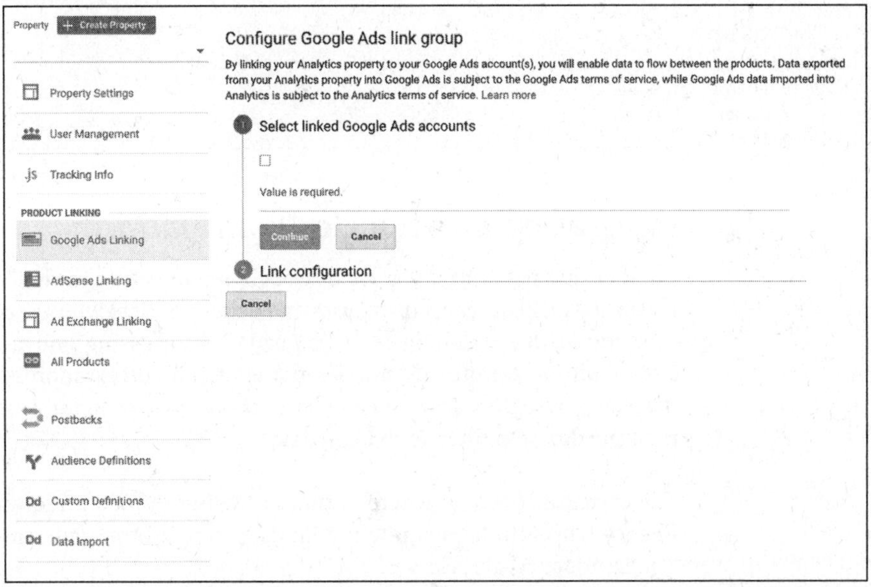

FIGURE 1-5: Connecting Google Analytics with a Google Ads account.

Google imports data from Google Ads (formerly DoubleClick for Advertisers), the Google search console, display and video ads, and paid search ads for Google Analytics 360 customers. In addition, segments created in Google Analytics can be enabled for remarketing campaigns via Google Ads. However, note that these remarketing lists are not retroactively updated, so users in your segment prior to the segment being shared to Google Ads are not included in the remarketing list. Only users who become a part of your segment *after* it is shared as a remarketing audience are available for remarketing.

Calculated metrics in Google Analytics and Google Analytics 360 are limited to the four basic arithmetic operators (add, subtract, multiply, divide) and can be used only in custom reports and created only by administrators. Some calculations are pre-built into reports, but they are often simple divisors of other metrics already in the report. Analysts often need more complex operators and functions, such as distinct/unique counts, means, medians, percentiles, and logical operators (if, then, and, or, greater than, and less than). The interface for creating a calculated metric in Google Analytics is shown in Figure 1-6.

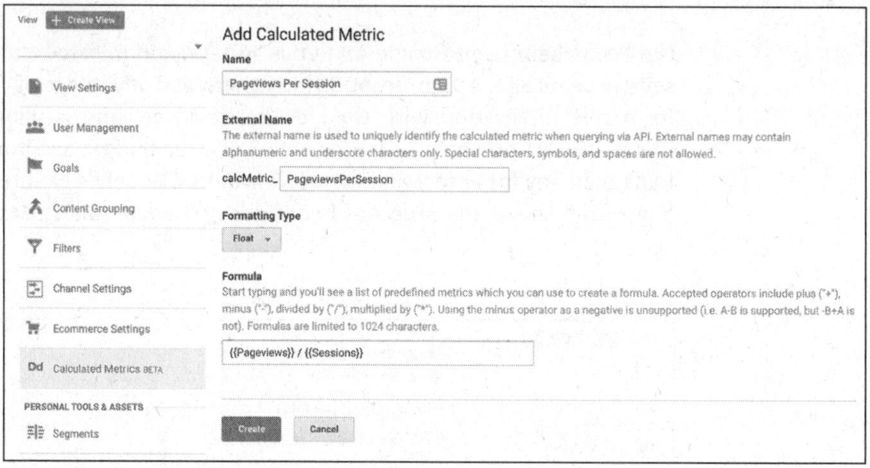

FIGURE 1-6:
Creating a
calculated metric
in Google
Analytics.

Integrating with Google Cloud Platform

Another distinguishing feature of Google's tool is integration with Google Cloud Platform (GCP). Advanced analysts and data scientists who are comfortable in SQL (Structured Query Language, a language for accessing and manipulating databases) will be able to run queries thanks to the integration of Google data into BigQuery, Google's fast-moving SQL-based platform for complex analyses of multiple datasets filled with huge data.

The caveat or downside here is that accessing this data requires a high level of fluency with SQL to generate the kinds of reports that you can generate without SQL in Adobe Analytics.

Surveying Google's Advanced Analysis interface

Google's recently released interface for Analytics 360 is called Advanced Analysis. It includes a few key features not previously available in standard Google Analytics. For example, Advanced Analysis increases a user's ability to break down a report, such as breaking down the marketing channel report by landing page. Google's Advanced Analysis allows for ten breakdowns in a report, whereas the old interface allows for a maximum of five.

Segment Overlap is the second report in Advanced Analysis. This report provides analysts with a Venn diagram of segments that show the percentage of users who share a segment. Finally, Google has expanded custom funnel capabilities in Advanced Analysis. Google Analytics 360 customers love the ability to create custom funnels on the fly, whereas non-360 customers have to create the funnel before data flows into it. In Advanced Analysis, Google has expanded these custom funnels to max out at 10 funnel steps, doubling the maximum in Google Analytics.

When compared to Adobe's Analysis Workspace, Google's Advanced Analysis tool is far less robust, but we're excited to see what Google cooks up in future releases.

Evaluating plusses and minuses

As noted, Google gets high marks for their integration with other Google platforms. However, Google Analytics has only one significant non-Google integration, with Salesforce, so all other data sources require a custom setup via API.

Google Analytics evolved from, and retains significant evolutionary holdovers and limitations based on, its origin as a much simpler tool for reporting, as opposed to a full-fledged analytics tool. The limitations associated with calculated metric capabilities, dimensional breakdowns, and custom funnels may be debilitating to analysts who are unable or uninterested in using SQL.

The most significant shortcoming may be that Google Analytics, even the premium Analytics 360 solution, uses data sampling in its reports, so some reports may not show a complete view of visitor behavior. Similar to election polling, Google Analytics reports show data associated with a percentage of the full set of data (20 percent, for example) and then multiply that number by the total number of site visitors (by five, in this example).

Of course Google's real sampling algorithm is more complicated than this (visit `https://support.google.com/analytics/answer/2637192?hl=en` for details) but the end result is important: Data may provide you with different answers depending on how it is sliced. In Analytics 360, sampling minimums are increased in many reports.

In short, the free version of Google Analytics plays a valuable role in opening the door to data analysis for a wide range of small-scale developers, including individual website designers who create their sites with WordPress, Wix, or other tools. It allows them to generate basic reports and perform a limited array of essentially predefined analyses.

The less widely known and implemented Google Analytics 360, with the Advanced Analysis interface, adds a few features that overlap in some ways with those in Adobe Analytics. Limitations include the need for SQL programming to get the most from the collected data and, significantly, data accuracy issues. Google Analytics has the advantage of providing the most direct path to data analysis with a focus on advertising and publishing.

Noting other analytics options

We've compared and contrasted the dominant options for professional-level data analytics. Here we briefly acknowledge some of the other players in the field. These analytics products are often more niche oriented, focusing on event-based tracking, real-time stats for publishers, mobile application frameworks, or data built for product managers.

Each of these vendors, including MixPanel, Heap, Amplitude, and Localytics, provides more focused but fewer features than Google Analytics 360 or Adobe Analytics. None have aimed to compete with the more complete cloud offerings in Google Marketing Platform or Adobe Experience Cloud.

Building a Positive Relationship with Your Data Team

We've surveyed a wide range of issues related to collecting and analyzing data in this chapter. But before we move on, it's important to talk about how humans fit into this process!

It can be valuable to formulate a plan before reaching out to your future analytics partner(s). It's always a good idea to learn about the history of an implementation before criticizing it. Websites, including the installation of tags, often contain years of history tied to acquisitions, mergers, and bolted-on technologies, which often turn an analytics solution into a multi-headed monster that hasn't been given the requisite love to keep data clean and actionable.

Our point is to be aware of office culture, personalities, and politics when digging into the depths of your data. Don't start your new potential friendship with the question "How did our data get so bad in the first place?"

TIP

A better approach is available. Think about the overview we've provided on where data comes from and how data is mined from user activity. Also listen to and learn from people who know the history and constraints of the resources at hand. Then work *with* your data team to find ways to maximize the value of what gets collected and poured into the mix from which you'll be extracting analysis, which will in turn be used to drive results.

In Chapter 2, we build on this overview of how Adobe Analytics works, survey and break down the building blocks of reporting and analysis, explore the report suite, and dig into the all-important challenge of accurately defining and measuring success events.

Chapter **2**

Basic Building Blocks of Reporting and Analysis

I n this chapter, we introduce you to the essential concepts for a solid foundation in analyzing data and show you how to implement these concepts in Adobe Analytics.

Step one of this phase of your journey is to survey the three basic ways of sifting through data, regardless of whether the tool is Adobe Analytics, Google Analytics, Excel, or even weather forecasts! The three key components analysts use to work with data are dimensions, metrics, and segments.

Getting your head around these three concepts and how they interact with each other is essential to doing meaningful work with Adobe Analytics. The data community worldwide uses these building blocks.

Step two in this leg of your journey is exploring Adobe's least granular structure for organizing data: a report suite. If you haven't been introduced to the term *granular* in relation to data analysis, you might have guessed its meaning based on the metaphor it draws on: The tiniest, most specific thing on a sandy beach is a *grain* of sand. It is the *most granular* element on the beach. But if you pull back the lens and view the entire beach, which might be isolated and empty, or full of people, you are taking in the *least granular* view of the beach, and you can draw more overarching conclusions about the nature of the beach.

Double negatives can be confusing, but by *least granular,* we mean that report suites are analogous to looking at the entire beach, not just grains of sand. Report suites are the highest level of looking at data.

Before you dive into working with Analytics, you should understand report suites. We share a few tricks to quickly get you on top of how your company's data is organized into report suites by introducing Adobe Experience Cloud Debugger, the best way to see what where data is being sent from your website and where it's going.

Standard Categories of Measurement

As in many industries, users of data often speak in their own language. That language includes some standard vocabulary words and an array of acronyms. We usually speak this language everywhere — in the office, at home, and even at happy hour.

You must be comfortable speaking this language if you want to make the most of your time in the industry — but you'll be welcome at happy hour regardless. After you learn these terms and concepts, you'll begin to find them in everyday life! In fact, finding ways to connect the terminology and concepts used in analytics with everyday activity is our favorite method of teaching the initial set of concepts: metrics, dimensions, and segments.

Here's the short story:

>> **Dimensions** are used to categorize data. Examples of dimensions include a date, a range of dates, a location, a set of locations, and characteristics of visitors to a website (such as geolocation or age group).

>> **Metrics** are quantitative measurements that answer questions such as "how many?" or "how much?"

>> **Segments** are subsets of visitor traffic filtered based on a combination of dimensions or metrics. For example, individuals could be segmented into those who accessed a website on a mobile device compared to those who accessed it from a laptop or desktop.

Let's start exploring how these terms are used to analyze data by inspecting a simple weather forecast in Table 2-1. You'd probably agree that the table shows a standard weather forecast, if a bit warm.

TABLE 2-1

Weather Forecast for New York City

Day of Week	High	Low	Chance of Precipitation	Humidity
Monday	77	71	70%	83%
Tuesday	79	72	90%	86%
Wednesday	80	67	90%	84%
Thursday	82	63	10%	70%
Friday	78	65	10%	69%
Saturday	84	67	10%	74%
Sunday	78	63	20%	68%

The average, non-data-equipped citizen would look at this weather forecast and see days and numbers. The data analysts in us see something a bit different — dimensions and metrics and even an applied segment. Let's discuss.

Defining Dimensions

We start by digging more deeply into the definition of a dimension. In Chapters 6 and 7, we walk through how to use dimensions in more detail. Here, we establish what we mean by a dimension. A *dimension* is a structure used in analytics to categorize data. Commonly used dimensions are based on time, location, or a person's characteristics.

In our weather forecast example, Day of Week is the only dimension in Table 2-1. Dimensions are usually made up of words rather than numbers, and are most often found in a table's left column. However, tables can have multiple dimensions, in which case the left two or more columns are usually dimensions.

In our weather example, consider a column to the left of Day of Week that categorizes each day into a Day Type (Weekday or Weekend). In that case, each of these two columns would be a dimension. Dimensions are named after the header (for instance, Day of Week and Day Type) and their values are, not surprisingly, called *dimensional values* (Monday, Tuesday, Wednesday, Weekend, Weekday, and so on).

Web and mobile analytics have a broader set of dimensions that are used when performing an analysis. Analysts must consider the day of the week when behavior is occurring on their website or app, but it's often more important to categorize digital behavior by dimensions such as device type, marketing channel, and product!

Just think about how useful it would be to understand whether more people purchased from your site using an iPhone versus an Android device. You'd be able to tailor your advertising so that you spent more on one type of device or another, or offer coupons for the device type with a lower propensity to purchase. This example shows the power of dimensions and the values they contain.

Using the page dimension

The most basic dimension used in digital analytics is the page dimension. Analysts use the *page dimension* to understand where activity on their website or app is occurring.

If you've used Google Analytics before, you may recognize that the page dimension is usually tied directly to the URL and sitting in the Behavior > Site Content report hierarchy. Using URLs as page names can be problematic because URLs can be *very* long, distorting attempts to view them in tables. Plus, URLs aren't always intuitively named.

Adobe Analytics users can define page dimensions with titles that are much friendlier than a URL. For example, administrators who set up Adobe Analytics configurations might replace the forward slashes with colons or space, or build custom logic to group product pages, or even capture dynamic text on the page and ignore the URL.

Are you thinking, "Hey! I better get clued in to how pages correspond with URLs before I start wrestling with data from our site"? You're right. As an analyst, you need to put your head together with the folks who configured your installation of Analytics to see how they populate page dimensions on your site.

Knowing when a page is not a page

Understanding how dimension titles in Analytics correlate with pages in your website is important in any situation. But it is especially important if your website is designed in parallax or a similar technology that provides a user experience that looks like multiple pages but is actually a single page.

Parallax sites are generally built with a single, long-scrolling HTML file. These sites are growing in popularity with the increasing dominance of mobile interaction with the Internet.

And to make the mobile user experience more accessible, sites also employ JavaScript to display and hide different sections of an HTML page as users interact with content (such as tabs).

In both examples, the content is a single HTML page, but simply measuring visits to that page isn't sufficient to get exact data on user interaction with the site. To capture user data from a site where a single HTML page appears to the user as multiple pages or at least sections of a page, you can tag several breaks in the content. An analytics team then uses the tagged breaks to distinguish page values *within* a page. (We explain how user interaction data is captured from websites in Chapter 1.)

Appreciating the foundational role of the page dimension

Now that you understand that Adobe Analytics does not necessarily have a direct correlation between a URL and a page, you can appreciate the importance of asking questions, looking at documentation, understanding how Analytics is configured in your environment, and knowing what page dimensions refer to.

Analyses often use the page dimension, which is shown in Figure 2-1. If your goal is to better understand site behavior in your most popular content, you'll start with the page dimension.

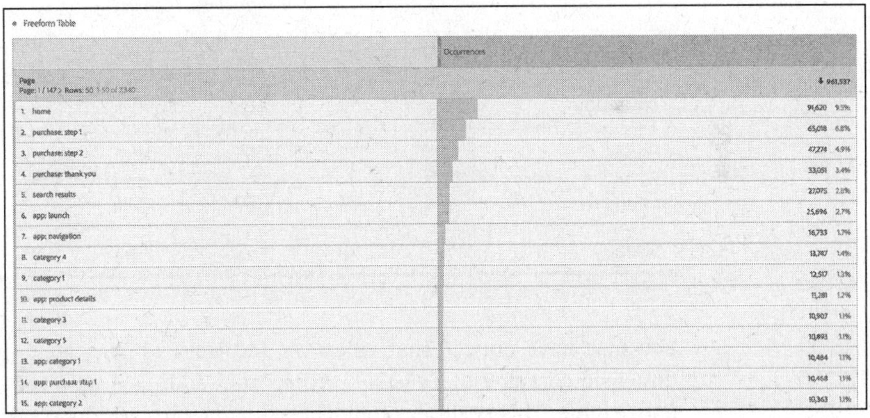

FIGURE 2-1:
A page dimension in a freeform table in Analysis Workspace.

You'll need the page dimension when you're analyzing the differences between visits to the website that resulted in a purchase versus those that didn't. Even if you're analyzing the success of a change to the navigation menu's structure, you'll still need to understand the pages where people are interacting with the menu.

The page dimension is the most fundamental part of your Adobe Analytics implementation, so be sure to master it and use it.

Splitting dimensions with breakdowns

The next definition is related to dimensions and easy to understand after you've grasped the concept of a dimension. A *breakdown*, or *drilldown*, is the method by which dimension values can be split by another dimension.

In the weather forecast example, suppose you wanted to know what time the rain is expected to start on Tuesday. You could break down the dimensional value of Tuesday by another dimension, Hour of Day. (See Table 2-2.)

TABLE 2-2 **Weather Forecast with an Hour of Day Breakdown on Tuesday**

Day of Week	Time	High	Low	Chance of Precipitation	Humidity
Monday		77	71	70%	83%
Tuesday		79	72	90%	86%
	6 am	75	75	10%	70%
	12 pm	79	79	10%	70%
	6 pm	73	73	90%	90%
Wednesday		80	67	90%	84%
Thursday		82	63	10%	70%
Friday		78	65	10%	69%
Saturday		84	67	10%	74%
Sunday		78	63	20%	68%

You may have noticed that when we add Hour of Day, we only break down the dimensional value of Tuesday, rather than adding it as a second column to the entire table. This is similar to how freeform tables in Adobe's Analysis Workspace solution work. (See Chapter 4 for a thorough walkthrough in creating and analyzing freeform tables.) This breakdown shows that the rain is more likely to reach the area later in the day, so good weather analysts would want to bring an umbrella for their commute home.

Digital analysts are similarly interested in using breakdowns to make decisions. A media publisher may use Adobe Analytics to discover that the majority of traffic comes to its site on Fridays. The publisher would then want to break down the dimensional value of Friday to see when the majority of Friday traffic arrives. This data-driven publisher would now want to make sure that their breaking news stories are always online well ahead of the rush.

Measuring with Metrics

In the preceding section, we mentioned the counterpart to dimensions and dimensional values without giving it a name. *Metric* is the quantitative measurement that answers the question "how many" or "how much."

In our weather forecast, metrics are all the numbers in the table — the high, the low, the precipitation percentage, and the humidity percentage. Metrics are exclusively numbers but you can format them as percentages, currencies, decimals, and more.

Metrics are often the most commonly discussed category of measurement for digital analysts. A standard question that an analyst at a B2B company receives is "How many leads did the website generate this week?" This question refers to the leads metric and is one of the most critical metrics captured on a B2B's website.

Having explored how metrics are posed in real life, let's take a look at how metrics are applied in Analysis Workspace. We describe additional metrics in more detail in Chapter 5.

Defining hits

One key metric that is essential when discussing Adobe Analytics but isn't available in the Workspace interface is called hits. A *hit* describes any interaction on your site or app that results in data being sent to Adobe Analytics. It's a catchall for page views, download links, exit links, and any custom tracking. The term will be useful as we go deeper into the capabilities of Adobe and need a generic way to describe any type of data sent to your report suite.

Measuring page views

Let's start with the most simple of metrics in Adobe Analytics — page views. The *page views* metric displays the number of times your HTML files or web pages (or sections of a page) were loaded. When analyzing a mobile app, page views correspond to the number of times your app's screens were loaded in the app. Mobile phone screens are much smaller than laptops and desktop monitors, and the definition of an app's screen is often unique within a company. Work with your Adobe administrators for a complete list of app screens, or at least request the rule of thumb they use to decide whether new content should be considered a new screen, and therefore a page view.

Every time your home page is loaded by a person browsing your site, that's a page view. Similarly, every time your Contact page is loaded by a person browsing your site, that's also a page view. The total count of page views increases with every page load.

As is the case with page dimensions, the definition of page views can be complicated on parallax sites and single-page applications. The good news is that your company's definition of pages and page views will be aligned because of a bond between the dimension and metric so that any time a page is viewed, page views will be increased.

In Figure 2-2, we applied the page view metric to a range of dates, which provides a quick overview of traffic to pages over that date range.

FIGURE 2-2:
A page views
metric in a
freeform table in
Analysis
Workspace.

Counting visits

Another standard metric in the web analytics world is the visits metric, also known as the sessions metric in Google Analytics. A *visit* is defined as an interaction or set of interactions by an individual that consists of one or more actions. The actions in a visit can occur on the same page or on multiple pages.

Following are a few simple examples:

Visit example 1:

On Monday, Eric lands on your home page at 1 pm, and closes his browser at 1:05 pm.

Visit example 2:

On Tuesday, David lands on a product page at 11 am and watches a video on that page.

David gets distracted and closes his laptop at 11:08 am.

Visit example 3:

On Wednesday, Heidi lands on your home page at 7 pm.

She performs a search on your site and is taken to the search results page.

Heidi clicks the first link to a product.

She adds the product to the shopping cart is taken to the shopping cart page.

She successfully checks out and makes the purchase on the checkout page.

Heidi confirms her purchase on the purchase confirmation page at 7:22 pm.

Each of these three examples contains a different numbers of page views (one, two, and six). However, each of them would count as just a single visit.

Bottom line: Visits and page views are related, but they are not the same thing. A visit can, and often does, involve more than one page view, as shown in Figure 2-3.

You may have noticed that we included a time at the end of all three examples. Including a time when the last interaction takes place is important because that is how we measure when a visit ends.

Why, by the way, can't we simply measure when a visit ends by identifying when a user leaves a page? The reason is that technical limitations keep analytics platforms such as Adobe Analytics and Google Analytics from being able to detect the action of a browser tab or a window being closed. As a result, we've had to get creative in how we define the end of a visit. A *visit ends* after a set amount of time passes without any data being sent from the individual.

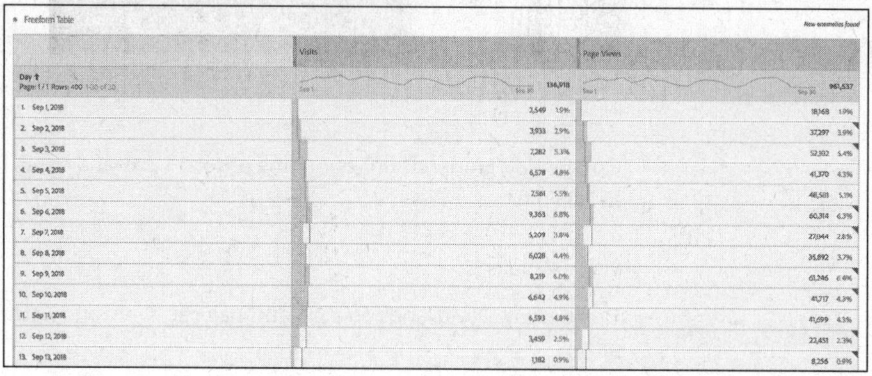

FIGURE 2-3:
The visits and
page views
metrics in a
freeform table in
Analysis
Workspace.

By default, most analytics platforms, including Adobe Analytics, use 30 minutes of inactivity to define the end of a visit. However, you can adjust the amount of time that results in a visit's end. We walk through how to adjust the visit timeout in Chapter 9, where we describe virtual report suites and context-aware sessions.

Identifying unique visitors

The page views metric is the most granular and detailed standard metric. Multiple page views within a timeframe roll up into a visit, a less granular standard metric. Multiple visits roll up into a single unique visitor, which is the least granular standard metric.

The number of *unique visitors* to a site or a page is the number of individuals with activity consisting of one or more visits to a site, an app, or a page. (Google Analytics uses the term *users* instead of *unique visitors*.) Note that *unique visitors* is different than *individual people*. Adobe Analytics has no way of knowing the difference between two people who share a computer or one person who accesses the same site from two different browsers on the same computer. Figure 2-4 is a table in Analysis Workspace displaying visits, page views, and unique visitors.

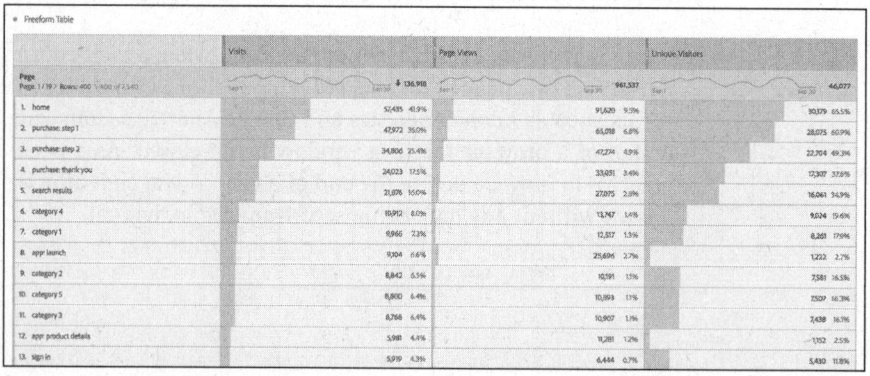

FIGURE 2-4:
Viewing visits,
page views and
unique visitors in
a freeform table
in Analysis
Workspace.

The unique visitors metric is based on cookies. If a cookie that identifies a browser is deleted, Adobe can't tie that individual's visit history to any new visits. As a result, new visits will generate a new cookie and therefore appear as a new unique visitor. A more accurate definition for unique visitor would state that it's the unique count of *browser cookies*, but that's not as much fun as just calling them people.

Earlier, we describe unique visitors as the least granular standard metric. Well, we fibbed a bit. Adobe Analytics has an even less granular standard metric than unique visitors called the people metric, but it's accessible only to Adobe customers who participate in Adobe's Device Co-op. Head to Chapter 5 to learn about the people metric and some of the technical details in how it's derived.

Understanding deduplication

Now that you've learned about metrics with three different levels of granularity (page views, visits, and visitors) but only one dimension (page), it's important to think about how they all come together. The flexibility of Adobe Analytics demands that you have a certain level of understanding of deduplication. A *duplicate* is an identical copy of something. When measuring user interaction with a website, it's often helpful to *deduplicate* — to strip out duplicate activity.

Let's explore an example:

1. Nolan views a home page.
2. Nolan views an article page.
3. Nolan views the home page again.

Even though this is a simple example, things get confusing quickly. A table containing the page dimension and a page views metric would look as you would expect: The home page has two page views and the article page has one page view.

But if you add a second metric of visits to this table, the home page has one visit and two page views and, the article page has one visit. Why one visit but two page views for the home page? The visits metric is deduplicated, meaning it is counted only one time during the entirety of the visit. In fact, Nolan could have gone back and forth between the home page and the same article page 50 times, and each of those two pages would still get only one visit each.

Adobe deduplicates the visits metric regardless of dimension; no matter how many times a dimensional value is sent in a visit, the visits metric is counted only once.

Let's expand our example by adding a second visit, this one coming a week later:

1. Nolan views the home page.
2. Nolan views a product page.
3. Nolan views the home page again.

If you were to view a report table with dates that spanned both visits, you could consider how each metric would align with each dimensional value in the page dimension. The home page gets four page views, two visits, and just one visitor. The article page earns one page view, one visit, and one visitor. The product page also earns one page view, one view, and one visitor. This means the unique visitors metric is also deduplicated, but it's done across visits for the full history of the visitor.

Trending metrics

If you think about your future as an analyst, you might imagine yourself discovering an incredible change in data that saves your company millions. In this dream, perhaps you've discovered several expensive products that customers can't buy due to a website coding error! For you to discover this error, you'd have to take advantage of trending, one of the most common activities you'll do with metrics in Adobe Analytics. *Trending* a metric means that you're analyzing a specific metric's change over time.

You can trend metrics in Adobe Analytics over any period of time with any granularity. You can trend page views per month for an entire year, or trend page views per hour for just a day. In both examples, you still have a metric and a dimension. The metric is page views and the dimension is the unit of time granularity you've specified for your table. In Analysis Workspace, you can build this table on your own, dragging in the metric and dimension, or you can use the one-click Visualize icon in any row in any table.

To learn more about one-click visualization of table rows, head to Chapter 8, which focuses on productivity tips and techniques.

Calculating metrics

Analysts must be able to apply calculations to their metrics that are flexible and adjustable on the fly, an area in which Adobe excels. To continue with our weather forecast example, you may want to convert the high and low temperatures in the forecast from Fahrenheit to Celsius. The formula is subtract 32 from the Fahrenheit temperature, and then multiply by 5/9. This new metric can be considered a calculated metric.

Let's take an example in the analytics world: An Adobe analyst is in a situation where unique visitors shoots up. Before declaring success, the analyst digs in further to some additional context by adding page views as a metric. In our example the analyst notices something strange — page views has barely increased, just a few more than the increased number of visitors.

The best recommendation that we have for the analyst is to create a calculated metric of page views per visitor. This simple metric, dividing page views by unique visitors, is one of the most basic calculated metrics in the digital analytics industry. In our example, the analyst may end up trending the calculated metric and discovering that although visitors increased significantly, page views per visitor dropped precipitously. Most likely this means that unqualified traffic is accessing the site, so our recommendation is to break that data down by other dimensions to better understand these disinterested visitors.

Calculated metrics get significantly more complex than dividing one metric by another. In Adobe, calculated metrics utilize all the standard math operators (division, multiplication, subtraction, and addition) and a wealth of advanced functions, such as square root, exponents, and percentiles. You can also apply logical operators (such as greater than and less than) and even segments to calculated metrics!

If you're looking to learn about all of your options for leveraging calculated metrics in Adobe Analytics, Chapter 10 is for you.

Measuring with Segments

Our last standard category of measurement to define is a segment. A *segment* is a subset of visitor traffic that is filtered based on behavior or attributes. If we go back to our weather forecast example from earlier, the closest concept to a segment that we have is the location of the forecast. New York is the original location. If we change the location to Maui, the metrics will change. A segment in Adobe Analytics is similar.

Let's imagine you're analyzing basic traffic patterns on your site. You grab the page dimension and add the page views, visits, and unique visitors metrics to the table, and discover that the top page on the site is the home page. You might then break down home page by the mobile device dimension to see the top devices on that page. Figure 2-5 shows a table that breaks down which devices people are using to interact with the site's home page.

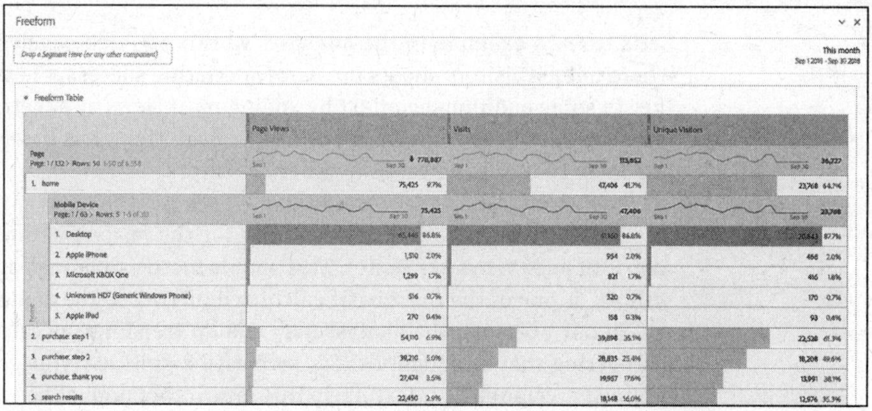

FIGURE 2-5:
A freeform
table without a
segment applied.

Note that the top device in the table is overwhelmingly desktop, but the data varies greatly for mobile devices such as the iPhone. An inquisitive analyst like you
would then want to know what the top pages are for mobile devices. In doing so,
you would create your first segment! By dragging the mobile device dimension,
you're now able to filter the data to a segment of visitors who came to the site via
a mobile device, as shown in Figure 2-6.

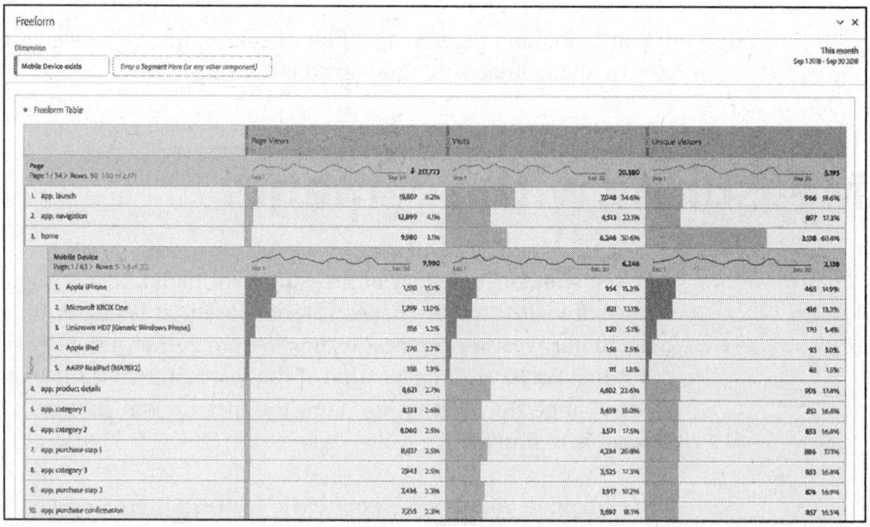

FIGURE 2-6:
A freeform table
with a mobile
device segment
applied.

Segments don't always have to be this simple. You can create a segment that combines multiple dimensions, metrics, and even powerful logic to include or exclude
your data based on behavior.

Chapter 9 defines the segment design process and digs into all of these capabilities.

Using Report Suites

Now that we've defined several standard categories of measurement, let's add one Adobe-specific category to the mix. A *report suite* defines a complete and independent set of data associated with one or many sets of websites. It's the highest-level data construct in Adobe Analytics and is similar to a Google Analytics profile.

Note that report suites are not reports. A report is a combination of any number of dimensions and metrics in a table. A count of page views, visits, and unique visitors distributed across all the values of the page dimension is a report. This basic report could be analyzed in any report suite to which you have access. Think of a report suite as a different database of underlying data, metrics, dimensions, and settings in which segments can be applied.

Report suites in Adobe Analytics have a number of settings that make them unique. All report suites have access to standard metrics and standard dimensions such as those discussed in this chapter. However, report suite administrators can hide those metrics and dimensions from view. In addition, Adobe has an impressive amount of custom metrics and dimensions that are defined and created by the managers of your Adobe implementation. These custom metrics and dimensions, as described in Chapters 5 and 7, respectively, can be different based on the report suite.

In addition to custom metrics and dimensions, report suites can also have unique currency codes, marketing channel settings, advertising account connections, and real-time report setup. Administrators also use report suites to define access rights within a company. These features are the key ingredients for understanding why report suites may be organized one way or another at your company.

Almost every company has more than one report suite in their Adobe Analytics implementation, so the data, settings, metrics, and dimensions will be different depending on the report suite that is being analyzed.

In this section, you walk through a few examples of report suite architecture and then discover the tools you need to find the report suite on your website.

Breaking it down in the real world

Some customers have just a single "global" report suite. Every website and mobile app sends data to one place, and data is consolidated into a single set of reports, dimensions, and metrics that often requires additional segmentation to focus on a single site or app. Other Adobe customers use a different report suite for every website; each report suite is organized differently with unique settings and custom metrics and dimensions.

The simple single website suite

Some companies have it easy. Brands that have a single domain and do business in one country often like to keep their analytics data simple too. Having a single online presence makes possible a simple report suite architecture: a single report suite that focuses on production data and a second report suite for all data generated in their development and staging environments.

REMEMBER

You may be surprised to see that second report suite, but it's imperative for analysts who value clean data (and we all do). Filtering data that comes from non-production environments is a best practice that we can't stress enough. Make sure your company is doing this. However, we still find it useful to capture non-production data. It's generally used for ensuring both data quality before site releases and that the IT team is aware of all code in use.

The biggest advantage in a single-production report suite environment is that your data is consolidated. If you need to focus on just one section of the site or one type of behavior, segments will do that for you. We're increasingly seeing brands move to a single-report suite configuration, especially as Adobe releases additional capabilities for virtual report suites, a newer feature in Adobe Analytics that allows administrators to globally apply a segment to a report suite to grant users a more focused experience. For more details on virtual report suites, check out Chapter 13.

The multi-country, multi-product corporation

We were recently working with an Adobe Analytics customer on the other side of the complexity spectrum. This customer has over 650 unique web domains spanning dozens of products in dozens of countries. Each domain has its own report suite.

You'll be glad to hear that configuring all these separate report suites was not done by accident. The company has over 100,000 employees based all over the world, and they used these report suites to ensure that each employee had access to the right data in the right report suite. If analysts for Product X in Romania were inaccurately provisioned for Product Y in Lithuania, they couldn't get their job done. In addition to access rights, report suite settings enabled the company to ensure that currency was displayed accurately in each country.

The good news is that the brand was rigorous with their analytics deployments. Every report suite had the same base set of custom metrics and custom dimensions, so it was easy for analysts to migrate from one brand to another or analyze data across countries without having to learn a new taxonomy for their data.

In addition, the company went a step further by leveraging *multi-suite tagging*, which is a technique used by some Adobe customers to send data to more than one report suite at a time. Separating different websites into specific report suites, and then leveraging multi-suite tagging to combine data when necessary is valuable to the brand because they send data to each individual domain's report suite as well as to a global report suite — the same one for every report suite. This combination of report suites and multi-suite tagging allows the brand to see a truly global view across all their products in all countries too.

Using Adobe Experience Cloud Debugger to identify your report suite

You may be wondering how simple or complicated your report suite architecture is. We thought this would be a great time to introduce you to a helpful, free tool called Adobe Experience Cloud Debugger. This tool provides an analyst with all the information necessary to identify a website's report suite, see what dimensional values are being sent, and more. At the time of this writing, the tool is available only for Google Chrome and can be accessed at https://marketing.adobe.com/resources/help/en_US/experience-cloud-debugger/.

After you've installed the extension, you'll see an Adobe Experience Cloud icon in your browser to engage the debugger. The final step is to head to your website (or any website that has Adobe Analytics implemented) and click the icon. A new window opens in your browser, displaying a list of all the Adobe solutions installed on the page along with a wealth of information about each.

You'll initially land on the Summary screen of the debugger. The left column displays a Page Information module with a screenshot of the page, URL, and page title. Below Page Information is the Adobe Analytics module, as shown in Figure 2-7.

In the Adobe Analytics module, note the Report Suite(s) entry. This is where you'll find the ID aligned with the website you're browsing.

We show you how to use this ID in Adobe Analytics as you begin to conquer the user Interface in Chapter 3.

IN THIS CHAPTER

» Interacting with the Analysis
Workspace tool

» Exploiting the value of prebuilt
Workspace templates

» Creating custom templates and
Workspace projects

Chapter **3**

Conquering the Analysis Workspace Interface

I n this chapter, you find out how to get around in Analysis Workspace, where you'll spend almost all your time in Adobe Analytics. You also create your first project.

This chapter sets the table, both metaphorically and literally, for what you explore in most of the remaining chapters. *Literally* because as you explore the basic interface in Analysis Workspace, you use tables — the non-graphical way to look at and work with data — as a way to learn the basics of setting up a project.

Next, you survey the templates in Analysis Workspace. Templates provide prebuilt starter projects that your company can use to kick-start your analyses and that users can employ to interact with and adjust data.

Even though you'll be spending most of your time in Analysis Workspace, you should be at least aware of other features of Adobe Analytics, which we describe in this chapter as well.

After you become familiar with these basics, you'll be armed with the knowledge and experience to begin analyzing data in Adobe Analytics. The goal is not just to analyze data, but to effect meaningful change at your company by creating better experiences for your customers, identifying successful advertising channels for your company, and more!

Surveying the Analytics Environment

The action in Adobe Analytics overwhelmingly takes place in Analysis Workspace. This is where you crunch, digest, and analyze data.

But as noted, there is more to Adobe Analytics than Workspace, so first you take a quick look at its additional features. Each has a place in an analyst's toolbox. You may have any number of the following features, depending on your Adobe Analytics version and configuration:

>> **Analysis Workspace** is Adobe's browser-based and visualization-heavy analysis tool. Analysis Workspace is built for the modern business user, analyst, and data scientist. And looking to the future, Analysis Workspace is where we expect to see new features appear as Adobe Analytics continues to evolve.

>> **Report Builder** is a plug-in that automatically imports Adobe Analytics into Microsoft Excel. It is used by analysts who prefer to work with data generated in Adobe Analytics in an Excel spreadsheet. Report Builder is available only for the Windows version of Excel.

>> **Activity Map** is a browser extension that overlays a *heat map* (a color-coded graphic overlay) to summarize information. For example, a heat map on your own website might display in a deeper shade of blue the links or images that were clicked more often, and display in a lighter shade of blue the areas that were clicked less often. You install Activity Map in your browser by choosing Tools ➪ Activity Map and downloading the plug-in for your browser. If you can't install Activity Map, talk to your Adobe Analytics administrator. The tool is useful for quickly identifying where on your site visitors are clicking but is not ideal for deep analysis. For more details on Activity Map, skip ahead to Chapter 16.

>> **Data Workbench** is Adobe's most advanced analysis tool. It enables Adobe customers to import and integrate non-Adobe datasets to perform advanced analyses, multitouch attribution, propensity modeling, and more. Adobe will often avoid recommending that a company buy Data Workbench unless the company's needs are aligned with specific use cases. The technology is more complicated to use than all other Adobe Analytics tools and is available for an additional cost. Data Workbench is used successfully by a small and mature set of data-driven companies.

>> **Ad Hoc Analysis** is a Java-based tool that was once the preferred tool for advanced analysis of Adobe data. Its features were migrated to Analysis Workspace. Adobe has announced that access to Ad Hoc Analysis will end soon and the tool will no longer be supported.

>> **Reports and Analytics** is the browser-based precursor to Analysis Workspace. If you've heard long-time Adobe users talk about SiteCatalyst or Omniture, they're describing this interface. The tool is inflexible, and companies are migrating towards Workspace.

Zooming In on the Workspace

Now that you understand the lay of the land when it comes to Adobe's tools, it's time to zoom in on the Analysis Workspace interface. It's Adobe's most widely used, flexible, and user-friendly tool and the place where Adobe is adding new analysis tools and gadgets all the time.

The key aspects of a sample Workspace project are labeled in Figure 3-1. As you can see, the interface has three main components:

>> Left rail

>> Left rail selector

>> One or more panels

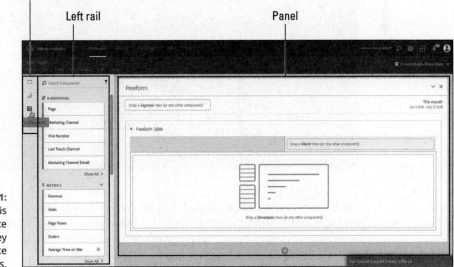

FIGURE 3-1: A sample Analysis Workspace project with key user interface annotations.

In this chapter, you explore all three components in detail, starting with the main panel. All analyses take place in the main panel. It's where you build data tables and visualizations by weaving together metrics, dimensions, and segments. However, first you need to log in and open a project, so that's what we describe next.

Creating Your First Project

Adobe made it easy to start working in Analysis Workspace. You log in at https:// experiencecloud.adobe.com. If you don't have your ID and password saved in your browser, you will be prompted for an ID and a password. Your Adobe ID is most likely your work email, although you should check with your Adobe administrator if you're unsure.

Adobe Experience Cloud has other solutions and platform-wide core services in addition to Adobe Analytics, so depending on your installation setup, you might see the Solution Selector when you log in to Experience Cloud. If that is the case, click Analytics, which should be highlighted in purple to let you know that you have access to it as shown in Figure 3-2.

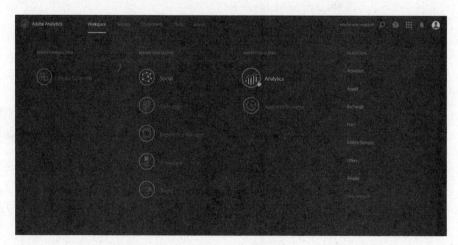

FIGURE 3-2:
Choosing Adobe Analytics in the Solution Selector.

You've now loaded Adobe Analytics in your browser, but let's make sure you have access to and are in Analysis Workspace. Click Workspace in the top row, as shown in Figure 3-3. Note how the Workspace is highlighted with an underline and a brighter font color because it's the currently open tool.

FIGURE 3-3:
Verifying that you
are logged into
Workspace in
Adobe Analytics.

If you don't see Workspace in the top row or you're unable to click it, reach out to your Adobe administrator. Every Adobe Analytics installation has access to Analysis Workspace, so if you don't see it as an option, it's still there! You just need to ask your administrator to enable your username so you can access it.

Analysis Workspace appears, as shown in Figure 3-4. You're ready to create your first project.

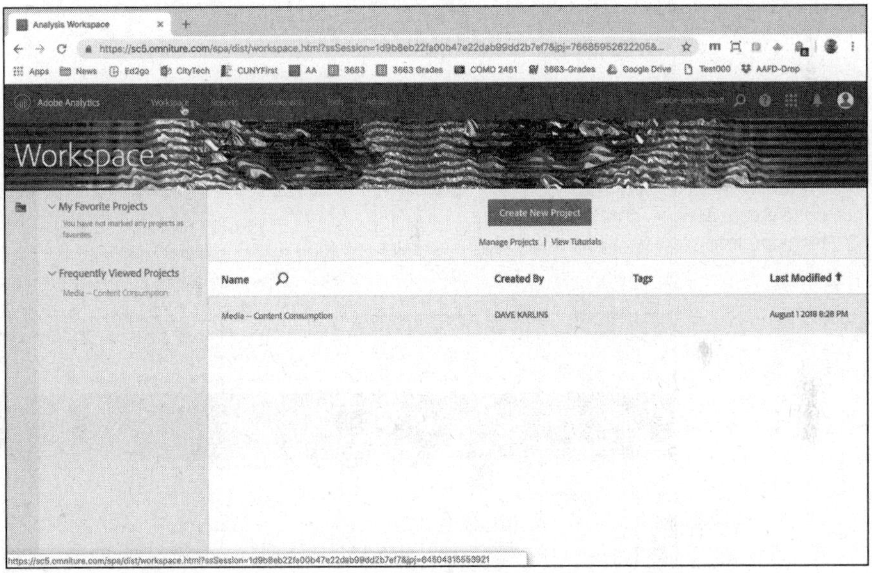

FIGURE 3-4:
Analysis
Workspace,
with a single
project created.

1. **Click the blue Create New Project button.**

   The dialog shown in Figure 3-5 opens, displaying optional templates. In Chapter 4, we explore these optional templates and share tips and advice on how to get the most out of them. Here, we focus on building a new project from a blank template.

2. **Double-click the Blank Project template.**

   You could also click the template once and then click the blue Create button in the bottom-right corner. A new blank project opens with a freeform panel, as shown in Figure 3-6. The freeform panel is essentially a blank slate, ready for you to begin to analyze data.

3. Pat yourself on the back.

Congrats, you're ready to analyze!

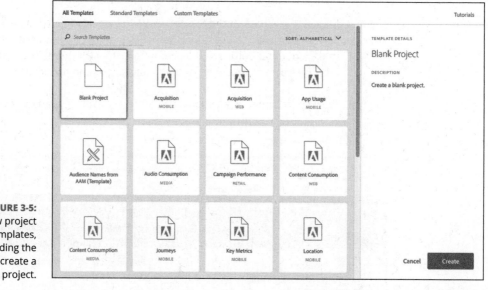

FIGURE 3-5:
New project templates, including the option to create a blank project.

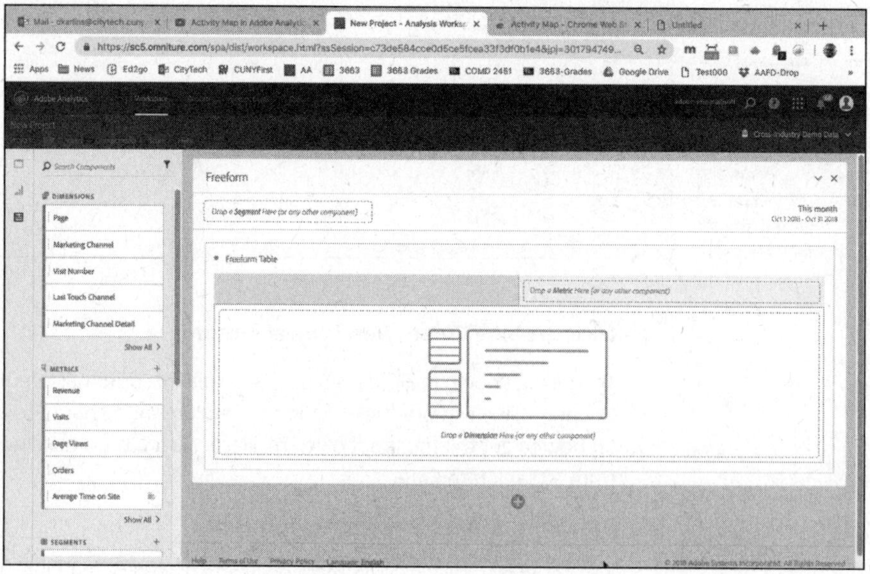

FIGURE 3-6:
A new blank project in Analysis Workspace.

Understanding the Calendar

Every analysis that you perform needs to be associated with a timeframe, so we begin examining the Workspace interface with a detailed explanation of the calendar and your options for interacting with it.

Mastering the calendar in Analysis Workspace is a must for users because every dataset you create is tied to a set of dates. Nothing is more frustrating than thinking you've found an interesting anomaly or insight only to realize that you were looking at the wrong timeframe. The Adobe calendar interface is intuitive and flexible, but it does have a few quirks, which we note in this section.

When you first open a blank project, the default date is set to This Month (refer to Figure 3-6).

To define a timeframe, follow these steps:

1. **Access the calendar by clicking any part of the date in the top-right corner of the main panel (refer to Figure 3-6).**

   The calendar dialog appears with the current month highlighted in gray and the current day in bold.

2. **Click one date and click again to select a second date.**

   The selected date range is shaded, as shown in Figure 3-7.

   Note that you can select the dates in any order; you don't have to select the starting date and then the ending date. To change months, click the left or right arrowhead, or click either of the visible months to see a drop-down list of all 12 months. To jump to a date in a different year, click the current year. See Chapter 7 to discover how to create custom date ranges.

FIGURE 3-7: Selecting a range of dates for a timeline.

3. **After you define your timeframe in the calendar, choose Apply or Apply to All Panels.**

A calendar's timeframe is limited to its own panel. You can add multiple panels to a project, each with its own unique calendar. The blue Apply button changes the dates associated with the calendar in only the panel where it exists. The Apply to All Panels button aligns the data in every panel in your Workspace project with the changed date.

TIP

To select the date quickly, simply double-click the month (or year) to select the entire month (or year).

In addition to selecting dates as described in the preceding list, you can also choose a *preset range,* which lets you quickly apply a frequently used timeframe. To select a preset time range, such as yesterday, last week, or the last 20 days, use the Select a Preset drop-down list (refer to Figure 3-7).

When you choose a preset range, the Use Rolling Dates check box becomes selected. As a result, data in your table will be updated when you log into the Workspace project. Updating takes place depending on the date range you define. For example, if you choose a date range of a few days, data is updated daily, if you chose an initial date range of a month, data is updated next month, and so on.

To view additional details about rolling dates, click the blue Rolling Daily — Rolling Daily link. You can now define when a day starts and ends, as shown in Figure 3-8.

FIGURE 3-8:
Viewing details
for rolling dates.

<	July 2018							August 2018						>
SU	MO	TU	WE	TH	FR	SA	SU	MO	TU	WE	TH	FR	SA	
1	2	3	4	5	6	7			1	2	3	4		
8	9	10	11	12	13	14	5	6	7	8	9	10	11	
15	16	17	18	19	20	21	12	13	14	15	16	17	18	
22	23	24	25	26	27	28	19	20	21	22	23	24	25	
29	30	31					26	27	28	29	30	31		

Shift+click or right click to append to range.   Selected Days: 90

☑ Use Rolling Dates (rolling daily - rolling daily)   Hide Details

Date Preview: Jul 4 2018 - Oct 1 2018

Start: Start of current day minus 89 days

End: End of current day (none)

Last 90 days   × ⌄

Cancel   Apply To All Panels   Apply

OVERRIDING CALENDAR TIMEFRAMES

You may override the calendar's timeframe. An example of this topic is described in detail in Chapter 8's section on time comparisons; we're noting it here because the option can confuse new users.

Adobe has included the Time Ranges component type, which is useful for filtering a metric, dimension, or segment based on a set of dates. These time-based components override the timeframe defined in the panel's calendar. This feature can be useful for a number of reasons. A simple example is comparing last month to the current month in a single table. You simply add the revenue metric to a table twice and apply to the second instance of the metric a time range set to the previous month, even though the calendar is still set to the current month.

The start date for this preset is the Start of Current Day Minus 89 Days and the preset ends on End of Current Day (None). Click each part of that definition and notice how you can customize the statement. You can define rolling dates in a virtually unlimited number of ways.

Using Analysis Workspace Panels

A *panel* is a collection of data presented in tables and *visualizations* (graphs and charts). Panels in Analysis Workspace are an easy way to keep your data visualizations organized. Adobe analysts use panels to organize projects by time period, business unit, geography, marketing channel, and more.

What are the advantages of grouping tables and visualizations in a panel, as opposed to having each one in its own panel? Well, for one, grouping tables and visualizations in a panel makes them visually coherent and easy to compare and look at as a set. Also, panels are assigned their own calendar, so all the tables and visualizations within a single panel can be updated by changing a single calendar.

Click the Panels icon, shown in Figure 3-9, to toggle between displaying and hiding the available panels.

Adobe has created four types of panels in Analysis Workspace, as shown in the left rail selector:

>> **Blank panel:** Our advice, especially as you acclimate to Adobe Analytics, is to start with the blank panel, shown in Figure 3-10. It's similar to the freeform panel but comes with a list of commonly used visualizations instead of a blank freeform table.

FIGURE 3-9:
When the left
rail selector is
set to Panels,
you see the four
types of panels.

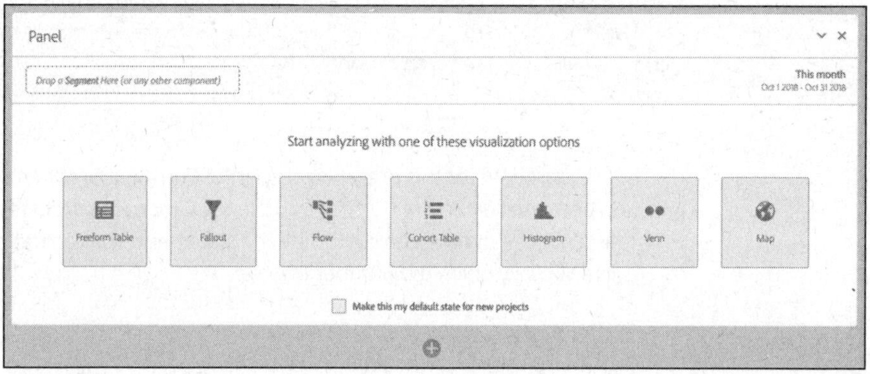

FIGURE 3-10:
The blank panel
in Analysis
Workspace.

>> **Attribution panel:** Adobe built the attribution panel to enable analysts to compare multiple models that weight a metric against multiple dimensional values. The panel starts with a drop zone for a metric, a dimension, and a menu to select the models for comparison, as shown in Figure 3-11. We describe the attribution panel in detail in Chapter 12.

>> **Freeform panel:** This panel is the most basic and is the default panel when you open a new blank project, as shown in Figure 3-12. It is comprised of the calendar (which is defined by clicking the date but is not usually displayed), the Dimension drop zone, the Metric drop zone, the Segment drop zone, and a blank freeform table.

>> **Segment Comparison:** This panel, shown in Figure 3-13, compares two segments. The panel starts with two drop zones for comparing segments, a date link through which you can define a calendar, an area to define advanced settings, and a Build button. Segment Comparison performs a massive set of calculations to compare different segments, and produces a set of values, charts, and tables that summarize the relationship between the selected segments. See Chapter 15 to learn more about the segment comparison panel, its functionality, and some of the associated statistics.

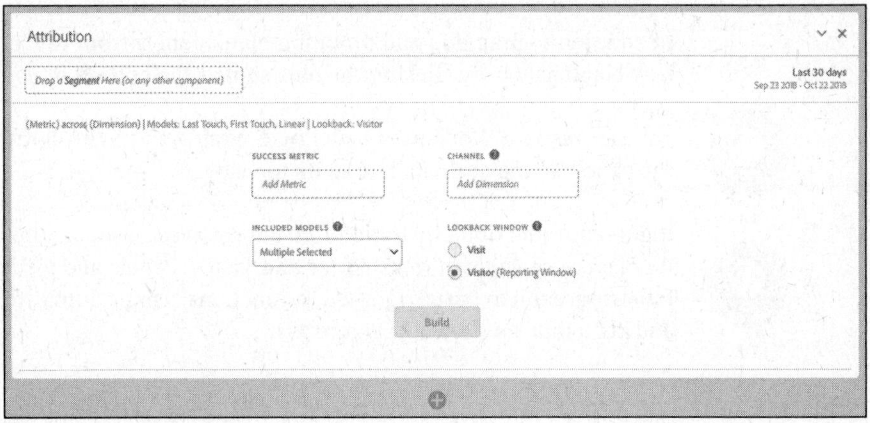

FIGURE 3-11:
An empty
attribution panel
in Workspace.

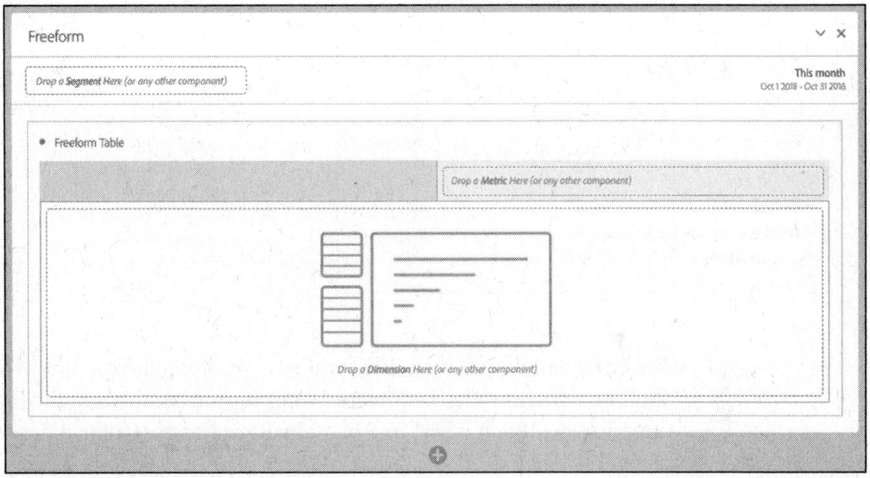

FIGURE 3-12:
A freeform table
ready to be
configured.

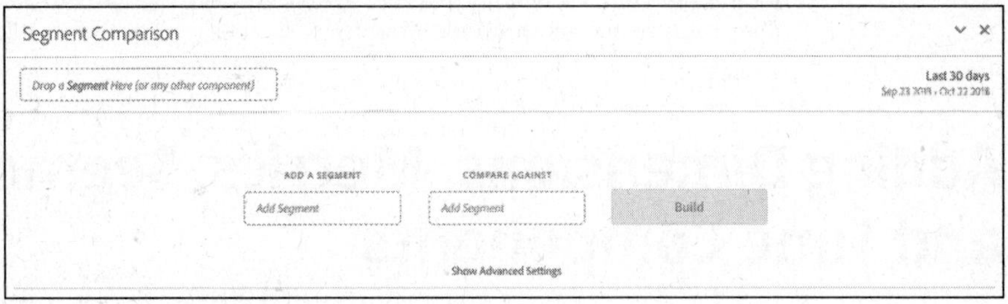

FIGURE 3-13:
A Segment
Comparison
panel is ready for
segments.

In addition to dragging and dropping blank panels from the left rail, you can add new blank panels by clicking the plus sign at the bottom of your project.

You can resize a Workspace panel by dragging the right, bottom, or left sides of the panel. To move a panel, drag its top side.

Right-click functionality is built into almost every visualization and component in Workspace so you can work better and faster. Panels and visualizations have the following similar basic right-click functions: copy, duplicate, edit description, and get a link, as shown in Figure 3-14.

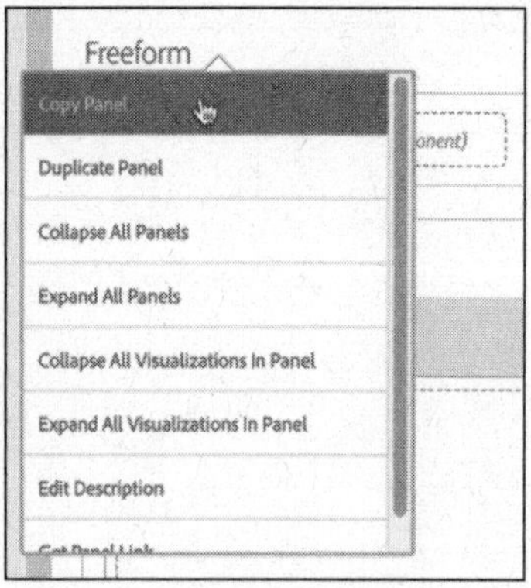

Freeform

Copy Panel

Duplicate Panel

Collapse All Panels

Expand All Panels

Collapse All Visualizations In Panel

Expand All Visualizations In Panel

Edit Description

FIGURE 3-14:
A freeform
panel's right-click
context menu.

The Copy Panel option enables you to copy a panel from one Workspace project to another, whereas the Duplicate Panel option simply replicates the panel in the same project. Each panel and visualization has room for a description, which you can edit by right-clicking and using a rich text editor. After you save a project, choose Get Panel Link to provide the user with a URL that links directly to the panel. This option is a great way to share a specific analysis to a colleague, but it does require access to Adobe Analytics.

Adding Dimensions, Metrics, Segments, and Time Components

The next step for leveraging data in Analysis Workspace is getting comfortable with adding components — metrics, dimensions, segments, and time — to the panels.

To view the list of components, click the Components icon, which is the third icon in the left rail selector, as shown in Figure 3-15.

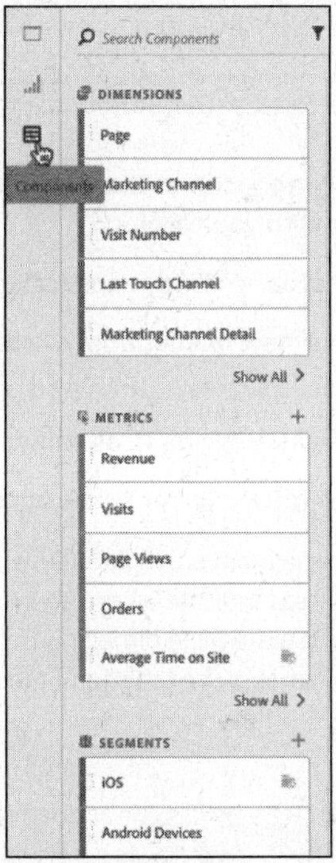

FIGURE 3-15:
Displaying
components.

The left rail is divided into four component types: Dimensions, Metrics, Segments, and Time. (Scroll down the left rail to see the Time component.) You can quickly find the components you use most often because each component type lists the top five most frequently used components.

You can also use the left rail to search for a component in several ways. You can manually browse for the component, or you can use the search bar at the top to search by the component's name or metadata tag.

You can drag all kinds of things into the Workspace, but they might not work together. That is, you could drag a combination of dimensions, metrics, and segments during a timeframe for which data does not exist in the report suite. Don't panic; instead, press ⌘+Z on a Mac or Ctrl+Z on a PC to undo your most recent action and try again.

Adding a dimension

Not to get too existential here, but just as there is no universe without dimensions (x, y, z, space, and so on), there is no analysis without dimension. So the starting point in defining a new freeform panel is to drop in a dimension.

To start a new blank project with a freeform panel, follow these steps:

1. **Add a blank panel by clicking the Panels icon at the top of the left rail selector, and dragging a blank panel to your project.**

   Or click the plus sign at the bottom of your Workspace project.

2. **Click the freeform table icon in your new blank panel to add a freeform table.**

3. **Select any dimension listed and begin dragging it, as shown in Figure 3-16.**

   To follow along with the example, select Page under Dimensions.

   As soon as you grab the component, the main panel dims several areas and highlights others. These highlighted areas indicate where you can drop the component. In Figure 3-16, you can drop the page dimension in the Segment drop zone at the top, the Metric drop zone in the table, and the Dimension drop zone.

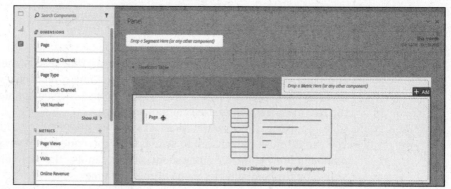

FIGURE 3-16: Dragging the page dimension into an empty freeform table.

4. **Drop the dimension in one of the highlighted areas.**

   Adding a dimension to a table means that you've created your first table in Analysis Workspace — congratulations!

Because dimensions are linked to metrics, when you add a page dimension, Adobe Analytics automatically places a relevant metric — the occurrences metric — in the second column of the freeform table. *Occurrences* are the sum of visits to a page and activity on that page (such as watching a video).

Adding a metric

Drop zone guides are the blue helper statements that appear as you bring a new component into a *visualization* (a table or graphic). These guides help ensure that the visualization reacts to having components added in a way the user expects by identifying breakdowns, filters, and additions to your work. For example, grab a metric other than occurrences in the left rail and drag it next to the occurrences metric in your table; the drop zone guide reads *Add*, as shown in Figure 3-17.

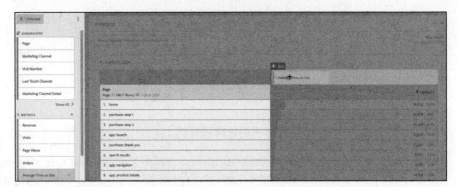

FIGURE 3-17: Adding a second metric to a freeform table.

Adding a dimensional breakdown

Now that you've successfully added a dimension and a second metric to a table, it's time to create your first dimensional breakdown.

A *dimensional breakdown* allows you to intervene anywhere in a hierarchy of data to break down any particular statistic. So, for example, if you don't want to break down an entire table to show what marketing channel users came through, you could make marketing channel users a breakdown that you applied only to a particular dimension (such as page) within a table.

Let's walk through how that would work — using the marketing channel dimension as a breakdown to identify which channels are driving people to our home page. To do that, drag Marketing Channel from the left rail, over the Home dimensional value (which is a row in the Dimensions column) in a table. As that happens, the drop zone guide reads *Breakdown*, as shown in Figure 3-18.

The result is a breakdown of the top marketing channels driving people to the home page, as shown in Figure 3-19.

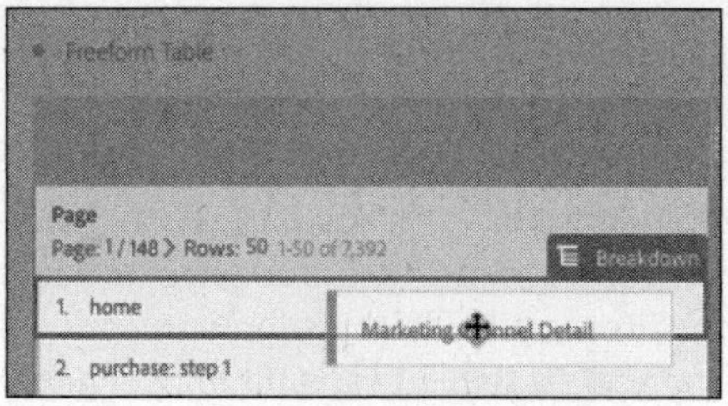

FIGURE 3-18:
Dragging the marketing channel dimension into a freeform table to create a dimensional breakdown.

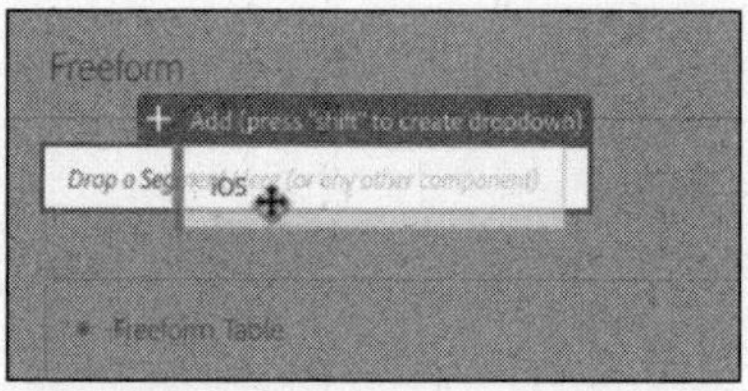

FIGURE 3-19:
Identifying top marketing channels driving users to the site home page.

Adding a segment

Segments enable you to identify subsets of visitors based on characteristics or website interactions, and to further filter data. For example, you might want to see table data filtered to show only Android users or only iOS users.

Segments are listed in the Segments area of the component section of the left rail. To take the next step in zeroing in on user activity, apply a segment to your panel by dropping a segment listed in your project into the Segment drop zone at the top of your panel. In Figure 3-20, the segment is iOS users. You may use whatever segment you have available. The data in the table is updated so that it applies to this segment.

FIGURE 3-20:
Dragging a segment into the drop zone to filter for iOS users.

REMEMBER

If you make a mistake, you can always press the undo keyboard shortcut (⌘+Z on a Mac or Ctrl+Z on a PC).

Adding a time

Finally, you look at how you can quickly and easily filter for a set time range using segments. For example, you might want to quickly zoom in on last week's data.

To apply a new date range to a panel quickly, without hassling with setting a new range in the calendar, you can drag a component from the Time section of the components area in the left rail right onto the date in the upper-right corner of the panel. For example, if you want to change the calendar to reflect data over the past two weeks, you can drag the Last Two Full Weeks time component over the date.

You may have noticed that time components have the unique capability to be dropped on top of the calendar, replacing the timeframe. This feature can be a nice way to save a few clicks if the time range you need is quickly accessible.

Thankfully, we have many more components than those listed for metrics, dimensions, segments, and time ranges. Adobe automatically displays the five most commonly used components in the left rail. Below each of these component types, note the Show All link, which provides a complete list of components. A quick inspection of this list reveals many more components, sorted alphabetically. The number of components that appear is based on the access you have as well as the complexity of your company's Adobe implementation.

Hover your cursor over any component to display an information bubble that provides useful details about that component:

>> Metrics display a metric definition if one exists as well as a trend of that metric over the last 90 days.

>> Dimensions display the top five items captured over the last 90 days.

>> Segments display the definition as well as a graph depicting the percentage of page views, visits, and visitors that make up that segment.

>> Time ranges display the definition of the range.

When you hover your cursor over a dimension component, a second icon appears — a caret pointing to the right. Click this useful icon to see an interactive set of all values captured in that dimension over the last 90 days. You can drag these dimensional values to a panel in Analysis Workspace for more tailored filtering and segmentation.

Users can also right-click a component in the left rail to tag, approve, share, or delete the component or make it a favorite, based on the component and your rights as a user.

The smart search box makes it easy to find what you're looking for in this unwieldy list of components. In addition to the standard typing-based search, the icon to the right of the search box (refer to Figure 3-16) filters based on component type, tag, and components you've approved or made a favorite.

To select multiple components, use Shift to highlight a set of adjacent dimensions, dimensional values, metrics, segments, or time ranges. Use Control (PC) or ⌘ (Mac) to select specific items in the left rail one-by-one.

Navigating the Menu Structure

The last section of the interface to understand is the second-level menu structure in the Adobe Analysis window or tab of your browser. The menu consists of six top-level items: Project, Edit, Insert, Components, Share, and Help as well as a list of report suites in the top right. Most menu items have keyboard shortcuts, which help make the Workspace feel more like an application and less like browser-based software.

Here's what each of these menu options does:

>> **Project menu:** Focuses on project-level adjustments, similar to the File menu in an application. Users can open a new project, save a project, refresh data, download a CSV or PDF file with the project data, and adjust the settings for a project. These are the most commonly used menu items.

If you select Project Info & Settings, a panel appears that tells you about the project and allows you to change or update information about a project, as shown in Figure 3-21. The panel is similar to the file properties box in an operating system application. Users can rename a project, see who created it, see when it was last modified, add metadata tags, create or edit the project description, and adjust the project color palette.

>> **Edit menu:** Provides undo and redo functionality, which can often be a blessing for users. The Clear All option deletes everything in the project. Adobe thankfully asks "Are you sure?" before clearing all your data from a project.

>> **Insert menu:** Offers an alternative to dragging and dropping panels and visualizations from the left rail.

>> **Components menu:** Provides an alternative to creating metrics, segments, date ranges, and alerts from the left rail or main panel. The Refresh Components option can be useful in multi-user organizations. For example, if a co-worker creates a new segment and shares it with you, the segment won't appear instantly in your Workspace instance. The Refresh Components feature instantly checks whether there are changes to the components you have access to so you can start using them without closing your current project.

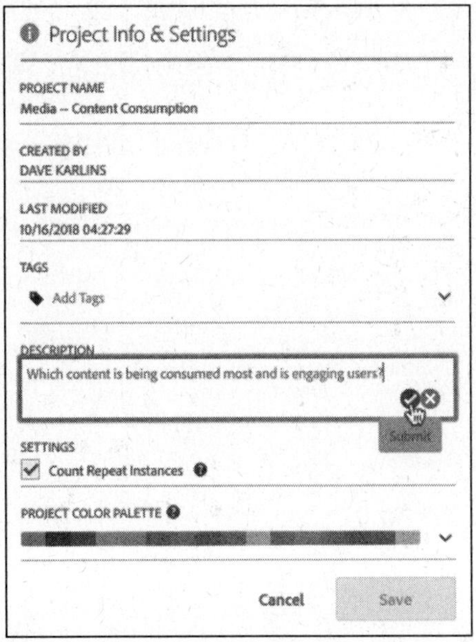

FIGURE 3-21:
Changing project
information and
settings.

>> **Share menu:** Deals with the myriad of ways that projects can be shared among users. Chapters 14 and 16 go into these functions in detail.

>> **Help menu:** Provides a set of useful user resources, including the Adobe knowledge base, the Adobe Analytics YouTube channel, and the Experience League help forum.

2

Analyzing Data

Chapter 4

Building Analytic Reports with Freeform Tables

The more adept you get at putting together combinations of dimensions, metrics, segments, and time constraints, and then comparing and filtering data in a report, the more effectively you can identify patterns, trends, and warning signs that lead to improving success rates online. In this chapter, we dig more deeply into how to do just that.

Reports can include graphical visualizations (charts and graphs) and tables. In this chapter, our focus is on building tables with a single dimension and with multiple dimensions, managing metrics, and then using different techniques to sort and filter the data that is revealed so it is easy to analyze and share.

We end the chapter with a look at templates in Adobe Analytics. Templates are useful, and exploring them is a valuable way to further acclimate to the interface and logic issues and solutions involved in creating or editing reports.

Working with Dimensions and Metrics

We introduce dimensions, metrics, and segments in Chapter 2, and you'll hear (if you're reading out loud, otherwise you'll read) about them in every chapter of this book. Let's revisit these terms in detail before you plunge into building reports.

Wrapping your head around dimensions

Dimensions are the essential characteristics of a set of data. Whereas metrics are quantitative, dimensions are qualitative. Dimensions set the parameters and define the framework for what is measured.

A dimension is something from which you can make a list. For example, color is a dimension with a seemingly unlimited number of values: red, blue, green, orange, and so on. In data analysis, common dimensions include the following:

- ❱❱ Page
- ❱❱ Products
- ❱❱ Day, week, month, quarter, or year
- ❱❱ Demographic (such as age)
- ❱❱ Day, week, month, or any other measurement of time
- ❱❱ Device, for example, mobile, laptop/desktop, or operating system (such as Android or iOS)

Combining dimensions and metrics

Metrics are the quantitative measurements of a dimension. Metrics show quantitative information about visitor activity, such as page views, click-throughs, reloads, average time spent, units, orders, and revenue. In a report, metrics are displayed in columns. Broad categories of metrics include the following:

- ❱❱ **Traffic metrics:** Measure the volume of visits to a page.
- ❱❱ **Conversion metrics:** Measure success events, such as satisfied users of a customer support site, purchases, or completed input forms.
- ❱❱ **Video metrics:** Quantify aspects of user engagement with videos, including the number of views, the time spent watching a video, or the rate at which users are watching a complete video.
- ❱❱ **Calculated metrics:** Are created by combining metrics. We dig into calculated metrics in Chapter 10.
- ❱❱ **Segments:** Consist of custom subsets of data, or data filtered by rules that you create. In Analysis Workspace, segmentation can be applied to individual tables, or to an entire panel.

Effectively piecing together dimensions and metrics can reveal ever-deepening levels of understanding of the effect of your web presence. To take a minimalist example, Figure 4-1 shows a table with product as the dimension and visits as the sole metric. It tells us that a product with a SKU of prd1006 is the most visited product on the site.

Product ▼pr Page: 1 / 20 > Rows: 10 1-10 of 198	Visits	
	Sep 16	Oct 15 ↓ 178,327
1. prd1006		5,263 3.0%
2. prd1009		5,250 2.9%
3. prd1016		4,973 2.8%
4. prd1014		4,686 2.6%
5. prd1052		4,403 2.5%
6. prd1149		4,225 2.4%

FIGURE 4-1:
A report with a single metric identifies products with the most visits.

But before recommending that our organization devote more resources into promoting the product that is getting the most visits, it would be judicious to enhance our understanding of which products are generating the most *revenue* per visit. That information is revealed when we add a revenue/visits metric. As you can see in Figure 4-2, although prd1014 is getting the most visits online, a different product produces much more revenue each time the associated page is visited. On this basis, you can make more informed decisions about marketing investments.

Product ▼pr Page: 1 / 20 > Rows: 10 1-10 of 198	Visits		Revenue / Visits	
	Sep 16	Oct 15 ↓ 178,327	Sep 16	Oct 15 $416.75
1. prd1006		5,263 3.0%		$47.79 11.5%
2. prd1009		5,250 2.9%		$138.50 33.2%
3. prd1016		4,973 2.8%		$89.94 21.6%
4. prd1014		4,686 2.6%		$107.46 25.8%
5. prd1052		4,403 2.5%		$255.41 61.3%
6. prd1149		4,225 2.4%		$11.76 2.8%

FIGURE 4-2:
An additional metric identifies more essential information about product revenue.

TIP

Tables are paginated, and you can control the number of rows that are displayed in any page of a table by clicking the Rows link at the top of the first column and choosing the number of rows to display. Click page numbers or the back (<) or forward (>) icon to navigate from page to page.

Adding Dimensions to a Table

Data analysis does not exist without dimensions. As a data analyst, you'll deploy your training, expertise, talents, and instincts to select dimensions to use to begin to analyze data. And as you do, you'll get plenty of help from Adobe Analytics, which supplies a set of frequently deployed dimensions in the Dimensions pane of the components section.

You can break down dimensions by other dimensions to analyze and compare nearly anything. For example, you can start with the cities dimension (which shows which geographical city your visitors are accessing your site from) and break it down by marketing channel (the technique used to bring your visitors to your site). You could then apply a metric such as revenue to see how these channels affected your bottom line in each city. This knowledge will then help your advertising team hone their marketing tactics based on geography.

REMEMBER

You add dimensions to a freeform table by dragging them from the Dimensions pane into the Drop a Dimension area of the table.

Adding the page dimension

When dimensions are applied to data analysis of web traffic, the page dimension often plays a defining role, identifying the page (or part of a page) with which metrics are associated. The page dimension is the most basic dimension used in digital analytics and tells you where activity is taking place on a website or an app.

If you're building report tables from scratch (using the blank project template), often the first place to start is by adding a page dimension to a freeform table. To add a page dimension to a freeform table, simply drag the dimension into the body of the table, as shown in Figure 4-3.

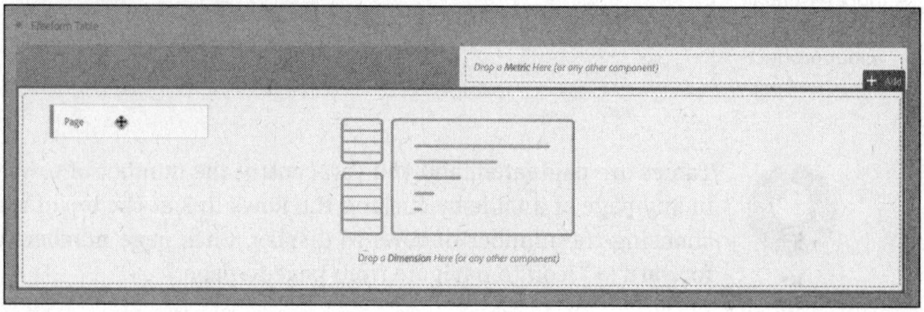

FIGURE 4-3:
Initiating a freeform table with a page dimension.

To understand what a *page* means in Adobe Analytics, including how page views are effectively measured in parallax sites and sites that employ JavaScript to show and hide page content, see Chapter 1.

Dimensions are meaningless without associated metrics, so as soon as you add a page dimension to a table, Adobe Analytics helpfully supplies your first metric: occurrences, shown in Figure 4-4.

FIGURE 4-4:
A page dimension with an added metric: occurrences.

We explore adding metrics later in this chapter. For now, remember that an *occurrence* is the sum of page views and subsequent page events. A *page view* is counted for each server call that is sent for a page. *Page events* are other user interactions with content that can be quantified, distinct from opening a page, including downloads, ad clicks, viewing a video, or submitting a registration form.

Analyzing a second dimension using the visit number dimension

The visit number dimension quantifies which customer visit numbers on your site most influenced your success metrics. A visitor making a first visit to your site is counted in the Visit Number 1 line item. Visitors that return to the site for a second visit are counted in the Visit Number 2 line item, and so forth.

A report using visit numbers helps answer questions such as: Do customers who purchased on their fourth visit generate more revenue than those who purchased on their first visit? And how can a site be enhanced to maximize conversions for return visits?

Figure 4-5 shows the increasing success rate for visitors who return to a website frequently.

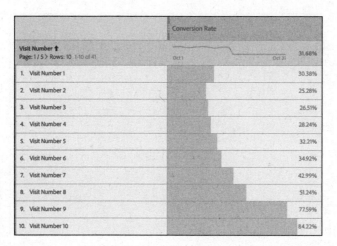

Visit Number ↑	Conversion Rate	
Page: 1 / 5 > Rows: 10 1-10 of 41	Oct 1 Oct 31	31.68%
1. Visit Number 1		30.38%
2. Visit Number 2		25.28%
3. Visit Number 3		26.51%
4. Visit Number 4		28.24%
5. Visit Number 5		32.21%
6. Visit Number 6		34.92%
7. Visit Number 7		42.99%
8. Visit Number 8		51.24%
9. Visit Number 9		77.59%
10. Visit Number 10		84.22%

FIGURE 4-5: Increased conversion rates for repeat site visitors.

You can use a table like this to see how conversion rates change as your visitors get more familiar with your site.

Mixing in the marketing channel dimension

Marketing channel data lets you know how much revenue your marketing channels generate. Depending on how your Adobe Analytics installation is set up, marketing channel dimensions can include email, paid search, directed traffic from affiliates, external campaigns, and social media campaigns (with varying levels of detail).

You create a basic marketing channel table by creating a new freeform table and dragging the marketing channel dimension into the table.

Zooming in with Multiple Metrics

As you've seen, the minute — no, make that the nanosecond — you drag a dimension into a freefrom table, Adobe Analytics helpfully plugs in a metric. By default, that metric is occurrences. You can replace that metric and you can add additional metrics.

Replacing a metric

Replacing one metric with another is easy. The trick, if you can call it that, is to drag the replacement metric over the original metric so that the Replace screentip appears. In Figure 4-6, we are replacing the occurrences metric with the conversion rate metric.

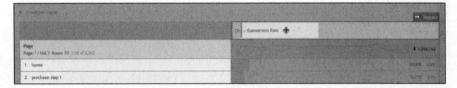

FIGURE 4-6:
Replacing a
metric.

WARNING

Depending on how you position a new metric in a column, you either replace the existing metric or add a new one. If you want to *replace* a metric, make sure that Replace screentip is displayed. If you don't see that message, adjust the position of where you drop the replacement metric until you do see the message.

Adding a second metric

In addition to replacing an existing metric, you can clarify your analysis by *adding* metrics.

Let's mix a second metric into this scenario: revenue/order. Adding that metric will help us understand the relationship between when a user makes a purchase, and how much they spend. Do users who wait until they've been to the site ten times before making a purchase spend more than users who grab an item and head for the shopping cart on their first visit? And if so, what can you do to maximize this information to improve success rates?

The results, shown in Figure 4-7, reveal that in this case, tenth visits yield a higher conversion rate *and* higher revenue per order.

FIGURE 4-7:
Comparing
conversion rates
and revenue per
order for repeat
visitors.

		Conversion Rate			Revenue / Order	
Visit Number ↑ Page: 1 / 5 › Rows: 10 1-10 of 41		Oct 1	Oct 31	31.68%	Oct 1	Oct 31	$1,373.91
1. Visit Number 1			30.38%		$519.84	37.8%
2. Visit Number 2			25.28%		$468.56	34.1%
3. Visit Number 3			26.51%		$570.06	41.5%
4. Visit Number 4			28.24%		$757.20	55.1%
5. Visit Number 5			32.21%		$955.30	69.5%
6. Visit Number 6			34.92%		$1,452.18	105.7%
7. Visit Number 7			42.99%		$2,032.21	147.9%
8. Visit Number 8			51.24%		$2,828.09	205.8%
9. Visit Number 9			77.59%		$3,300.69	240.2%
10. Visit Number 10			84.22%		$4,735.01	344.6%

Throwing a third metric into the mix

To further get a handle on visitor activity and how visits translate into sales, let's add a third metric to our table: orders.

As Figure 4-8 reveals, adding the orders metric sheds a different light on the data than was revealed simply by looking at revenue/order and conversion rate. It reveals a radically decreasing number of orders placed by users on visits beyond five. In addition, in terms of absolute numbers of orders, over half of all orders are placed during a user's first or second visit to our site.

FIGURE 4-8:
Adding a third
metric sheds new
light on how
many orders are
placed in relation
to the number of
user visits.

		Conversion Rate			Revenue / Order			Orders	
Visit Number ↑ Page: 1 / 5 › Rows: 10 1-10 of 41		Oct 1	Oct 31	31.68%	Oct 1	Oct 31	$1,373.91	Oct 1	Oct 31	31,783
1. Visit Number 1			30.38%		$519.84	37.8%		11,261	35.4%
2. Visit Number 2			25.28%		$468.56	34.1%		5,818	18.3%
3. Visit Number 3			26.51%		$570.06	41.5%		3,877	12.2%
4. Visit Number 4			28.24%		$757.20	55.1%		2,619	8.2%
5. Visit Number 5			32.21%		$955.30	69.5%		1,840	5.8%
6. Visit Number 6			34.92%		$1,452.18	105.7%		1,193	3.8%
7. Visit Number 7			42.99%		$2,032.21	147.9%		847	2.7%
8. Visit Number 8			51.24%		$2,828.09	205.8%		578	1.8%
9. Visit Number 9			77.59%		$3,300.69	240.2%		516	1.6%
10. Visit Number 10			84.22%		$4,735.01	344.6%		395	1.2%

Robust tables have five, six, or even a dozen metrics to allow analysts to pull out important observations on user behavior that leads to success or failure. Adobe doesn't place a limit on the number of metrics or dimensions in a freeform table.

Sorting and Filtering Data

Filtering and sorting tables in Adobe Analytics is intuitive and useful. Filtering can be as simple as isolating a set of SKUs with common character sets (such as *prod*, which appears in a range of numbered products), or as complex as adding a string of criteria.

And columns can be sorted high-to-low value using numerical criteria.

Sorting freeform tables in ascending and descending order

By default, tables are sorted in descending order (highest number to lowest number), and by the first metric added to the table. Some dimensions, such as those based on time, default to chronological sorting (Sunday, then Monday, Tuesday, and so on). Click the sort icon to toggle between descending and ascending, as shown in Figure 4-9.

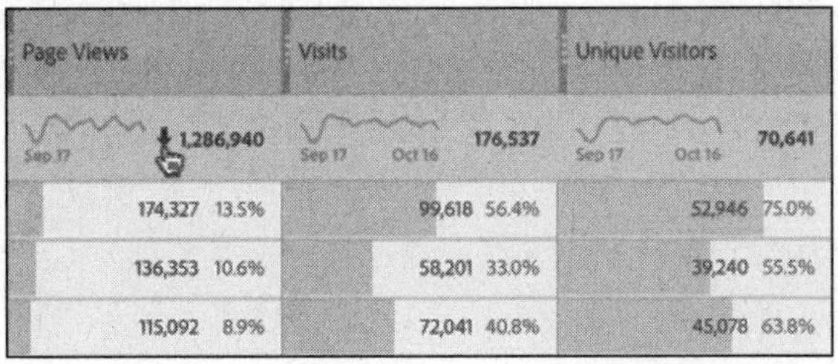

FIGURE 4-9: Toggling between a descending and an ascending column sort.

You can change the metric column to which sorting is applied by hovering your cursor just to the left of the total value at the top of the column until a sort icon appears, as shown in Figure 4-10, and clicking that icon.

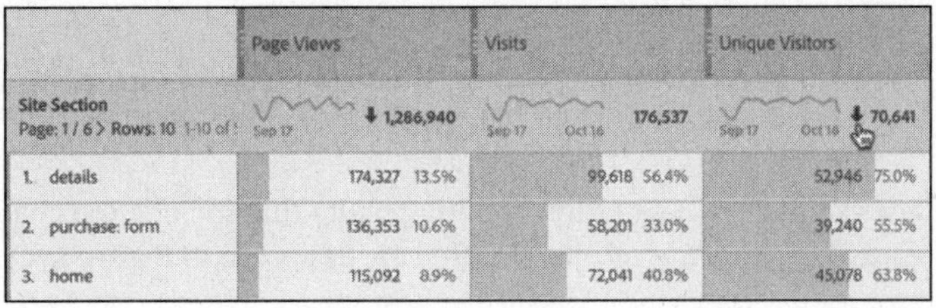

FIGURE 4-10: Choosing a new sort column.

Can you sort by dimension? Sometimes. If you're using a value dimension (such as a series of dates or the visit number dimension), the sort option becomes operative, as shown in Figure 4-11.

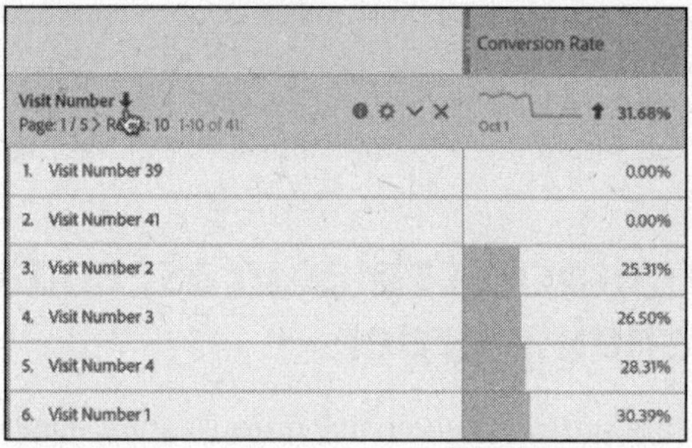

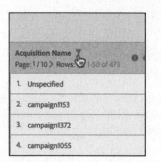

FIGURE 4-11:
Sorting a dimension column with numeric values.

Filtering freeform tables based on a word or phrase

It's easy to filter dimension columns in a freeform table based on a string of characters. Just hover your cursor over the header row at the top of your listed dimension, and click the filter icon, shown in Figure 4-12.

FIGURE 4-12:
Opening the filter dialog.

In the filter dialog, you can simply enter a character string in the Search Word or Phrase box and click Apply. The filter will now be in effect.

For example, you can filter for any results that include the character string "category" by entering *category* in the box, as shown in Figure 4-13.

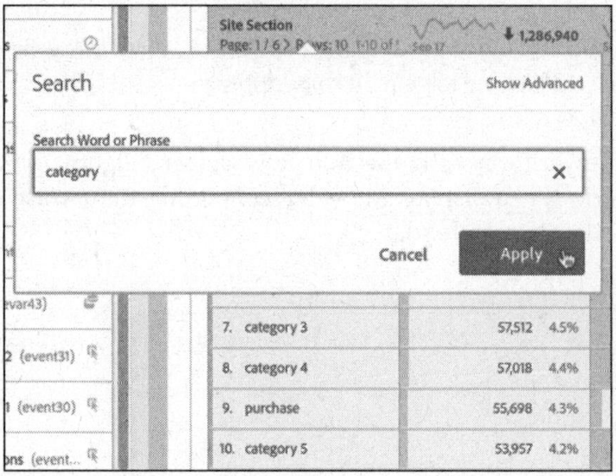

FIGURE 4-13:
Filtering data
results for
anything with the
characters
category.

Advanced filtering of freeform tables

The Show Advanced link in the Advanced Filtering dialog, as you may have guessed, displays more advanced options for filtering your freeform table:

» **Contains the Phrase:** Filters for items that contain a specific phrase some-where in their value. Characters can exist before or after the phrase.

» **Contains Any Term:** Allows you to list a set of space-delimited terms (use a space, not a comma, between terms). One of the terms must be contained somewhere in the item.

» **Contains All Terms:** Is defined the same way as Contains Any Term, but filters only results that include each term.

» **Does Not Contain Any Term:** Filters *out* any results that contain any of a set of space-delimited terms.

» **Does Not Contain the Phrase:** The opposite of Contains the Phrase, filters to display only results that do not contain the characters somewhere in the dimensional value.

» **Equals:** Filters to the values that exactly match your text. If any characters in a dimensional item exist before or after the phrase, they will not be included in your filtered data.

» **Does Not Equal:** As the name suggests, the opposite of Equals. All rows that match the exact phrase are removed from your filtered table.

» **Starts With:** Can be a useful filter to ensure that the table displays only data where each row begins with the same set of characters.

>> **Ends With:** The opposite of Starts With, ensures that the ending of each of the rows in your filtered table match your phrase.

You add filter criteria with the Add Row button. Figure 4-14 shows advanced search criteria set to display any value containing the phrase *category* that does not include the characters 10.

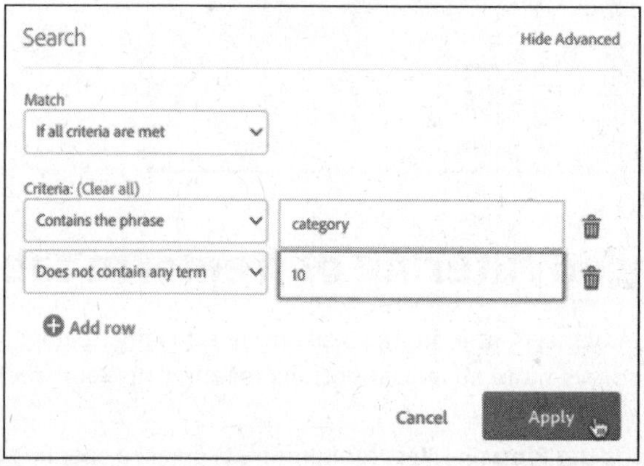

FIGURE 4-14: Filtering to show a select set of categories.

Dropping into the Segment Drop Zone

The *Segment drop zone* is located at the top of every panel. Despite (or perhaps appropriate to) its daredevil-connoting name, it's a flexible tool for isolating and focusing on just about any kind of data using segments, metrics, dimensions, or time ranges.

In addition, you can convert a set of such criteria into a drop-down menu (here we are with that evocative *drop* terminology again), allowing you to quickly pivot from one set of data to another. So, put on your jump suit and explore different ways to use the drop zone.

Dropping one or more segments into the drop zone

You start with dropping segments into the drop zone. To focus a report on just iOS users who come to our site from their mobile Apple devices, you can drag iOS into the drop zone for a panel, as shown in Figure 4-15. All tables (and any other visualizations) in the panel will now display data *only* for iOS users.

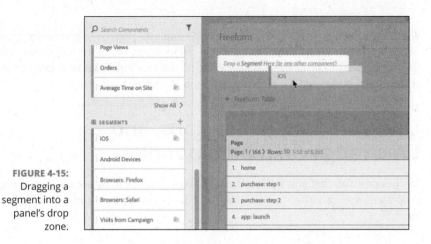

FIGURE 4-15:
Dragging a segment into a panel's drop zone.

You can add multiple segments to the drop zone, creating a drop-down menu that accesses any of them. Do this by holding down the Shift key while dragging one or more segments over the drop zone guide, as shown in Figure 4-16.

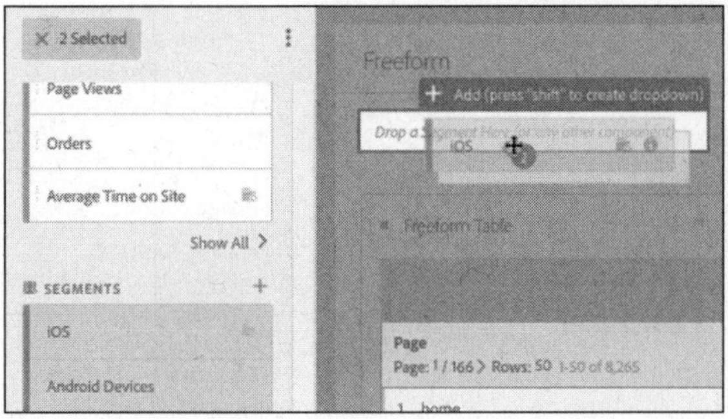

FIGURE 4-16:
Dragging multiple segments into a panel drop zone to create a drop-down menu.

The result is a drop-down menu that enables you to toggle between two choices, as shown in Figure 4-17.

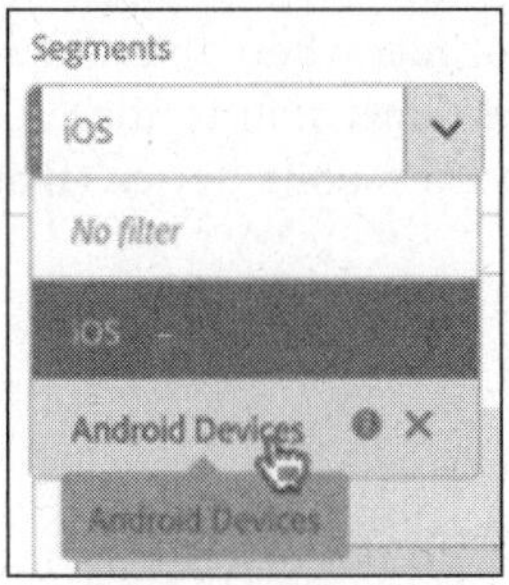

FIGURE 4-17:
Toggling between data for iOS and Android users.

When multiple segments are added next to each other in the Segment drop zone, Adobe stacks them together. For example, if you were to drag the iOS segment and then a segment that focuses on new visitors, the resulting data will apply to both segments as if they were one: iOS devices on their first visit.

Using metrics, dimensions, and time ranges in the drop zone

In the same way that you walked through adding one or more segments to a panel drop zone, you can also drag any metric, dimension, or time range into the drop zone.

For example, suppose you want to be able to quickly and easily toggle between a set of time ranges to explore how data changes over those time periods. You could drag a set of time components into the drop zone, make them function as a drop-down menu, and easily access those time ranges, as shown in Figure 4-18.

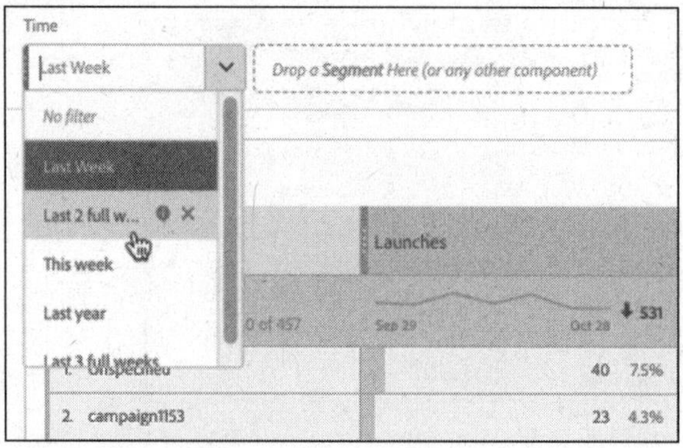

FIGURE 4-18:
Toggling between time ranges in a drop zone drop-down menu.

Adobe automatically assumes that you want to focus on metrics that you drag into the drop zone. So if you drag in revenue, your data is filtered to hits where revenue was collected. The same rule applies to dimensions dragged into the drop zone; they create a segment that filters only for hits where that dimension was set. For example, if you apply the mobile device dimension to the drop zone, your data is segmented based on visitors who have a mobile device (that is, desktops and laptops are filtered out).

Exploiting the Value of Templates

Sometimes, instead of starting with the blank slate of an empty freeform table, you'll want to start your analysis with a prebuilt set of tables and visualizations. When you choose Project⇨New from the Workspace menu, you can explore the standard templates in Adobe Analytics as well as custom templates. The standard templates are available in all installations, but custom templates (if you have any) are put together by your administrator.

When you click a template in the New Project dialog, details of the template are shown to the right. For example, the acquisition (web) template, shown in Figure 4-19, creates a report revealing the top traffic drivers to your website.

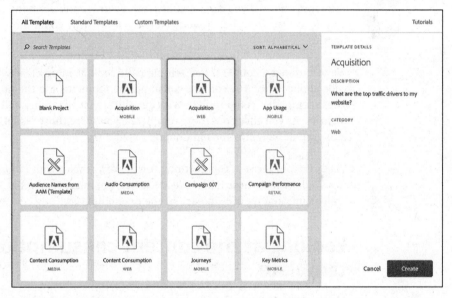

FIGURE 4-19: Previewing reports associated with standard templates.

In this example, the acquisition (web) template generates a set of highly useful tables, including the top search engine sources and top referring domains driving visits to your site, as shown in Figure 4-20.

When you set out to create a report, see whether you can base it on prebuilt visualizations from one of the standard templates. You can easily edit, analyze, and interact with the visualizations in a template. In addition, it's easy to duplicate visualizations so you can keep the original data intact (both tables and graphs): Right-click the top row of a visualization and choose Duplicate Visualization from the context menu. Then customize the duplicate.

Top Search Engine

Search Engine Page: 1/6 > Rows: 10 1-10 of 60	Visits		Unique Visit		Bounce Rate
	171,847		↓ 64,765		30.40%
1. Unspecified	159,077	92	62,923	97	32.43%
2. Google	1,146	0.7%	1,106	1.7%	4.54%
3. Yahoo!	552	0.3%	541	0.8%	6.16%
4. Google - Ireland	401	0.2%	397	0.6%	4.99%
5. Google - Canada	400	0.2%	395	0.6%	6.00%
6. Google - Denmark	379	0.2%	378	0.6%	2.64%
7. Google - United Kingdom	377	0.2%	375	0.6%	5.84%
8. Google - Netherlands	370	0.2%	367	0.6%	3.51%
9. Yahoo! - Russia	370	0.2%	361	0.6%	5.95%
10. Google - Korea	349	0.2%	348	0.5%	4.30%

Top Referring Domains

Referring Domain Page: 1/19 > Rows: 10 1-10	Visits		Unique Visitors		Bounce Rate
	↓ 171,847		64,765		88.8%
1. t.co	3,452	2.0%	3,111	4.8%	7.0%
2. dailymotion.com	3,113	1.8%	2,957	4.6%	9.1%
3. facebook.com	2,723	1.6%	2,454	3.8%	7.4%
4. tumblr.com	1,822	1.1%	1,786	2.8%	10.5%
5. yahoo.com	1,754	1.0%	1,666	2.6%	5.9%
6. reddit.com	1,798	1.0%	1,519	2.3%	5.5%
7. pinterest.com	1,706	1.0%	1,500	2.3%	8.2%
8. opendiary.com	1,623	0.9%	1,584	2.4%	9.4%
9. blogster.com	1,330	0.8%	1,302	2.0%	11.7%
10. google.com	1,278	0.7%	1,256	1.9%	6.2%

FIGURE 4-20:
Top search engine and referring domains generated by the acquisitions (web) template.

TIP

Take some time, if you can, to study and reverse-engineer templates. The process is a good way to build up your comfort level with combining dimensions and metrics.

We've curated a couple if key templates to look at more closely because of their wide applicability: the content consumption template and the products template. These templates come replete with graphical visualizations and other advanced features. As you check out these templates, you'll see those visualizations. We dive into graphic visualizations in Chapters 13 and 14.

That said, our focus in this section is on building tables with dimensions and metrics. And because those tables are at the heart of many templates, we'll explore the dimensions and metrics in each of the two templates.

Looking at the content consumption template

The content consumption template shines a light on which content is consumed most and is engaging users. It includes prebuilt graphic visualizations, but its core is a table that measures activity at different pages of your site based on the following:

>> **Page views:** Count of server calls to a page.

>> **Visits:** Measures a sequence of page views in a sitting.

>> **Unique Visitor:** Counts visitors who visit a site for the first time within a specified time period.

- » **Entry Rate:** Calculates the number of entries divided by the number of visits.

- » **Bounce Rate:** Calculates the percentage of visits that contain a single hit by dividing Bounces by Entries.

- » **Exit Rate:** Measures the percentage of traffic where a page (in the Dimension column) was the last place a visitor engaged.

- » **Content Velocity:** Measures how fast users are viewing your content and how long it takes them to move to another part of the site.

This template also includes a table based on the site section dimension, which measures activity at defined sections of your site by using similar metrics.

The other visualizations in the template are called flow visualizations. They focus on analyzing how users are traversing from the first page they enter to each of the next pages they view. Adobe prebuilt other flow visualizations that work backward from the exit page as well as forward from site section to site section. Chapter 14 explains the flow visualization and its capabilities in detail.

Examining the products template

The core of the products template is three valuable tables that focus on the top viewed products, the products that are performing well, and the products that aren't performing well.

The main table uses the product dimension, combined with metrics that measure product views, cart additions, orders, units, revenue, and orders/visit. The tables that focus on the top and lowest converting products are populated with just the orders/visit metric. This metric helps you easily find products that are visited and do and do not result in orders.

One key visualization in this template that isn't a freeform table is the *fallout* — a visualization that shows where visitors leave and continue through a sequence of touchpoints. The fallout in the products template is configured to show all of your visitors, those who viewed a product, added a product to the cart, and purchased. Chapter 14 provides a detailed explanation of building and analyzing the fallout visualization. In addition, Chapter 13 helps explain the other key visualization in this template, which is the area chart showing trended revenue.

Using custom templates

It's great to be able to use Adobe standard templates, but sometimes an organization will decide that it needs a custom template. Custom templates are useful in organizations that want to share the same starter project to all Adobe Analytics users.

When you create a project, you see the All Templates tab, the Standard Templates tab, and a third tab, Custom Templates. Any templates that administrators have created are displayed in the Custom Templates tab. Figure 4-21 shows the Custom Template dialog with a few custom templates we've created for use in our environment. We needed administrator status to create these templates, but they're available to any user.

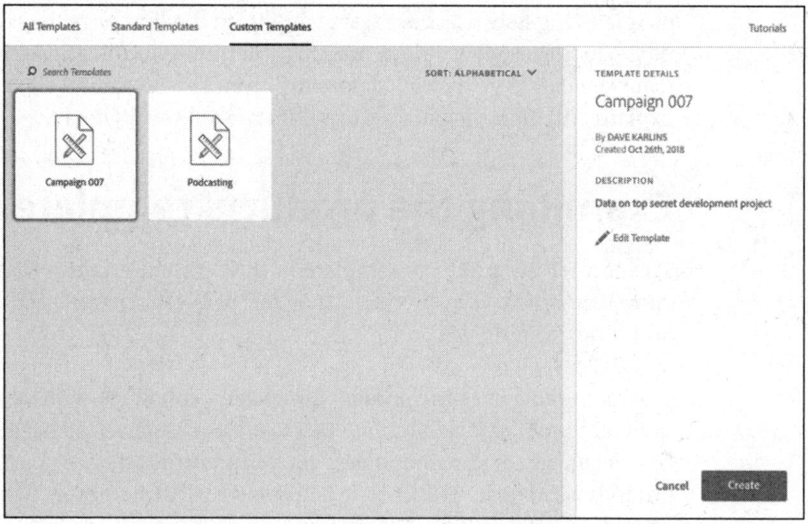

FIGURE 4-21:
Custom
templates.

Creating custom templates

Only users with access to create custom templates, generally admins, can create and build them. They do this by creating a set of visualizations and tables, adding tags so users can find the template, and saving what is really a built-from-scratch custom project.

If you do have access, you can convert any project into a custom template by choosing Project ⇨ Save as Template from the main Workspace menu, as shown in Figure 4-22.

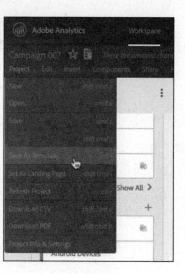

FIGURE 4-22:
Saving a
workspace as a
template.

If you do not have access, you can suggest items you think would be productive to build into a template for frequent reuse. For example, if you've worked hard to create a workspace with panels that present data needed to analyze paid search campaigns, and these panels could save you or someone else in the organization a lot of time and effort when repurposed for similar campaigns, you might present your administrator with that workspace and suggest that he or she save it as a template.

Chapter **5**

Using Metrics to Analyze Data

I n this chapter, you start digging several layers deeper into the metrics you have at your disposal in Adobe Analytics. We discuss page views, visits, and visitors in Chapter 2, but you may have already noticed that many more metrics are available to analyze — some that are important to your business and others that are not.

Which of the dozens of built-in metrics are most valuable? That depends on your environment, your goals, and the mission of your digital presence. Here we break widely applicable metrics into four categories:

» Metrics that analyze time spent

» Metrics that isolate bounces (quick departures) or single page visits

» Metrics that measure engagement with shopping carts or other forms or purchases

» Custom metrics — ones you define yourself

As you explore each set of metrics, you zoom in on specific metrics as examples — both because they are widely used and to provide examples of techniques that you can apply more broadly to metrics in general. Along the way, we warn you about potential pitfalls to avoid.

Some metrics are generic. Both Adobe Analytics and Google Analytics, for example, measure page views. But in the course of surveying metrics in this chapter, you also explore Adobe-specific metrics, which are unique to the Adobe Analytics toolset, uniquely defined in the Adobe Experience Cloud, or both.

Finally, you deploy metrics at another level with an overview of the plethora of options available for analyzing custom metrics in Adobe. Where necessary, we provide the specification you need to use your debugger to discover how these metrics are getting set on your site.

In this chapter, our focus is metrics. We also mention the basic techniques for creating projects in Analysis Workspace, configuring Workspace panels, and adding metrics, dimensions, and segments to panels, but cover those topics in Chapters 3 and 4.

Analyzing Time Spent

Before you set off to analyze time spent by visitors, let's quickly identify one complicated (but not *too* complicated) concept: *deduplication,* which means removing redundant data in a dataset by providing a unique count rather than the sum. Deduplication is usually most effective when applied to metrics such as visits and visitors. As we deploy metrics to measure visitor time spent, you'll see us apply techniques that deduplicate (strip out duplicate data).

You know time, right? You've been reading clocks since grade school. When it comes to analytics data, time plays an important role. Visits are comprised of multiple page views during different intervals, and visits end when inactivity during a set amount of time passes.

Adobe has incorporated several time-related metrics into Analysis Workspace. These metrics can be useful, are often fickle, and have some significant drawbacks worth mentioning. By default, Adobe incorporates four different metrics associated with the amount of time spent on site: total seconds spent, average time on site, time spent per visit (seconds), and time spent per visitor (seconds).

It's important to point out how fickle these metrics can be before we dig into them. Time-based metrics always need additional context to be valuable; in essence, time metrics by themselves are neither good news nor bad news. For example, suppose a colleague says, "The average time spent on our website has doubled this month." Is that good or bad? As with many data-related topics, it depends. Perhaps the example website is for a newspaper and the increase in time spent on site has taken place specifically on article pages. That news is starting to sound much better. But if the increased time on site was spent by frustrated users hassling with a broken registration form, the news would be significantly worse!

A reverse example could be suggested for a decrease in average time spent. Declining time spent may be good news that users are getting to the content they need faster. Or it could mean that the content isn't engaging enough, so visitors are exiting the site.

See how time spent, by itself, is not enough? Instead, consider the context. What pages? Which types of visitors? How did these visitors discover the website? Are they new to the site or loyal users? That additional lens is required to find valuable insights from any metric but especially time-based metrics.

Counting total seconds spent

The total sum of seconds spent for all visitors to your report suite is captured in a metric labeled *total seconds spent.* The metric can be broken down by any dimension in Analysis Workspace, like most metrics, so you can easily see the total seconds spent per page or day, or even break the metric down by multiple segments.

This metric is shown in the Adobe interface as an integer or a whole number, so you don't have to worry about decimal points or fractions.

Metrics that are integers, such as total seconds spent, are difficult to use by themselves but easy to use in calculated metrics. For example, you could easily divide total seconds spent by the count of product orders to see the average time spent on site per order. Seconds can also be an unwieldy level of granularity, so you could consider dividing it by 60 to get the number of minutes instead. Figure 5-1 shows both the seconds and minutes that users spent at a marketing channel.

A key caveat of most web-based time metrics has to do with the last page view in a visit. Analytics products such as Adobe Analytics calculate time spent by subtracting the time of the first page view from the time of the last page view of the visit. This methodology is accurate but has one glaring omission: the amount of time spent on that last page.

Freeform Table				
		Total Seconds Spent		Total Minutes Spent
Marketing Channel Page 1/1 Rows: 400 1-12 of 13	Sep 1	↓ 63,851,873	Sep 1	1,064,197.9
1. Email		16,205,114 25.4%		270,085.2 25.4%
2. Paid Search		11,173,805 17.5%		186,230.1 17.5%
3. Social Campaigns		10,071,349 15.8%		167,855.8 15.8%
4. Display		7,418,963 11.6%		123,649.4 11.6%
5. Comparison Shopping		4,423,424 6.9%		73,723.7 6.9%
6. Referring Domains		4,215,486 6.6%		70,258.1 6.6%
7. Print		2,319,214 3.6%		38,653.6 3.6%
8. Podcasts		2,162,855 3.4%		36,047.6 3.4%
9. Text		2,062,050 3.2%		34,367.5 3.2%
10. Direct		1,673,292 2.6%		27,888.2 2.6%
11. Social Networks		1,251,165 2.0%		20,852.8 2.0%
12. Natural Search		875,156 1.4%		14,585.9 1.4%

FIGURE 5-1:
A freeform table showing total seconds spent and a calculated metric of total minutes spent per marketing channel.

REMEMBER

As we explain in Chapter 2, technical limitations keep analytics platforms such as Adobe Analytics and Google Analytics from being able to detect the action of a browser tab or a window being closed. A workaround can send data to Adobe after every 30 seconds of inactivity on a page, but this approach has other consequences that may cause more trouble than it's worth.

A second, related caveat to most web-based time metrics is on visits that only last a single page. These minimal visits are called *bounces* and will cause some havoc on time metrics. If time metrics subtract the time of the first page view from the time of the last page view, bounces last 0 seconds because there was only a single page view.

Measuring time spent per visit (seconds)

Time spent per visit, a built-in calculated metric that Adobe includes by default in every report suite, is used to represent the average amount of time (as opposed to the total amount of time) visitors interact with a dimensional value during each visit, as opposed to the *total* amount of time. The calculation deals with the bounces caveat to time spent by simply removing it from the denominator. The definition is as follows:

total seconds spent / (visits – bounces)

Time spent per visit is one of the more commonly used time-based metrics in digital analytics platforms. Like total seconds spent, Analysis Workspace presents the metric as an integer in seconds. If you use this metric, consider creating a calculated metric to divide it by 60 for a friendlier minute-based metric.

Identifying time spent per visitor (seconds)

Time spent per visitor, another built-in calculated metric that Adobe provides based on time, is used to represent the average amount of time visitors interact with a dimensional value across the visitor's entire cookie-based history. Adobe defines it similarly to the preceding metric, filtering out bounces:

total seconds spent / (unique visitors – bounced unique visitors)

If you're analyzing this metric alongside time spent per visitor, you can expect to see higher numbers when visitor is the denominator because visitors can never be higher than visits.

TIP

Consider leveraging this visitor-based average instead of the previous visit-based time spent metric when analyzing activities that take multiple visits to complete. Multistep registrations or big, pricey product purchases may lend themselves more towards using time spent per visitor rather than per visit.

Calculating average time on site

A separate metric exists for average time on site. Adobe made it easy to visualize average time on site; Workspace shows the metric formatted as *mm:ss*.

In addition, Workspace provides an out-of-the-box average time on site (seconds) metric, which is the same metric formatted as an integer. The *average time on site* metric represents the total amount of time visitors interact with a dimensional value *per sequence of that value.*

The difference between average time spent on site and time spent per visit is subtle: time spent per visit uses a simple non-bounced visit metric as the denominator, while average time on site is more complicated because it focuses on the count of dimensional value sequences.

A *dimensional value sequence* is best described as a consecutive set of page views where the value does not change. The following table demonstrates an example that uses a custom dimension we named page type:

Page View #	1	2	3	4	5
Page Type	Product Category	Product Page	Product Page	Product Category	Product Category
Seconds Spent	30	50	10	40	60

An example of a sequence is in page views 2 to 3; product page is set as the page type twice in a row. Similarly, page views 4 and 5 are a sequence with a dimensional value of product category. The following table displays the calculations for each of the time-based metrics based on this scenario:

	Total Seconds Spent	Time Spent per Visit	Count of Sequences	Average Time Spent on Site
Product Category	30+40+60 = 130	130/1 = 130	2	130/2=65
Product Page	50+10 = 60	60/1 = 60	1	60

Note how different the time spent per visit metric data is from the average time spent on site metric due to the denominator change from visits to sequences. The difference is significant for dimensions such as page type, where it would be possible to have sequences of the same value in a row.

Assessing mobile app time spent

Adobe customers who have implemented Analytics in their mobile app have two additional time metrics at their disposal: total session length and average session length. Mobile apps can provide additional information to Adobe that helps solve for the caveats that analysts have to deal with on the web.

Apps provide Adobe with the amount of time spent on the last page before the app is closed or the phone is powered off — hooray, more accurate time spent data! However, the ability to identify when a user exits an app comes with its own caveat: The time spent on that last page view isn't available to send to Adobe until the next time the app is opened. Mobile app users who use the app only once do not have any time associated with their usage during that single visit.

Other than that caveat, mobile-app-focused metrics are defined as you would expect. *Total session length* calculates the number of seconds where the app is in the device's foreground. *Average session length* divides total session length by the number of *launches* (mobile-speak for visits) but subtracts first launches to handle the mobile app caveat mentioned previously. Figure 5-2 shows the built-in time-based metrics in Analysis Workspace.

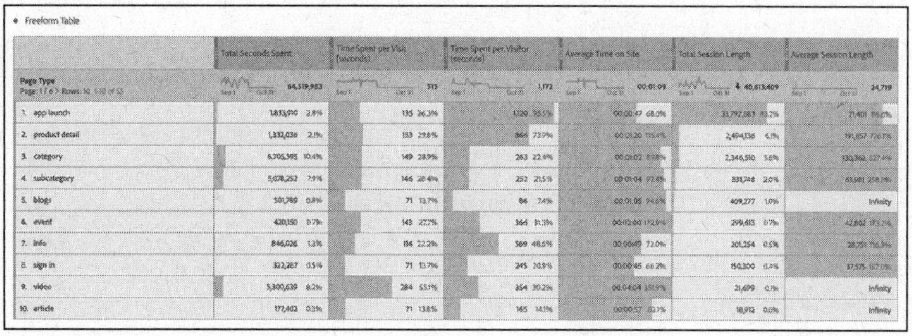

FIGURE 5-2: A freeform table with data from both the web and a mobile app showing built-in time-based metrics.

Using Metrics for Bounces, Bounce Rate, and Single Page Visits

Another highly discussed set of metrics in the digital marketing industry is bounces and bounce rate. The industry defines a *bounce* as a visit to a site or app that views only a single page. This same definition applies to Adobe except for one small change. In Adobe, a *bounce* applies to visits that navigate away from a site or an app after firing only a single tag. This difference is important. If a visitor lands on the home page, watches a video, and then closes her browser, that is not considered a bounce in Adobe Analytics. It is, however, considered a single-page visit. A single-page visit is identical to the more generic definition of a bounce because it ignores hits that aren't page views, such as a link click or file download.

Adobe also has a pre-built metric for *bounce rate*, which shows the percentage of visits that have bounced. Adobe analysts will often create a calculated metric of single page bounce rate that more closely mirrors the industry definition of bounce rate:

single page visits / visits

All of these metrics can be valuable to analysts to help identify visitors who erroneously came to the site, commonly referred to as *unqualified traffic*.

REMEMBER

However, analysts should beware that a bounced visit doesn't necessarily mean that the visit failed. Like the time spent metrics, bounce-focused metrics can be fickle. A visit that accesses only a store's address and contact information would technically be considered a bounce, but the visitor may have found the necessary information and left the site. To resolve what a bounce actually indicates, be sure to always leverage precise segments and dimensions when using these metrics. Pronouncing success because a website's bounce rate decreased is not valuable analysis. Figure 5-3 demonstrates bounces, bounce rate, and single page visits.

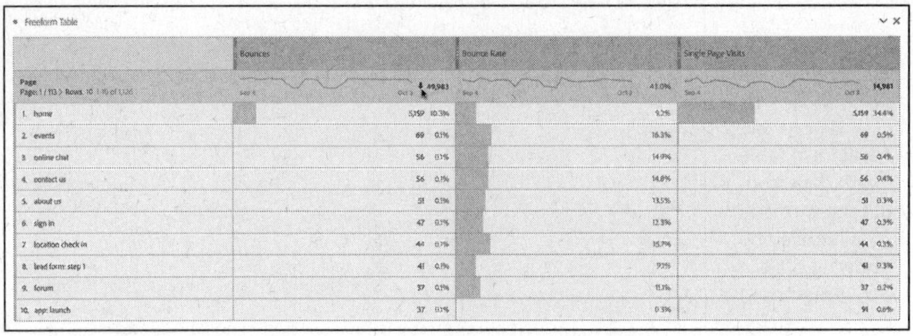

FIGURE 5-3:
A freeform table showing bounces, bounce rate, and single page visits by page.

Understanding Metrics Unique to Adobe

You're probably noticed that Adobe has customized a few definitions for metrics uniquely for the Adobe Analytics platform. In addition, Adobe also has an abundance of metrics that are not commonly used concepts in other platforms. Understanding these is crucial to making the most of your time in Workspace.

Counting instances

Adobe has hundreds of dimensions with potentially hundreds of thousands of unique dimensional values per dimension. Analysts need a way to know how many times each value was sent to Adobe regardless of the type of *hit* (page view or link). *Instances* are the total count of hits where a specific dimensional value was sent in a tag to Adobe Analytics.

Analysis Workspace provides a unique instance metric for almost every dimension in the platform. Tracking code instances, for example, would show you the number of times each tracking code was passed into Adobe Analytics. This feature is often useful when debugging data or creating custom metrics after data has been collected, but can be used reliably only with its partner dimension. Suppose that an Adobe customer forgot to set a custom metric that captures video starts. If the brand sends the video name in a dimension every time a video starts, instances of the video name dimension could act as a replacement for the missing video starts metric. Figure 5-4 compares video starts to video instances.

Measuring occurrences

One of the most commonly accessed and, perhaps, most misunderstood metric in Analysis Workspace is the occurrences metric. *Occurrences* are a count of the number of times a specific dimensional value is captured, plus the number of hits for which the value persisted. To explain *persistence* in Adobe Analytics, let's use an example. When a visitor accesses your site by clicking through a paid search ad, the marketing channel dimension is set to paid search. The value of paid search must persist for the marketing channel dimension through the entire visit so that all behavior is properly tied to paid search. The occurrences metric in this example would be a count of all hits associated with the visit.

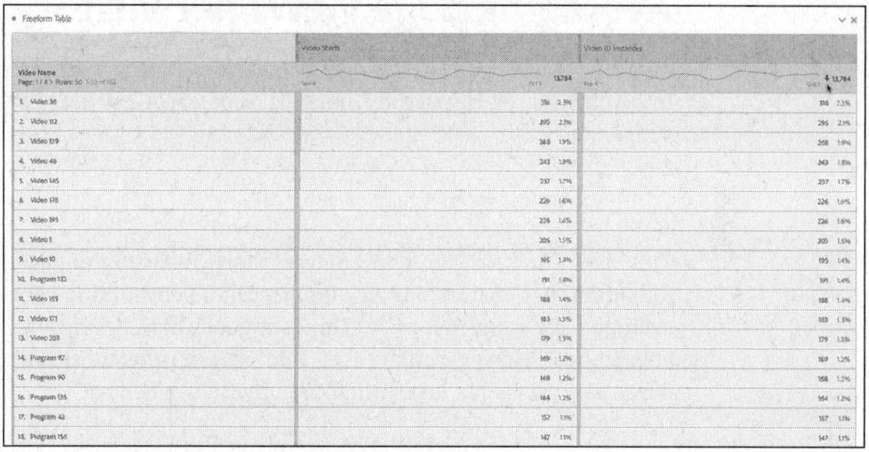
Freeform Table

Video Name	Video Starts	Video ID Instances
	13,784	13,784
1. Video 36	316 2.3%	316 2.3%
2. Video 112	295 2.1%	295 2.1%
3. Video 139	268 1.9%	268 1.9%
4. Video 46	243 1.8%	243 1.8%
5. Video 145	237 1.7%	237 1.7%
6. Video 178	226 1.6%	226 1.6%
7. Video 195	226 1.6%	226 1.6%
8. Video 1	205 1.5%	205 1.5%
9. Video 10	195 1.4%	195 1.4%
10. Program 132	191 1.4%	191 1.4%
11. Video 185	188 1.4%	188 1.4%
12. Video 171	183 1.3%	183 1.3%
13. Video 203	179 1.3%	179 1.3%
14. Program 97	169 1.2%	169 1.2%
15. Program 90	168 1.2%	168 1.2%
16. Program 135	164 1.2%	164 1.2%
17. Program 42	157 1.1%	157 1.1%
18. Program 156	147 1.1%	147 1.1%

FIGURE 5-4: A freeform table showing video starts and video ID instances.

In Analysis Workspace, occurrences is the default metric for every dimension. Every time a dimension is added to a table that doesn't contain any metrics, the occurrences metric will be added by default.

Generally, the ability to combine data into an occurrence is useful because it guarantees that data is shown in your table (as long as some data is associated with the dimension). Plus, it allows you to easily perform dimensional breakdowns because occurrences span all dimensions, whereas instances are dimension-specific.

Unfortunately, the occurrences metric isn't a very actionable. As an analyst, you'll rarely make a decision based on an increase or decrease in occurrences. However, the metric is still useful when building tables, breaking down dimensions, and confirming that data exists. Figure 5-5 shows occurrences, page views, downloads, and exit links. Note how occurrences equals the sum of the other metrics for each row.

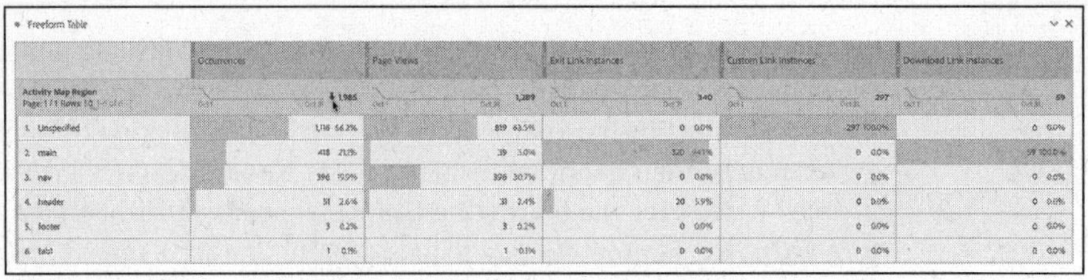

Freeform Table

Activity Map Region (Page: 1 / 1 Rows: 10 1-6 of 6)	Occurrences	Page Views	Exit Link Instances	Custom Link Instances	Download Link Instances
	1,985	1,289	340	297	59
1. Unspecified	1,116 56.2%	819 63.5%	0 0.0%	297 100.0%	0 0.0%
2. main	418 21.1%	39 3.0%	320 94.1%	0 0.0%	59 100.0%
3. nav	396 19.9%	396 30.7%	0 0.0%	0 0.0%	0 0.0%
4. header	51 2.6%	31 2.4%	20 5.9%	0 0.0%	0 0.0%
5. footer	3 0.2%	3 0.2%	0 0.0%	0 0.0%	0 0.0%
6. tabl	1 0.1%	1 0.1%	0 0.0%	0 0.0%	0 0.0%

FIGURE 5-5: A freeform table showing a occurrences, page views, and instances of custom, download, and exit links.

Averaging page views per visit

Adobe has saved analysts some time by incorporating a standard calculated metric into Analysis Workspace by default: *page views per visit.* The calculation is a simple one:

page views / visits

This useful metric can help analysts start analyzing engagement on their site. The more that visitors are viewing pages and consuming content, the higher the average page views per visit. This is a good, high-level metric to quickly gauge engagement. However, like time- and bounce-related metrics, it's best to break down page views per visit into more precise segments.

Averaging page depth

Analysts will often ask how far into a visit was a dimensional value set. For example, an analyst might ask, "How many page views does it take to get a customer to the first step of our purchase funnel?" This is a great question to ask, and the average page depth metric helps answer it. *Average page depth* provides the number of instances of a dimension that are viewed prior to any specific value. Figure 5-6 compares visits, average page views per visit, and average page depth.

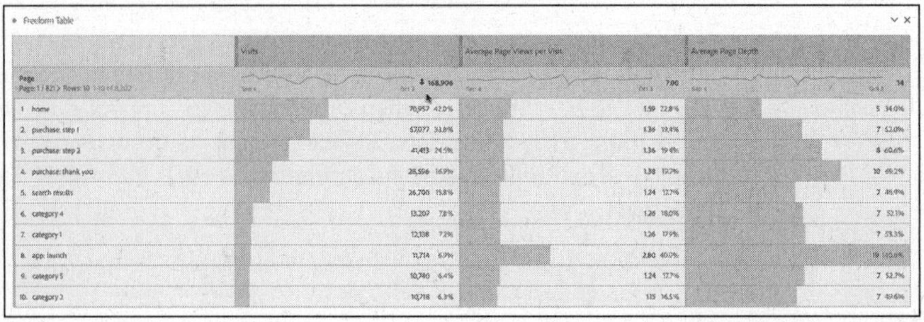

Freeform Table

Page (Page: 1 / 821 Rows: 10 1-10 of 8,202)	Visits	Average Page Views per Visit	Average Page Depth
	168,906	7.00	14
1. home	70,957 42.0%	1.59 22.8%	5 34.0%
2. purchase: step 1	57,077 33.8%	1.36 19.4%	7 52.0%
3. purchase: step 2	41,413 24.5%	1.36 19.4%	8 60.6%
4. purchase: thank you	28,556 16.9%	1.38 19.7%	10 69.2%
5. search results	26,700 15.8%	1.24 17.7%	7 49.9%
6. category 4	13,207 7.8%	1.26 18.0%	7 52.1%
7. category 1	12,138 7.2%	1.26 17.9%	7 53.3%
8. app: launch	11,714 6.9%	2.80 40.0%	19 140.0%
9. category 5	10,780 6.4%	1.24 17.7%	7 52.7%
10. category 2	10,718 6.3%	1.15 16.5%	7 49.6%

FIGURE 5-6: A freeform table showing visits, average page views per visit, and average page depth broken out by the page dimension.

It can be useful to sort calculated metrics such as average page depth by visits to provide additional context on the calculation. Additional context provided by the visits metric will ensure that your analysis of this metric is warranted due to a significant amount of traffic.

Analyzing entries and exits

Entries and exits are often highly useful metrics for analysts who are digging deep into an analysis. The *entries* metric provides the number of times a dimensional value is captured as the first value in a visit, whereas the *exits* metric is the number of times a dimensional value is captured as the last value in a visit. Both metrics can occur only a single time within a visit, but they are not necessarily set only on the first hit in a visit. If a dimension is not set during the first three page views of a visit but does get set on the fourth, the entries metric would count the value of that dimension on the fourth page view.

Entries and exits can be valuable to analysts when answering questions related to the order that actions were taken. What was the first product that was viewed? What was the last search term that the visitor searched before making a purchase? Entries and exits are used more often than you think.

Counting reloads

Reloads, like browser reloads, are counted when the same dimensional value is sent in subsequent hits. The reload metric is interesting because it can be applied to any dimension, not just the page dimension. Figure 5-7 shows entries, exits and reloads associated with the page dimension.

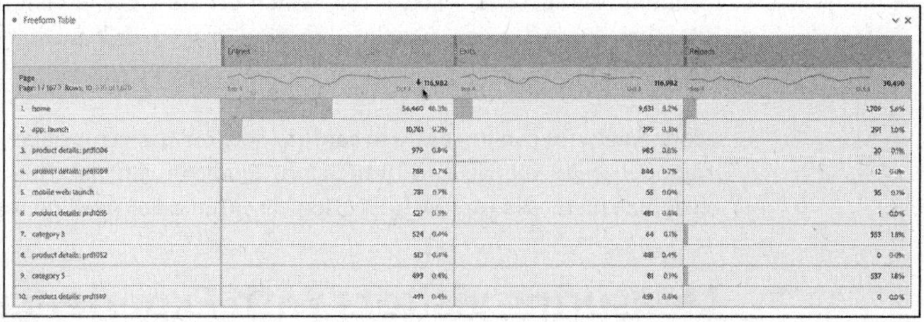

FIGURE 5-7: Entries, exits, and reloads broken out by the page dimension.

Distinguishing page hits from page events

As we explain in Chapter 2, not all Adobe Analytics hits are page views. Some actions taken on a website or in an app should be categorized as download links, exit links, or custom links without wrongly increasing the count of page views.

For example, a PDF download is an action that should be tracked in Adobe Analytics, but it shouldn't count as a page view. Instead, Adobe customers categorize it as a download link. Another example is tracking link clicks to another website, such as a partner brand to your company. These clicks would be tracked as an exit link. Adobe has one additional bucket — a catchall called *custom links* — for any other actions that need to be tracked and aren't page views, exits, or downloads. The summation of instances of download, exit, and custom links is provided in an out-of-the-box metric called *page events*. Page events metrics can help you analyze how many actions took place as a result of a dimensional value. Figure 5-8 illustrates a table with different page events.

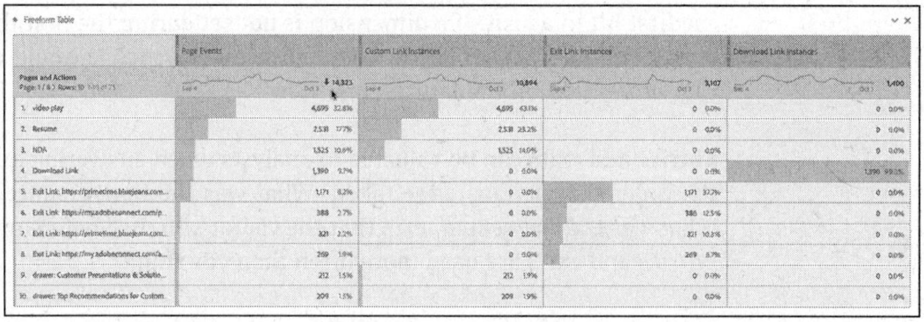

FIGURE 5-8:
A freeform table
showing how
page events are
the summation
of instances
of custom,
download, and
exit links.

Identifying pages not found

Have you ever been to a web page where an error occurred and the page didn't load? We hope you weren't on your company's website, but we all know that mistakes on the web happen. Luckily, Adobe Analytics is there to help! The most common web error is a 404 error, which occurs when a visitor tries to access a URL that doesn't exist, usually due to a broken link or someone sharing the wrong URL.

Adobe Analytics can be set up to capture data on 404 error pages by populating the *pages not found* metric and dimension. Analysts can use this metric to quickly recognize increases (or, we hope, decreases) in error page views.

Measuring visitors with Experience Cloud ID

All Adobe customers have access to a free technology called Experience Cloud ID Service, which is used to better integrate the Adobe Experience Cloud solutions. The technology rarely fails, but when it does, a fallback is engaged to ensure that data is still tracked in Adobe Analytics. When that happens, the unique visitors metric will be increased but the *visitors with Experience Cloud ID* metric will not.

Analysts rarely use the visitors with Experience Cloud ID metric. More often than not, it is identical to the unique visitors metric that we explore in Chapter 2.

Analyzing single access

Analysts often are interested in utilizing metrics similar to single page visits but for dimensions other than page. The *single access* metric is defined by the number of visits that contain a single unique dimensional value. As analysts, we've used the single access metric to analyze visitors who started just one video in a visit.

An example is media, as illustrated in the table in Figure 5-9, which combines media initiates, single access, and single page visits by video name (different programs).

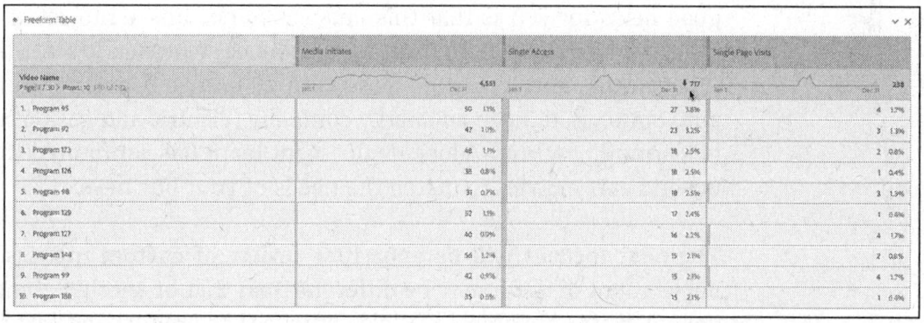

FIGURE 5-9:
Media initiates,
single access, and
single page visits
by video name
are shown in a
freeform table.

According to the media initiates in Figure 5-9, Program 95 was started 50 times and, per the single access metric, was the only video watched in a visit (and was watched just once) 27 times. As a reminder from earlier in this chapter, the 4 single page visits for Program 95 describe visits where Program 95 was the only video watched, but that video could have been watched several times.

Analyzing visits from search engines

Adobe Analytics is often used to analyze visits from search engines. The *searches* metric measures visits coming from search engines and is identical to applying a segment of search engine visits to the visits metric.

Using the people metric

You walk through the standard metrics of page views, visits, and unique visitors in Chapter 2. Page views is the most granular metric and visitors is the least granular. Adobe has one more trick up its sleeve when it comes to a less granular traffic metric, people. The *people* metric helps analysts attribute and deduplicate multiple browsers and devices into a single person. The metric provides a people-based view of marketing, letting an analyst measure activity across all their devices.

One big caveat with the people metric is that it is available only if your company is a member of the Adobe Experience Cloud Device Co-op. We detail the Device Co-op in Chapter 16. If you're not sure whether your company is a member, check the list of participating companies at https://cross-device-privacy.adobe.com.

Exploiting Product and Cart Metrics

Adobe analysts love to help affect and improve their company's bottom line, so the analysis generally must focus on product-related metrics and content. The good news for you is that this analysis is not limited to retail businesses. Every industry has some definition of a product, whether it's a financial institution (credit cards and mortgage loans), an insurance company (home insurance and auto options), or even an energy company (electric and gas options). The fun part is learning how your Adobe deployment team has configured the pre-built product and cart metrics to match the needs of your business.

The next metrics will be your first review of custom metrics. Your company's deployment of them may be different than that of another company, especially if your website or business model is unique. The product and cart metrics are in a bit of a gray area because they are standard metrics that every company has access to, such as visits and visitors, but they can be customized. Adobe has set aside a specific variable in an Adobe Analytics tag for each of these metrics.

In each of the following descriptions, we assume that your Adobe deployment is following best practices and standards, but it's worth confirming this with your Adobe administrators.

Chapter 1 describes getting to know your implementation team, and these metrics are a great way to expand that relationship.

Identifying product views

The most basic metric associated with product analysis is product views. By default, the *product views metric* captures the total number of views of your company's product detail page. You can use Adobe Experience Cloud Debugger to check on what pages the product views metric is being set. Simply load the page, open the debugger's tab for Analytics, and then scroll down to the Events row.

If prodView is listed in the Events row, as in Figure 5-10, the product views metric was increased on that page.

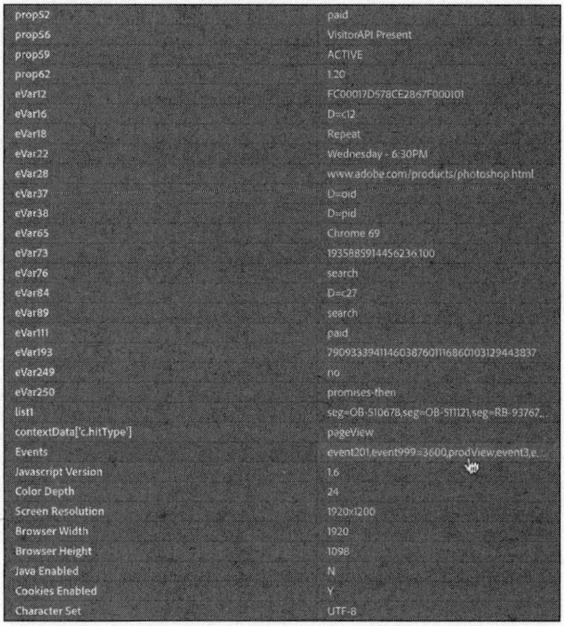

propS2	paid
propS6	VisitorAPI Present
propS9	ACTIVE
prop62	1.20
eVar12	FC00017D578CE2867F000101
eVar16	D=c12
eVar18	Repeat
eVar22	Wednesday - 6:30PM
eVar28	www.adobe.com/products/photoshop.html
eVar37	D=oid
eVar38	D=pid
eVar65	Chrome 69
eVar73	1935885914456236100
eVar76	search
eVar84	D=c27
eVar89	search
eVar111	paid
eVar193	2909333941146038760111686010312944383
eVar249	no
eVar250	promises-then
list1	seg=OB-510678,seg=OB-511121,seg=RB-93767...
contextData['c.hitType']	pageView
Events	event201,event999=3600,prodView,event3,e...
Javascript Version	1.6
Color Depth	24
Screen Resolution	1920x1200
Browser Width	1920
Browser Height	1098
Java Enabled	N
Cookies Enabled	Y
Character Set	UTF-8

FIGURE 5-10: Adobe Experience Cloud Debugger shows a tag firing with multiple events, including prodView.

The product views metric is most often used to answer questions related to the top of the product conversion funnel, such as, "How many times was Product X viewed?" However, simply knowing how often a product was viewed often isn't sufficient for a proper analysis. Analysts will often use product views as the denominator in product-related calculated metrics, such as the following:

cart adds / product views

A calculation of cart adds per product view could help show the effectiveness of the product detail page.

Metrics for shopping carts

Adobe Analytics has several built-in metrics that measure activity in the shopping cart. If your company doesn't have a shopping cart, these metrics have probably been disabled or renamed and repurposed. However, if you do have a shopping cart on your website, you will want to take advantage of these metrics.

Adobe has five cart-related metrics, as shown in Figure 5-11. You can identify them with Adobe Experience Cloud Debugger by inspecting the Events row on the Analytics tab (as described in the preceding section):

- **_Carts_ is a count of the shopping carts that have been started on your site.** It is normally set once per flow through the purchase funnel. You can recognize the variable getting sent to Adobe Experience Cloud Debugger by looking for scOpen in the list of Events.

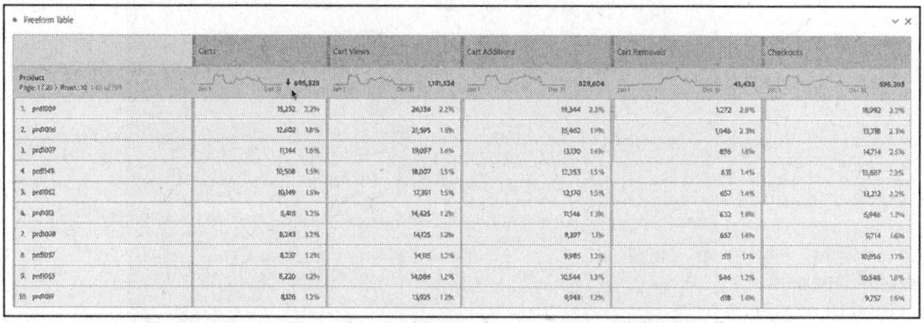

Freeform Table

Product Page: 1 / 20 > Rows: 10 1-10 of 199	Carts		Cart Views		Cart Additions		Cart Removals		Checkouts	
	695,328		1,191,524		829,604		45,433		596,203	
1. prd1009	15,252	2.2%	26,136	2.2%	19,344	2.3%	1,272	2.8%	18,992	3.2%
2. prd1036	12,602	1.8%	21,595	1.8%	15,462	1.9%	1,046	2.3%	13,798	2.3%
3. prd1007	11,144	1.6%	19,097	1.6%	13,130	1.6%	836	1.8%	14,714	2.5%
4. prd1149	10,508	1.5%	18,007	1.5%	12,353	1.5%	631	1.4%	13,887	2.3%
5. prd1052	10,149	1.5%	17,391	1.5%	12,170	1.5%	657	1.4%	13,212	2.2%
6. prd1012	8,418	1.2%	14,425	1.2%	11,546	1.3%	632	1.4%	6,946	1.2%
7. prd1008	8,243	1.2%	14,125	1.2%	9,307	1.1%	657	1.4%	9,714	1.6%
8. prd1037	8,237	1.2%	14,115	1.2%	9,985	1.2%	511	1.1%	10,056	1.7%
9. prd1053	8,220	1.2%	14,086	1.2%	10,544	1.3%	546	1.2%	10,548	1.8%
10. prd1039	8,126	1.2%	13,925	1.2%	9,943	1.2%	618	1.4%	9,757	1.6%

FIGURE 5-11: The five cart metrics for the top 10 products sorted by carts.

- **_Cart additions_ is the count of products that have been added to a shopping cart.** Adobe customers will often increase cart additions for each unit of a product added to the cart. If Product X is added to the cart three times, cart additions will also increase by three. The event name for to look for in Adobe Experience Cloud Debugger is scAdd.
- **_Cart removals_ is the number of times an item was removed from a shopping cart.** We've noticed that companies often forget the plethora of ways in which products can be removed from their cart, so be sure to work with your implementation team to ensure that they have them all covered. Adobe Experience Cloud Debugger shows scRemove as the event name.
- **_Cart views_ counts the number of times a shopping cart is viewed by visitors.** This metric can be useful to analyze when considering the different paths users take to get to the shopping cart. Are users going back and forth between products and the cart, perhaps to get their subtotal high enough to qualify for free shipping? The cart views metric can help with this type of analysis. scView is the event to look for in the debugger.
- **_Checkouts_ is the last step in the purchase conversion funnel.** It is often the page where users enter their payment information and click submit to confirm their purchase. Our analyses have shown that websites often leave a lot of money on the table at this step due to customers who get cold feet during this last step of the purchase funnel. It's a fantastic place to start your

analysis anytime you're looking to positively affect your company's bottom line. Look for checkout as an event in your debugger to ensure that the metric is set properly.

Using purchase metrics

Websites that sell things are always most interested in one thing: the amount of revenue generated. However, that information doesn't tell the full purchase story. Adobe has been sure to incorporate metrics that capture the count of orders and units purchased.

Orders are the total number of purchases made and *units* count the number of individual products that were sold. This additional context can be enlightening. Imagine if revenue increased by 200 percent due to a single high-value order. As an analyst, you would consider either filtering out that order from your analysis, or perhaps zeroing in on that order to try to drive additional high-value orders in the future.

It might be valuable, for example, to piece together a picture of orders, units, and revenue per product, as shown in the table in Figure 5-12. Note how revenue includes a dollar sign because it's currency.

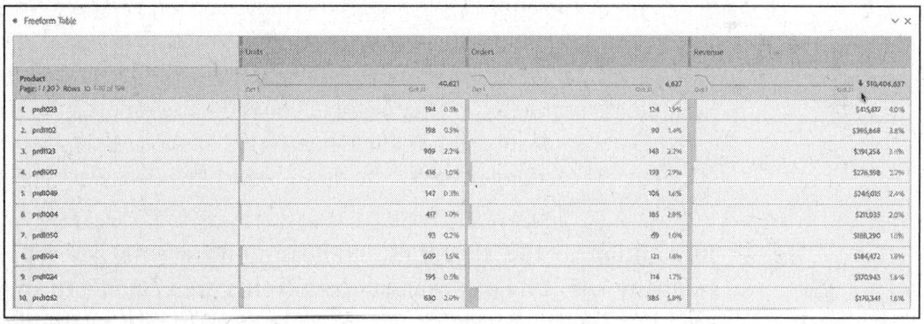

FIGURE 5-12:
Orders, units, and revenue per product in a freeform table.

The Adobe Analytics deployment specification requires that these three metrics be populated in a complicated fashion. The orders metric is the simplest: Look for the purchase variable in the Events row of Adobe Experience Cloud Debugger. To tie the orders metric to any products, a complex implementation variable called s.products must be populated. It's in this variable that product name/SKU, the number of units purchased, and the revenue associated with each product is captured. We describe s.products in more detail in Chapter 7.

Working with Custom Metrics in Adobe

You may have noticed that we haven't provided an exhaustive list of all the metrics available in your report suite. This is because companies can deploy up to 1,000 custom metrics per report suite! These custom metrics can be used to capture something as simple as a click on a navigation menu or as complicated as each step of a 10-step registration form.

Adobe Analytics uses the term *success events* to describe custom metrics. You can format success events in one of three ways:

>> **Counter events:** Act just as they sound. Every time the event is set, the metric increases by one. Adobe implementation teams can choose to pass whole numbers to counter events so that they increase by more than one in a single tag. Analysis Workspace formats counter events as an integer.

>> **Numeric events:** Are rarely used these days but are worth mentioning. They act similarly to counter events but can be increased also by numbers that have decimals. Analysis Workspace formats these as an integer, so a calculated metric with a decimal place is required to view any numbers to the right of the decimal.

>> **Currency events:** Used for passing a monetary value to Adobe Analytics. Three features combine to make currency events unique. First, like numeric events, currency events accept decimals. Second, Analysis Workspace formats currency events with a currency symbol (similar to revenue in Figure 5-12). Finally, Adobe automatically performs a currency conversion on them. If data is sent to a currency event in euros but the report suite is set to capture US dollars, Adobe automatically performs this conversion for you, using the current exchange rate for the day on which the data was captured.

In addition to the seemingly endless 1,000 events per report suite that your company has at its disposal, success events are valuable to analysts because they are highly flexible metrics. They can be used in any segment, visualization, and calculated metric, just like the built-in metrics discussed earlier in this chapter.

Success events are designated using a number between 1 and 1,000, the value of which is translated to a friendly name such as *registrations* or *logins*. Your admins set the friendly names and the event type (such as counter, numeric, or currency) in Adobe Analytics Admin Console. Because this translation is not done in the tag, you may have to do a bit of reconnaissance work to understand how data is populated when using your debugger.

In the left rail in Analysis Workspace, the event number for each metric appears in parentheses next to each success event. For example, in Figure 5-13, the right rail lists success event 32 along with its translation into a friendly name (Leads); event 37 with its translation (Sign-Ins), and so on. These success events are shown alongside the marketing channel dimension in Figure 5-13.

REMEMBER

You walk through the content of the left rail and how to use it in Chapter 3.

You can search for events by using the search box in the left rail. For example, if you enter *event1* as your search keyword, the friendly name will appear.

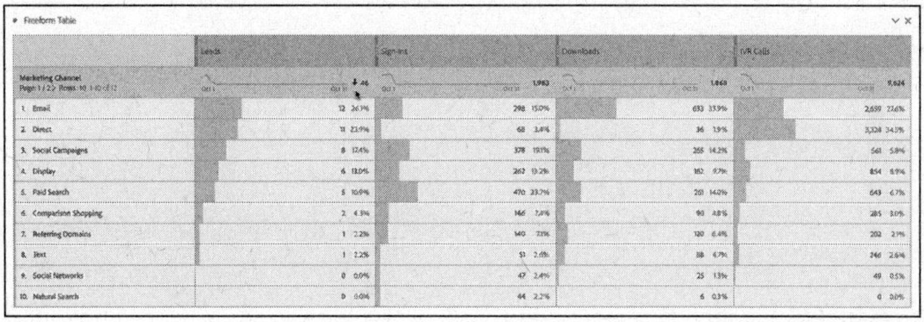

TIP

FIGURE 5-13:
Several success
events are
aligned with
marketing
channel in a
freeform table.

Freeform Table								
	Leads		Sign-Ins		Downloads		IVR Calls	
Marketing Channel Page 1 / 2 > Items 10 1-10 of 12	Oct 1	Oct 31 ↓ 44	Oct 1	Oct 31 1,993	Oct 1	Oct 31 1,469	Oct 1	Oct 31 9,624
1. Email	12	26.7%	798	15.0%	613	33.9%	2,659	27.6%
2. Direct	11	23.9%	68	3.4%	36	1.9%	3,324	34.5%
3. Social Campaigns	8	17.4%	378	19.1%	265	14.2%	561	5.8%
4. Display	6	13.0%	262	13.2%	167	9.7%	854	8.9%
5. Paid Search	5	10.9%	470	23.7%	261	14.2%	643	6.7%
6. Comparison Shopping	2	4.3%	146	7.4%	90	4.8%	285	3.0%
7. Referring Domains	1	2.2%	140	7.1%	120	6.4%	202	2.1%
8. Text	1	2.2%	51	2.6%	88	4.7%	146	2.6%
9. Social Networks	0	0.0%	47	2.4%	25	1.3%	49	0.5%
10. Natural Search	0	0.0%	44	2.2%	6	0.3%	6	0.0%

As noted, in the example in Figure 5-13, the first metric — leads — is event32. That's important to know because if you were to run Adobe Experience Cloud Debugger on your website on the leads page, you would see event32 listed in the Events row of the Analytics tab.

Chapter **6**

Using Dimensions to Analyze Data

E very table combines one or more dimension with one or more metrics. In Chapter 5, you dig into key metrics — both standard metrics such as bounce rate and visits as well as custom metrics. In this chapter and the next, you zero in on exploiting the use of dimensions to analyze data. This chapter pays particular attention to Adobe's powerful built-in advertising dimension.

Dimensions are key to any analysis, and a good analyst knows when to use them to properly break metrics into useful *buckets* — that is, data with associated characteristics that feed into insightful analysis.

Before you set off to explore dimensions, be aware that Adobe provides a wide array of built-in dimensions that focus on traffic, time, advertising, technology, product, and more. Many of these dimensions are standard in every implementation, but it's worth confirming with your analytics admins that the descriptions you find here align with the data in your report suites.

Wielding Content Dimensions

In Chapter 2, we define and begin to use the page dimension, the most basic of the content-focused dimensions. Content and traffic dimensions are used to identify specific areas or actions on your site or app. Let's examine a couple of examples to dig deeper into what we mean by a content-based dimension:

>> An analyst for an online newspaper wants to understand the difference in behavior in the sports section compared to the financial pages.

>> Analysts for a retail company want to understand whether new visitors are landing on men's clothing pages or women's accessories.

In these analyses, content will be analyzed, so an analyst would use content-focused dimensions. In the next few sections ,we focus on several dimensions that may prove useful as you're analyzing data. We outline the best practices for implementing each dimension, but your company may have chosen to deploy a few dimensions in a different way. Don't let this disorient you. If your implementation differs from ours, a conscious decision was probably made to use (or not use) different dimensions in your Adobe Analytics configuration. Communicate with your admin team to understand these decisions; doing so will make you a better analyst and possibly improve your implementation.

Identifying server sources

We start with a dimension that has one of the highest levels of granularity in your report suite: the *server dimension.* Companies, institutions, and other enterprises utilize the server dimension in different ways. The original use case for this content dimension was to capture the server hosting the website, such as the west coast server or the east coast server. In these current days of unlimited cloud-based servers and multi-tenant hosting companies, the dimension has migrated to a better and simpler use: identifying the particular branch of an institution's online presence.

Think about it: A large clothing company has multiple brands; a large publisher has a variety of imprints; an activist organization has multiple campaigns. You get the idea. And most enterprises push data from a wide array of domains into a single report suite. That's helpful to get a meta-picture of the performance of enterprise-spanning ad campaigns, social media initiatives, email blasts, and so on. But sometimes analysts need to look at data for a particular branch of the enterprise — a brand, an imprint, or a campaign.

If each of these components of an enterprise has its web presence hosted on distinct servers (which is often the case), the server dimension can distinguish each domain and app in a global report suite architecture.

TIP

The server dimension is optional. You can identify whether or not this dimension is implemented by checking to see what, if any, data is populated there. To see whether data is being sent to this dimension, use Adobe Experience Cloud Debugger on your website. The debugger will display data sent to this variable in a row labeled *Server* in the Analytics tab.

Figure 6-1 shows server used as a dimension with a visits metric. This table displays visits at three servers, identified as A.com; B.com; and D.co.uk, along with traffic through separate servers hosting iPhone and Android apps (which usually require host servers with special software).

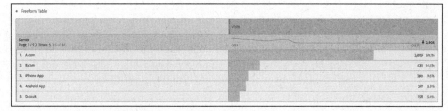

FIGURE 6-1:
A global report
suite breaks out
each domain and
app in the server
dimension.

If your company is using server in this fashion, it's most likely the dimension with the highest granularity in your report suite.

Looking at the site section dimension

The site section dimension is one level more granular than server. *Site section* is a content dimension designed to be organized the same way your website is organized, into sections. However, site section, like server, can be custom-populated based on the deployment of your Adobe Analytics tags. Our preferred method for populating site section is to have the dimensional values mirror the navigation menu on your website. Analysts can then easily identify the site section of any page they visit, without having to invoke the debugger to learn how data is populated.

TIP

You may have launched Adobe Experience Cloud Debugger on your site to look for the site section but were confused because there isn't a row associated with it on the Analytics tab. (You walk through using Adobe Experience Cloud Debugger in Chrome in Chapter 2.) Fear not, because you might be looking for the wrong item. Site section has a pseudonym on the tagging side of Adobe Analytics. Your implementation team will know that *site section* is defined as *channel* in their tags, and channel is also how site section appears in the debugger. So give the debugger another try and look for channel instead. Now you'll see the values getting populated into site section in Analysis Workspace.

Figure 6-2 shows a site section dimension displaying visits to sections of a website corresponding to top-level menu items at the site.

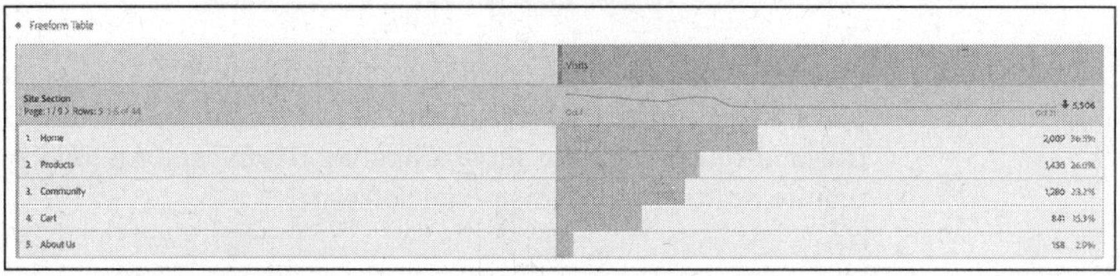

FIGURE 6-2:
Site section mirrors a site's navigational menu.

If your report suite isn't showing any data associated with site section, it may be time to have a chat with your implementation team. The site section dimension can be an extremely valuable way to slice and dice your data and getting the dimension up and running is usually a painless process.

Examining hierarchy

You've examined two different levels of content granularity: server (highest granularity) and site section (second-highest). In Chapter 2, you examine a third level — the page dimension (lowest granularity). The nice thing about these levels is that every website has them, so they are always useful and there is minimal need for extreme customization when making decisions about how to push data into each variable.

However, most websites have many intermediate levels of granularity, such as a content site organized into multiple directories and sub-directories. Perhaps an enterprise product company has strict site categories ordered by geography, industry, and solution. Think about your company. How many levels deep into your site can visitors browse?

Adobe Analytics is flexible enough to handle the most complex websites and apps regardless of industry or geography. The hierarchy variable is often the content dimension that can help fill the vast gap between server and page. It's a dimension that can accept many levels of data (up to 98!) at the same time in a single hit.

You can implement up to five hierarchy variables, each with its own maximum number of levels as defined by admins. In addition, for each of the five hierarchy variables, admins can decide on a unique delimiter, or character, to indicate new levels in the hierarchy.

For example, hierarchy 1 and the pipe delimiter would look like this:

widgets.com|products|widget A|reviews

Each item would populate into a different hierarchy level in hierarchy 1. So one dimension would capture widgets.com; another would capture products; another, widget A; and the fourth level, reviews. This feature can be especially valuable because analysts can easily compare all values populating a single hierarchy level, or even break down one level by another, as shown in Figure 6-3.

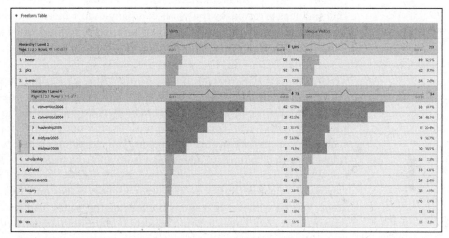

FIGURE 6-3: A hierarchy's level 2 with a value broken down by level 4 in a freeform table.

Hierarchy variables are often not in use — most Adobe customers who we've worked with haven't implemented them. The variables are difficult to implement, and the old Adobe Analytics interface, Reports & Analytics, made it difficult to work with them. Nowadays, Analysis Workspace has made them more useful and relevant!

Another limitation is that hierarchy variables max out at 255 characters per hit. For example, if you have 98 levels worth of data to pass in, delimiters will use up 97 characters, and Adobe implementers will have only 158 character to divvy up between 98 levels — that's an average of less than 2 characters per level! Thankfully, most report suites that use hierarchy variables need 10 or 20 levels at the most.

The last drawback to hierarchy variables is that they are not available in Report Builder, Adobe's Excel plug-in. (You can learn more about Report Builder in Chapter 16.)

The hierarchy variables are identified in Adobe Experience Cloud Debugger as hier#, where the hash is used to identify which hierarchy variable (1–5) is receiving data. Keep in mind that administrators can customize the name of each hierarchy level, so you may want to reference your Solution Design to find the name that appears in Workspace. (A *Solution Design* is a data dictionary that your company uses to keep all data in your Adobe Analytics instance organized and accessible.)

Finding error pages

Analysts need to understand behavior everywhere on your site, and sometimes that includes error pages that your company didn't mean to direct your users to. These error pages are called 404 errors and are usually accessed by users via broken links with misspellings in the URL.

The bad news is that your site's visitors are definitely finding these error pages on occasion. The good news is that Adobe Analytics can help find them so you can get them fixed. Error pages are categorized in their own dimension in Adobe Analytics called *pages not found*. For technical reasons, it's not possible for Adobe to automatically collect data in this dimension; your implementation team has to teach Adobe how to differentiate a real page from an error page.

Deploying Adobe Analytics on 404 error pages requires only two implementation steps. You, or whoever is responsible for tagging pages, can try this test to see if data on your error pages is being collected properly in Adobe: Try manually going to a URL on your site that doesn't exist (we suggest *yourdomain*.com/EricAnd DavidRock.html) and run the debugger on it to see if an Adobe Analytics tag fires. If a tag fires, the first step of the error page tracking is set up properly.

The second step is teaching Adobe to treat this as an error page. A variable called pageType set to errorPage is used to differentiate error pages. At the time of this writing, the debugger doesn't have the capability to display the value of pageType, so your best bet is to check the pages not found dimension to see whether data is populating there.

Analyzing links

A large portion of the behavior that you want to analyze occurs on a website or in an app after the page has finished loading. For example:

>> What files are being downloaded?

>> Which videos are watched to completion?

>> When users exit the site, which affiliate sites are they going to most often?

Each of these actions happens well after a page has already loaded, so analysts can't use any of the other content dimensions you've examined up to now. Instead, Adobe Analytics admins implement tracking of this behavior by using download links, custom links, and exit links.

TIP

If you're familiar with Google Analytics, you can see that links are similar to events: Links allow behavioral data to be captured without increasing the number of page views.

Link dimensions are often used as a container for sending additional metrics and dimensions to Adobe. Let's walk through an example: A company may be interested in capturing the name of a PDF that is downloaded. The PDF filename will most likely be captured in the download link dimension, but other metrics and dimensions should be captured too, including the URL where the PDF is hosted, the product associated with the PDF, and a metric counting the number of times the PDF is downloaded.

REMEMBER

Keep this in mind as you read the data captured in the link dimensions: The values sent to these dimensions are often not as important as the other data points sent in the same hit.

Examining download activity with the download link dimension

The *download link dimension* is used to capture file downloads from websites. The data captured in the download link variable is customizable, so it is worth spending some time with your implementation engineer to understand how it's populated.

Adobe provides two options for your team to implement data capture in download links:

>> **Automatic tracking:** Takes advantage of a customizable list of file extensions (such as PDF, PPTX, or XLSX) to automatically capture clicks on downloadable files.

>> **Manual tracking:** Requires custom definitions for downloads. Most implementation specialists prefer to manually capture download links so that they have more control over the data sent in the tag.

Figure 6-4 shows the top downloads from a site. The table includes automatically tracked items (MP3 audio files and PDFs) as well as downloads that have been manually defined.

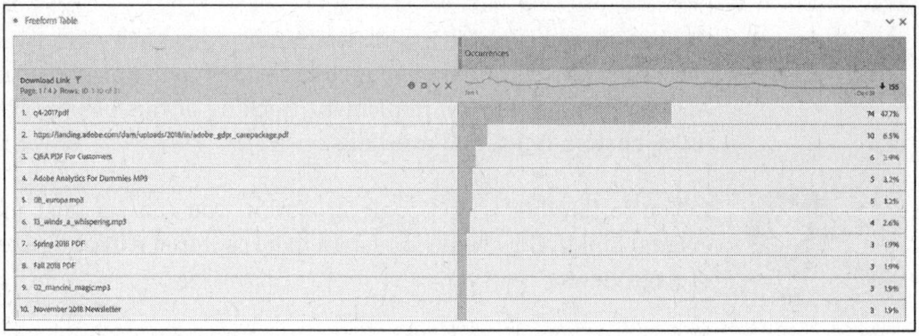

FIGURE 6-4:
The top ten downloads from a site with partial automatic and partial manual tracking.

If you use the debugger, it shows how three different variables help differentiate a page view tag from a download link tag:

» **Link type:** Helps differentiate the type of link — download, exit, or custom. When link type is set to lnk_d in your debugger, that hit is a download link.

» **Link URL:** Populated when automatic tracking is enabled for download links. It automatically captures the URL of the content being downloaded. The value of link URL is populated in the download link dimension in Analysis Workspace when the link type is set to lnk_d.

» **Link name:** Populated when manual tracking is in use for the download link. It is manually set by your implementation team, as you would expect. If lnk_d is set as the link type, the download link dimension is populated with link name if it is set, even if link URL is also set in your tag.

Analyzing download links can be a worthwhile task. Not all businesses capture revenue on their website, but almost all businesses have some kind of download activity. A lead-based B2B company may not accept orders online, but they have PDFs available to help differentiate product offerings. A good analyst will analyze the download link dimension to understand which products are most interesting to prospective customers to help inform the rest of the organization of changes in product trends.

Measuring when people leave with the exit link dimension

Another type of link dimension is the *exit link*, which is used to capture exits to other domains from your site. The exit link dimension may be used to capture exits to partners, affiliates, or different brands within your organization. Exit links are similar to download links in several ways:

>> **The data captured in the exit link dimension is customizable based on your implementation and does not increase the count of page views.** Adobe still charges you for collecting this data.

>> **Adobe provides both an automatic exit link and a manual exit link capture mechanism.** Automatic tracking uses a list of domains that should not be considered exits, and then automatically captures clicks on links to any other domain as exit links. Adobe also provides manual exit linking options, in which admins decide where, when, and how to capture exit links.

>> **The link type, link URL, and link name variables are populated in Experience Cloud Debugger to distinguish exit links from others.** However, exit links differ because the link type variable is set as lnk_e, ending in *e* for *exit*.

>> **The relationship between link URL and link name remains the same for exit links.** The link name takes precedence over link URL, which means if both are populated, the exit link dimension is populated with link name.

In Figure 6-5, we can see where visitors to our site are headed as they leave the site.

FIGURE 6-5: Identifying where users go when they exit a site.

Exit links are similar to download links in that they help analysts understand behavior that can lead to product purchases. Consumer package goods (CPG) brands sell thousands of products but rarely sell them direct-to-consumer, which means they link to a retail store website for consumers to buy them. The page dimension helps an analyst understand the product pages being viewed, but the exit link dimension helps an analyst understand buying actions!

Analyzing activity that isn't a page, an exit, or a download

If you were to write down a list of all the types of behavior on your website, the majority could be categorized under three content dimensions: page, download link, and exit link. But a significant number of items on your list wouldn't be tied to a page loading, a file download, nor an exit being clicked.

This other activity includes interactions with videos, chatbots, photo galleries, forms, internal search, product filters, navigational menus, and more. All of these can be useful to an analyst, and none of them fit into the page/download/exit format. Therefore, we need a catchall for the remaining interactions — and that catchall is the custom link. As you would expect, a custom link is similar to download and exit links but does have a few unique features:

» **The data captured in the custom link dimension is customized based on your implementation and does not increase the count of page views.** Adobe still charges you for collecting this data.

» **Adobe provides only a manual custom linking option, in which admins decide where, when, and how to capture custom links.**

» **The link type, link URL, and link name variables are populated in Experience Cloud Debugger to distinguish custom links from others.** Custom links can be recognized in the link type variable because it is set as lnk_o, ending in o for other. (The reason why it doesn't end in c for custom is a mystery.)

» **Custom links never populate the link URL variable, just link name.**

Figure 6-6 shows the custom link dimension with a curated set of actions.

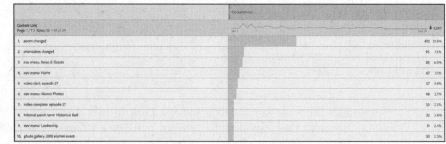

FIGURE 6-6: Custom links capture several unconventional interactions.

The value of custom links is hard to oversell. Custom links capture the nuance associated with visitors beyond simple page views, downloads, and site exits. The difference between converting visitors and non-purchasers might be whether or not they watch a video until the end; analysts need that data at their fingertips to discover that key differentiating moment.

Specifying Activity Map dimensions

The last built-in content-focused dimension to cover is actually several dimensions tied to a separate, visually compelling Adobe tool: Activity Map. Activity Map is a browser plug-in that uses visual overlays to rank link activity on your website. Think of Activity Map as a heat map for clicks on your site.

Chapter 16 provides a deeper dive into using the tool to visually map your site's activity. But in addition to Activity Map's usefulness for visual representation of data, it also populates four useful dimensions: Activity Map region, Activity Map page, Activity Map link, and Activity Map link by region. Data in these dimensions is captured *automatically* as long as your administrator has enabled the Activity Map feature in your report suite. Data is captured in these dimensions on every click because the goal of the feature is to map all clicks visually.

Using Activity Map dimensions

Let's look at the four Activity Map dimensions and how they're used:

» **Activity Map link:** Automatically captures the text in any link on every page. The text is captured verbatim, so beware of any pages where a user's PII (personally identifiable information, such as an email address, a full name, or a social security number) may be clicked. It's also important to realize that many pages have the same text linked in multiple locations. Adobe has thankfully thought of this, which is why two other Activity Map dimensions differentiate multiple links with the same text.

>> **Activity Map region dimension:** Captures the location in the HTML where the link was clicked. The Activity Map region dimension is one way that Adobe combats the problem of having multiple links with the same text. It can be a helpful way to distinguish two links to the home page on a site, one in the nav menu and another in the body of the page. Adobe does use complex logic to populate the data in this dimension, but we've found it valuable to know that the Activity Map region dimension is always available to aid our link analyses.

>> **Activity Map link by region:** Combines the Activity Map link dimension with the Activity Map region dimension and separates them using a vertical pipe. If a user clicks to the home page via a link in the divGlobalBanner HTML object, for example, this dimension will appear as home|divGlobalBanner.

>> **Activity Map page:** Captures the name of the page where the user is coming from. (Activity Map link captures the text of the link where a user is going to.) This dimension can be useful when analysts are trying to understand the links that users are clicking from any specific page; an analyst can break down Activity Map page by Activity Map link and easily obtain the answer.

Avoiding pitfalls with Activity Map dimensions

Although Activity Map dimensions may sound perfect, we should mention a few caveats. Analysts rarely start an analysis with an Activity Map dimension, but they often find them useful when digging deep with a need to break down data in an unusual or unplanned way. Before they do this, however, they must understand the idiosyncrasies of the data.

The biggest caveat: To avoid firing unnecessary tags, each dimension is captured on the subsequent page view. For example, if a user is clicking from the home page to a product page, the Activity Map data for the home page is captured on the product page. This behavior can be useful to the analyst who understands it and frustrating to the analyst who doesn't, so you walk through an example in Table 6-1.

The first hit is simple: The visit's first page view is on the home page, so there is no need to populate any data associated with Activity Map there.

The second hit is where things get complicated. Because the visitor clicks a link to Product A on the home page, it's important to capture the associated data in the Activity Map dimensions. Activity Map page captures Home because the user clicked from that page. Activity Map link captures Product A because that was the text clicked from the Home page. Activity Map Region captures divProd because that was the HTML surrounding the link.

TABLE 6-1 | **Sample Visit with Three Hits across Three Pages**

Hit Number	Page (Standard Dimension)	Link Clicked	Activity Map Page	Activity Map Link	Activity Map Region
1	Home	Product A			
2	Product A	Shopping Cart	Home	Product A	divProd
3	Shopping Cart		Product A	Shopping Cart	header

The third hit occurs on the shopping cart page. Similar to the second hit, Activity Map dimensions are delayed. Activity Map link is set to Shopping Cart, Activity Map region is set to header, and Activity Map page is set to Product A.

Understanding this complexity is key to using these dimensions in Workspace. Figure 6-7 demonstrates how the data would look in a freeform table.

Note how in Figure 6-7, everything lines up as expected except for the page dimension. Because the data is captured on the subsequent page, the value of page aligns with the value of Activity Map link and not Activity Map page. Activity Map page is populated with the previous page's value.

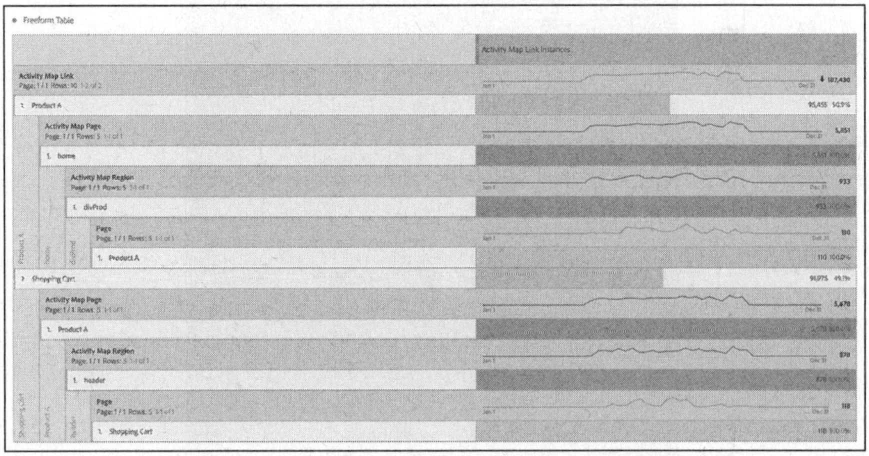

FIGURE 6-7: The data from Table 6-1 is shown using Activity Map and page dimensions.

We hope that complication didn't scare you away from using these useful dimensions. If it didn't, this next caveat might.

Activity Map dimensions do not capture all links. A lot of complicated websites use technologies new and old. If your website is using legacy technology such as Flash, Adobe has no way of detecting link clicks. It's okay to assume that your data is being collected in Activity Map, but if you think that data from some links is missing, it's valuable to know how to check that data is being sent to Adobe. Thankfully, the vast majority of links are automatically captured, so the dimensions are highly useful.

You can use Adobe Experience Cloud Debugger to confirm the data sent by Activity Map. As you can see in Figure 6-8, each dimension is populated in the Analytics tab in the Debugger as follows:

» contextData['c.a.activitymap.page']

» contextData['c.a.activitymap.link']

» contextData['c.a.activitymap.region']

Be sure to open the debugger before clicking the link that you're inspecting. This way, the debugger can capture any tags that fire during your click on the link as well as tags that fire on the subsequent page view.

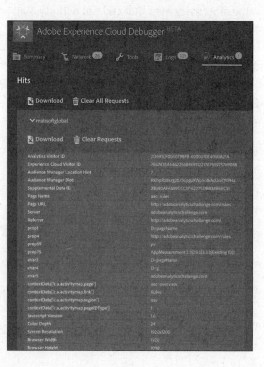

FIGURE 6-8:
The debugger with the Activity Map dimensions populated.

Connecting Behavior to Advertising

One key use case for web analytics solutions such as Adobe Analytics is to attribute the success of your digital marketing campaigns.

Adobe has several variables that are built into the product to make it easier to perform these marketing attribution analyses. Most of them populate with data after little customization to your report suite, so they are almost all capturing data for your company. Each dimension retains their value for the extent of the visit that drove them to the site, which means that analysis is easier because all activity is properly attributed to the advertising dimensional value that drove that activity.

TIP

This behavior is different than in Google Analytics, which has some dimensions that are available only on the landing page and others that persist through the visit.

Analyzing referrer dimensions

Referrer-based data is some of the most basic advertising data in a web analytics platform. An *HTTP referrer* is a field that identifies the address of the web page that linked to the page being accessed. Because the data is automatically available in a browser, the analytics tool just needs to capture it. Adobe has broken out the referrer into three dimensions to make the data more manageable.

Dissecting the referrer

The referrer dimension is the most basic advertising dimension. It accepts the HTTP referrer verbatim, exactly as it is passed to the browser. Referrer captures the full URL where your visitors came from before they arrived at your site.

For the referrer to be populated, the visitor must have clicked from the previous site to yours and the previous site must not have proactively blocked referring site information. Therefore, visitors to your website from a browser bookmark will not have a value for referrer even if they were on a different website when they clicked the bookmark. Visits that don't have a referrer are bucketed by Adobe with a value of Typed/Bookmarked, as shown in Figure 6-9.

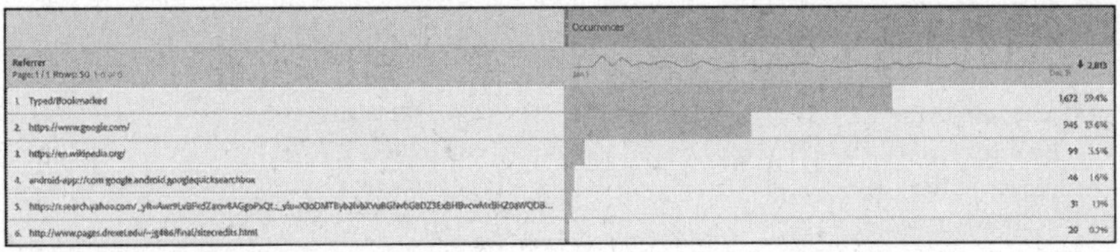

FIGURE 6-9: Referrer shows some complete URLs while others such as google. com are limited.

Referrer	Occurrences
	♦ 2,813
1. Typed/Bookmarked	1,672 59.4%
2. https://www.google.com/	945 33.6%
3. https://en.wikipedia.org/	99 3.5%
4. android-app://com.google.android.googlequicksearchbox	46 1.6%
5. https://r.search.yahoo.com/_ylt=AwrtLvBPeSZaceoEAGgivhQt_ylu=X3oDMTByb2IvbXVuBGNvbGsDDZIExBHBvcwArdlHZowVQDA...	31 1.1%
6. http://www.pages.drexel.edu/~gd4w/Final/sitecredits.html	20 0.7%

Simplifying the referrer into the referring domain

Let's face it: Some URLs are long. Microsoft's Internet Explorer browser has a max length of over 2,000 characters, and some developers still need more!

Adobe realizes that URLs can be lengthy and ugly, so they helped by cleaning up referrer a bit by focusing the dimension on just the domain. This change makes it easier to analyze the data because the values end after .com, .net, .org, and so on. However, because data is cut off, it may be more useful to start with the referring domain dimension and then drill down to referrer if necessary. As with referrer, Adobe buckets visits without a referring domain with a value of Typed/ Bookmarked.

Figure 6-10 illustrates how the referring domain dimension appears in a freeform table.

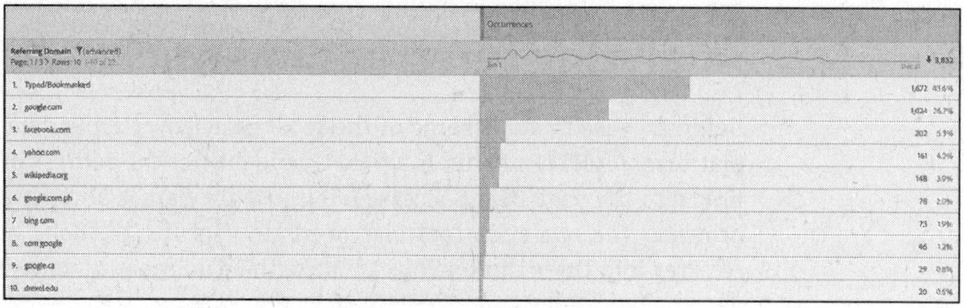

FIGURE 6-10: Referring domain populated in a freeform table.

Categorizing referrers into referrer type

Adobe applies one more bucket to the referrer to make the data more manageable. The referrer type dimension classifies referrers into one of four categories:

>> Typed/Bookmarked

>> Search Engines

>> Other Websites

>> Social Networks

Figure 6-11 shows the referrer type dimension in a freeform table.

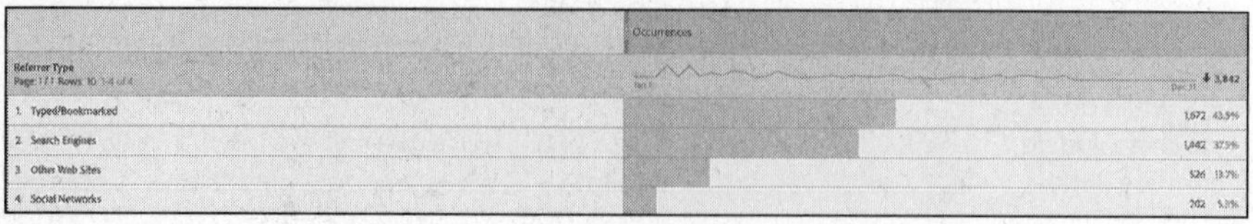

FIGURE 6-11: Referrer type categories are shown in a freeform table.

TIP

Adobe manages the definition of these categories, and we've found analysts to be dissatisfied with their breakout. To temper this dissatisfaction, Adobe provides a significantly more flexible dimension named marketing channel.

Tracking marketing channels

As an analyst, you will inevitably need a considerably more detailed view into the channels driving visitors to your site than the referrer-based dimensions. Referrer type automatically buckets referrers into a few categories, but analysts need much more detail to properly distinguish visitors that click-through on paid search versus natural search, or display ads versus organic links.

The *marketing channel dimension* provides a complete view into each of the categorizes of referrers and ads that drive traffic to your site or app. It is built on a custom set of rules defined in your report suite's Admin Console. These rules are called the *marketing channel processing rules.* You would be smart to sync with your Adobe admins to understand how these rules have been defined and, if possible, even help decide how they are set up and prioritized.

Identifying marketing channel dimensions

By default, Analysis Workspace has six marketing channel dimensions. To keep things simple we group them into two sets: channel and channel detail.

Marketing channel, last touch channel, and *first touch channel* are the dimensions associated with a higher granularity bucketing of visits, often containing values of paid search, natural search, email, display, social networks, and referring domains. These dimensions are defined by the first drop-down in the channel settings within a rule set.

The key difference between the three channel dimensions is tied to attribution: Which value, over time, should apply to the corresponding metrics? Attribution is defined in more detail in Chapter 12, but the following presents a simple example to help you grasp the concept:

Visit Number	Channel	Action
1	Display Banner Click	Research
2	Paid Search	Purchase

Note how the table describes two separate visits, the first driven from display and the second driven from paid search. The head of advertising will want to know whether to put the budget for next quarter in display or paid search. As an analyst, you will want to attribute the revenue to one of those two channels, but which one?

For years, analysts have been using a *last touch attribution model* to associate the revenue to paid search. In this model, whichever channel is the most recent deserves 100 percent of the credit for the revenue.

In this instance, the advertisers responsible for display would argue that the visitor wouldn't have even known about the brand without their display-driven awareness campaign, so they should deserve 100 percent of the credit. This approach is known as *first touch attribution*.

As you may have guessed, the last touch channel attributes metrics to the channel value by using a last touch attribution model. The first touch channel attributes metrics by using a first touch attribution model.

When Adobe released Attribution IQ, a powerful way of changing the attribution model of any metric tied to any dimension, they were concerned that the dimensions of last touch channel and first touch channel could be misleading, because technically the last touch channel could be tied to metrics where the attribution model has been adjusted to first touch! To resolve this potential conflict, Adobe created a more generic marketing channel dimension. *Marketing channel* has a default attribution of last touch, but doesn't carry the confusing *last touch* name distinction because metrics are more customizable now.

TIP

The best practice is to always use (or migrate your old projects to use) marketing channel and ignore the first touch and last touch dimensions.

The second set of dimensions created by marketing channel processing rules are set by the value in each rule set, which is the second drop-down in the channel settings. Marketing channel detail, last touch channel detail, and first touch channel detail provide a more detailed view into the channel. These dimensions are set to capture the keyword for paid search, the campaign name for display, or the search engine for natural search. Because these values are customizable, be sure to work with your Adobe admin team to see how each channel's value is set in the marketing channel processing rules for each of your report suites.

Adobe provides three separate *channel detail dimensions* just as they provide three channel dimensions: first touch, last touch, and marketing channel detail. *Marketing channel detail* is a duplicate of last touch channel detail and is similarly less confusing when new Attribution IQ models are applied to it. Therefore, the best practice is the same as with marketing channel: Use (or start migrating to) marketing channel detail.

Figure 6-12 shows the marketing channel dimension, further broken down by marketing channel detail.

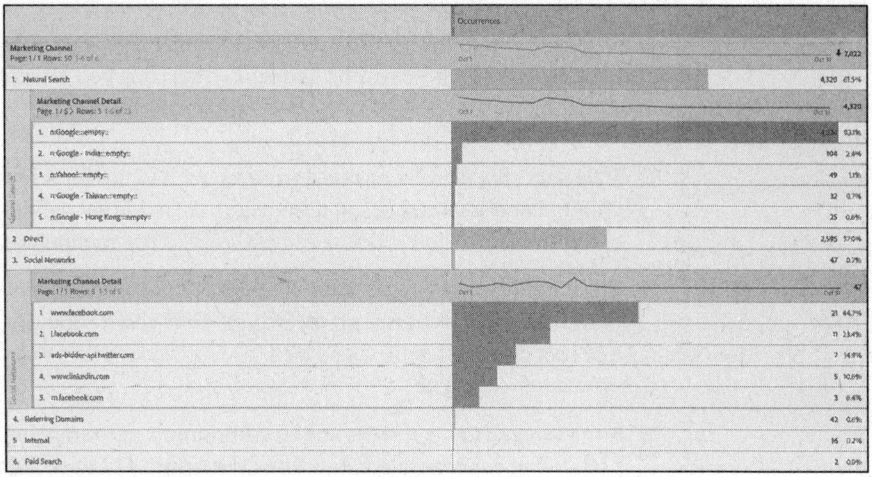

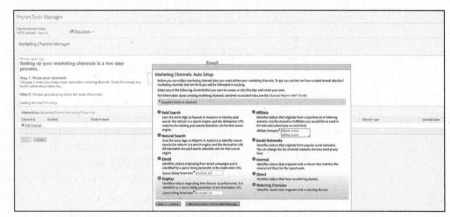

FIGURE 6-12:
Breaking down marketing channel by channel detail.

Defining marketing channels

Marketing channel processing rules are defined using a combination of dimensions based on referrer, search engine, query parameter, page, any eVar, and more. If you're unfamiliar with the concept of an eVar, skip ahead to the last section of this chapter, which is focused on custom dimensions in Adobe.

WARNING

Be careful! Processing rules are permanent, so be sure to avoid accidents when adjusting them.

If your report suite isn't yet capturing data in the marketing channel dimension, Adobe will suggest a default set of rules the first time an admin accesses their settings (available in Admin Console⇨Report Suites⇨Edit Settings⇨Marketing Channels). Figure 6-13 shows the setup screen.

FIGURE 6-13:
The automatic setup screen to define marketing channel rules.

A report suite's marketing channel processing rules are comprised of three key elements. Only an administrator can edit them, but you should understand their capabilities:

>> **Rule sets contain one or more rules to set a value for a marketing channel and channel detail dimension.** Each rule set defines a single value to the channel dimension and a single value to the channel detail dimension.

>> **Rules define how visits should be bucketed into the channel and channel detail dimensions based on conditions that you define.** For example, a rule's condition could be configured to identify whether a visit's referrer is from a search engine.

>> **Processing order is a well-named component of marketing channel processing rules because it defines the priority of each rule set.** As soon as a visit matches a rule set, the visit's channel and channel detail are set based on that rule set. For example, you may have one rule set that defines paid search (based on a search engine referrer and the existence of a CID query parameter) and a second rule set that defines natural search (based only on the existence of a search engine referrer). If the rule set for natural search is prioritized above the rule set for paid search, the paid search channel will never be set because all search engine visits, regardless of the existence of the query parameter, will be bucketed as natural search.

Figure 6-14 provides a useful visual to understand how priority affects rule sets.

Tying back to search engines

A key advertising channel for all brands occurs on search engines such as Google, Bing, and Yahoo! Companies apply two types of tactics to increase the visibility of their brand on search engines: search engine optimization (SEO) and search engine marketing (SEM, or paid search).

Analysts need to analyze behavior coming from search engines as a channel as well as distinguish between paid and natural. The data helps them determine how the channel affects behavior and conversion rate.

Adobe collects data in several search-focused dimensions, but they are unfortunately less reliable than the marketing channel and referrer dimensions. Our recommendation is to follow Adobe's best practice by ignoring data in these dimensions and instead using marketing channel, referrer, referring domain, and the dimensions associated with Ad Analytics for Paid Search (see Chapter 16 for the last one).

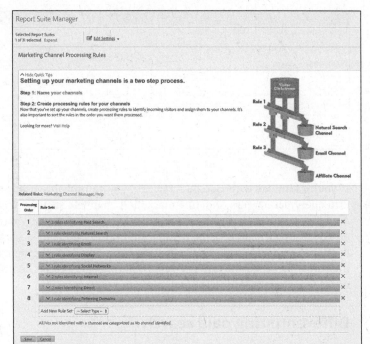

To be thorough, and because your installation of Adobe Analytics may be configured this way (it might not be possible or prudent to attempt to change that, at least not quickly), it is useful to provide details on the original goals of these dimensions. That said, please consider the recommended best practice instead if you are in a position to do so.

Detecting paid search visits

Adobe provides administrators with the ability to define rules to help differentiate paid search from natural search. The rules are set in a report suite's Admin Console, listed under Report Suites ⇨ Edit Settings ⇨ General ⇨ Paid Search Detection. One automatic rule that Adobe provides is that a visit must have a referrer that is a known search engine.

Adobe thankfully keeps this list updated so admins do not have to concern themselves with it. The remaining paid search detection rule definitions are based on a query string parameter, for example: *cid=PS*. Companies can set up different query string parameters based on the search engine, but we've found it preferable to use a single variable across all engines to keep data clean more simply.

Figure 6-15 shows how to configure paid search detection, which mirrors Google Analytics standards.

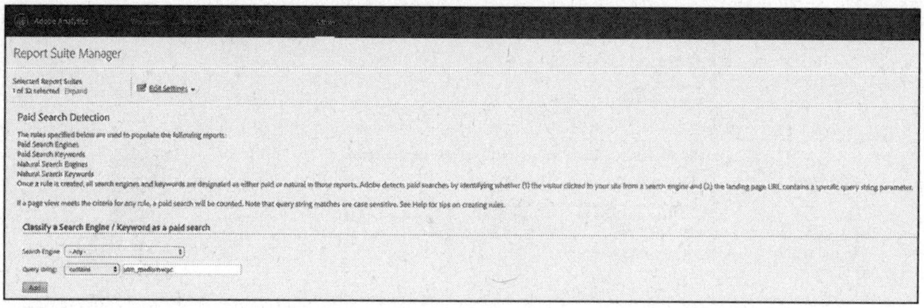

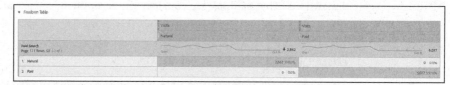

FIGURE 6-15:
A report suite's
paid search
detection mirrors
Google Analytics
standards.

TIP

If you're familiar with Google Analytics, you're probably used to the concept of utm query parameters to define marketing channels such as paid search. Google Analytics requires that you use *utm_medium=cpc* as the query parameter to properly bucket paid search visits. Because Adobe can define paid search based on any query parameter, brands that transition from Google to Adobe tracking can keep the same query parameter. The report suite's paid search detection rule simply needs to be taught to look for *utm_medium=cpc*.

Differentiating paid search

The simplest of the dimensions focused on search engine data is the paid search dimension, as shown in Figure 6-16. The paid search dimension helps analysts break down search engine behavior as either paid or natural. This high-level breakdown can be used to easily differentiate behavior at a very high granularity.

FIGURE 6-16:
A freeform table
shows the
simplicity of the
paid search
dimension.

Analyzing paid and natural search engines

All behavioral data from all search engines, regardless of paid search detection, is tied to the search engine dimension. The dimensional values are thankfully friendlier than just domains. As you can see in Figure 6-17, Adobe returns the data as text, such as Yahoo! or Google — Denmark.

The friendlier view of your search engine data can be useful when filtering or segmenting data to find exactly the engines you're trying to analyze. Figure 6-17 shows the search engine dimension with a paid search segment.

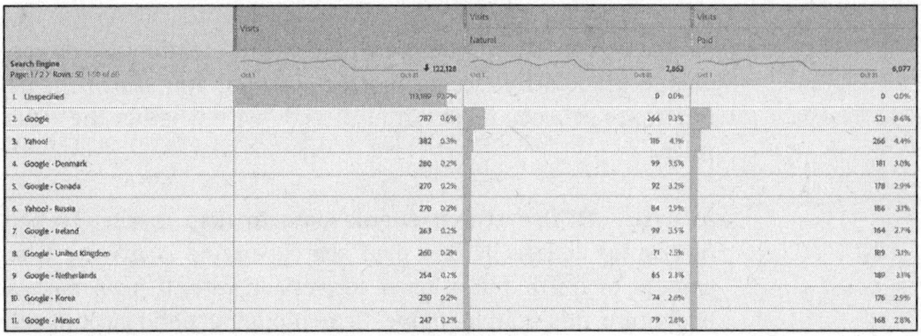

Search Engine Page: 1 / 2 > Rows: 50 1-50 of 60	Visits 122,128	Visits – Natural 2,862	Visits – Paid 6,077
1. Unspecified	113,189 92.7%	0 0.0%	0 0.0%
2. Google	787 0.6%	266 9.3%	521 8.6%
3. Yahoo!	382 0.3%	116 4.1%	266 4.4%
4. Google - Denmark	280 0.2%	99 3.5%	181 3.0%
5. Google - Canada	270 0.2%	92 3.2%	178 2.9%
6. Yahoo! - Russia	270 0.2%	84 2.9%	186 3.1%
7. Google - Ireland	263 0.2%	99 3.5%	164 2.7%
8. Google - United Kingdom	260 0.2%	71 2.5%	189 3.1%
9. Google - Netherlands	254 0.2%	65 2.3%	189 3.1%
10. Google - Korea	250 0.2%	74 2.6%	176 2.9%
11. Google - Mexico	247 0.2%	79 2.8%	168 2.8%

FIGURE 6-17: Search engine is shown with a paid search segment applied.

Take a few seconds and analyze Figure 6-17. See anything strange? Because the data is sorted by visits, which doesn't have a segment applied to it, the first line item is listed as *Unspecified*.

Unspecified is listed at the top because it is the result of all the visits that didn't come from a search engine. If an analyst were to sum all the visits to each of the individual search engines, there would be a significant difference between that sum and the total count of visits to the site; *Unspecified* acts as the remainder. Adobe adds an Unspecified row by default for almost all dimensions to make it easier to focus on behavior where the dimension was not set (or unspecified) when that metric was captured.

Adobe makes it easy for analysts to remove that dimensional item from view through the table filter feature. Figure 6-18 illustrates the details to remove Unspecified now. See Chapter 8 for a walk-through on how to apply filtering.

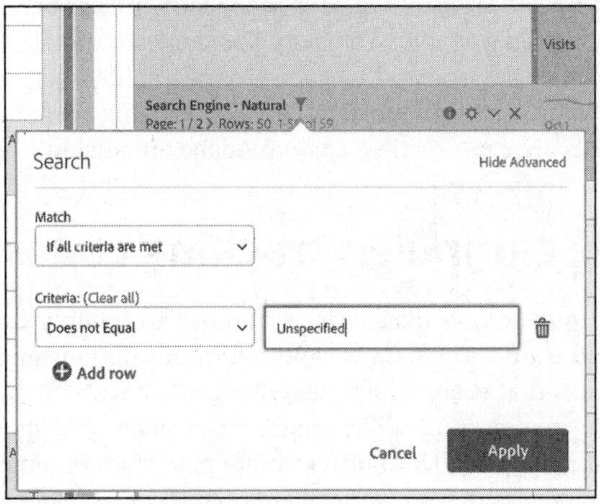

FIGURE 6-18: An advanced filter is applied to exclude Unspecified.

Paid search detection rules help analysts by creating two dimensions at the search engine granularity: *search engine — natural* and *search engine — paid*. The only difference between these aligns directly with whether the visits met the detection rules.

Analysts can use search engine data to help marketers better attribute their marketing dollars. If one paid search engine is driving a significantly higher amount of traffic but a lower conversion rate, it may make sense to adjust the budget for this search engine. Search engine alone isn't usually enough to make this recommendation. As you would expect, Adobe also provides similar dimensions focused on the search keyword rather than the engine.

Initiating search keyword analysis

Search keyword allows analysts to dig deeper into their search advertising data to identify what keywords are driving prospects and consumers to visit their site. These keywords can often become some of the most useful dimensional values to an analyst; when else do consumers tell you exactly what they're looking for?

Unfortunately, there's a catch. Years ago, in the name of privacy, Google blocked natural keywords from view by all analytics platforms. Other search engines soon followed suit, and now our beloved natural search keywords have been removed from Adobe Analytics (and Google Analytics, Webtrends, Coremetrics, and so on).

The search engines did, however, continue to provide advertisers with access to capture the search keyword if a user clicked through on a paid search ad, but only if that keyword as sent via query parameter on the landing page. So what does this all mean? All three of these dimensions are mostly useless because they generally list just Keyword Unavailable. You may see some minimal data in them from search engines that have not yet blocked paid search, but you should instead collaborate with your Adobe admin team and advertising team to ensure that paid search keywords are captured in a custom Adobe dimension.

Applying campaign tracking codes

The *campaign tracking code dimension* is another commonly used dimension for identifying paid traffic. The data is captured in this dimension in a custom fashion, which means that every Adobe customer could have a unique way of populating data in the dimension. Adobe customers usually add query parameters to campaign landing page URLs to differentiate paid from organic traffic. The most used query parameters that we've seen are CID (short for Campaign ID) and utm_ campaign (which is the Google Analytics query parameter).

Tracking code data, like most dimensions in Adobe Analytics, can be classified to more friendly buckets. You can easily find all the dimensions associated with tracking code by searching for it in the left rail, as shown in Figure 6-19.

Unspecified is Adobe's way of showing metrics that were captured at a time without out a value set for the dimension being analyzed. Visits aligned with an Unspecified tracking code mean that there was not a tracking code set for that visit, so it was most likely organic.

REMEMBER

Having a detailed yet easily understood taxonomy for defining the values passed into the campaign tracking code is key to a well-governed analytics deployment. Be sure to work with your Adobe admin team to understand the taxonomy. If the taxonomy is not being followed, it is imperative to work with your agencies or advertising team to clean up the data passed into tracking code.

Chapter **7**

Using Device, Product, and Custom Dimensions to Analyze Data

I n Chapter 6, you step back and examine the value and role of content-based dimensions (such as sections in an online newspaper, or product lines at a fashion-based site) and advertising dimensions (such as referrer and marketing channel). So if, in the course of this chapter, meta-questions pose themselves about the nature and role of using dimensions to analyze data, keep Chapter 6 handy for reference.

But you can do much more with dimensions when analyzing data in Adobe Analytics! In this chapter, you discover dimensions that identify and isolate behavior related to different device technologies, including mobile devices. You walk through how to discern the products variable to analyze products and product categories as well as purchase quantity, purchase price, and more.

Finally, you open the door to yet another level of customization and specific focus through the use of custom dimensions.

Defining Key Technology Dimensions

The visitors who come to your brand's website or app use different types of technology to interact with your company. They may be using the latest and greatest iPhone on the fastest gigabit mesh Wi-Fi on a new version of iOS that hasn't even been released yet. Or they may be using a 2008 Palm Treo (probably the only one that still has battery life) running Windows Mobile 6.1 on a slow 2G cellular connection.

These two people will have a vastly different experience on your website. If the iPhone user converts in lightning-fast time and the Palm user can't even click anything on the home page, your conversion rate for these two visitors is 50 percent. Wouldn't you want to know what caused the failed conversion? For these reasons, and plenty more that don't involve comically ancient smartphones, Adobe provides a wide variety of technology-related dimensions.

Distinguishing browsers and operating systems

The *browser dimension* in Adobe captures the name of the browser in use as well as the browser version. This data is then automatically bucketed into a *browser type dimension*, which captures the technology company that developed the browser.

Both dimensions are helpful to analysts when trying to analyze errors, bugs, and even significant drop-offs in key metrics. How so? Identifying browser type identifies which browser was used to view your site, such as Google's Chrome, Apple's Safari, Microsoft's Edge, and Mozilla's Firefox. These browser types have general characteristics in common in terms of the features they support, and your site development team will be interested to know how your browser data breaks down to make sure your site's code works for the vast majority of visitors.

But both to get a more granular picture of users and to assist in making the user experience function smoothly (and avoid features not yet supported by a critical mass of users' browsers), it is helpful to see more detail — What *version* of a browser do visitors of your site use? The additional levels of detail that browser and browser type provide is shown in Figure 7-1.

In addition, Adobe also captures browser-specific data in the *browser width* — *bucketed* and *browser height* — *bucketed* dimensions. These dimensions provide analysts with the count of pixels in width and height in 100-pixel buckets. Analysts often find these pixel buckets convenient when trying to analyze the difference in behavior between visitors with widescreen monitors, laptops, tablets, and phones. We walk through even better ways to identify device types later in this section.

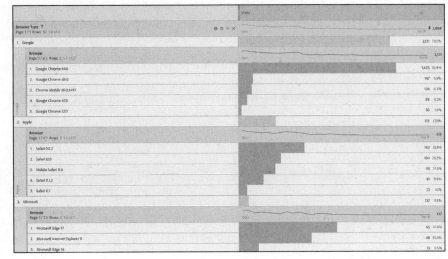

FIGURE 7-1:
The browser
dimension
provides more
details than the
browser type
dimension.

Additional technology dimensions that are automatically captured are *operating system types* and *operating systems*, which capture the O/S and the O/S version, respectively. We've seen some interesting analyses take place based on operating system, so don't discount this dimension just because the data is generic. Guess which operating system drives a higher conversion rate on your site, and then use data to see if you were right. You might be surprised.

Differentiating mobile device dimensions

It's clear that the mobile revolution isn't going away, and analysts need to stay attuned to rapidly evolving ways in which people use technology to engage online digital content. Adobe provides two key out-of-the-box dimensions to help analysts on their mobile analysis journey. *Mobile device type* provides a categorized list of mobile devices: mobile phones, tablets, gaming consoles, TVs, and more.

Sorting out what "Other" devices means

One potential source of confusion in your mobile device type is the value of Other. This is one of the rare times that Adobe is inconsistent in their naming, because in this dimension, Other means Desktop/Laptop.

Strangely, Adobe follows their own Unspecified standard in the other device dimension: mobile device. That's why in Figure 7-2, for example, you see Other listed as the mobile device type with the most visits, yet no actual "other" devices are listed in the breakdown!

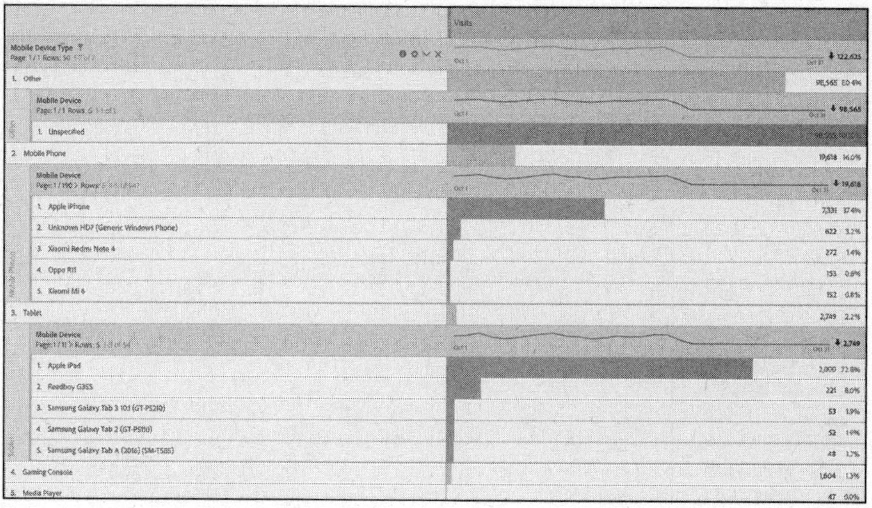

FIGURE 7-2: The many levels of device data.

Mobile device provides a more granular view into the devices visiting your property. The mobile device dimension differentiates between Apple iPhones and Samsung Galaxies, Apple iPads and Samsung Galaxy Tabs, and Microsoft Xboxes and Sony PlayStations. After you get past the confusing Other value, Figure 7-2 illustrates the relationship between the mobile device dimension and the mobile device type dimension.

Identifying mobile device data

Dozens of mobile device dimensions are built into Adobe Analytics. To see the list, type *mobile* in the Components search box, as shown in Figure 7-3. Many if not most of these dimensions are intuitively named. Some other useful and self-explanatory dimensions associated with mobile devices follow:

>> Mobile carrier

>> Mobile screen size

>> Mobile manufacturer

Companies that have mobile apps will have additional mobile-focused dimensions that expand on these dimensions, such as the following:

>> Device name

>> Operating system version

>> Resolution

FIGURE 7-3:
Exploring mobile
device
dimensions.

Mobile apps historically provide Adobe with more reliable and more granular details about these dimensions than the web browsers. If you're analyzing an app, the best practice is to use the dimensions just listed, which are generated by the Mobile App SDK.

Locating users with geographic dimensions

Understanding where in the world your visitors are accessing your digital property can provide valuable insights. For example, when analyzing conversion, brands that are not global will want to consider applying segments that filter their traffic to countries where they do business. Similarly, we've seen situations where global marketing enterprises have benefited from analyzing how site behavior varies depending on country, region, and state.

Adobe provides analysts the ability to break down their traffic at several levels:

>> Countries

>> Regions

>> US states

» US DMA (designated marketing area)

» Cities

» Postal/ZIP code

Figure 7-4 shows visits broken into countries, regions, and US DMA.

FIGURE 7-4:
Visits distributed
across many
levels of
geographic
dimensions.

Each of these listed dimensions, except ZIP code, is automatically captured in report suites. For ZIP code, admin teams must manually pass the ZIP code in via code or work with Adobe Customer Care to have the data automatically captured.

Not all countries populate data automatically into regions and ZIP codes. Use the following helpful resource to learn which countries do and don't populate those dimensions: https://marketing.adobe.com/resources/help/en_US/reference/ reports_geosegmentation_reference.html.

WARNING

Dissecting Product Dimensions

Adobe has properly reserved the most power for the dimension in their analytics product that has the highest demand and the highest need for flexibility and control: products.

The *products variable* tracks products and product categories as well as purchase quantity, purchase price, and more. After companies implement the products variable, several dimensions result: product, category, customer loyalty, days since first purchase, and days since last purchase. Each is valuable to an analyst in any industry, but they are especially valuable if your company has e-commerce. Note that the last two listed dimensions involve time, so we include them in the next section of this chapter.

Zooming in on product

Most Adobe customers use the product dimension to capture one of two types of values: product SKU or product name. Either is useful to analysts, although product name will probably be easier to analyze. Inspect your product dimension to see what type of data is populated there.

The news isn't all bad if the data is an unfriendly alphanumeric SKU. Admins can apply *classifications* (buckets based on lookup tables) to convert product SKU into product name or any other dimension. See Chapter 11, which provides a full walk-through of classifications, if you need to make your product dimension friendlier.

Regardless of the friendliness of the data in the product dimension, the value should be obvious. The *product dimension* enables analysts to examine behavioral data correlated to the associated SKU or product. Metrics such as product views, carts, cart views, orders, units, revenue, and checkouts (described in Chapter 5) should all connect to the product dimension.

The product dimension is more powerful than most because it's one of only a few multi-value dimensions. It properly distributes metrics such as units and revenue during the purchase of multiple products. For example, suppose a customer makes the following purchase:

Product Name	Quantity	Revenue Per Unit
Car	1	$30,000
Tee shirt	4	$15
Sunglasses	2	$45

At the time of the purchase, $30,060 in revenue is collected in a single transaction across three products. The product dimension needs to be smart enough to capture all three product names and associate the correct revenue and number of units purchased for them. If Adobe instead distributed the revenue by dividing the total revenue by three, they'd be out of business.

Work with your Adobe admin team to better understand how and when the product dimension is populated. You'll get a feel for the complete list of metrics that should be tied to this dimension, beyond just transactional ones. For example, some metrics such as video starts may not be tied to the product dimension if the videos that are watched aren't product related. However, if they are product related, they can be distributed by the product dimension as long as your implementation team has set up your video tags correctly.

Adopting product category . . . or not

Product SKUs and names are often too granular for analysts to use reasonably during an analysis. For example, ten colors of the same jacket will each generate their own product SKU, but an analyst needs to understand only how all jackets are performing. This example — of the relationship between trackable SKUs and larger classes of jackets — illustrates the need for multiple levels of classification of the product dimension. Chapter 11 goes into classifications in significant detail.

Adobe includes one level of classification tied to product automatically: category. The *category dimension* was built to show how various groupings of products affect your metrics. This category dimension means data buckets can be applied to your product dimension data so that product SKU becomes product name, product type, product category, product version, or anything else you can dream up. Unfortunately, the dimension is rarely used because it's inflexible. We've seen only a handful of Adobe customers use this dimension over the years, and they usually migrate to the more flexible classification option as we explain in Chapter 11.

Identifying customer loyalty

Understanding the difference between prospects, new customers, and repeat customers is crucial for all businesses interested in customer retention, especially those with e-commerce.

The difference in behavior between a customer you've had for years and one who has never purchased is significant and worthy of any analyst's time. To handle these needs, Adobe created the *customer loyalty dimension*, which displays purchasing patterns based on four categories of loyalty: not a customer, new customer, return customer, and loyal customer. Although they may seem self-explanatory, let's walk through each briefly:

Not a customer	Visitors who have never purchased
New customer	Visitors who have made a single purchase
Return customer	Visitors who have made two purchases
Loyal customer	Visitors who have made more than two purchases

Each category is tied to the full history of the visitor based on the Adobe cookie ID associated in that browser (or the device's ID if your report suite includes mobile app data). So even if you're analyzing one day's worth of data, several repeat customers may have come to the site because they made multiple purchases last month. Conversely, a customer may have made a purchase in Safari and then another in Chrome, and that customer would appear as two different visitors, each labeled as new customer.

Sifting through Time Dimensions

Analysts are constantly considering time as they do their job. Last month's data may have shown a significant decrease in a metric that turned around for the better this month. If you were to analyze the sum of both months, you might not have noticed the roller coaster that had occurred. You'd have that power with the right dimensions at your fingertips.

Adobe fortunately provides you with the ability to sort each of these dimensions chronologically, which we find to be useful compared to sorting by only metric data as in most dimensions.

Applying time-parting

Analysis Workspace includes several dimensions that are prebuilt to help solve the types of questions you may have of your data. These dimensions help answer the question: When?

Consider two caveats when using these dimensions:

» Time-parting dimensions are based on your report suite's time zone settings, not on the location of the visitors to your site.

» Built-in time-parting dimensions are available in only Analysis Workspace, not in any of the other Adobe Analytics tools. Companies will often capture time-parting data in a classified custom dimension so that the data can be used in Report Builder. If you're not familiar with custom dimensions, keep reading; we review them at the end of this chapter.

Here is a complete list of each time-parting dimension available in Analysis Workspace:

» **Hour of day:** Identifies the hour number in which activity is occurring on-site. Hour of day is presented as a whole number between 0 and 23. (0 is midnight,

7 is 7 a.m., and 23 is 11 p.m.) This dimension is helpful in answering a question such as, What is the most popular time of day for visitors to access my site or app?

>> **AM/PM:** Identifies whether the activity you're analyzing happened in the morning (AM) or afternoon/night (PM).

>> **Day of week:** Enables you to break your data out by a friendly day name, Monday through Sunday, and identify whether conversion rates are consistently higher on particular days. The fun part is then digging into the data further to understand why.

>> **Weekend/Weekday:** Categorizes the day of week dimension into values of weekend or weekday. Although you might be tempted to use this dimension to identify whether you have higher revenue numbers on weekends or weekdays, consider taking advantage of a conversion rate such as revenue per visitor instead of using just revenue. Conversion rates normalize the data because there are five weekdays and only two weekend days.

>> **Day of month:** Returns the numerical day of the month between 1–31. This information can be useful when building segments focused on campaigns that are limited to a set timeframe.

>> **Day of year:** Returns the numerical day of the year between 1–366.

>> **Month of year:** Provides you with the friendly month name of January through December.

>> **Quarter of year:** Breaks down all 12 months into Q1, Q2, Q3, and Q4 using standard monthly quarters (January-March, April-June, July-September, and October-December). Note that you can't adjust this dimension to align with your business's fiscal quarters, if they are different from the calendar year.

Measuring time spent

Chapter 5 provides significant detail into the many time spent metrics, and it's important to include the same level of detail for the time spent dimensions. The *time spent dimensions* have fewer options, so the concepts are simpler.

REMEMBER

Adobe captures time only between the first and last hits of a visit. Bounced visits that send just a single hit will have a time spent of 0 seconds, and these visits are generally excluded from any time spent calculations. In addition, any time that visitors spend on their last page in a visit performing actions that are not tracked by Adobe Analytics are also excluded from your dataset.

The *time spent per visit* dimension is populated with the total time spent during a visit. Adobe provides you with two versions of this dimension.

Time spent per visit — granular is available only in Analysis Workspace and is comprised of the exact number of seconds captured by the dimension. *Time spent per visit — bucketed* is available in Workspace, Report Builder, and the old Reports & Analytics interface. As you would expect from the name, this dimension buckets the seconds into useful containers: less than 1 minute, 1–5 minutes, 5–10 minutes, 10–30 minutes, and so on. Figure 7-5 shows time spent buckets sorted chronologically with granular breakdowns.

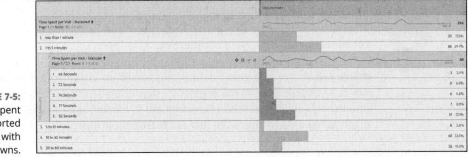

FIGURE 7-5: Time spent buckets sorted and with breakdowns.

The time spent on page dimension is perhaps one of the more cryptically named Adobe dimensions. *Time spent on page* counts the total time spent on each hit and includes both page views and link events. It's not limited to the page dimension, as the name suggests, but can be tied to any other dimension or action in Adobe. For example, you might use the time spent on page dimension to understand how much time people are spending looking at each product. Time spent on page comes in the same two flavors as time spent per visit: granular and bucketed.

Time spent on page — granular is similarly available only in Workspace and shows the number of seconds captured. Time spent on page — bucketed classifies the data into buckets: less than 15 seconds, 15 to 29 seconds, 30 to 59 seconds, 1 to 3 minutes, and more.

Analyzing visit number

Although visit numbers are not necessarily *time* dimensions, we categorize these types of dimensions here because they are captured and change over time.

During your time as an analyst, you'll often wonder how behavior changes as visitors come back to your site often. You may assume that after a few visits, visitors get used to the site's user interface and are able to find the content they're looking for faster and more easily.

That's a nice hypothesis, but only data can prove that it's happening. You would need to break down your data by *visit number*, the number of times each visitor visits your site. The dimension is based on the entire lifetime of the visitor, not just the selected date range. You could, for example, see whether more visits during a time period were from visitors who came to your site for the first time or the tenth time. We find that the visit number dimension is especially valuable when building basic segments such as new visitors, returning visitors, or loyal visitors.

Let's explore and illustrate three scenarios, all used in segments. Chapter 9 provides extensive detail on building segments like these, but we include some basics of the interface here to get you accustomed to the experience.

REMEMBER

Chapter 2 points out that segments are subsets of visitor traffic filtered based on a combination of dimensions or metrics.

Figure 7-6 shows a segment definition focused on visits from new visitors. Note how the box reserved for the segment's definition demands that the visit number dimension is *equal* to 1. When this segment is applied to any panel, table, or visualization, all data is filtered to just visits from new visitors.

| DESCRIPTION |
| Enter a description for this segment |
| TAGS |
| 🏷 Add Tags |
| DEFINITION * |
| Show Hit ⌄ |
| Visit Number   equals ⌄ |
| ☐ Make this an Experience Cloud audience (for Cross-Industry Demo Data) ❓ |
| * All fields with an asterisk are required in order to save. |

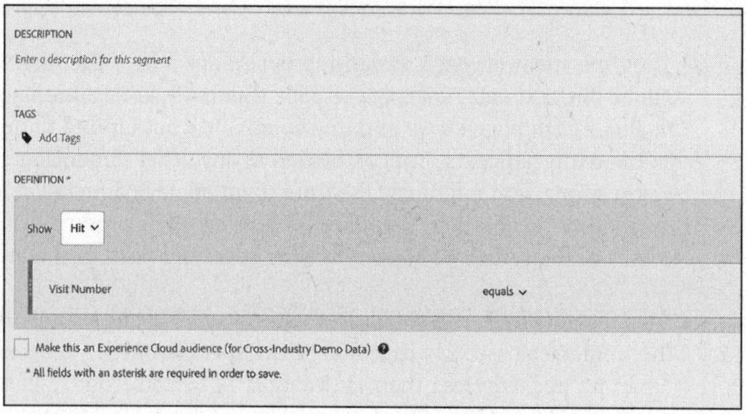

FIGURE 7-6:
A segment definition focused on visits from new visitors.

Figure 7-7 shows a segment definition focused on visits from repeat visitors. The definition differs from the definition in Figure 7-6 because the segment demands that visit number *is greater than* 1, rather than equals 1. This requirement ensures that all data in the segment is limited to visits from visitors who had previously been to the site at least once.

Figure 7-8 is a segment definition focused on visits from loyal visitors. You may have noticed that the definition for this segment demands that visit number *is greater than or equal to* 5, a somewhat arbitrary number we chose to define our loyal visitors.

Chapter 9 goes into more detail on building precise segments like these as well as other ways you can define and deploy segments that bucket your audience.

Identifying days before first purchase

E-commerce brands are constantly aiming to better understand the journey someone takes to become a customer. One of the key components of understanding this journey is time: How much time passes between a visitor's first visit to your site and his or her first purchase. The *days before first purchase* dimension is automatically derived for you as long as purchase data is captured using the standard products dimension, revenue, unit quantity, and purchase event.

This data can be useful when analyzing the lag between your first touchpoint and your first sale. From there, you'll want to look for trends and then consider identifying the key moments during that time period that convinced the prospect to become a customer. The conditional formatting deployed in Figure 7-9 identifies trends concerning when visitors make purchases in relation to how many times they've visited the site. (We explain how conditional formatting is defined in Chapter 8).

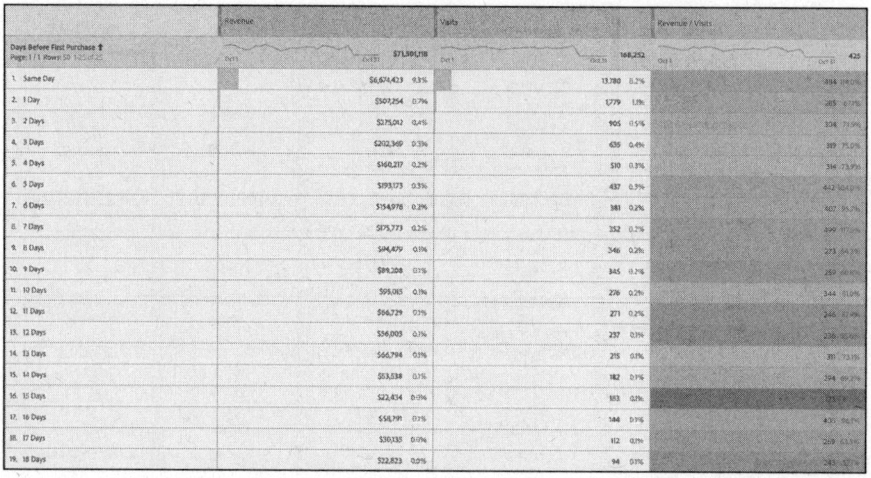

FIGURE 7-9: Revenue based on the number of days between first visit and purchase.

Data is populated in the days before first purchase dimension as Same Day (for visitors who purchase on the same day as their first visit to your site), 1 Day (for visitors who purchase on the day after their first visit), 2 Days (for visitors who purchase two days after their first visit), 3 Days, and so on.

Analyzing days since last purchase

Another time-based question about lag that brands ask of their data focuses on how much time has passed since a customer made their most recent purchase. You'd want to learn as much as possible about a subset of customers who previously purchased a big-ticket item and are researching another big-ticket item but haven't purchased for months. What products are these customers are researching? What marketing channels are driving them to the site?

The *days since last purchase dimension* helps answer these questions; it provides a count, similar to days before first purchase, of the number of days that have passed since your customer's latest purchase. Figure 7-10 deploys the days since last purchase dimension with metrics to quantify visits, product views, product reviews, and video starts. This combination gives us an interesting perspective into how users are interacting with different site content in relation to how long it has been since they last made a purchase.

Days Since Last Purchase ↑ Page: 1 / 1 Rows: 50 (1-17) M 22	Visits 168,439		Product Views 164,544		Product Reviews 18,096		Video Starts 47,400	
1. Same Day	40,039	23.8%	52,335	31.9%	5,733	31.7%	12,676	26.7%
2. 1 Day	11,448	6.8%	8,447	5.1%	903	5.0%	2,168	4.6%
3. 2 Days	6,009	3.6%	4,365	2.5%	459	2.5%	1,230	2.6%
4. 3 Days	4,156	2.5%	2,903	1.8%	313	1.7%	728	1.5%
5. 4 Days	3,133	1.9%	2,243	1.4%	236	1.3%	554	1.1%
6. 5 Days	2,502	1.5%	1,879	1.0%	184	1.0%	468	1.0%
7. 6 Days	1,977	1.2%	1,341	0.8%	146	0.8%	370	0.8%
8. 7 Days	1,686	1.0%	1,193	0.7%	128	0.7%	259	0.5%
9. 8 Days	1,518	0.9%	1,090	0.7%	113	0.6%	337	0.7%
10. 9 Days	1,325	0.8%	917	0.6%	82	0.5%	257	0.5%
11. 10 Days	1,162	0.7%	811	0.5%	93	0.5%	200	0.4%
12. 11 Days	1,087	0.6%	751	0.5%	75	0.4%	252	0.5%
13. 12 Days	877	0.5%	601	0.4%	79	0.4%	222	0.5%
14. 13 Days	754	0.4%	548	0.3%	67	0.4%	188	0.4%
15. 14 Days	698	0.4%	514	0.3%	71	0.4%	138	0.3%
16. 15 Days	543	0.3%	407	0.2%	43	0.2%	97	0.2%
17. 16 Days	476	0.3%	347	0.2%	30	0.2%	112	0.2%

FIGURE 7-10: Key activity based on the days since customers' most recent purchase.

Measuring return frequency

Brands have been reaping the benefits of advertising campaigns focused on remarketing for years. The thinking behind remarketing goes like this: We know this segment is interested in our product, so let's advertise to them about that product again and get them back on the site. The more consumers are on our site, the better chance we have at conversion.

With that concept in mind, the *return frequency dimension* was created. This dimension shows the length of time that passes between visits from returning visitors in easy-to-consume buckets. You can use the dimension to see the average amount of time that returning visitors go without visiting your site and the trends your site has in repeat customers.

By default, this report has the following time lengths:

>> Less than 1 day

>> 1 to 3 days

>> 3 to 7 days

>> 7 to 14 days

>> 14 days to one month

>> Longer than one month

The most obvious consideration with this dimension is that it does not record any data for first-time visitors because there is no prior visit to compare against. The other consideration is a little less obvious. The date range uses the time in which the visit occurred. For example, suppose a visitor comes to your site in May, and then returns twice on the same day in August. The return frequency dimension for the month of August would therefore show one visit under longer than 1 month and another visit under less than 1 day.

Figure 7-11 gives a picture of the length of time since a user's last visit to a site, measured with the visits metric.

Return Frequency ↑ Page: 1 / 1 Rows: 50 1-5 of 5		Visits	
	Oct 1	Oct 31	114,503
1. less than 1 day			51,630 45.1%
2. 1 to 3 days			25,050 21.9%
3. 3 to 7 days			21,072 18.4%
4. 7 to 14 days			14,140 12.3%
5. 14 days to 1 month			2,671 2.3%

Identifying single-page visits

The last dimension that relates to time is the *single page visits dimension*. Chapter 5 discusses each of the differences between bounces and single page visits; head there if you need a refresher. In Analysis Workspace, the single page visits dimension returns just a single value: Enabled. You must break down a single-value dimension, but doing so is easy. In Figure 7-12, we've broken down the single page visits dimension by the page dimension.

You can break down or segment any data point by visits that were limited to just a single page view. The dimension is most used with the page dimension.

Note how the data in Figure 7-12 shows identical numbers for the page views and visits metrics? Each of those visits had just a single page view, so it's a one-to-one match.

Single Page Visits [Page: 1 / 1 Rows: 50 1-1 of 1]		Page Views		Visits	
		Oct 1 Oct 31 ↓1,217,243		Oct 1 Oct 31 14,191	
1. Enabled		14,191 1.2%		14,191 100.0%	
Page Page: 1 / 90 > Rows: 6 1-5 of 445		Oct 1 Oct 31 14,191		Oct 1 Oct 31 14,191	
1. home		4,815 33.9%		4,815 33.9%	
2. product details: prd1006		242 1.7%		242 1.7%	
3. product details: prd1009		179 1.3%		179 1.3%	
4. product details: prd1003		130 0.9%		130 0.9%	
5. product details: prd1052		126 0.9%		126 0.9%	

Working with Custom Dimensions

As you've probably noticed by now, Adobe provides a wide assortment of built-in dimensions for you to use. These built-in dimensions will help you analyze products, device technologies, advertising, content, and more.

Unfortunately, it's never enough. We analysts are a demanding bunch, so Adobe has created two types of custom dimensions to help us capture even more useful data about the behavior occurring online. You can use these custom dimensions to capture data that is necessary for you to complete your analysis but not available in the preconfigured dimensions you've read about. For example, a custom dimension could capture internal search terms that visitors have used on your website. The number of custom dimensions that your company has access to is tied to your Adobe Analytics SKU, but most companies have close to 300 custom dimensions per report suite.

Defining expiration and allocation dimensions

Adobe provides administrators with several options for customizing the definition of these custom dimensions. Before you dig into the different variable types and how to find them in your report suite, let's discuss two pieces of terminology: expiration and allocation. Because these options involve complex concepts, you walk through them in some depth. Expiration is the simpler concept, so you start there.

Understanding expiration

Expiration focuses on how long the values in a dimension should persist. Should the value expire at the end of the page view, like the page dimension, or should it expire at the end of the visit, like a marketing channel? Adobe gives admins the ability to define expiration from as short as the hit that the tag fires to the length of the visitor's cookie (in other words, never). This consideration is important for administrators because the expiration of custom dimensions needs to extend long enough for the metrics that matter to correlate with the persisted dimensional value.

Table 7-1 illustrates an example visit where a custom dimension is capturing the name of the video being watched with several metrics firing along the way.

The visit example in Table 7-1 describes a simple visit: a consumer comes to a website, watches a video to completion, starts a second video, but doesn't complete it. In this implementation, a custom dimension called video name is set at the start of each video. The company's Adobe administrator needs to decide the expiration for the custom dimension so that the metrics correlate to the dimension properly. If the expiration is set to expire on *page view*, hits 3, 4, 6, 7, and 8 will not be tied back to any video names that were set. Those hits would align with *Unspecified* in your reporting.

TABLE 7-1 **Sample Visit with Custom Dimensions and Metrics**

Hit Number	Consumer Action	Video Name Dimension	Metric Name
1	Landing page		Page view
2	Video start	Intro to analytics	Video start
3	50% of video reached		50% milestone
4	Video end		Video complete
5	Video start	Advanced analytics	Video start
6	50% of video reached		50% milestone
7	Product added to cart		Cart add
8	Browser closed		

If the expiration is set to expire when the *video complete* metric fires, all hits will accurately tie back to their assigned video name. In addition, if the expiration is set to expire *never*, the metrics in this example will also tie back to the video name correctly. However, any additional metrics from the next visit (perhaps downloads or registrations) will also align back to the Advanced Analytics video name because the dimensional value persisted and never expires.

REMEMBER

Unspecified is Adobe's way of showing metrics captured when a value was not set for the dimension being analyzed. This includes custom dimensions that have expired. Therefore, any metrics aligned with an Unspecified video name did not have a value set for that dimension when the metric was captured. If the video name dimension was set to expire at the page view, no value is assigned to the custom dimension.

Defining allocation

The other half of the admin settings for custom dimension is called allocation. *Allocation* decides what value of a custom dimension should get credit when multiple values are sent to the dimension before expiration. Another common name for allocation is attribution, which you may be familiar with already. The section on marketing channels in Chapter 6 takes advantage of the same concepts described here, and Chapter 12 goes into even more detail on Adobe's attribution models.

In the visit example in Table 7-1, the consumer is sending two values to the custom dimension: intro to analytics, and advanced analytics. If the Adobe administrator for this company sets a *visit expiration* for this dimension, how will each of the metrics align with these two dimensional values?

By default, custom dimensions apply a most recent/last touch model, meaning that the metrics are attributed back to the most recent value captured in the dimension. This allocation method would be ideal in the stated scenario: 1 video start, 1 50% milestone, and 1 video complete would be attributed to intro to analytics; 1 video start and 1 50% milestone would be attributed to the advanced analytics video. Based on our experience, a vast majority of custom dimensions are set to a most recent/last touch allocation, so it's probably safe to assume that's how yours are set. Of course, it's always worth checking with your admin team to confirm.

Another option for custom dimensions is to set the allocation to original/first touch model. This approach would not bode well for the scenario in Table 7-1 because it would attribute both video starts, both 50% milestones, and the video complete to the original value that the custom dimension received: intro to analytics. This result is clearly inaccurate and last touch allocation for this video name dimension seems like a no-brainer. But as an analyst, you're always thinking about the product purchase cycle, so you probably got excited to see that a product was added to the cart after the second video was partially watched. In this example, which video would you assign credit to — the first one watched or the last one watched? Perhaps partial credit for both?

Partial credit is where the last custom dimension allocation comes into play. In addition to first and last touch, admins can set custom dimensions to have linear allocation. In a *linear allocation*, every value sent to the dimension gets a percentage of the metric being analyzed. If video name in Table 7-1 were set to a linear allocation, each video would get 50% credit for the add to cart that occurs at the end of the visit.

The best news we can share is that Adobe's Attribution IQ set of features enables more flexible models than these three and gives you the ability to change the attribution model on the fly for any dimension. So between the two settings, expiration and allocation, the more important one these days is expiration.

Distinguishing between props and eVars

Now that you have a good feel for the settings that you can apply to custom dimensions, let's dig into the two types of variables that exist in your implementation. Adobe has several names for both of them. The first are often referred to as "props" but are synonymous with sProps and traffic variables.

Props are custom dimensions that always expire on the hit. Your company has access to 75 props. They can be quite useful because of their simplicity. Because they expire on the hit, you don't have to worry about allocation because only a single value can be passed into a dimension per hit. Because props expire instantly, they are often considered to be a little less useful than eVars, their custom dimension counterpart. However, analysts who know when props are set can find plenty of uses for props.

eVars are custom dimensions that have settings aligned with allocation, expiration, and more. They are more flexible and powerful than props but also more complex. Most companies have between 100 and 250 eVars, depending on their contract with Adobe. If you jump back to the sample visit in Table 7-1, you would almost definitely want to use an eVar to capture video name so that the dimensional values persist and the video metrics properly attribute back to them.

Your trusty debugger can be used to easily identify all custom dimensions that are firing in any hit. Note how Figure 7-13 shows the URL being passed into prop4 and just the domain passed into eVar5. You'll be glad to know that administrators have an interface, known as Admin Console, to create friendly names for all props and eVars. You don't have to memorize that prop4 means URL and eVar5 means domain; Analysis Workspace would simply show the friendly names automatically.

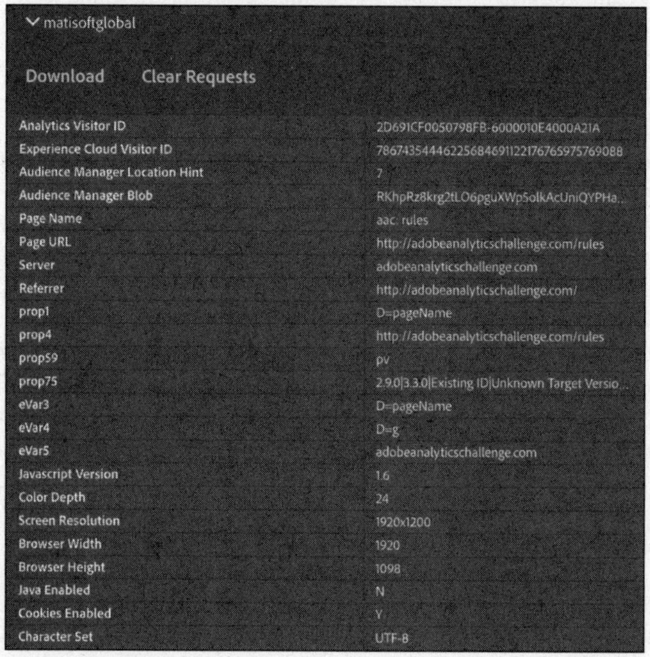

FIGURE 7-13: Experience Cloud Debugger captures values in both props and eVars.

TIP

Because you will often find yourself going back and forth between the debugger and Workspace, it makes sense that you will occasionally forget the friendly for an eVar or a prop. Fear not, for Adobe has already made that process easier: eVars and props can be searched in the left rail search box. Try searching for eVar1 or prop2 in your report suite to see how the process works.

Applying date ranges

The final custom dimension to discuss is a unique one. Chapter 3 provides a detailed view into using the calendar, but did you know that you can also add date ranges to your freeform tables?

You can drag preset date ranges (which are listed at the bottom of the left rail) into a table. Any of these can be used as dimensions in freeform tables. In addition, you can easily create new date ranges based on your needs. Let's create a new date range that focuses on the last full 5 days:

1. Click the plus button in the left rail next to the word Time, or click Components in the main menu and choose New Date Range.

Or use the keyboard shortcut Shift+⌘+D on a Mac, or Shift+Alt+D on a PC. A dialog appears requesting you to define your date range. The interface is intuitive and mirrors the calendar in panels.

2. Use the calendar to select a date range, such as the last five days.

3. Select the Use Rolling Dates check box (see Figure 7-14), and then click Apply.

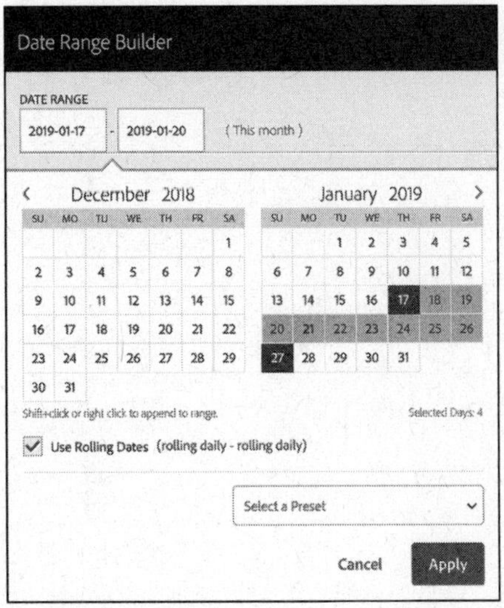

FIGURE 7-14:
Defining a date range with rolling dates.

CHAPTER 7 **Using Device, Product, and Custom Dimensions to Analyze Data** 153

4. **Add a friendly name in the Title text box of the date range (such as Last 5 Days), and then click Save.**

Rolling dates allow you to decide whether the dates should update as time passes. If you have a date range of the last 5 full days and choose the Use Rolling Dates option, when you log into Adobe tomorrow, the date range will be updated to include that day's data.

After you've defined a custom date range, you can drag that dimension into a table, as shown in Figure 7-15

FIGURE 7-15: Applying a custom date range.

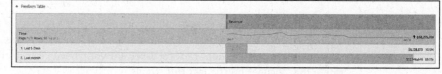

Dimensions such as eVars, props, and custom date ranges will be useful tools for analysis in Adobe. Stay involved with your Adobe administrator to ensure that the custom dimensions you need are tracked accurately and consistently.

Chapter **8**

Productivity Tips and Techniques

I s productivity an issue in your work environment? Would it be helpful to have at your fingertips essential techniques to perform functions in Adobe Analytics quickly and mindlessly so you can focus on analyzing data? Interested in exploiting some features of Adobe Analytics that you might not have thought of, but that bulk up your capacity to work with data?

With the tips in this chapter, you can quickly generate graphs and time comparisons, as well as identify trends in a metric by using colored backgrounds that make positive and negative data pop.

If any of this sounds useful, read on!

Exploiting Essential Keyboard and Mouse Shortcuts

Almost anything you do in Analysis Workspace has a keyboard or mouse shortcut. As you make menu selections, keyboard shortcuts are displayed for your operating system, as shown in Figure 8-1. As you get comfortable with menu options, and integrate those shortcuts into your workflow.

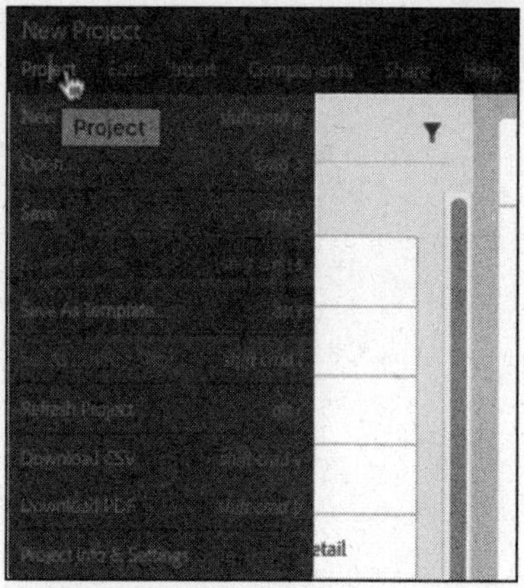

FIGURE 8-1:
Keyboard
shortcuts for the
Project menu in
Analysis
Workspace.

Based on our experience and observations, we're sharing our list of essential keyboard shortcuts and mouse selection techniques. Perhaps you're already using some of them, but let's make sure you're getting your money's worth out of the shortcuts in Adobe Analytics.

Opening projects and saving work

To create a new project, open an existing one, or save an open project, use these shortcuts:

>> **Create a new project:** Shift+⌘+P on a Mac or Shift+Ctrl+P on a PC

>> **Open an existing project:** ⌘+O on a Mac or Ctrl+O on a PC

>> **Save a project:** ⌘+S on a Mac or Ctrl+S on a PC

Creating content

Here are a few of our "most wanted" shortcuts to create new content, starting with panels and tables:

>> **Create a new blank panel:** Option+B on a Mac or Alt+B on a PC

>> **Create a new freeform panel:** Option+A on a Mac or Alt+A on a PC

>> **Create a new freeform table:** Option+1 on a Mac or Alt+1 on a PC

And here are shortcuts for creating commonly used charts:

>> **Create a new bar chart:** Option+3 on a Mac or Alt+3 on a PC

>> **Create a new line graph:** Option+2 on a Mac or Alt+2 on a PC

Undoing and redoing edits

Adobe Analytics keyboard shortcut for undo can bail you out whether you make a cataclysmic error or a tiny mistake. Similarly, redo shortcuts help you when you realize your error wasn't an error after all and want to redo what you just undid. The keystrokes, particularly for redo, might vary from other apps you're used to:

>> **Undo:** ⌘+Z on a Mac or Ctrl+Z on a PC

>> **Redo:** ⌘+Shift+Z on a Mac or Ctrl+Shift+Z on a PC

Making quick selections for breakdowns

Here are a few handy moves to select data in freeform tables:

>> Single-click a row to select it in its entirety.

>> Double-click the upper-left cell, located above the header used to describe the row, to select the entire table at once.

>> Select a range of contiguous cells by clicking once, then holding down the Shift key, and then clicking somewhere else in the table.

>> Deselect cells that are already selected in a table by holding down ⌘ on a Mac or Ctrl on a PC and then clicking.

>> Hold down the ⌘ key on a Mac or Ctrl on a PC while you click on noncontiguous cells to select that set of data, as shown in Figure 8-2.

These selection techniques are useful for all kinds of purposes, from simply copying data, applying breakdowns to sets of data, or even dynamically creating segments. Let's explore that second option: By first selecting a set of rows (including noncontiguous rows), and then dragging a breakdown component into *any* of those rows, you can apply the breakdown to those selected rows.

In Figure 8-3, for example, we're using the Marketing Channel dimension to break down when users visited pages associated with an app launch.

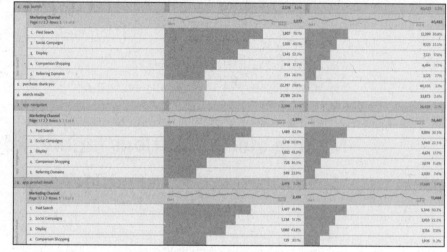

FIGURE 8-2:
Selecting a
noncontiguous
set of rows
in a table.

FIGURE 8-3:
Applying a
breakdown
to a set of
noncontiguous
rows in a table.

Using the clipboard to move data to other apps

Here's another valuable tip for what you can do with selected rows, columns, or cells, whether they are contiguous or noncontiguous: ⌘+C on a Mac or Ctrl+C on a PC copies data to your clipboard.

Many people you interact with and share data with will not be conversant (let alone fluent) in Adobe Analytics, and will prefer to have you pull out specific tables to share via spreadsheet apps that they are more comfortable with. You might be surprised to know that data copied from a table in Adobe Analytics easily drops into an email or any spreadsheet program. Figure 8-4 demonstrates the clean, nicely formatted results when you simply use ⌘+V on a Mac or Ctrl+V on a PC to paste copied cells.

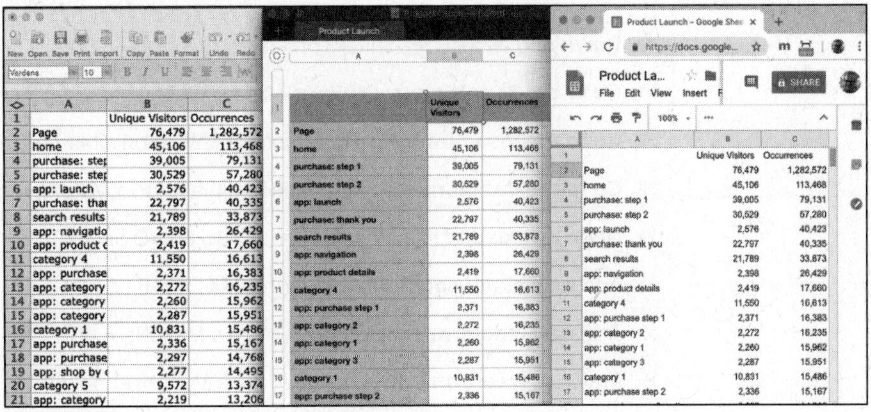

FIGURE 8-4:
Pasting a table
into spreadsheets
(left-to-right:
Microsoft Excel,
Numbers for Mac,
Google Sheets).

Refreshing content

Because Adobe Analytics runs in the cloud, you may find a need to periodically refresh the display. One such example is if a co-worker shares a new calculated metric that he created. Adobe doesn't force you to log out and log back in or even refresh your browser. Instead, just refresh the components. To refresh your components in the left rail or the data in all of the visualizations in your open project, do the following:

>> **Refresh components:** Option+Shift+R on a Mac or Alt+Shift+R on a PC

>> **Refresh a project:** Option+R on a Mac or Alt+R on a PC

Deploying key keyboard shortcuts

As noted, Adobe Analytics has dozens and dozens of keyboard shortcuts. Some are specialized, and others you'll use all the time. We've sifted through the list and pulled out some selected shortcuts that you'll find handy in Workspace:

>> **Clear all:** Option+E on a Mac or Alt+W on a PC

>> **Create an alert:** ⌘+Shift+A on a Mac, Ctrl+Shift+A on a PC

>> **Create a calculated metric:** ⌘+Shift+C on a Mac, Ctrl+Shift+C on a PC

>> **Create a date range:** ⌘+Shift+D on a Mac, Ctrl+Shift+D on a PC

>> **Create a new project:** ⌘+Shift+P on a Mac, Ctrl+Shift+P on a PC

>> **Create a segment:** ⌘+Shift+E on a Mac, Ctrl+Shift+E on a PC

>> **Download as CSV:** ⌘+Shift+V on a Mac, Ctrl+Shift+V on a PC

>> **Download as PDF:** ⌘+Shift+B on a Mac, Ctrl+Shift+B on a PC

>> **Go to the Panels pane:** Option+Shift+1 on a Mac, Alt+Shift+1 on a PC

>> **Go to the Visualizations pane:** Option+Shift+2 on a Mac, Alt+Shift+2 on a PC

>> **Go to the Components pane:** Option+Shift+3 on a Mac, Alt+Shift+3 on a PC

>> **Open an existing project:** ⌘+O on a Mac, Ctrl+O on a PC

>> **Add new blank panel:** Option+B on a Mac, Alt+B on a PC

>> **Add new freeform panel:** Option+A on a Mac, Alt+A on a PC

>> **Add new freeform table:** Option+1 on a Mac, Alt+1 on a PC

>> **Save project as:** ⌘+Shift+S on a Mac, Ctrl+Shift+S on a PC

Taking Advantage of One-Click Visualize

In Chapters 13 and 14, you explore using the visualizations section of the left rail to craft all types of charts and graphs. If you're taking some time to focus on and carefully craft a visualization, you start by clicking the visualizations icon in the left rail selector, and then build a chart or graph piece by piece.

But sometimes, fine-tuning a visualization isn't critical, and instead you need to quickly generate a basic trended line or area or bar chart. For that scenario, Adobe Analytics offers one-click visualization.

One-click visualizations, like all visualizations linked to freeform tables, come in two flavors: locked and unlocked. By default, when you generate a one-click visualization, that graph is unlocked. Unlocked visualizations are based on the cell in the table that is *selected*, not the row number or the dimensional value. Therefore, if you click a different item in the linked table, the data in the chart changes to the newly selected item.

If, instead, you want to lock the visualization to either the *dimensional value* or *row number*, you must apply a lock to your visualization. The dimensional item displayed in the graph doesn't change, even if you click other rows in the linked freeform table. Let's walk through both scenarios.

Generating unlocked visualizations

To instantly generate a visualization for a row of data, click the Visualize icon shown in Figure 8-5. By default, as we noted, that visualization is linked to the selected cell in the table, not the data itself.

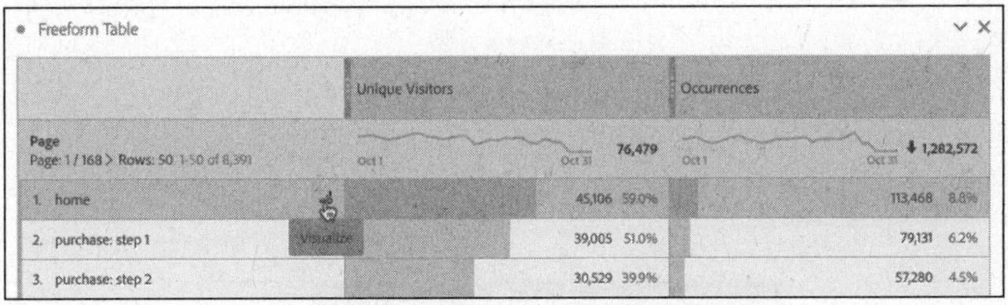

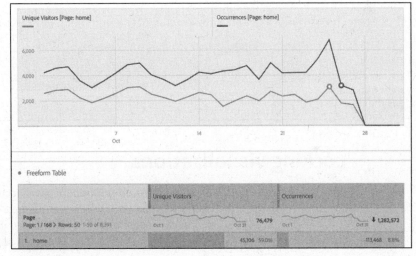

FIGURE 8-5:
Generating a
line chart
with one-click
visualization.

So, for example, if we select the first row in a table to visualize, as we are in Figure 8-5, the visualization will always display data in the first row — in this case, the most viewed page in our site — even if we change the panel's dates and the most viewed page changes. The result, by default, is a line graph, as shown in Figure 8-6.

FIGURE 8-6:
A line graph
generated with
one-click
visualization.

Again, if fine-tuning your visualization is necessary, head over to Chapters 13 and 14. Here we're looking at throwing up a quick visualization, and one-click does the trick.

Don't want a line graph? It's easy to change the type of chart by clicking the Visualization Settings gear, shown in Figure 8-7.

In the dialog that opens, choose a different visualization type from the drop-down list. That new visualization is applied to the selected data. Figure 8-8 shows an area chart applied.

FIGURE 8-7:
Accessing
visualization
settings.

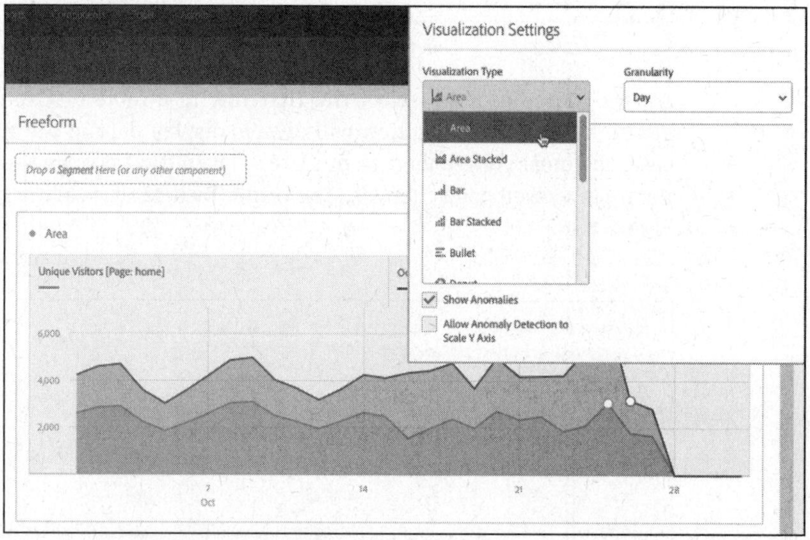

FIGURE 8-8:
Changing to an
area chart.

Locking visualizations

Again, by default, a one-click visualization is based on the selected cells — not a data item — in the linked table. How does that play out? Figure 8-9, for example, shows a visualization of data in the second row of a table based on the marketing channel dimension. That item, in the month of June, was paid search.

But look what happens when the calendar is changed to reflect data in July. As shown in Figure 8-10, the visualization now reflects the *new* row two, social campaigns.

This functionality is the default for linked visualizations. If the data in the linked table changes, the selected cell stays in place and the graph therefore is updated based on the new dimensional item.

Sometimes you'll want the freedom to click elsewhere in your table without affecting the data displayed in the linked visualization. To do this, you'll have to ask yourself a question: Do you want to lock to the row number or the dimensional value? You can lock a visualization to either choice by clicking the Manage Data Source icon, shown in Figure 8-11.

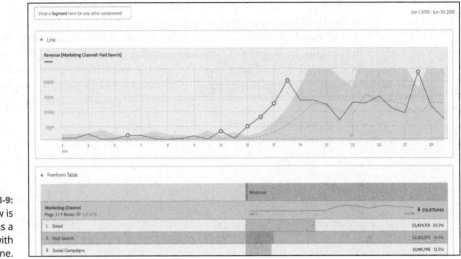

FIGURE 8-9:
A selected row is visualized as a line graph with data from June.

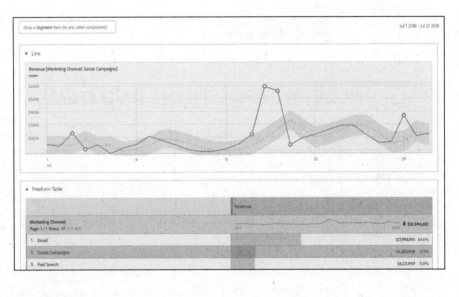

FIGURE 8-10:
Visualizations locked to position automatically change when the data position changes.

FIGURE 8-11:
Accessing data source settings.

In the Data Source Settings dialog that appears, choose Lock Selection, and then choose items in the drop-down menu to marry the visualization to selected *data* in the table. In Figure 8-12, we are choosing to lock to Selected Items. Choosing to lock to Selected Positions would marry the visualization to the currently selected cells and gives you the freedom to click around elsewhere in the table.

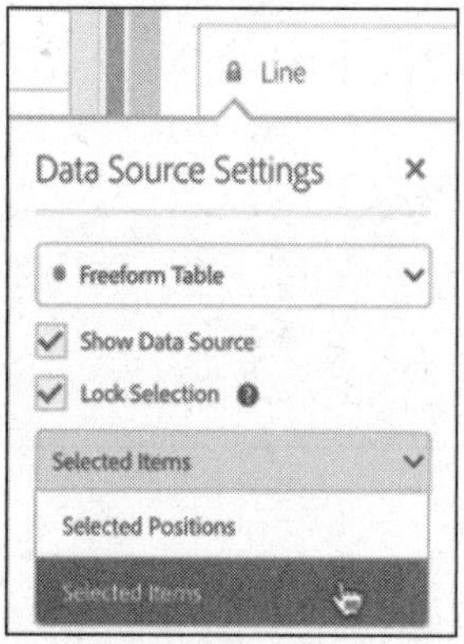

FIGURE 8-12: Locking selected items.

LOCKING POSITIONS AND ITEMS

When do you lock positions, and when do you lock items when using one-click visualization to get a quick chart or graph? Let's explore a couple scenarios.

You might *lock positions* when you are interested in tracking the performance or want the visualization of the top five performers in a table. As the data changes month to month or week to week, or due to the application of a segment, visualizations locked to positions will reflect the trending items. For example, choose this option if you want to show the top five marketing channels in this visualization at all times, no matter what those channels might be.

On the other hand, you should *lock selected items* when you want the visualization to stay focused on the specific items currently selected in the corresponding data table. These items will continue to be visualized, *even if they change their ranking among items in the table*. For example, choose this option if you want to show the same three marketing channels in a visualization at all times, no matter where those channels rank.

Saving time with visualization shortcuts

While we're on the subject of quickly generating visualizations, we want to point out the options that appear when you right-click a visualization, opening the context menu. These options vary depending on the type of graph or chart:

>> **Copy Visualization/Panel:** Copy a visualization or panel to the Workspace clipboard.

>> **Insert Copied Visualization/Panel:** Add a visualization or panel that was copied to the Workspace clipboard into another place within the current project or into a different project.

>> **Duplicate Visualization/Panel:** Duplicate the current visualization, which you can then modify.

>> **Collapse all Visualizations in Panel:** Save space by collapsing all visualizations in the selected project panel.

>> **Expand all Visualizations in Panel:** Expands all visualizations in a selected project panel, making the most of every pixel.

>> **Edit Description:** Add (or edit) the text description for the visualization/panel.

>> **Get Visualization Link:** Copy a link to the selected visualization that you can use to send others directly to this visualization. (Users have to log in to your Adobe Analytics project with access to Analysis Workspace and the report suite.)

>> **Start Over:** Delete the configuration for a flow, Venn, or histogram.

Again, these options are context-dependent, but appear when you need them most and are precious productivity tools when working with visualizations.

Invoking Time Comparisons

Adobe Analytics has a quick and easy way to compare date ranges in a table. This feature is essential for putting current data in perspective. Current data is valid for comparative analysis within the time range selected in the calendar, but without historical context, it's not enough to properly confirm success. Imagine if your company saw a huge spike in sales on Black Friday and considered it a success without comparing it to the huge spike in sales from the same "holiday" last year. Historical context is essential to successful analysis.

Because this concept is so essential, let's dig into it a bit before walking through the intuitive quick-steps method for time comparisons in Analysis Workspace.

Applying time comparisons can reveal the following:

» How user visits have increased, decreased, or stagnated over any period of time

» Which marketing channels have been factors in changes in visits, purchases, and other measures of success over time

» Whether there are trends that set off alarms, indicating a need for intervention in marketing or other factors affecting success rates

» Whether positive trends exist that should be seized on and maximized

We're sure this list of time comparison use cases has your head buzzing with trends and patterns that can only be identified and analyzed by comparing time periods. You can gather the information that matters, analyze it to find patterns or problems, and then take action based on those insights.

Because time comparison is such an essential component in data analysis, Adobe has made it easy to generate basic comparative data in a table. Let's walk through an example. In Figure 8-13, we see orders for each marketing channel. That data is valid for the time range selected, but it doesn't tell us how the data has changed over time. Are my metrics going in the right direction, or are they stalled, or are they going in the wrong direction?

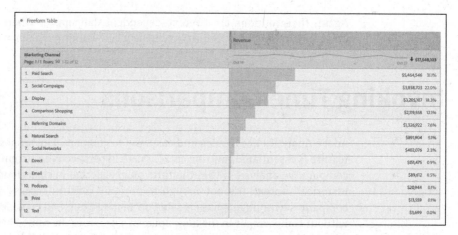

FIGURE 8-13: Without date comparison, you can see the relationship between marketing channels, but you can't see historical trends.

Adobe Analytics provides two quick ways to add date comparisons. By right-clicking any metric column, you can choose from two options, shown in Figure 8-14: Add Time Period Column and Compare Time Periods. Let's examine both options.

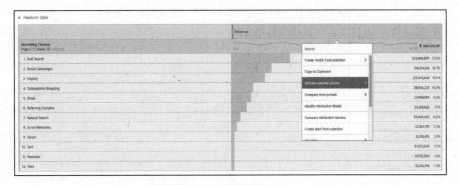

Adding a time period column

When you select Add Time Period Column from the context menu for a metric column, Adobe provides a best guess at what time periods make sense given your project calendar. In other words, the options will be different based on the context that Adobe knows about your project's data timeframe.

You also have the option of defining a custom date range with which to compare your defined date range. A Select Comparison Range dialog appears, as shown in Figure 8-15, and you can click start and end dates to define that custom range.

FIGURE 8-15:
Choosing a
custom date
range for a
custom time
period column.

After you select one of the suggested date ranges or define your own, a new column appears with comparative data from the added range. Figure 8-16 is an example of two columns of data based on different date ranges.

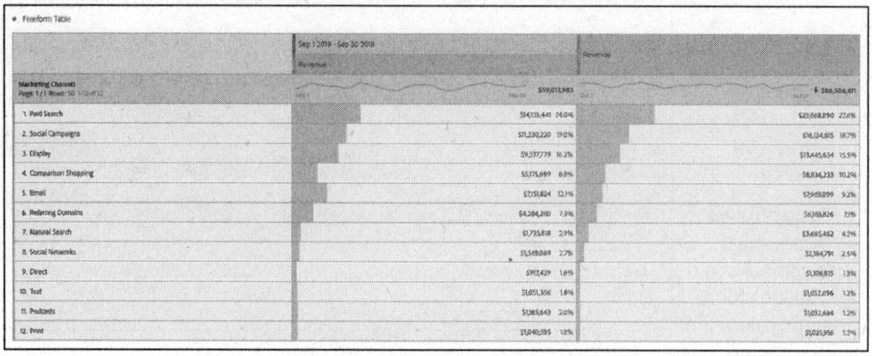

FIGURE 8-16:
Displaying marketing channel revenue for two time periods.

Comparing time periods

If you select Compare Time Periods from the context menu for a metric column, you see the same options that appear when you choose to add a time period column: suggested time periods and an option to define a custom time period. When a time period comparison is completed, Adobe adds a column to show the percent change between time periods instead of just adding a raw number column, as shown in Figure 8-17.

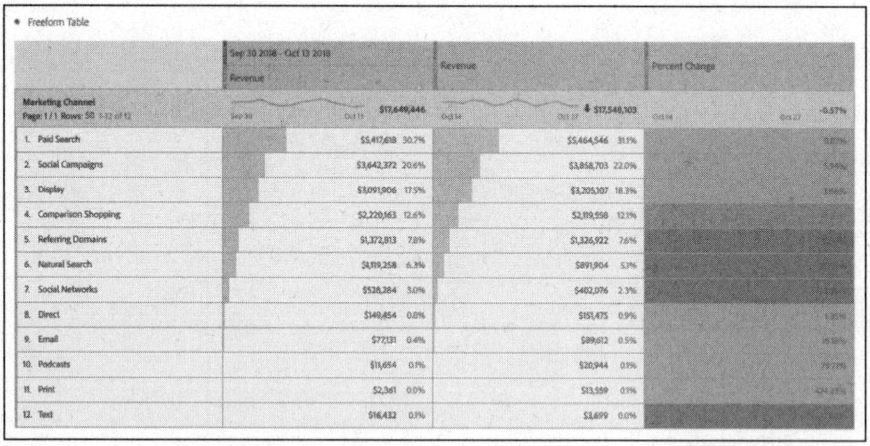

FIGURE 8-17:
Viewing a percentage change from one time period to another.

REMEMBER

If you have a time dimension as your rows, the only available option is Add Time Period.

By default, Adobe applies conditional formatting to the percent change column, where green shading indicates an increase in value and red shading a decrease.

Applying Conditional Formatting

We can't close this chapter without acknowledging and addressing the colored shading generated by the percent change column in the time period comparison. If you're adept at Excel, you may already be familiar with the concept of conditional formatting. *Conditional formatting* provides visual cues to help you quickly make sense of the data in your freeform tables. The coloring is based on rules that are predefined by Adobe but can be customized easily. So, how is this kind of conditional formatting defined?

As mentioned in the preceding section, Adobe applied green for an increase in value and red for a decrease in value. To reveal the settings behind that conditional formatting, hover your cursor over the column heading that has conditional formatting applied and click the middle icon, the Column Settings gear. As shown in Figure 8-18, formatting has been defined so that any positive value that reaches 1% (or more) is displayed as green, and the higher the number, the darker the green. Conversely, any negative value that meets the criteria of –1% (or less) displays as red, and the farther from zero, the darker the red.

Let's walk through another, simpler scenario. You can set conditional formatting to any column in any freeform table to flag values within the high, low, and middle value ranges. Do that by clicking the Settings gear for a metric column, and choosing Auto-generated, as shown in Figure 8-19. Try applying conditional formatting to any metric in any freeform table, regardless of dimension.

Understanding conditional formatting options

When you choose the Auto-generated option in the conditional formatting options for a column, you're telling Adobe Analytics to format cells in that column based on a paradigm defined by the highest value in the column on one end, and the lowest value on the other end. Adobe will intelligently divide cell values into high, middle, and low values and format them accordingly.

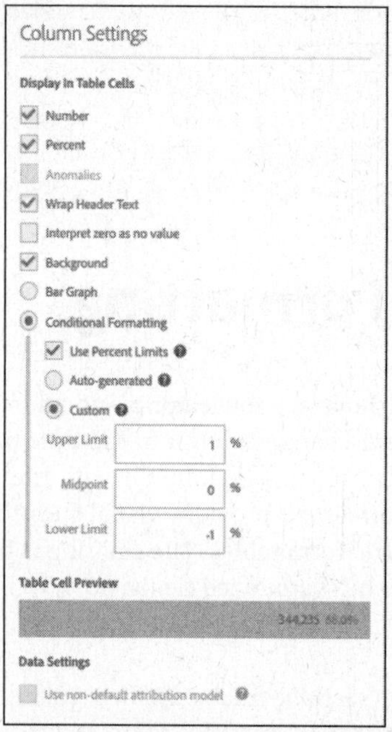

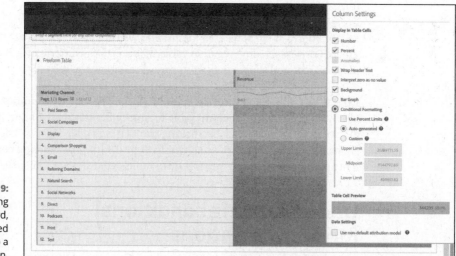

FIGURE 8-18:
Examining
conditional
formatting for
percentage
change values.

FIGURE 8-19:
Applying
standard,
auto-generated
formatting to a
metric column.

If you choose to use percent limits to define conditional formatting, Adobe applies formatting based on dividing the percentage values for the selected metric instead of the raw numbers. Using percent limits to define conditional formatting works for metrics that are percentage based (such as bounce rate) and for metrics that have a count and percentage (such as page views).

If you choose the Custom option in the conditional formatting options of the Column Settings dialog, you can define your own breakpoints for upper limits, a midpoint, and lower limits. Defining your own breakpoints is often useful for datasets that vary only slightly or if you have a defined goal that must be met before your metric should appear as green.

Conditional formatting rules continue to persist even as the data in the column changes. So if a change in date causes a cell's value to change from below the lower limit to above the upper limit, the cell's color will change from red to green.

3

Massaging Data for Complex Analysis

Define segments based on precise audience traits for advanced analyses.

Define and apply calculated metrics to focus on and identify highly specific trends and issues.

Classify data in Adobe Analytics to make it more accessible to different audiences and stakeholders.

Use basic attribution models and Attribution IQ to identify the factors that lead to a success event, and their relationship to each other.

Chapter **9**

Designing Precise Segments

I n Chapter 2, we explain that *three*, not two, required categories of measurement exist. In addition to dimensions and metrics, *segments* are a required category in analyzing data. Did you just shout, "What? Reports don't require that a segment is applied, so how can you say they are required?" We understand your reaction (although your colleagues might not, so maybe it's better to just shout to yourself).

Yes, metrics and dimensions are the two *technically* required categories of measurement to build a report. And Adobe Analytics will insist that you supply a dimension and a metric before you can generate a simple freeform table.

In the real world of analytics, segments are required not because you can't build a report without them but because you can't perform a proper analysis without them.

Without segments, the picture you get of user behavior is too static and decontextualized to be valuable. Or, to put it bluntly, without segmenting data, the picture you get of what's happening at your website is downright misleading.

YOU CAN APPLY SEGMENTS TO METRICS

Adobe segments can be applied to metrics, to create calculated metrics (as described in Chapter 10). These segments can also be wholly applied to a report suite, via a component called virtual report suites, to redefine your data view. Plus, did you know that when you drop metrics, dimensions, and time ranges into the Segment drop zone (as described in Chapter 4), you're creating on-the-fly segments? Well, you are!

And to invoke personal experience here, we've spent decades analyzing data, and in that time we have never once been involved in a project where analysis was done without applying a segment. Segments are the lifeblood of your analyze, confirming, among other things, whether anomalies apply to all of your visitors or a small faction.

Because segments are so fundamental to the successful use of Adobe Analytics, we can't stress their value enough. Let's dig into that before we get to the nuts and bolts of deploying them. You'll enjoy this!

Understanding and Defining Segments

A quick refresh of the thorough definition of segments from Chapter 2 may be valuable: A *segment* is a subset of visitor traffic filtered based on behavior.

Following is a non-analytic table with a single dimension, day of week, as well as two metrics, high and low temperatures. But this data is useless at best without being segmented to identify *where* it applies, and when. If this data is from International Falls, Minnesota in mid-January, that's one thing. If it's from Honolulu in April, that's an anomaly! Something extreme and strange is going on:

Day of Week	High	Low
Monday	22	–8
Tuesday	15	–4
Wednesday	22	2
Thursday	12	5
Friday	18	5
Saturday	24	15
Sunday	32	21

Identifying segment containers

Our weather table demonstrates the essential role of segmentation to make any meaningful analysis. Let's dig deeper.

Adobe Analytics segments are created based on combinations of the following:

>> Dimensions (such as page)

>> Dimensional values (such as order confirmation page)

>> Metrics (such as orders)

>> Time ranges (such as last 30 days)

To set conditions in an Adobe segment, you set rules to filter visitors based on visitor characteristics or navigation traits or both. To further break down visitor data, you can filter based on specific visits or page view hits or both for each visitor. Adobe's Segment Builder provides an architecture to build these subsets and apply rules as a nested hierarchy: visitor ⇨ visit ⇨ hit containers. When you define a segment, Adobe will apply the segment based on the container that you use. For example, if you define a segment that focuses on order purchases, the three Adobe containers will handle that segment as follows:

>> A visitor container segmented on order purchases will include all hits from all visits from visitors who have ever purchased.

>> A visit container segmented on order purchases will include all hits from visits where purchases were made. All visits that didn't include a purchase are excluded. If a purchasing visitor has multiple visits, only the purchasing visits will be included in this visit container segment.

>> A hit container segmented on order purchases will include all hits where purchases were made. All other hits are excluded. If the hit isn't capturing order and revenue data, it will not be included in the hit container segment.

Containers are Adobe's way of helping you decide how much data should be included in your segment based on the segment's definition. Let's walk through a more in-depth example in Table 9-1.

TABLE 9-1

A Visitor Makes a Purchase Spanning Several Days and Locations

Hit #	Action	Day	City
1	Go to home page	Monday	New York, NY
2	Go to product page	Monday	New York, NY
Visit ends			
3	Go to product page	Tuesday	Philadelphia, PA
4	Add to shopping cart	Tuesday	Philadelphia, PA
5	Go to blog page	Tuesday	Philadelphia, PA
Visit ends			
6	Go to shopping cart	Wednesday	Lehi, UT
7	Enter credit card info	Wednesday	Lehi, UT
8	Order confirmation for $1,300	Wednesday	Lehi, UT

Distinguishing segment containers

As an analyst, you may have many segments to create based on the visitor whose visits are described in the Table 9-1. These segments help answer questions such as these:

> How much revenue is captured in Lehi, Utah?

> In what city do visits occur that view the product page and add a product to the shopping cart?

> How many pages are viewed from visitors who have been to the site in New York?

Different granularities of segments are required to answer these three questions.

Let's start with a very simple example: Figure 9-1 envisions an ancient-era data analyst segmenting revenue by the source of a hit to the website.

Understanding hit-based containers

As noted, *hit-based containers* are the narrowest and strictest (most granular) type of segment container. (A *hit* is any interaction on your site or app that results in data being sent to Adobe Analytics.) The data returned from hit-based segments is limited only to those hits where the segment definition is true; all other data is excluded.

FIGURE 9-1:
Sorting revenue
by the city that is
the source of a
hit to the site.

New York City hits   Philadelphia hits   Lehi hits

So to answer the question as to how much revenue is captured in Lehi, Utah, we could define a segment that focuses on *hits* sent to Adobe while the visitor is in Lehi, Utah. If we were to create this hit-based segment and apply it to a freeform table on a website with just the one visitor in Table 9-1, our revenue metric would only show $1,300.

You may then want to know what happens when you keep the segment applied and add the page views metric. Because three page views occurred in Lehi, the data would show three. The pages viewed in Philadelphia and New York are filtered out from your segment because those values don't match the definition of the segment in hits 1, 2, 3, 4, and 5.

As of the time of this writing, hit-based containers are unique to Adobe Analytics and unavailable in Google Analytics.

Using visit-based containers

Visit-based containers include more data than segments built with hit-based containers. The *visit container* is the most commonly used container because it captures behaviors for the entire visit if the definition is met. In addition, visit containers can be used to analyze a single dimension that changes during a visit. The second question aligns with this need, identifying the city where visits contain a page view of the product page and add a product to the shopping cart.

For example, you might create a segment definition requiring a custom dimension of page type equal to product and the cart additions metric firing. The product page view is captured in one hit and the cart addition is captured in a second hit. Therefore, we can't use a hit-based container because no single hit contains both.

If we were to define this segment, focusing on product page type and cart additions to the website capturing the data in the Table 9-1, the cities dimension would display only Philadelphia.

The fun part of visit-based containers is aligned with the behavior outside the segment's definition — in this instance, that third hit, a page view on the blog page. Our segment would include that hit, which means the data would return two page views, one cart addition, and one visit.

REMEMBER

When you use visit-based containers, you will see results that fall outside the values specified.

Zooming out to visitor-based containers

The broadest segment container is tied to the visitor. *Visitor-based containers* apply the segment definition to the entire history of the visitor to include all associated hits in the report timeframe.

If we created a visitor container where cities equals New York, and applied this segment to the example visitor in the table, *all data* associated with that visitor would be included in the segment, even though only part of the activity occurred in New York. Think of this visitor container as asking the question: Has the visitor ever been in New York? If so, include all of that visitor's behavior in my segment — every page view, visit, custom link, cart addition, order, and revenue.

Factoring in the calendar

Before we describe how to define custom containers in Adobe Analytics, let's not forget to factor in time. All the segmentation examples we've discussed up to this point rely heavily on a defined timeframe. Let's walk through a few examples to illustrate how the calendar factors into segmentation.

In the example table, a defined segment focusing on hits that occur in Lehi, Utah, would include the data in hits 6, 7, and 8. It's important to recognize that this is true only if the data you're analyzing includes data from Wednesday. (Table 9-1 shows that Wednesday is the day of the Lehi, Utah visit.) If instead our timeframe had been focused on Monday or Tuesday, Adobe Analytics wouldn't return any data because there were no hits in Lehi on those days.

The same applies to a segment applied to a freeform table with a timeframe set to Monday or Wednesday. In that case, there would be no associated data. Visit containers are similar to hit-based containers: If the visit with the segment's behavior didn't occur during the timeframe, data is not returned. Visitor containers are unique because they potentially span multiple visits and days. So, if the segment identifying visitors who have visited the site from New York is applied to data in a freeform table limited to just Wednesday, then hits 6, 7, and 8 would be included in the freeform table. The visitor segment says "find me all the visitors who have ever visited the site in New York" and the table's time range is limited to data from that segment that occurred on Wednesday.

Defining a Segment and Setting the Container

Now that we've explored a few ways that segments can be defined for hit, visit, and visitor, let's walk through defining segments and setting the container.

Adobe makes the process easy. Follow the next set of steps in Analysis Workspace to create a segment. If you don't have access to follow along, your administrators have most likely removed your access to create segments — work with your administrator to regain access.

WARNING

In rare cases, companies disable segment creation for non-administrators. In that situation, you could work with an administrator who will define segments.

1. **On the menu, choose Components ⇨ New Segment, as shown in Figure 9-2.**

   In Analysis Workspace, you can create new segments several ways, but the menu command is the easiest to remember. You can also click the plus button in the left rail just to the right of the section dedicated to segments or press Shift+⌘+E (Mac) or Shift+Control+E (PC). You are now brought to the Segment Builder dialog.

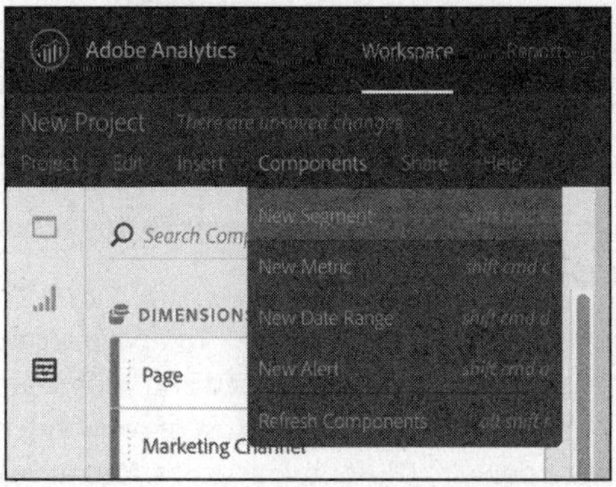

FIGURE 9-2:
Two ways to create a new, blank segment.

2. **Drag and drop any combination of dimensions, metrics, other segments, and time ranges into the Definition box in the Segment drop zone to create segments.**

   Try dragging the page dimension from the left rail into the drop zone.

3. **To change the operator, use the drop-down menu, as shown in Figure 9-3.**

   By default, Adobe assumes you want to set newly dropped dimensions equal to a value. To follow along with this example, leave the drop-down set to Equals and click the field to the right to set Page equal to your site's Home page. Note how the segment preview in the top-right adjusts to display what percentage of your data is now included in your segment.

FIGURE 9-3: A hit-based segment where Page Equals Home.

4. **Drag a second page dimension into the Segment drop zone, below the one that you just set, as shown in Figure 9-4.**

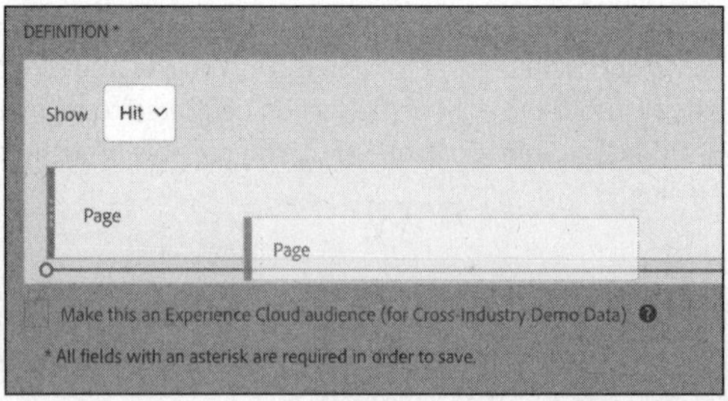

FIGURE 9-4: Dragging a second page dimension into a segment.

5. **Set the second page dimension in this segment to any other page available in the drop-down menu.**

   In Figure 9-5, we've chosen the Purchase: Thank You page. In the example here, two page dimensions have been combined and your segment preview (in the upper-right corner of the dialog) shows 0% of your data is included in the segment. Data went down to 0% for two reasons: You have a hit-based container and the two components of the definition are bound by an *and*, meaning both have to be true. Of course, this is impossible. No single hit could have two different values for the page dimension. Change either of these and you should have data.

FIGURE 9-5: Identifying an impossible combination of segments.

6. **Change the logical operator in your segment definition from And to Or.**

   You'll now include all hits on the Home page *or* on the Purchase: Thank You page. If instead of changing the segment's logical operator you changed the *container* from hit to visit, your segment would include visits where both the Home page and the Purchase: Thank You page were viewed.

7. **Name your segment and click Save.**

   You've just created your first segment!

   Several other fields are available to make it easier to find this segment and understand its definition. Let's quickly go through them.

Governing your segments properly

All segments that you create have several optional fields to make them easier to describe and categorize. Each of these fields can be edited and are tied to the segment when it is shared from one user to the next.

TIP

We highly recommend using intuitive names that properly describe your segment at a glance. For example: *Purchasing iOS Visitors* is a clear segment name that specifies the filtering components (purchase and iOS) as well as the container (visitor). In addition to using intuitive names, add context in the description field. Our preference is to include in the description information about how the segment is defined and where it should be used. You'll be able to quickly access the segment description by hovering your cursor over the segment in the left rail and clicking the information icon, as shown in Figure 9-6.

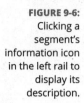

FIGURE 9-6:
Clicking a
segment's
information icon
in the left rail to
display its
description.

Segments can also have one or more *tags* applied to make them more organized and easier to find. We find it useful to apply tags that are aligned with the type of analysis (such as marketing channel) or the department at your company most likely to use it (such as operations or advertising).

Consider adding one or more tags for every component used in the segment's definition. Doing so will make it easy to find all segments related to page type or cart additions without having to remember the segment's name.

TIP

Adobe Analytics administrators have access rights to designate any number of shared segments as approved. *Approved* segments are often designated as such because your admins have fully vetted the definitions. If you're an admin who can do this, be careful to approve (and share) only segments that you have thoroughly audited for accuracy.

All users of Adobe Analytics have their *favorite* segments, so the interface has a feature to make it easier to find them. Favorite segments are at the user-level (they aren't tied to the segment when it's shared).

After you've defined segments and components, you can easily find them using the search box at the top of the left rail, as shown in Figure 9-7. You can search your segments (and all components) by tag, approval status, and favorite.

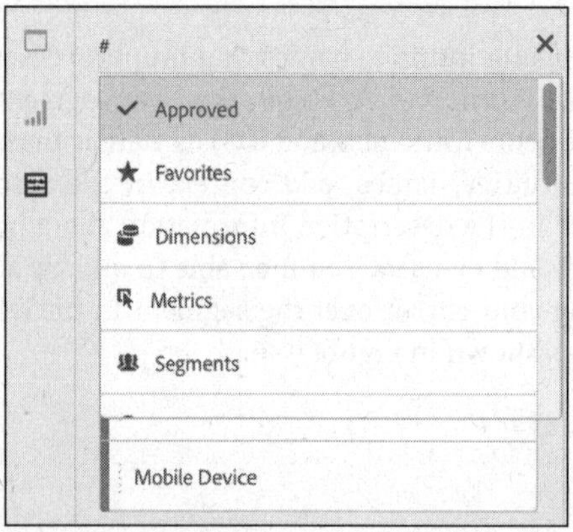

FIGURE 9-7:
The left rail
search box can
filter based on
tag, approvals,
and favorites.

Creating segments dynamically in a freeform table

The process for creating new segments using Segment Builder isn't too complicated, but it can be time-consuming. A lot of clicking, dragging, dropping, and typing is required to create even simple segments.

Analysis Workspace, however, lets you create simple segments easily and without interrupting your analysis. Give these simple steps a try to create a hit-based segment with multiple values:

1. **Drag any dimension into a freeform table.**

2. **Use Shift to select contiguous rows in the table.**

   You can also use Shift+⌘ (Mac) or Shift+Control (PC) to select noncontiguous rows in a table.

3. **Right-click any of the rows that are highlighted and select Create Segment from Selection from the context menu.**

   Workspace pre-fills each of the rows you selected into a hit-based segment with Or separating each value.

This shortcut will be a huge time-saver when you're performing an analysis. Think how much longer it would've taken to drag and drop the dimension multiple times, type the individual dimensional values, and then switch the functional logic from And to Or.

Several other visualizations also enable you to right-click to create a segment. We discuss these additional time-saving segment creation features in Chapter 14 as we go through each visualization.

Sharing segments between users and Adobe solutions

After you become a master of creating segments, you'll want to share your creations — not to show off but to share the wealth! Why let your co-workers waste time recreating what you've already built? And sharing defined segments will help with segment governance to make sure that everyone is using the same segments.

You can share saved segments with others in your organization by hovering the cursor over the Components menu and selecting Segments. You're quickly brought to Segment Manager, where you can share, delete, tag, rename, approve (if you have access as an admin), copy, and export segments. You can even add new segments from this interface rather than through Workspace if you'd like.

The process for sharing segments is a simple one: Click the check box next to one or more segments and then click Share from the top menu. A dialog box similar to Figure 9-8 appears, so you can share the segment(s) with any other Adobe Analytics users in your organization. If you're an admin, you'll also be able to share segments to all users or groups of users, as defined in your organization.

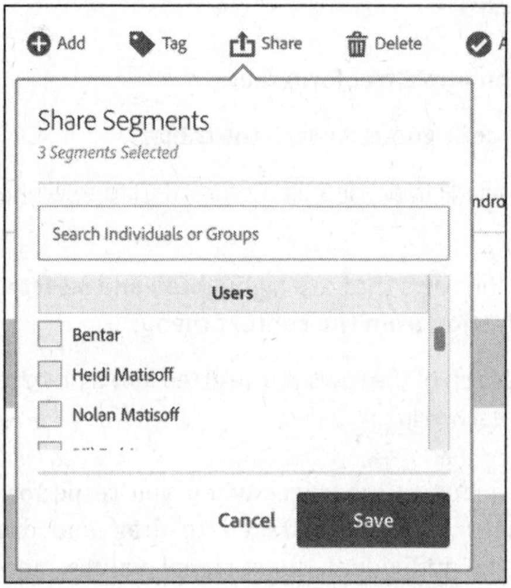

FIGURE 9-8:
The dialog box
that appears
when sharing
from Segment
Manager.

Another way to share segments is from Adobe Analytics to the rest of Adobe Experience Cloud. If your company uses Target, Audience Manager, Ad Cloud, or Campaign, you'll get value from shared segments.

Segments can be shared to Experience Cloud by accessing the Segment Builder interface. Below the segment's definition but above the option to save is the Make This an Experience Cloud Audience check box, as shown in Figure 9-9. Click this check box and then click Save to share the segment to other solutions that your company has integrated to Adobe Analytics.

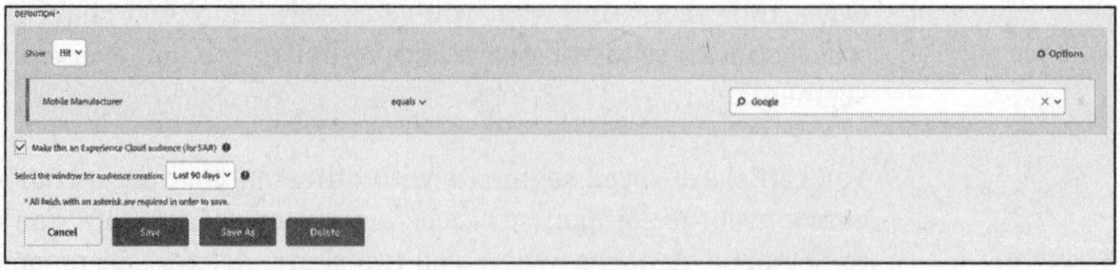

FIGURE 9-9:
A segment is
shared to
Experience Cloud.

If you know you have other Experience Cloud solutions but you don't see the Make This an Experience Cloud Audience check box check box, you either don't have access to create shared segments or your solutions are not properly integrated. Follow up with your Adobe administrator if you can't create shared segments but think you should be able to.

Using Virtual Report Suites Based on Segments

Think of *virtual report suites* as report suites that your administrator has customized by segments, updated visit definitions, and curated components.

Your company has access to creating an unlimited number of virtual report suites. If any of them are useless, they can be easily deleted. You may not have access rights to create virtual report suites, so we focus on the options for virtual report suites and how to identify these report suites in Analysis Workspace and Report Builder. By the way, if you're interested in learning how to set up a virtual report suite, we suggest walking through the process with your administrator.

Virtual report suites are used for a variety of reasons. We describe two of the most common uses. All data for your company might be collected in one report suite, but your administrator(s) may have reasons to define access rights to certain sets of data. Some people in your company should have access to part of the data but not all of it. Report suite data might be divided by region, language, or brand. This way, the team that manages the website in the United States sees only the data that matters to them, while the team that manages the Canadian website sees only data from that region.

Another common use for virtual report suites is associated with sharing data outside the walls of your brand. Think about the ad agencies and consultancies that you work with. It's in your and their best interest for them to have access to data, but it may make sense to limit what data they can see. For example, you can define a virtual report suite by applying a segment that focuses only on traffic driven by paid search. This way, the ad agency that manages paid search has access to just the data they need.

Identifying virtual report suites

Virtual report suites are interspersed into the report suite drop-down menu of Analysis Workspace. You'll be able to find them easily thanks to the blue dot to the left of each virtual report suite's name. Figure 9-10 shows a mix of standard report suites and virtual report suites. The virtual report suites are

>> 5 minute timeout (AAC)

>> 60 minute timeout (AAC)

>> AOS

>> AOS (with RPT)

>> Bixby 1-minute timeout

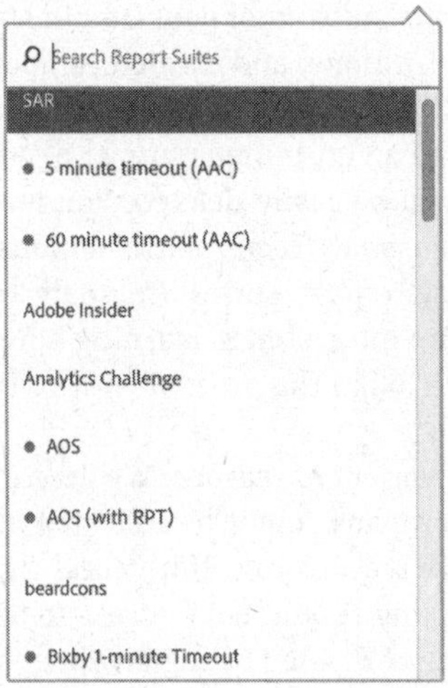

FIGURE 9-10:
The report suite selector drop-down menu with five virtual report suites.

Hover your cursor over a report suite in the drop-down list and click the information circle that appears. You'll see how data has trended in the report suite (virtual or standard) during the past 90 days.

Virtual report suites are accessible also in Report Builder, Adobe's plug-in for accessing analytics data. Virtual report suites are listed with the word *Virtual* in parentheses in the report suite drop-down list, as shown in Figure 9-11. Chapter 16 provides a more thorough review of the capabilities of Report Builder.

Curating via virtual report suites

Virtual report suites are fantastic simply because administrators can curate the components that are accessible to analysts like you. Imagine if instead of having thousands of metrics, hundreds of dimensions, and dozens of segments, you had just the components that mattered to your analysis.

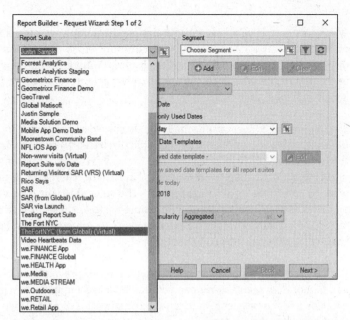

This feature is called *curation,* the ability to limit components accessible to users. Workspace projects can also take advantage of this feature when they are shared; we discuss this topic in detail in Chapter 14. Virtual report suite curation expands on this with the ability to rename components too. So not only are the metrics, dimensions, and segments tailored to your needs, they're also given friendlier names based on the context defined by the virtual report suite. A good example is renaming the visits metric to app launches if your virtual report suite limits your data to just mobile app data.

Redefining visits with context-aware sessions

In Chapter 2, we walk through the definition of a visit and discuss how Adobe uses 30 minutes of inactivity to define the end of a visit but that the time interval is flexible. A powerful feature of virtual report suites makes that flexibility possible. *Context-aware sessions* grant virtual report suites the capability to recalculate data based on an updated definition of a visit via either a different timeout or the occurrence of a specified metric. Let's walk through an example of each.

Many brands these days are building skills for voice assistants powered by Amazon Alexa, Google Assistant, and Microsoft Cortana. These brands also see the value in capturing behavioral data associated with these skills, as you would expect.

When this data is sent to Adobe Analytics, the default visit timeout is 30 minutes of inactivity. In a conversation, a 30-minute block could pass with dozens of different and unrelated conversation topics. Companies building voice skills are beginning to consider each conversation as separate, so they naturally align with a visit in Adobe Analytics.

But, like a real conversation, the topic discussed at the top of the hour is usually different from and unrelated to the topic discussed 29 minutes later. To solve for this, brands are changing the criteria for context-aware sessions to redefine the visit timeout definition to 30 seconds of inactivity. Therefore, if 30 seconds passes where a consumer hasn't engaged with the voice skill, the next voice request will be considered a new visit. As you would expect, these brands are often using virtual report suite curation to rename visits to something that better aligns with their voice skill, such as conversation.

Digital analytics is now starting to become more prevalent in brick-and-mortar stores too! How many stores can you name where you interact with a tablet kiosk, a touchscreen, or a salesperson who is armed with a digital device? Digital is being introduced to the in-store experience. Brands that are doing this realize the expense associated with this new technology and need to be able to use data to ensure that they are enabling consumers with the best possible experience.

The brick-and-mortar stores that are using Adobe Analytics are also leveraging context-aware sessions to ensure high data quality. Every time a user taps the Start Over button, devices send a metric to Adobe Analytics, and the virtual report suite uses context-aware sessions to look for that metric to end the previous visit and start a new one. It's a simple yet powerful use case to better understand how in-store consumers are interacting with digital signage.

Chapter **10**

Creating Calculated Metrics to Accelerate Analyses

As you know, metrics — along with dimensions — are essential components of data analysis. Metrics are a key part of all reports, tables, and data visualizations in any analytics platform. Metrics such as page views, visits, orders, and revenue are imperative to incorporate into your daily life as an analyst.

In this chapter, you take metrics to another level by using calculated metrics.

Understanding and Defining Calculated Metrics

In Chapter 2 we define metrics as quantitative measurements that answer questions such as "how many?" or "how much?" Calculated metrics continue to answer these questions by incorporating mathematical computations.

You may be familiar with calculated metrics in Google Analytics, where you can combine addition, subtraction, multiplication, and division to create calculated metrics. The Google Analytics calculated metric feature is available in Admin Console. In current versions of Google Analytics and Google Analytics 360, you're limited in the number of calculated metrics you can define.

In Adobe Analytics, you can create an unlimited number of calculated metrics on the fly as you analyze data in Analysis Workspace. You walk through how to do that in this chapter, along with sharing insights into when and why calculated metrics can radically enhance the accuracy and focus of reports.

You also look at new features in Adobe Analytics that expand the amount of mathematical functions you have at your disposal, including distinct counts, mean, and standard deviations. If you're familiar with some of those statistical terms, you might be chomping at the bit to get into how to deploy them. Good! We get there soon.

If you're not familiar with those statistical analysis terms, don't worry. You walk through what you need to know to get the most out of Adobe's calculated metrics features.

TIP

Overwhelmingly, the calculated functions you explore in this chapter are available in all packages of Adobe Analytics, but some of the more complex and advanced functions are not, at this writing, available in the Select package. If you encounter issues with any of the calculation, consult with your administrator as to which package you have installed.

Calculated metrics in the real world

Let's take the example of the basic weather forecast that we use throughout this book, and incorporate some useful calculated metrics:

Day of Week	High (C)	High Adjusted to Fahrenheit	Low (C)	Low Adjusted to Fahrenheit
Monday	28	82.4	19	66.2
Tuesday	27	80.6	18	64.4
Wednesday	26	78.8	16	60.8
Thursday	26	78.8	14	57.2
Friday	22	71.6	12	53.6
Saturday	30	86	20	68
Sunday	32	89.6	25	77

The table has two calculated metrics, the Fahrenheit-adjusted high and low. We create these metrics by multiplying the Celsius temperature by 9/5 and adding 32.

If Adobe Analytics were capturing the temperature of your website in Celsius, you could easily apply this formula to convert it to Fahrenheit. We made an important decision when we added the new metrics: how many decimal places to include in the result. This detail is important to consider whenever you divide metrics or calculate data based on other metrics that have decimal places.

Let's think about a few other calculated metrics that could be derived from this dataset. If you were trying to plan a day at the pool and wanted to know what day will be the hottest day of the week, your brain makes it easy to recognize that Sunday has the highest high (32/89.6 degrees!). If you ask your analytics platform to tell you the highest high, you use a more apt term: column max. A fifth metric that applies a column max to Celsius high would return 32. Similarly you could apply a column min to Celsius low to find the lowest low, 12.

Another common question that you could ask of this data is the average Fahrenheit high for the week. You might not think that's a question that you would ever ask of a weather forecast. But have you ever asked "what's the weather there?" before traveling to a new region? If someone responds by saying, for example, "It's warm, in the 70s and 80s," you've asked your weather forecast for the average.

You can easily apply an average (commonly referred to as the *mean*) to any column in the table by adding each day's value and dividing by the number of days, 7. The result shows that the average high in Fahrenheit is 81.1 degrees for the week — pretty warm!

Calculated metrics in the data world

You may be thinking to yourself that we covered calculated metrics in Chapter 5 when discussing bounce rate, time spent per visit, and average page views per visit. That is true! Each of these are built-in calculated metrics that Adobe provides in every report suite. As analysts, however, we can't stop there. Our curiosity forces us to think beyond built-in metrics to properly complete our analyses.

In Adobe Analytics you have the chance to create simple calculated metrics using basic operations such as addition, subtraction, multiplication, and division. Having these operations at your disposal helps answer a wealth of questions, for example:

>> What was the average order value per visit?

>> How many visitors didn't come from paid search?

>> What is the total revenue coming from these three products?

Identifying the average order value per visit — *revenue/visits* — is one of the simplest and most valuable calculated metrics. Inspect the following table without this calculated metric and guess which marketing channel you should put more money in:

Marketing Channel	Revenue
Paid search	$800
Display	$270
Paid social	$3,000

With just this data, it's obvious that paid social is the most successful program. However, additional context is required to make a true analysis. See how the following table tells a different story?

Marketing Channel	Revenue	Revenue/Visits
Paid search	$800	$80
Display	$270	$3
Paid social	$3,000	50¢

The context that the calculated metric provides helps ensure that you don't make a rash decision: Paid social is driving the most revenue but it's also driving a slew of unqualified traffic that is buying either very low cost items or nothing.

TIP

When performing analyses, always make sure you consider the context of your data. A healthy combination of standard metrics and calculated metrics is required to understand both sides of the data story.

Just like when you calculate something in a three-ring notebook or a spreadsheet, calculations in analytics must consider the order of operations.

All analytics platforms gracefully handle the mathematical order of operations — multiplication, division, addition, subtraction. Parentheses are one of the preferred method for helping ensure that math is completed in the expected order. For example, if you want to calculate revenue per visit for the combined sum of paid searches and paid social media promotion, your formula will first define the sum in parenthesis, and then divide that sum by the combined total number of visits. A bit later in this chapter, you walk through exactly how to group calculations in building calculated metrics.

Like standard metrics, calculated metrics also need to take advantage of segments to be meaningful, but unlike standard metrics, segments can be applied to the entirety or a small component of a calculated metric. You can easily create segment-enabled calculated metrics such as these:

>> Paid search revenue

>> New visitors page views per visit

>> Percent of registrations from Philadelphia

The paid search revenue metric is simple. You apply a visit-based segment where marketing channel equals paid search to the revenue metric. Isn't it interesting how a calculated metric can technically not even contain a calculation? A segment applied to any standard metric can be saved as a calculated metric — you see how to do this a little later in the chapter.

The second metric in the list, new visitors page views per visit, is similar to the first metric, but instead of applying a segment to a standard metric, you apply a segment to a calculated metric.

The third metric in the list — percent of registrations from Philadelphia — is the most exciting. This calculation requires the following formula:

Philadelphia registrations/worldwide registrations

The numerator starts with a visit-based segment in which cities equals Philadelphia, which is then applied to the registrations metric. The denominator is set as registrations without a segment.

All three segmented metrics are necessary tools for your analysis toolkit. Keep reading to learn how to build them in Adobe Analytics!

Adobe gives you several ways to create calculated metrics:

>> On-the-fly

>> Using Calculated Metric Builder

>> Using an API (application programming interface)

We combed through these different options and found the most-used and most useful styles to use in your everyday life as an analyst. Each option has pros and cons, but it's invaluable to learn them all to more dexterously use Analysis Workspace.

Creating Basic Calculated Metrics in a Freeform Table

The fastest way to create a calculated metric is so simple you can do it with a few clicks.

Calculated metrics can be applied to a single metric, or to two or more metrics. The latter option is more typical, so you explore it first.

Calculating with two metrics

Imagine this scenario: You have a freeform table loaded with data and realize that you want to follow Eric and Dave's advice to incorporate context in your analysis.

Your table has one dimension, marketing channel; and two metrics, revenue and visits. You haven't created a calculated metric to divide revenue by visits to easily identify traffic with high revenue per visit. Your table would look something like Figure 10-1.

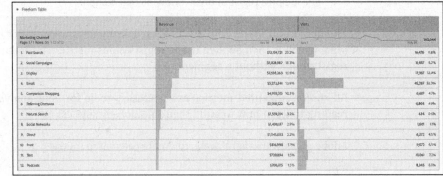

FIGURE 10-1:
A freeform table without a calculated metric for context.

In this scenario, you already have the ingredients for a great calculated metric — revenue per visit. To divide revenue by visits requires just four steps:

1. **Click in the revenue metric header cell at the top of the column to highlight Revenue.**

2. **With the header cell in the revenue column (still) selected, ⌘-click (Mac) or Control-click (PC) the visits metric header cell at the top of the column so Visits is also selected.**

3. **Right-click Visits and choose Create Metric from Selection in the menu that appears, as shown in Figure 10-2.**

4. **Left-click Divide.**

   Voila! A new column appears with revenue/visits data.

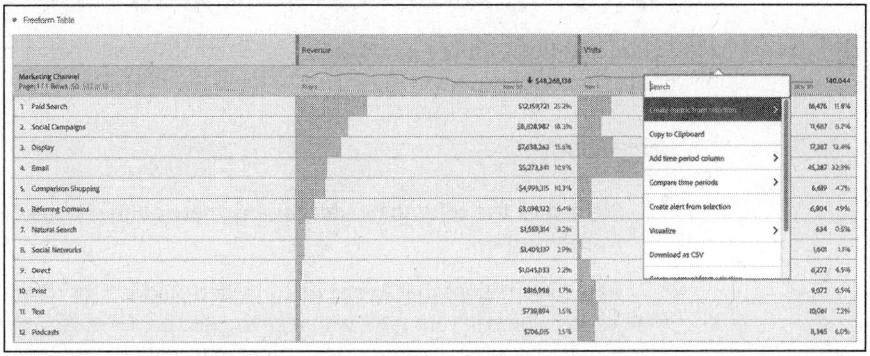

FIGURE 10-2: The right-click menu when two metrics are highlighted.

While going through that process, you might have noticed other options in addition to Divide. We use the divide operation at least nine times out of ten, but it's worth noting that other functions in this menu are subtraction, addition, multiplication, and percent change. There's also an option to Open in Calculated Metric Builder, which we get to that shortly.

A calculated metric that you create on-the-fly in a freeform table like this is accessible only in the table in which it was created. Therefore, you won't be able to pull it into other tables, visualization, or panels — you'd have to recreate it. If you're creating a metric that should be more accessible, you can either make the metric public, as shown in Figure 10-3, or use Calculated Metric Builder, as described in the next section.

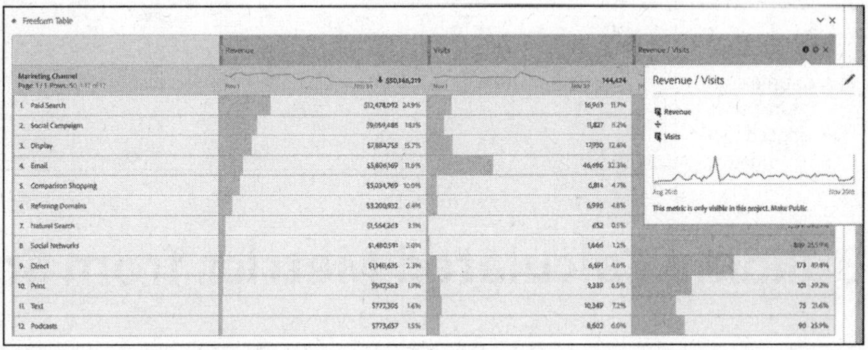

FIGURE 10-3: The information circle is clicked on an on-the-fly calculated metric.

Clicking the Make Public link shown in Figure 10-3 doesn't actually make the metric public, for all the world to see. Instead, it displays the metric in the left rail of the project. Give it a try and take a look at the metric at the top of the list of available metrics for easy access while working in the open project!

Applying functions to a single metric

Before moving to more complex ways of creating calculated metrics, it's worth noting that you can apply functions to a single metric too.

Here's how:

1. **Right-click the column header for any metric and choose Create Metric from Selection.**

    Note the functions that Adobe has provided quick access to. You can create a new column in your table with data focused on the mean (mathematic average), median, column max, column min, and column sum.

2. **In the resulting menu of function options, click Column Sum.**

3. **Note the result, displayed in a new column.**

    Because each of these functions applies to the full extent of the data in the table, every row is populated with the same value. Figure 10-4 illustrates this — every row in the calculated new column displays a value identical to the sum listed at the top of the first column.

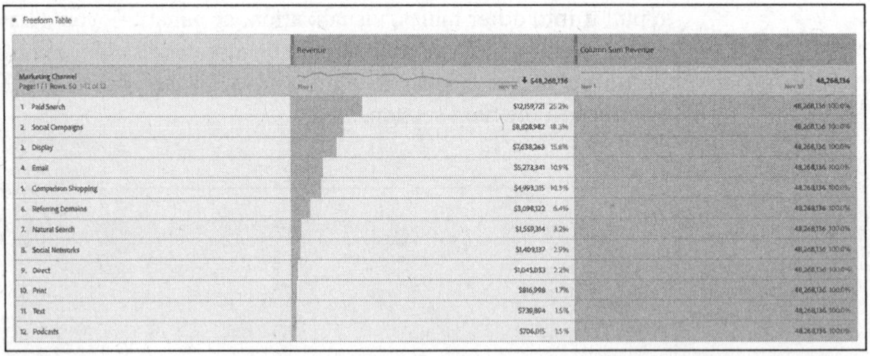

FIGURE 10-4:
A column sum function is applied to a metric.

Building Calculated Metrics from Scratch

Although we love the seamless process of creating metrics on-the-fly in a free-form table, sometimes we need more: more metrics, more functions, more control!

Adobe's Calculated Metric Builder is flexible and the interface is similar to Segment Builder, which you explore in Chapter 9. You have the option to create calculated metrics with unlimited base metrics, more powerful functions, containers (Adobe's way of incorporating parentheses into the drag-and-drop interface), static numbers, segments, and more!

You start with building a simple calculated metric — page views per visit — in Calculated Metric Builder and then advance to some of those more powerful capabilities:

1. **Open Calculated Metric Builder by using one of the options labeled in Figure 10-5.**

   You can click the plus sign in the left rail next to the metrics listing, click Components ⇨ New Metric from the navigation menu, or use the keyboard shortcut Shift+⌘+C (Mac) or Shift+Control+C (PC).

   REMEMBER

   One or two metrics can be prefilled in Calculated Metric Builder by right-clicking them in a freeform table, choosing Create Metric from Selection, and then choosing Open in Calculated Metric Builder.

Components menu

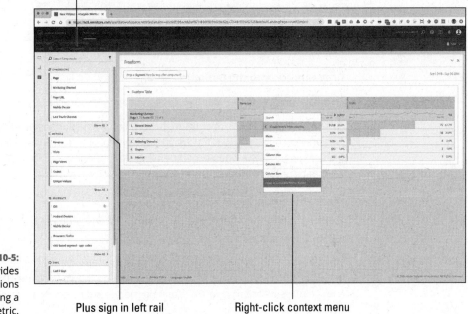

Plus sign in left rail   Right-click context menu

2. **After the blank Calculated Metric Builder appears in your browser, note the familiar list of metrics, dimensions, and segments in the left rail.**

Instead of time ranges, however, you see a section for functions, as shown in Figure 10-6. You come back to this list later. In the center of the builder is the Definition drop zone for these components.

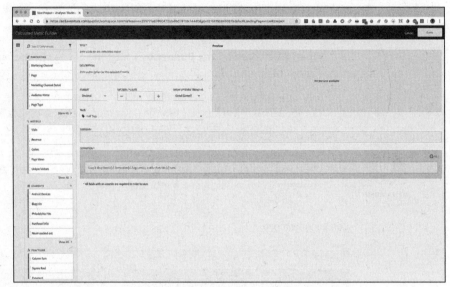

FIGURE 10-6:
Calculated Metric
Builder.

3. **Drag a metric into the Definition area.**

To follow along with the example, drag the page views metric.

A preview of your metric appears in the top-right corner, as shown in Figure 10-7. This preview helps you identify the 90-day trend of your current definition. This feature can be useful when experimenting with unfamiliar metrics, dimensions, segments, or functions.

4. **Drag the second metric into the definition.**

This step, taken before choosing a mathematical operator, may seem counter-intuitive, but bear with us.

To follow along with the example, drag the visits metric below the first metric in the Definition drop zone. A blue line appears, as shown in Figure 10-8. This line is a reassurance that you're dropping the second metric in an acceptable place.

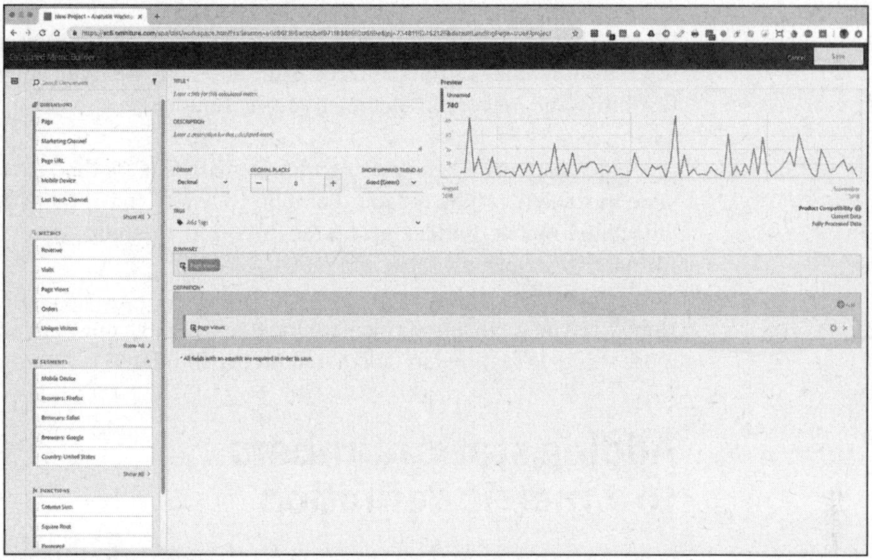

FIGURE 10-7:
Calculated Metric
Builder with page
views added to
the definition.

FIGURE 10-8:
A visual cue
assists you when
dropping a
second metric
into Calculated
Metric Builder.

5. **Choose a mathematical operator.**

   Adobe defaults to division, but note the down arrow in the division icon. Click the icon to switch to the other basic operations of addition, subtraction, and multiplication. To follow along with the example, keep the default division operator.

6. **Name the metric Page Views Per Visit and add a couple of decimal places.**

   You name the metric in the Title field, which is to the left of the preview. To change the number or decimal places, click + twice in the Decimal Places field. Your metric will now look like Figure 10-9.

7. **Click Save.**

FIGURE 10-9:
A completed
calculated
metric: page
views per visit.

Wasn't that easy? Sure, the process required a few extra steps compared to creating the same metric from the freeform table, but we hope you got a taste for the flexibility and power of Calculated Metric Builder.

One big advantage when creating metrics with this method is that they are accessible in the left rail by default. You don't have to make them public. In addition, Calculated Metric Builder grants enables you to apply decimal points, numeric formats, descriptions, tags, and more.

Now that you have a few calculated metrics under your belt, walk through a few more valuable features in Calculated Metric Builder.

Adding static numbers to a metric definition

Sometimes, you need to add hard-coded numbers to your calculations. A standard example is creating a metric that we call the *sticky rate*, which is the opposite of a bounce rate. Bounce rate shows you the percentage of users who bounced from the site whereas *sticky rate* shows you the percentage of users who stuck around.

The sticky rate calculation is simple — 1 minus the bounce rate. To create this calculation in Adobe Analytics, add a static number to the Calculated Metric Builder by clicking the Add button in the top-right of the definition box. Type the static number, 1, in the resulting text field. Finally, drag the bounce rate metric to the definition below the static number. To complete the sticky rate metric, you'll want to change the function from division to subtraction. The completed definition is shown in Figure 10-10. The figure also displays the Add drop-down menu, which we use to add static numbers to the definition.

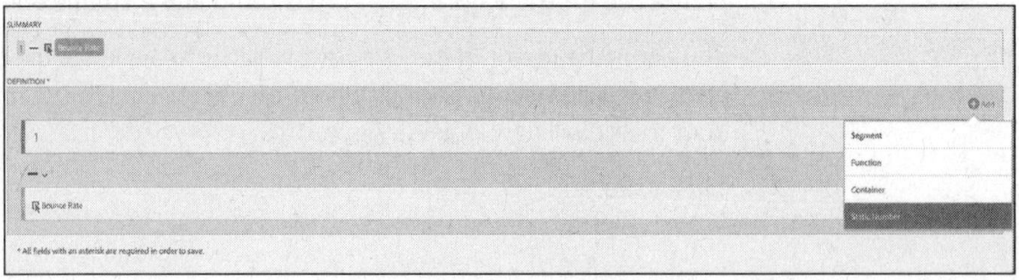

FIGURE 10-10:
A completed
sticky rate metric.

REMEMBER

All components in a metric definition can be dragged up or down.

Including parentheses when defining new metrics

As you may remember from math in grade school, parentheses are a highly necessary and valuable tool in your mathematic arsenal. They help you prioritize certain parts of your formula to ensure that the result matches your expectation. For example, the result of $(80 * 20) + 2$ is significantly different than $80 * (20 + 2)$. It's a difference of 158, for those counting.

Adobe provides you with an elegant solution to handle the need for parentheses when defining calculated metrics. The term is defined for segments but used in a different context for calculated metrics: containers.

Containers in calculated metrics enable you to prioritize and segregate sections of your definition, just like parentheses in math. Here's a great example of the value that containers, like parentheses, provide: A retail company is capturing a custom metric called potential revenue, which captures the amount of money that customers add to a cart. It's *potential* because cart revenue doesn't necessarily result in a purchase. The company realizes that a lot of money is lost in abandoned shopping carts and wants to understand how much money, on average, is lost.

To define this, you start by figuring out how much total potential revenue is being lost by subtracting potential revenue from revenue. The company then wants to understand, on average, the amount of revenue lost per person, so you divide that deducted amount of revenue by unique visitors.

In Adobe Analytics, you can create this metric with or without containers. Let's compare the data associated with these two options. Without containers, our calculated metric looks like Figure 10-11.

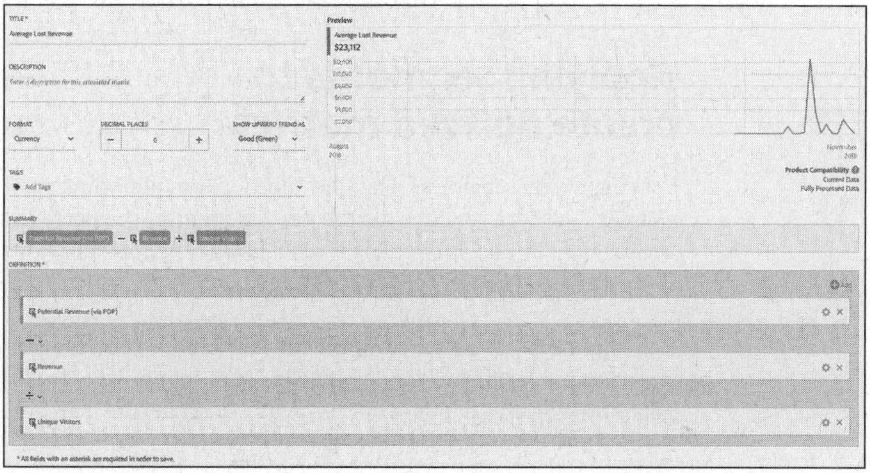

FIGURE 10-11: An inaccurate calculated metric set without containers.

As expected, Adobe follows the mathematical order of operations when containers aren't around to set priority. Revenue is divided by unique visitors first, and then that number is subtracted from potential revenue. As you've probably guessed, this calculation results in inaccurate data. The calculated metric preview shows that, on average, the website is losing $23,112 per person. This sounds way too high to be accurate!

Now compare $23,112 to the value provided by a calculated metric using containers. Figure 10-12 shows the metric definition with parentheses included. Instead of starting the calculation by dividing revenue by unique visitors, Adobe prioritizes the math in the container. This updated formula aligns with a significantly more accurate metric preview — as well as better news for the retail company: Only $108 is lost per person on average.

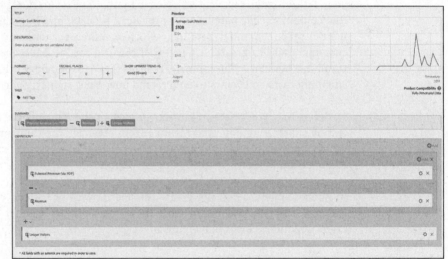

FIGURE 10-12:
An accurate
calculated
metric set
using
containers.

Applying segments to create derived metrics

You may remember the example metric example you explored earlier in this chapter — where we describe the need to identify the percentage of registrations occurring in Philadelphia. This is a no-brainer opportunity for applying segments to a calculated metric.

You might not have a registrations metric in your report suite, so we'll use a different example that we hope you can work along with in your configuration of Adobe Analytics. In this example, you calculate the percentage of page views occurring in Philadelphia. Follow along to learn how to create this metric, step by step:

1. **Open Calculated Metric Builder and search the left rail for the cities dimension.**

2. **Drag cities into the Definition box.**

   A dialog appears, as shown in Figure 10-13, giving you the chance to begin typing and begin your search for Philadelphia (Pennsylvania, United States).

FIGURE 10-13: The text box where you can search for cities.

3. **Choose Philadelphia (Pennsylvania, United States) and click Done.**

   A segment is created on-the-fly and placed in your metric definition. (If you had already created the segment, you could have just dragged it instead of the dimension from the left rail.)

4. **Drag the page views metric into the metric definition that the blue Philadelphia segment encapsulates.**

   The numerator is set for Philadelphia page views, and your definition looks like Figure 10-14.

FIGURE 10-14: The page views metric has been applied to the Philadelphia segment.

5. Add the total page views metric as a denominator.

Do a careful drag of the page views metric, as shown in Figure 10-15. Be sure to drag the metric outside the segmented region so that the horizontal blue line designating where the metric will drop appears below the vertical blue line designating the segment. When you release the second metric, a divisor appears between this new page views metric and the segmented one.

TIP

Because you're still getting used to how Metric Builder deals with the different locations where you can drop metrics, consider an easier way. After Step 2 is complete, add a container to the definition by clicking Add and selecting Container from the drop-down menu. Now you have a much bigger region to drop the page views metric for your denominator.

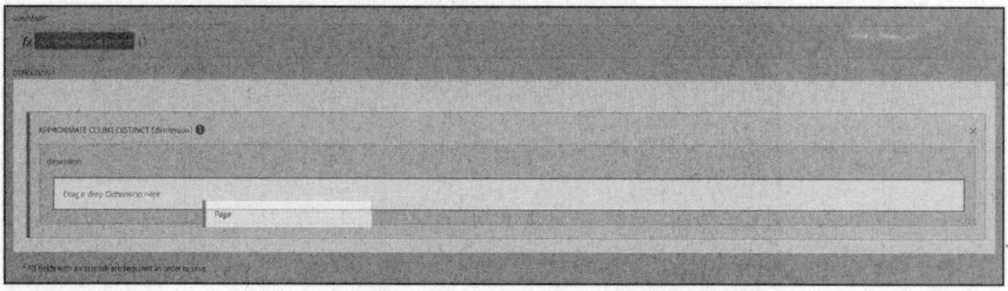

FIGURE 10-15:
Page views is added as a denominator, outside of the segment container.

6. Type a friendly metric name and add two decimal places.

To do so, use the fields to the left of the preview at the top of the screen. Then enjoy your first segmented calculated metric!

Getting the Most from Calculated Metrics

Now that you have a few calculated metrics under your belt, think about how you're going to get the most out of the power that comes with them.

Adobe's calculated metrics have so much power that we could probably write *Calculated Metrics For Dummies.* Instead, we give you the tools to get the most value from the key features without getting into statistics and linear algebra. In this section, we focus on just two more topics: applying functions and calculated metric governance. Ready, set, calculate!

Applying basic and advanced functions

As you've already seen, calculated metrics have several math functions available to them with minimal effort: division, multiplication, subtraction, addition, and parentheses. But sometimes you need to employ more advanced math when building metrics.

Calculated Metric Builder has a slew of functions, ranging from simple (if, then, greater than, less than) to advanced (count distinct, pi, mean, median, percentile) to way too complicated even for us (hyperbolic cosine, quadratic regression, and linear regression: correlation coefficient). Every calculated metric function is described in Adobe's knowledge base at https://experiencecloud.adobe.com/resources/help/en_US/analytics/calcmetrics/cm_reference.html.

One of the easier advanced functions is approximate count distinct, which returns a dimension's total count of unique values .

For example, suppose that a newspaper is considering adding a *paywall* (a message like the one on the NY Times and Medium websites that says you have to pay after reading a certain number of articles). The newspaper wants to know how many total paid customers are on their website today to calculate how much ad revenue would be lost due to the paywall. To begin calculating the number of paid customers, they use an eVar to capture a unique ID that identifies their customers whenever they log in.

The analysts at the newspaper could pass this eVar into the approximate count distinct function to see how many unique IDs they have collected. The truly powerful part of this function is that the calculated metric can be tied to any dimension! So the newspaper could align that metric with the first touch marketing channel dimension to see the channel that first drove eventual customers to the website.

REMEMBER

eVars are custom dimensions that persist. By passing a customer ID into an eVar, all metrics that take place after the ID is sent to Adobe are tied to the customer. Chapter 7 provides a thorough section on custom dimensions if you'd like a refresher.

Because there's a chance that your website doesn't have a login, let's walk through an example that you can probably recreate. In this example, a member of the team responsible for creating content, Ben, walks into your office and cries out that his boss, Jen, has been tasked with using advertising to drive more views of the blog.

The content team thankfully recognizes the value of data, so Jen and Ben have asked you to provide some analysis on the marketing channels that drive the most unique views of content. And like all requests that Jen makes, it's an answer she needs yesterday! So you roll up your sleeves to brainstorm, and wonder, "What if I count the distinct pages viewed in the blog site section, and then analyze that metric against the marketing channel dimension?"

Ben, not having a clue what you said, agrees profusely. Let's build it together!

1. Open Calculated Metric Builder.

2. In the left rail, find the approximate count distinct function and drag it into the metric definition.

To find the approximate count distinct function, do one of the following:

- Click the Show All link next to the Functions section in the left rail, and then scroll down to find it.

- Search for *approximate count distinct* in the search box at the top of the left rail.

- Click the Add button to the right of the Definition drop zone, choose Function, and then search for and select the function name.

You now have a container powered by your favorite function.

3. Again in the left rail, drag the page dimension and drop it into the center of the functional container, as shown in Figure 10-16.

If you wanted to simply count the unique number of pages viewed, your metric would be complete. However, Jen and Ben want the metric limited to views on the blog, so you need to apply a hit-based segment that is limited to hits on the blog.

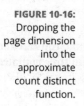

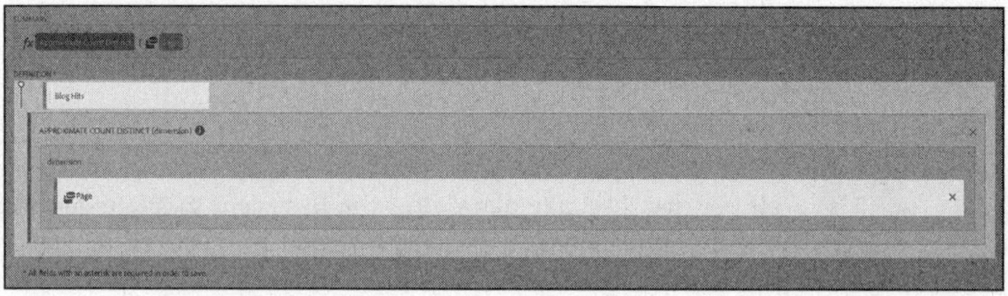

FIGURE 10-16:
Dropping the page dimension into the approximate count distinct function.

4. In the left rail, click the plus sign next to the Segments section.

Segment Builder will appear, ready for you to define a segment. If you need a refresher on building segments, head to Chapter 9.

5. Define the Blog Hits segment by dragging the Site Section dimension into your definition box, setting the value to Blog, and setting the container to Hit.

If your site doesn't have a blog, use a different site section value.

6. **Save your segment as Blog Hits by clicking the blue Save button.**

You return to the calculated metric you were creating.

7. **Drag the Blog Hits segment into the metric definition, taking care to place it at the top of the metric definition when the blue line is vertical, as shown in Figure 10-17.**

When your calculated metric looks like Figure 10-17, you've successfully created your first calculated metric with a function and a segment!

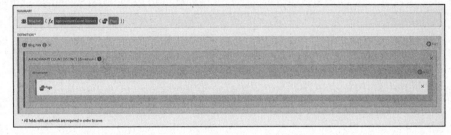

FIGURE 10-17: A segment is added so it applies to the function container.

8. **Name your new metric (we called ours Unique Blog Articles Viewed) and then save it by clicking the blue Save button.**

TECHNICAL STUFF

You may have noticed that the function is called *approximate* count distinct, not count distinct. To speed up your ability to analyze, Adobe uses an algorithm called HyperLogLog to bring the unique value back to you more quickly. Adobe promises that the data will be within 5 percent of the actual value 95 percent of the time. If statistics aren't quite your forte, that means the data is returned extremely quickly and very accurately, though with a potential for a small error.

Now that you're a master of calculated metrics, having created basic, derived, and advanced metrics, try playing around with Calculated Metric Builder to learn more about it. Use functions such as if, greater than, percentile, mean, and column max to see how they work. Try pulling in more than one segment or multiple containers into a metric to get a better feel for the interface.

TIP

Adobe provides three useful examples of advanced calculated metrics — filtered bounce rate, filtered bounce rate with percentile, and weighted metric — in the Analytics knowledge base at `https://experiencecloud.adobe.com/resources/help/en_US/analytics/calcmetrics/cm_weighted_metric.html`.

Governing all of your calculated metrics

Now that you're so well-versed in the capabilities of calculated metrics, you can start creating them, a *lot* of them. Just like we describe in Chapter 9 for segments, a wealth of options are available for keeping your calculated metrics organized and well-governed.

The most obvious way to keep your metrics clean is with friendly, intuitive names. Calculated metrics, like segments, have a description field. Use that field to describe the metric, including how it was defined and how it is best used. A calculated metric's description is shown in the left rail when you click its information circle, as shown in Figure 10-18 for the unique blog articles viewed metric you just created.

FIGURE 10-18:
A calculated metric's description is shown via the information circle.

Calculated metrics, again like segments, also have tags available to make the metrics easier to find. Consider using the same tags for both component types so it's even easier to find what you're looking for! You can apply one or more tags to a calculated metric.

TIP

Consider adding a tag for every component in the metric's definition. For example, consider the metric you just explored, which measures distinct pages viewed in the blog site section and analyzes that metric against the marketing channel dimension. That metric might have tags for page, blog hits, and approximate count distinct. These tags will make it easy to find all metrics related to those components without having to remember the name of each metric.

As a user, you can make it easier to find your most frequently used calculated metrics by designating them as *favorites*. To do so, go to the Calculated Metric Manager interface (from the main navigation menu, choose Components ⇨ Calculated Metrics) and simply click the star next to any calculated metric listed there.

You go to Calculated Metric Manager also when you want to share your creations with others in your organization. Like favorite segments, favorite metrics are at the user level and aren't accessible by other users in your organization.

Finally, Adobe Analytics administrators can apply an *approved* stamp to any calculated metrics they've vetted and shared with you. If you are an admin, be careful to approve (and share) only metrics that you've thoroughly audited for accuracy.

REMEMBER

Use the search box at the top of the left rail to filter your calculated metrics (and all components) by tag, approval status, and favorite.

Chapter **11**

Classified! Using Classifications to Make Data More Accessible

espite the intentional ambiguity of the chapter title, we are not addressing how to keep your data secret. Just the opposite, in fact. A *classification* is a way of categorizing reporting and analytics variable data and changing the way that data is displayed in reports. In short, classification has two main functions:

» **Organizing data** with a level of flexibility that supplements and goes beyond what you can do with even complex combinations of dimensions, metrics, and segments

» **Renaming data** with more user-friendly terms

Typically, categorizing involves both aspects, in combination. The objective is to make your data more *accessible* using classifications (with an *s*) to organize and package that data in a way that is most useful for the stakeholders who need to understand it.

In this chapter, you explore classification on three levels:

>> **Why you use classified data**

>> **How to use classified data**

>> **How administrators define classifications** and how you (whether or not you are an admin) can contribute to the process of identifying and creating needed classifications

Making Data Coherent and Accessible

Raw data can be unique and exceptional. For example, product SKU nomenclature is often interpretable only by a small audience, and even for them, a bunch of letters and numbers requiring a lookup on a product sheet is usually not a handy way to get an overview of patterns and trends. Even filtered data can be hard to decipher when it's presented with terminology that only those in a tiny inner sanctum of knowledge can understand. Classifications can help solve these issues, making reports accessible to a wide range of stakeholders.

Classifications can also pull together categories of data that aren't easily combined using just dimensions, metrics and segments. All this will make a lot more sense after you walk through some illuminating examples of how classifications make life easier for you as an analyst and for the people with whom you share reports.

Renaming unfriendly codes

One widely applicable role for classifications is to assign more user-friendly, accessible terms to unfriendly codes captured in Adobe Analytics. Examples include the ugly values captured in campaign tracking codes, long and unclean URLs, and SKUs for products. Scenario: You're pulling together a report that analyzes user behavior in relation to a product with a SKU of 12394809874xh-445. That may mean something to a small number of people, but not to the team for whom you're preparing an analysis of how well that product is selling, where it is being ordered from, who is ordering it, and so on.

Here, classifications (such as *Skateboard — 2019 model* or *New Balance 880 running shoes*) can make that data more intelligible.

And sometimes, SKU values are just awkward. Classifications can clean up those values, stripping extra spaces, correcting misspellings (yes, those happen in data entry), or shortening value names. Figure 11-1 illustrates what results after using classification to rename SKUs. The table on the left is a set of product SKUs decipherable only to a limited audience. The table on the right shows the SKU values renamed with more widely interpretable product names.

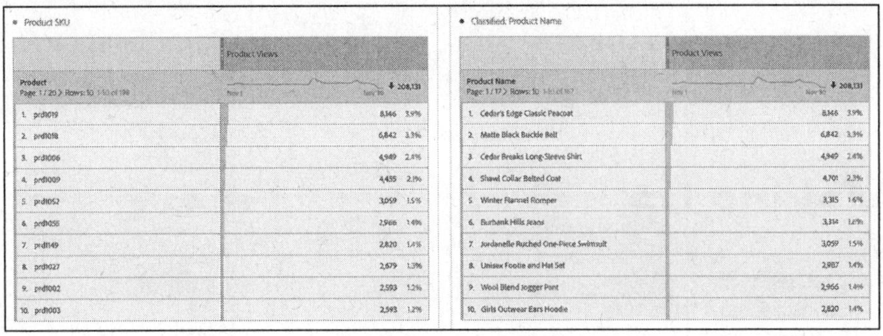

FIGURE 11-1: Renamed SKUs with classification.

Consolidating with classifications

Another feature that we've seen folks use classifications for to good effect is to simplify reports by using consolidation.

This consolidation can take the form of combining a set of values into a single value. To continue with our previous examples, there might be several sizes of the 2019 skateboard, each with distinct SKUs. However, the distinctions between these traits might not be important to some analyses.

Figure 11-2 demonstrates the result of consolidating values through classification. A set of paid marketing channels has been consolidated into the paid classification, and a set of earned marketing channels has been consolidated into the earned classification.

Think of all the ways your company's products and services could be organized. For example, size, color, price range, or age could each act as a different classification.

Another example of classification consolidation could focus on a dimension that tracks the length of time it takes to load web pages. This hypothetical dimension might draw on values broken down by a tenth of a second. But that number might provide too much detail when analyzing the accessibility of a site. In this situation, you could use classifications to consolidate and bucket the values that measure page loading into a few different sets of classifications. You might organize the values into one-second intervals: one second; two seconds; three seconds, and so on (effectively rounding off to integers). Or you might bucket the values into classifications of one to two seconds, two to four seconds, four to six seconds, and so on.

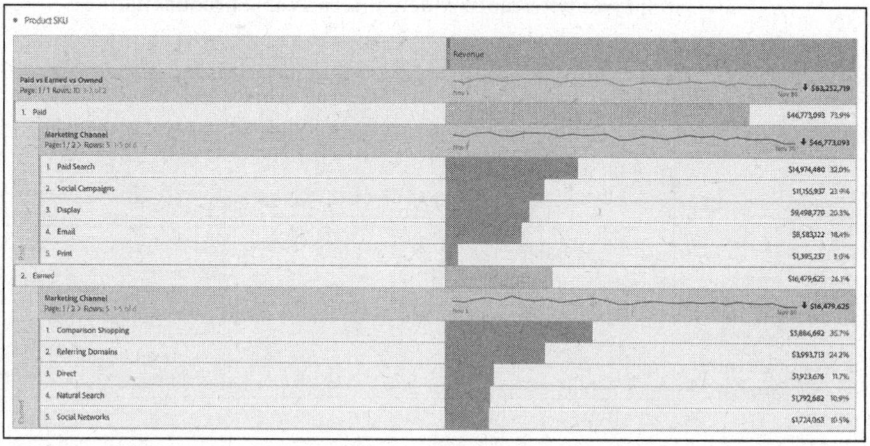

FIGURE 11-2:
Consolidated values with classification.

Consolidating retroactively

An applied classification is retroactive. If you've been collecting unfriendly data for six weeks and only just realized that you want to classify it to make it friendlier, you can make that change today! The classification will be applied to all data collected over the previous six weeks, so you can use these friendly new dimensions for historical data in addition to data collected in the future.

This feature has particular implications for when and how classifications are defined, something you explore in the last section of the chapter. Retroactive classification is also unique to Adobe Analytics; classifications in Google Analytics (commonly referred to as *dimension widening*) are not retroactive. In Google Analytics, you have to plan for how you want to classify your data and you can't update data that has already been processed.

Thinking outside product classifications

Adobe has made it possible to create classifications for almost all dimensions in Adobe Analytics. We mention some of them in Chapter 6 when we discuss marketing channels. That's right — those are the same classifications we discuss here! There are so many more use cases for classifications in Adobe Analytics that we couldn't possibly list them all. However, we can give you some ideas to get your creative juices flowing.

Besides product and marketing channel classifications, the most commonly classified dimension is page, generally because it's used so frequently — it's set on every page view and is essential to many analyses that you'll perform. However, because the data is so ubiquitous, the dimensional values often contain improper characters or misspellings. This unclean data occurs because Adobe Analytics implementations may have gone through a transition of ownership, or the strategy used to name the page might have changed, or perhaps different domains use a different strategy. Whatever the cause, we often see that the page dimension is most in need of cleanup and consolidation. The page dimension also aligns well with the need to bucket the values into similar groupings — based on page type or department, for example.

Finally, your custom dimensions — eVars and props — can also be classified, which means that any dimension that is critical (and perhaps unique) to your business can be classified for cleanliness, bucketing, and more — all retroactively! A great example is a media company that captures the byline, or author, of every article that is written on their site. That company would be able to use classifications to consolidate all authors by department (sports versus finance versus world news) or status (senior writers versus interns).

EVARS AND PROPS

Throughout this chapter (and elsewhere in this book), we reference eVars and props. We discuss them at length in Chapter 7, but if these terms are unfamiliar or confusing to you, you might want a short reminder of their definitions. Props and eVars allow your organization to report on custom dimensional data that standard out-of-the-box reports do not offer. *Props* are custom dimensions that always expire on the hit. Conversely, *eVars* are more flexible custom dimensions that can be set to persist beyond the hit by using features known as *allocation* — how metrics are distributed if multiple values are captured in an eVar — and *expiration* — the length of time an eVar's value should persist. For an in-depth exploration of the distinctions between eVars and props, how they are defined, and how they are used, see the last section of Chapter 7.

Applying classifications to breakdowns, metrics, and segments

Because classifications are applied to each individual dimensional value of the base dimension that is classified, they are extremely flexible. In essence, any time you' break down or segment data based on a specific dimension, the same data could be broken down or segmented by the classifications of that dimension.

For example, imagine that you're analyzing drop-off between skateboards that were added to the cart versus those that were purchased. You would start with your product dimension along with metrics associated with product views, cart additions, and orders.

Most likely, you would apply the techniques we explore in Chapter 10 to create a calculated metric of orders per cart addition. Your exploratory analysis would then bring you to an interesting segment of 25 different skateboard product SKUs, all accessed by paid search. But then you'd be stuck — you need to categorize the 25 SKUs based on size, color, model year, and more.

Thankfully, you have classifications set up for each of these traits. You can feel confident that every metric, calculated metric, breakdown, and segment that you previously created will also work with your classifications.

You get into some specific application of classified dimensions and metrics next, when you walk through how to work with classifications in freeform tables.

Working with Classified Data

We thought it was worth taking several pages to explore some of the ways in which you can use classifications. But we must emphasize that different administrators, working with different kinds of data, in different environments, filling different needs (that's a lot of "differents!") will apply classification — you guessed it — differently. No two Adobe Analytics environments will be the same. But what *is* the same is how Adobe Analytics presents classified dimensions.

Defining classifications in a report suite is the job of an Adobe Analytics administrator. As an analyst, you'll spend more time analyzing classified dimensions rather than creating them, unless you are also an administrator. Therefore, part of your job will be acclimating yourself to and familiarizing yourself with the particular set of classifications you have at your disposal. At the end of this chapter, you walk through how classifications are defined, but for most analysts, those classifications simply appear as available dimensions and metrics.

When classified dimensions are presented in the left rail, Adobe Analytics displays some hints that identify the source data behind the classified values. These hints help distinguish classified dimensions from standard unclassified dimensions as well as identify the base dimension that is classified. Next, you learn how to interpret these keys to dissect the data reflected in a classified value.

Identifying classified dimensions

Classified dimensions are so deeply integrated into your data that it's often hard to distinguish classifications from standard or custom dimensions. To the untrained eye, they're all dimensions. Thankfully, Adobe realized how important it is to know the dimension that a classification is based on, and that's the best way to identify a classified dimension.

You've probably noticed by now that Adobe includes useful information in the parentheses appended to components in the left rail. For example, if you search the left rail for *eVar1*, as shown in Figure 11-3, Adobe lists each of the dimensions associated with eVar1. Adobe also provides the actual eVar associated with each component in gray font in parentheses.

FIGURE 11-3: We are searching in the left rail for eVar1.

The additional context in gray parentheses is exactly how you can identify classifications from the left rail. Three types of values can appear: eVar numbers, prop numbers, and base dimensions for classifications. You see base dimensions for classifications when a dimensional classification is displayed.

Figure 11-4 is an example of a classified dimension called Company ID; evar97 in gray parentheses means that the component is a custom dimension — not a classification. Each of the other dimensions (Industry, Sub-Industry, Revenue Range, and so on) have the friendly name of the dimension listed in gray parentheses (Company ID). When a dimension has an item in gray parentheses that isn't an eVar or prop, it's a classification.

TIP

Try using this knowledge to your advantage to find some classifications in your report suite. In the left rail, filter to dimensions and then search for a closed parenthesis. Scroll through and see whether you can find any dimensions that have something other than an eVar or a prop listed in the gray parentheses.

Confirming: The best way to identify your classifications

Are you concerned that the left rail isn't the most comprehensive and substantial way to understand how classifications are defined? Well, you're right. Sometimes identifying classification properties from the left rail is sufficient, such as when you need to answer the question, "Is this component a classification?"

The more powerful way to understand your company's classifications is to work with your administrator. He or she will most likely have a solution design reference document that outlines every dimension that is classified and why.

However, this document might be out of date. Or, even worse, your classifications might be out of date! Keep reading to learn how classifications are defined, populated with data, and kept up to date. We also include some tips on recognizing classifications that are out of date.

Defining Classifications

Now that you've walked through how and why to use classifications, and how you, as an analyst, can identify classification components and their base dimensions, let's dig deeper and explore exactly how classifications are defined.

Our purpose in doing this is twofold:

» To enable analysts to better communicate with administrators to understand classification setup options and contribute to the process of defining new and improving current classifications

» To provide a step-by-step blueprint for those of you who have administrator access for creating classifications

Even analysts who do not have administrator access will likely find it worthwhile to read through and be aware of the process of defining classifications. Doing so will help open communication channels that can expedite the effective use of classifications.

Creating classifications is a two-step process:

1. Identify the base variables that you'd like to classify and name your classification variables.

2. Import data into the variables either in bulk or in a rules-based automation.

Next, you walk through each step in detail.

If you have administrator access to a report suite, you have access to view and edit existing classification definitions as well as create ones. If you don't have admin access, don't worry; the steps are simple enough to follow using our screenshots.

Adobe Analytics Admin Console is accessible by clicking Admin in the main navigation menu. The most commonly used resources in Admin Console is used to manage report suites, the link shown in Figure 11-5.

This section of Admin Console is where a lot of the magic that makes your report suite user-friendly happens: eVars and props are given names, marketing channels and rules are defined, and enough to fill an entire admin-focused book.

TIP

If you are looking to learn more about the Adobe Analytics Admin Console, you'll find detailed and frequently updated documentation at Adobe's knowledge base at `https://marketing.adobe.com/resources/help/en_US/reference/admin.html`.

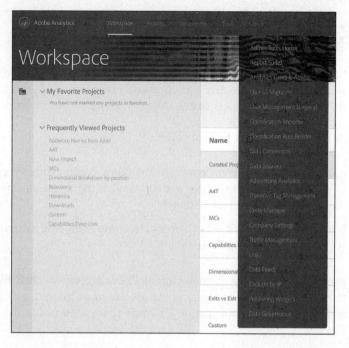

FIGURE 11-5:
An admin
prepares to click
report suites in
Admin Console.

As you now know, classifications can be built on top of most dimensions and Adobe has differentiated them into three areas of Admin Console:

» **Traffic classifications:** Used to create classifications based on the page, channel (aka site section), server, and prop variables.

» **Conversion classifications:** Used to enable classifications based on product, campaign (aka tracking code), ZIP code, and eVar variables. In addition, integration-focused variables such as TnT (for an integration with Adobe Target) are also categorized as conversion classifications.

» **Marketing channel classifications:** Used to classify the marketing channel dimensions, as described in Chapter 6.

For our example, we go through the process of creating a classification based on an eVar, but the process is identical for every other type of base variable. The difference is shown in Figure 11-6, where we choose to view the conversion classifications. Traffic classifications are listed in the traffic submenu whereas marketing channel classifications are listed under marketing channel. Each setting is available after selecting a report suite and then hovering your cursor over Edit Settings.

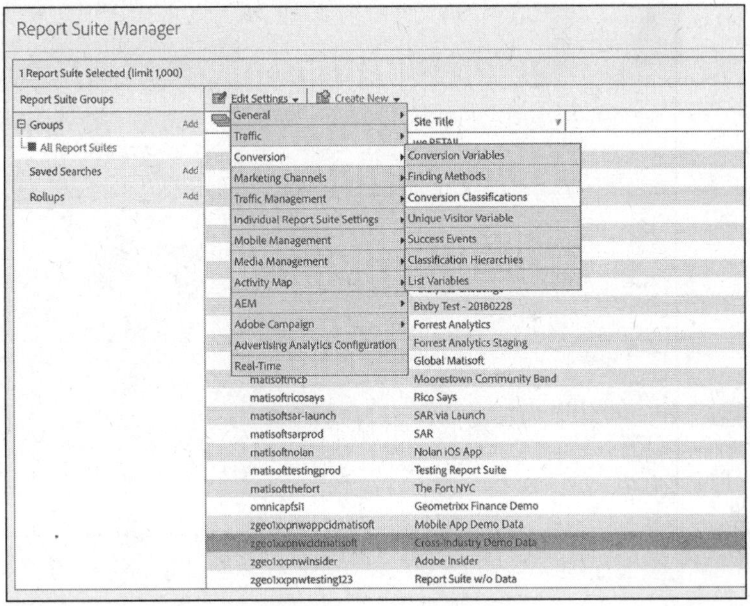

FIGURE 11-6:
Conversion classifications are selected after highlighting a report suite.

WARNING

Editing settings for report suites affects all users who have access to the report suite that you are making changes to. Work with your Adobe administrator if this is your first time accessing Admin Console.

The classification setup screen is now shown and the next step is to find the variable for which you want to create a new classification. The drop-down menu to the left under the Select Classification Type heading lists all the variables that set up in your report suite and available for classification.

Because most conversion classifications are applied to the product variable, we show the steps associated with adding a classification to it. Figure 11-7 shows how unfavorable the data in the product variable is in our report suite. How would anyone to know the difference between prd1019 and prd1016?

After you find the variable you need to classify, you will see a list of existing classifications. If there aren't any, as shown in Figure 11-8, hover your cursor over the arrow to the right of your variable and choose Add Classification.

The last step is to name your classification. We are fans of following our own best practices, so we've also provided a description for this new classification, product name, as shown in Figure 11-9.

Congrats — you have now created your first classification! In case you haven't actually created it, Figure 11-10 shows the experience.

FIGURE 11-7:
The product variable is collecting some very unfriendly SKUs.

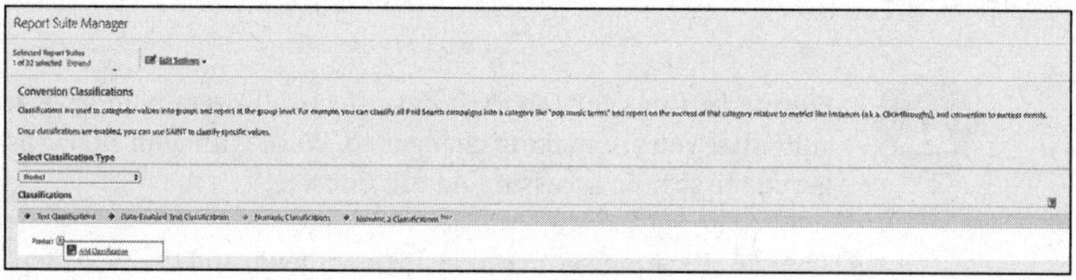

FIGURE 11-8:
The first classification to product is about to be added.

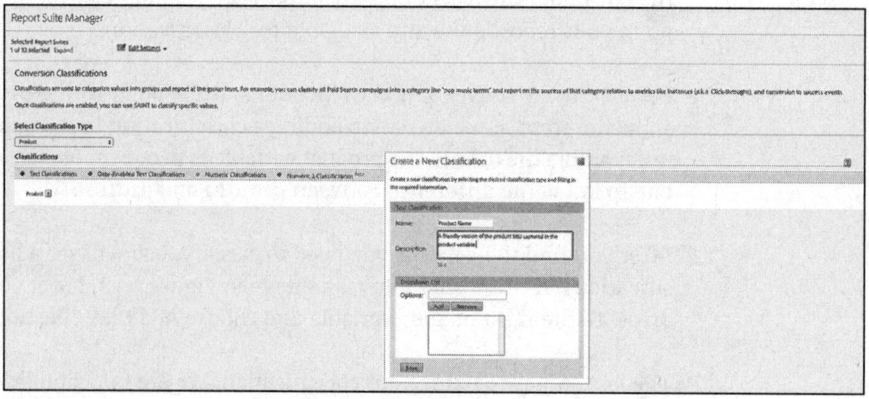

FIGURE 11-9:
A name and description are added to a new classification.

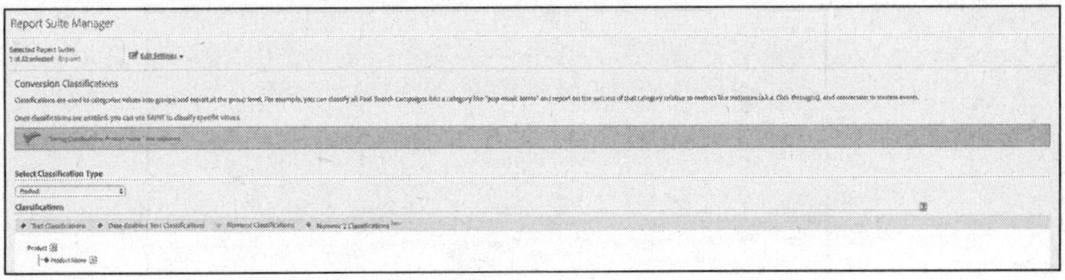

FIGURE 11-10:
A classification
was successfully
added to the
product variable.

Sending Data to a Classification

Now that you understand how classification variables are created, we need to discuss the ways in which data gets pushed into them. Data can be classified in two ways. Both methods are valuable and are not mutually exclusive. You walk through each option because a single variable's classification might be using them together!

Importing classification data in bulk

A bulk import of classification data is probably the easiest way to send data to Adobe Analytics to classify a variable. Remember all of those ugly product SKUs illustrated in a table in Figure 11-7? Someone at that company has a spreadsheet that ties each SKU with a friendlier product name. The goal of Classification Importer is to use a spreadsheet, commonly referred to as a *lookup table*, to connect the values of your base variable to the classification values that you prefer.

As of this writing, Classification Importer is finicky. The Adobe product team is actively working on an improved interface, but we walk through what's currently available:

1. **Open the importer by hovering your cursor over Admin in the main navigation menu and choosing Classification Importer.**

   The first steps in importing data in bulk are to see what data is available to classify and to check the values that have already been classified, if any.

2. **Click the Browser Export tab, and then select the desired report suite and variable, as shown in Figure 11-11.**

   Feel free to edit the default settings (they're self-explanatory); we've rarely found the need to do so.

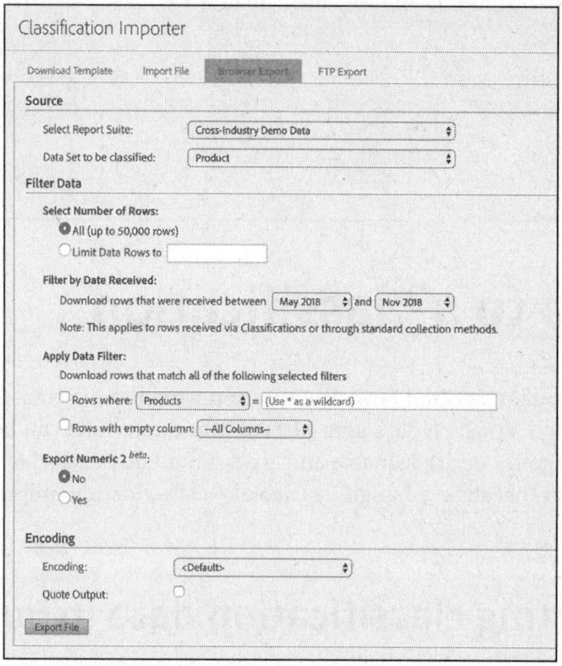

Classification Importer

Download Template   Import File   Browser Export   FTP Export

Source

Select Report Suite: Cross-Industry Demo Data

Data Set to be classified: Product

Filter Data

Select Number of Rows:
- ● All (up to 50,000 rows)
- ○ Limit Data Rows to [　　　　]

Filter by Date Received:
Download rows that were received between [May 2018 ▾] and [Nov 2018 ▾]

Note: This applies to rows received via Classifications or through standard collection methods.

Apply Data Filter:
Download rows that match all of the following selected filters
- ☐ Rows where: [Products ▾] = [(Use * as a wildcard)]
- ☐ Rows with empty column: [--All Columns-- ▾]

Export Numeric 2 *beta*:
- ● No
- ○ Yes

Encoding

Encoding: [<Default> ▾]

Quote Output: ☐

[Export File]

FIGURE 11-11:
Preparing a
classification
browser export.

3. **Click Export File, in the bottom left.**

   The browser export feature of Classification Importer provides you with a .TAB file. Don't let that weird file extension fool you — it opens fine as a spreadsheet in Microsoft Excel.

   The .TAB file contains a list of all the values in your base variable ready for classification. The .TAB file also acts as your template for additional import back into Adobe Analytics.

4. **Copy and paste (or manually enter) data into the .TAB file.**

   The data that you copy into the .TAB file should come from any source in your company that can explain the values in the base variable that you're classifying. This person might be you (hooray, if so!) or you might have to track down a friend in the company.

   WARNING

   Do not to adjust the first five rows of the .TAB file — Adobe Analytics uses them to ensure that the file is authentic. Figure 11-12 shows a section of a completed .TAB file, ready for import.

5. **Save the .TAB file in Excel, retaining the .TAB extension.**

   If Excel asks for a file type, Mac users may have to save the file as a tab-delimited text file. Now you're ready to import the spreadsheet into your report suite. Files can be imported directly in the browser or by FTP. Using FTP is valuable, but because it's an admin function we focus on the browser import.

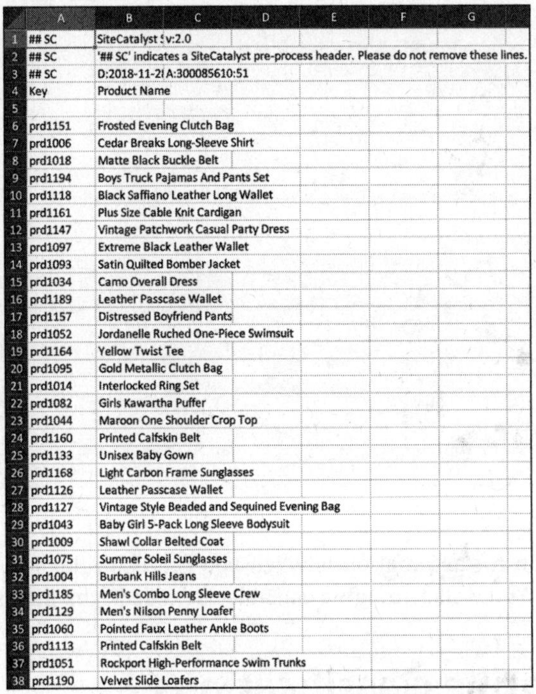

FIGURE 11-12:
The classification file is ready to be imported.

	A	B	C	D	E	F	G
1	## SC	SiteCatalyst : v:2.0					
2	## SC	'## SC' indicates a SiteCatalyst pre-process header. Please do not remove these lines.					
3	## SC	D:2018-11-2(A:300085610:51					
4	Key	Product Name					
5							
6	prd1151	Frosted Evening Clutch Bag					
7	prd1006	Cedar Breaks Long-Sleeve Shirt					
8	prd1018	Matte Black Buckle Belt					
9	prd1194	Boys Truck Pajamas And Pants Set					
10	prd1118	Black Saffiano Leather Long Wallet					
11	prd1161	Plus Size Cable Knit Cardigan					
12	prd1147	Vintage Patchwork Casual Party Dress					
13	prd1097	Extreme Black Leather Wallet					
14	prd1093	Satin Quilted Bomber Jacket					
15	prd1034	Camo Overall Dress					
16	prd1189	Leather Passcase Wallet					
17	prd1157	Distressed Boyfriend Pants					
18	prd1052	Jordanelle Ruched One-Piece Swimsuit					
19	prd1164	Yellow Twist Tee					
20	prd1095	Gold Metallic Clutch Bag					
21	prd1014	Interlocked Ring Set					
22	prd1082	Girls Kawartha Puffer					
23	prd1044	Maroon One Shoulder Crop Top					
24	prd1160	Printed Calfskin Belt					
25	prd1133	Unisex Baby Gown					
26	prd1168	Light Carbon Frame Sunglasses					
27	prd1126	Leather Passcase Wallet					
28	prd1127	Vintage Style Beaded and Sequined Evening Bag					
29	prd1043	Baby Girl 5-Pack Long Sleeve Bodysuit					
30	prd1009	Shawl Collar Belted Coat					
31	prd1075	Summer Soleil Sunglasses					
32	prd1004	Burbank Hills Jeans					
33	prd1185	Men's Combo Long Sleeve Crew					
34	prd1129	Men's Nilson Penny Loafer					
35	prd1060	Pointed Faux Leather Ankle Boots					
36	prd1113	Printed Calfskin Belt					
37	prd1051	Rockport High-Performance Swim Trunks					
38	prd1190	Velvet Slide Loafers					

6. **Click the Import File tab in Classification Importer.**

7. **Select your report suite and variable as the destination.**

8. **Click "Choose File" and then browse to and select your .TAB file.**

9. **Click Import File to begin the data import.**

It takes between a few minutes to 24 hours for your data to propagate to your report suite, depending on the size of your classification file and the amount of data in your report suite. Adobe is in the process of speeding up this data propagation, but at the time of this writing we didn't have a confirmed release date.

After data propagation has occurred, you'll have a new dimension populated with classification data based on your import. Figure 11-13 shows how data has changed in the classified dimension, along with some breakdowns to illustrate how the classification data is fully integrated.

Now that wasn't too hard, was it? Imagine if your company has thousands of constantly changing product SKUs. Just keeping the classifications current would be a full-time job. In a situation like this, the FTP option is valuable. Administrators can work with IT to define a weekly process in which a classification import happens automatically.

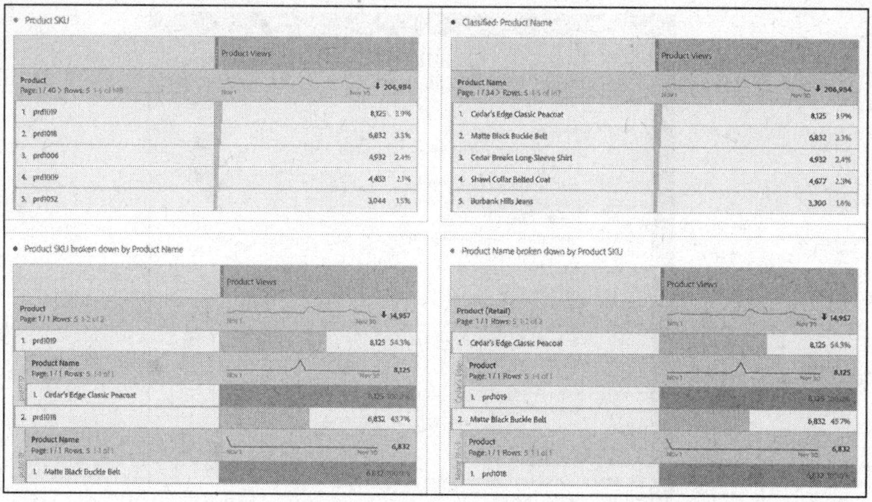

FIGURE 11-13: Classification data is shown and broken down.

Another reason for automation is when you can use rule-based logic to clean a base variable. You walk through a valuable use case in the next section.

Automating classifications with Rule Builder

We bet that the most used base variable for classifications after the product variable is page. The page dimension has a wealth of useful information about the pages contained in it. Often, a lot of thought goes into the page-naming strategy, but sometimes it is too granular. Upleveling and bucketing pages into page types can make it easier to find what you're looking for. Classifications to the rescue!

The bulk Classification Importer does not work well when your use case for a classification is to classify rapidly changing data. The bulk import is applied to pages that exist today, but what about the new pages, site sections, and microsites published tomorrow? Every time new content is created, you have to manually update and import the classification — not ideal! Instead, you need to build some logical rules that inspect the content in each dimensional value and then dynamically apply a classification.

Classification Rule Builder is the perfect tool when classifications can be automated based on the underlying data. The builder uses logical operators such as starts with, ends with, and contains to help you inspect the base variable's value and easily apply it to a grouping. For example, if you have a page named *purchase: step 1*, you might want to classify it as *cart flow*. You would simply create a rule in Classification Rule Builder that looks for a value that starts with *purchase*.

Adobe also handles the need for more complex logical operators through regular expressions. *Regular expressions* are a pattern-searching algorithm that provides advanced administrators more control over the rules they define in Classification Rule Builder. For example, an admin for a company with 30 registration steps might want to dynamically capture into a classification the step number in the *registration: step 1* page name. Rather than set up 30 rules, the admin can use regular expressions to extract the step number.

If you're not familiar with regular expressions, don't worry — they are advanced and not necessary to understanding Classification Rule Builder. If you're interested in learning more about regular expressions, check out the tutorial at `www.regular-expressions.info/`.

To keep things simple, let's highlight the key steps to creating a classification using Rule Builder — without regular expressions.

The data in our page variable has plenty of opportunity for bucketing via classification. Figure 11-14 shows how we can easily combine the category, purchase, and mobile web pages into their own groupings so our data is more generic.

FIGURE 11-14: Some values of the page dimension that are ready for classification rules.

The steps to using Classification Rule Builder may seem more complex than using Importer, but we love not having to concern ourselves with recurring manual imports. Here are the steps to deploy your first set of rules in Rule Builder:

1. **Access Classification Rule Builder by hovering your cursor over Admin in the main navigation menu and choosing Classification Rule Builder.**

2. **Click Add Rule Set, and then click your newly created rule set to see a blank set of rules.**

   A *rule set* is a container for a set of rules that are applied to one or more variables (in one or more report suites). A rule set lets you apply the same rules to several variables or several report suites.

   Figure 11-15 displays a rule set named page grouping. You need to teach Adobe what variable(s) you're planning to classify.

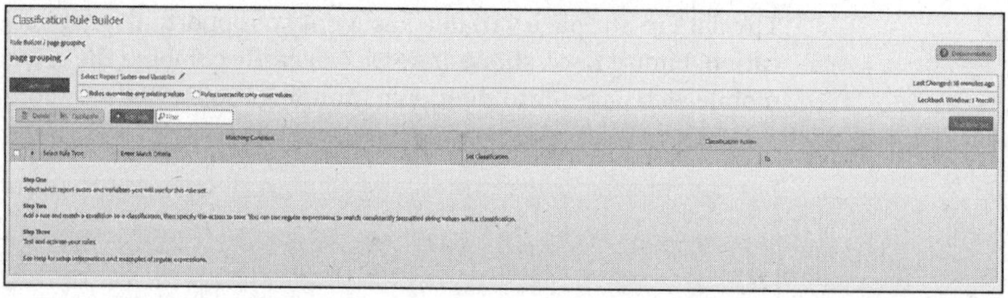

FIGURE 11-15:
A new rule set named page grouping.

3. **Click the Select Report Suites and Variables link to display the dialog box shown in Figure 11-16.**

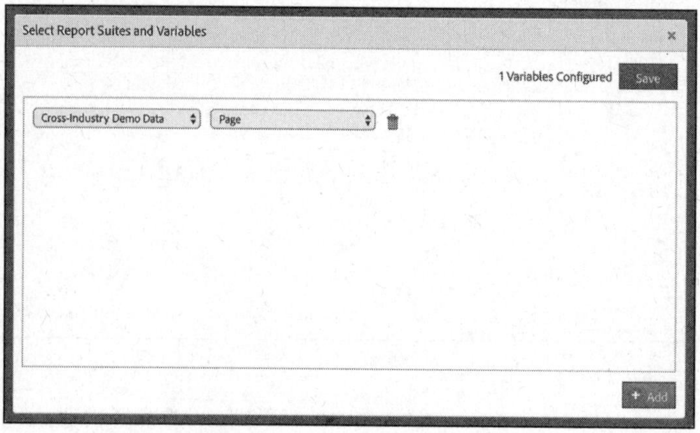

FIGURE 11-16:
A variable is included in the Variable Selection dialog box.

4. **Select as many variables as necessary, clicking the Add button in the bottom-right after each selection. Then click Save.**

   Note that you can select variables in different report suites. We selected the page dimension in our Cross-Industry Demo Data report suite.

   Next comes the fun part — defining the rules!

5. **Create your rules.**

   a. *Click the gray Add Rule button.* A blank rule appears and a drop-down under the Select Rule Type column opens.

   b. *Under Select Rule Type, select the logical operators to use.* We chose Starts With, as shown in Figure 11-17.

   c. *In the second column, type your matching criteria.* The *matching criteria* is the search term that Adobe uses to identify whether or not the rule is true. Figure 11-17 shows a rule that will bucket each page in the cart flow, so we use a rule that looks for pages that start with *purchase:*.

   d. *In the third column, use the drop-down to choose the classification you want to set.* We selected a classification called page grouping, as shown in Figure 11-17. You must choose the classification you're setting because you may have added multiple classifications to your rule set in Step 4.

   e. *In the last column, titled To, type the value you want to save in the classification.* Figure 11-17 shows how the Page Grouping classification will receive the value of *cart flow* any time the page variable starts with the text *purchase:*.

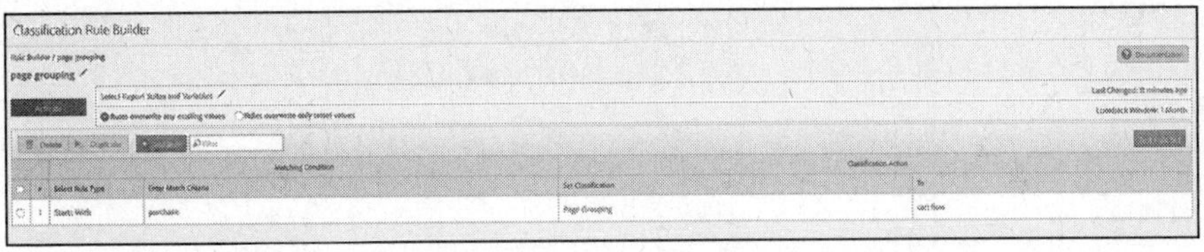

FIGURE 11-17: A rule classifies pages that start with *purchase:*.

6. **Repeat Step 5 to create as many rules as necessary.**

   In Figure 11-18, we created several more rules to create more buckets for our pages.

We highly recommend that you test your rules before activating them. Follow these steps:

1. **Click the Test Rule Set link in the top-right.**

   The Classification Rule Builder Test screen appears.

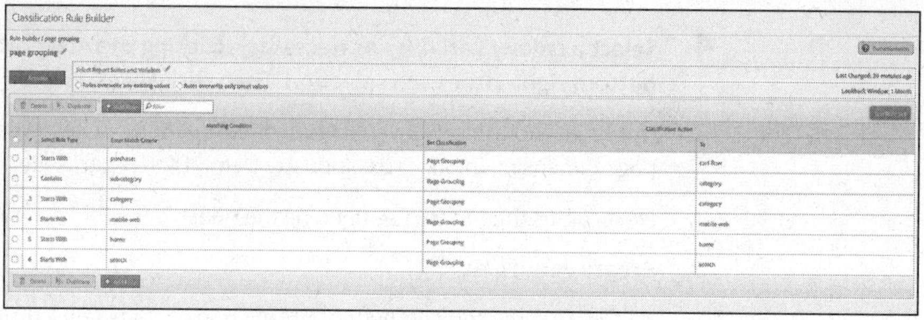

FIGURE 11-18:
A more complete rule set with six rules.

2. **In the text field on the left, add some the sample dimensional values.**

   You can type these samples, but we prefer to copy and paste them from a freeform table in Workspace with the base variable as the dimension.

3. **Click the Run Test button.**

   Any dimensional values that are not matched appear as ** *Unmatched* ** in the table results, as shown in Figure 11-19.

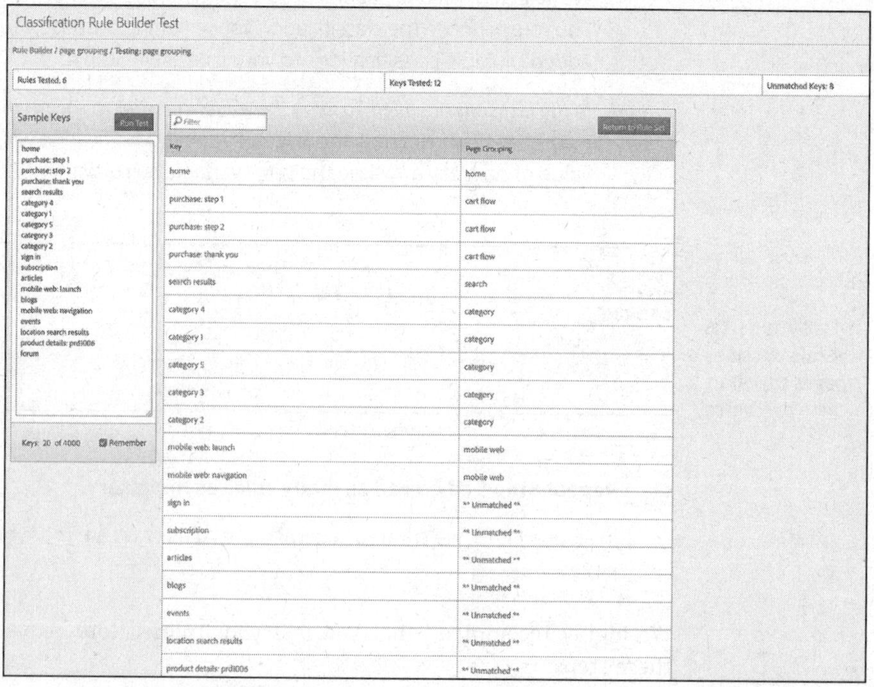

FIGURE 11-19:
Some values aren't handled in the classification rules.

4. **If your results contain unmatched values, some rules are missing in your rule set. Click Return to Rule Set to add them.**

To fix one of the unmatched items in Figure 11-19, we added a rule that deals with pages that start with product details and tested our rule set a second time.

REMEMBER

5. **Keep testing your sample values until all your results have a match.**

A proper rule set never returns an unmatched item.

You can see in Figure 11-20 that the rule set test with the addition of these two rules doesn't contain any unmatched items. Isn't that pretty?

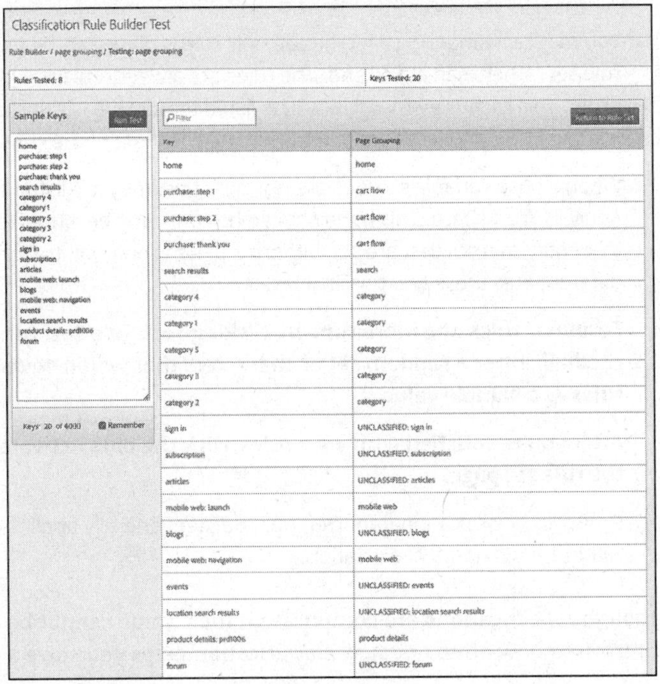

FIGURE 11-20:
All variables are matched in the rules in the rule set.

6. **As a best practice, always set the first rule of every rule set to match the rule displayed in Figure 11-21:**

   a. *Set the Select Rule Type drop-down to Regular Expression.*

   b. *Enter Match Criteria of .* (a period and asterisk) as the regular expression.*

   c. *In the Set Classification column, choose your classification.*

   d. *In the last column, set UNCLASSIFIED: $0 as the value.*

   The rule uses a regular expression to automatically copy the dimensional value into the classification with a prefix of UNCLASSIFIED:. This rule acts as a catchall, making it easy, as an analyst, to discover opportunities to improve your classifications.

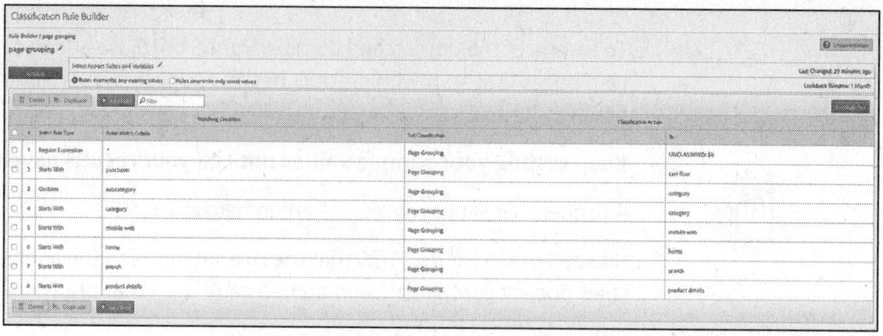

FIGURE 11-21:
Setting the first
rule of every rule
to use a regular
expression.

You may be wondering why the catch-all rule is placed at the beginning of the rule set rather than at the end. The rules are always run, for every value, in order. This means every value will be listed temporarily as unclassified. A value will get a friendly classification only if it matches one of the subsequent rules.

TIP

When a base variable's values are not classified, they are listed as None in Analysis Workspace. This behavior can be confusing because None is used also to identify metrics that are set without a dimensional value. Our catchall rule differentiates these two possibilities.

7. **Test your rules one more time by clicking Test Rule Set. To test your catchall, enter a random set of characters that would never meet your rules as a sample value.**

8. **After you're satisfied with your rules, click the blue Activate button on the rule set page.**

Similar to Classification Importer, Rule Builder generally applies rules to data within 1 to 24 hours of activation.

Although classifications are complicated, their value cannot be overstated. You'll be surprised how often one new classification helps you solve a data problem.

Chapter **12**

Applying Attribution Models for Sophisticated Analysis

L ife is complicated. Why are we bringing up this truism now? Because it has applicability in data analysis, and in particular, because the mix of user interactions that lead to a success event (such as a purchase or a sign up) is often the result of a complex set of factors — especially in today's multimedia world.

Attribution modeling with analytics tools helps identify and paint a picture of the set of factors that lead to a success event, and their relationship to each other.

And a careful approach to attribution helps analysts avoid conscious or unconscious biases built into how we look at data; attribution models can help uncover and dispel those biases.

In this chapter, you discover how you can enhance your ability to analyze the data in your report suites by taking advantage of the power of Attribution IQ — Adobe's expansive set of features that bring attribution to your fingertips.

First, you dig more deeply into what attribution is and why it's necessary. Then you uncover the definitions of the models that Adobe makes accessible. After you are armed with these basics, we provide a walkthrough of the Attribution IQ features. Get ready, get set, go!

Applying Attribution to Your Data

We now live in a world full of big data and constant commercials for AI technologies, and where data scientist is ranked by the Harvard Business Review as the sexiest job of the 21st century — we're not kidding about that last one. Look it up!

The inherent problem for analysts is that it's too easy to assume that our analyses are correct simply because we have so much data. A proper analysis is so much more than just having a bunch of data and applying a metric to a dimension. Your ability to use the data correctly is just as important as your ability to understand the definitions of the components that you're using.

This data comprehension is imperative in attribution. We begin our discussion of attribution in Chapter 6, where we describe the marketing channel dimensions and walk through a simple example of a visitor with two visits driven from two different marketing channels. In that scenario, analysts then have to decide which of those two marketing channels should receive credit for driving a conversion.

Sometimes that level of (non)complexity is sufficient to answer a particular question, such as who is ordering more overnight produce, iOS users or Android users? Other times, more nuance and complexity is required. Attribution helps explain which dimensional value(s), over time, should apply to corresponding metrics. This additional nuance and complexity in evaluating attribution for success events is especially necessary when analyzing marketing channels. Remember the famous quote by John Wanamaker: "Half the money I spend on advertising is wasted; the trouble is, I don't know which half." We can appreciate the irony and humor in that quote, but in today's world of complex, intersecting, and overlapping marketing channels, simply answering "which half" isn't always enough.

The need to accurately identify attribution for success events is the reason analysts spend so much time focused on dimensions such as marketing channel. The greater our ability to analyze advertising success in all its complexity, the more useful we become to our company.

Consider this journey a consumer might have to ordering a new product:

>> Avoiding getting out of bed on a Monday morning, our consumer browses Instagram and sees an ad for a stylish watch.

>> She clicks through, and the watch looks interesting. But she decides it's too early in the day to be spending money, so she closes the page.

>> Our consumer thinks about the watch all morning but can't remember the brand name. One Bing search later, and she finds a paid search ad to click through that leads to the watch.

>> After viewing the landing page, she watches a video to learn about the watch mechanics, and then clicks to the product page, which she bookmarks.

>> The next day she clicks the bookmark, views a few other products that the company sells, but doesn't make the purchase.

>> On Wednesday, she clicks the bookmark again, adds the watch to the cart, registers an account with the company, and then gets distracted because a neighbor improperly quoted something from the user's favorite TV show, *Rick & Morty*.

>> On Thursday, she receives a reminder email from the company that she left something in the cart. She clicks the email to complete the purchase online.

Rather than discuss how easily distracted this consumer is, let's organize this activity into five visits — listed in Table 12-1 — to consider how attribution can be applied to sort out which marketing channels deserve credit for the revenue from this purchase.

TABLE 12-1 **A Multi-Visit Example with Several Marketing Channels and Actions**

Day Of Week	Visit Number	Marketing Channel	Action
Monday	1	Social ad click (Instagram)	1 page view, then bounce
Monday	2	Paid search (Bing)	2 page views, 1 video view
Tuesday	3	Typed/bookmarked (direct)	8 page views, 5 product views
Wednesday	4	Typed/bookmarked (direct)	1 product view, 1 add to cart, 1 account registration
Thursday	5	Email	1 purchase, $50 revenue

Table 12-1 distills the most relevant pieces of the example consumer journey. Many questions should instantly come to mind. Most importantly:

>> Which marketing channels deserve credit for the purchase, and how much?

>> If our advertising budget suddenly increases, should it go to paid social or paid search?

Advertisers ask these two questions every day, and the answer is never simple for anyone. The answer is difficult for the local car dealer advertising on local news and just as difficult for Samsung, recently crowned the world's spendiest advertiser.

The analyst tool that helps answer these questions is attribution. We use *attribution* to link revenue and micro-conversions — non-purchase-related success metrics such as video views and account registrations — back to the marketing channels that we believe most helped to drive the consumer's actions.

Differentiating Attribution Models

Knowing that attribution is the answer is the easy part. Figuring out what model to use when attributing conversions back to dimensional values is hard. Attribution models might sound complicated — and they can be — but the concept isn't. If the goal of attribution is to link conversion to a dimension, an *attribution model* defines the rules of the links. Let's consider an example.

Applying last touch and first touch models

You can apply several different models of attribution to the data in Table 12-1 if you're trying to attribute the $50 of revenue to a marketing channel. The simplest attribution model to define is the *last touch attribution model*. The concept is simple — the dimensional value that was most recently set gets full credit. Last touch attribution would state that email drove $50 worth of revenue. Although this model is simple, it is heavily biased and ignores a potentially massive number of dimensional values.

For these reasons, companies try to avoid relying only on a last touch model to make advertising budget decisions. If the company in Table 12-1 were budgeting their ad dollars using a last touch attribution model, all of their budget would go to improving their email campaigns. Doing so would ignore the success that paid social had in driving awareness and how paid search reinforced the brand.

The inverse of last touch attribution is first touch attribution. As you may have guessed, the *first touch attribution model* applies full credit of the metric to the dimensional value that was first collected. In our watch purchase example, all $50 would be credited to the paid social ad on Instagram. As you now know, much more resulted in the purchase of that watch, and it would be unfair to the paid search and email teams to donate all ad budget to social because the first touch attribution model says so.

Interestingly, there are plenty of times where last touch attribution and first touch attribution are useful. Attribution can apply to any metric and any dimension — not just purchases and marketing channels. A good example of this would be asking a different question about the data in Table 12-1: What marketing channel drove the video view? Last touch attribution probably makes the most sense for this question because the video that was viewed exists on the campaign landing page. If the consumer hadn't clicked the paid search ad, the video wouldn't have been accessible or watched. Using first touch attribution would be undesirable.

A related question might be: What page should get credit for the video view? This is probably when you're going to hastily reply, "You just told me the video exists on the campaign landing page." That's true, but a page was viewed earlier in the day on Monday. Does that page also deserve some credit for that video view? The answer is an almost definite no. The video was viewed on the campaign landing page, so that page deserves the credit. Therefore we are asking to use a last touch attribution model without even thinking about it. This is the reason Adobe defaults to a last touch attribution model for almost all dimensions in Analysis Workspace; it's often the most intuitive.

CONSIDERING LOOKBACK WINDOWS

An additional consideration when applying attribution models is time. Because you're dealing with changing dimensional values that eventually result in a conversion, you need to think about how much history you want to include in your analysis.

If a consumer clicked a paid social ad a week before clicking a paid search ad that resulted in a purchase, should we include the paid social ad click when attributing the revenue from that order? If so, the reporting window needs to be at least 7 days. What if the paid social click had occurred a month prior to the paid search ad? For it to be included in your attribution-based analysis, your reporting window would have to be at least a month.

Adobe provides two options for lookback windows, but it's important to understand the concept as you get further into the attribution model options at your fingertips.

Considering linear and participation models

The next attribution models to consider using are similar: linear and participation. These attribution models aim to fix the biggest shortcoming of first and last touch models: All dimensional values are considered as helping drive the end result.

A *linear attribution model* takes the metric and divides it evenly among all the touchpoints of the dimension. In the watch purchase example, the $50 would be divided evenly between paid social, paid search, direct, direct, and email. No, the two instances of *direct* are not a typo. Direct drove visits on both Tuesday and Wednesday, so it gets two portions of the $50. The second column in Table 12-2 shows how revenue would be divvied among channels using a linear attribution model.

TABLE 12-2   **Data Using Linear and Participation Models**

Marketing Channel	Revenue (Linear)	Revenue (Participation)
Paid social	$10	$50
Paid search	$10	$50
Direct	$20	$50
Email	$10	$50

Instead of dividing the metric evenly among all touchpoints like a linear model, the *participation attribution model* gives *full credit* to all dimensional values. Each channel that drove a visit in our watch purchase example would receive $50. Participation in Adobe is unique from linear because values are deduplicated. This means that when a dimensional value is seen more than once, the participation model gives it credit only once — a specific value can't have more than 100 percent credit. Even though direct drove two visits in our watch example, the third column in Table 12-2 shows how it would receive $50.

WARNING

If you were to sum all of the numbers attributed based on a participation model, they would be significantly higher than the actual total. It is clear how the total of the linear column in Table 12-2 would accurately sum up to $50, whereas the participation column sums to $200! Be careful to avoid summing participation metrics.

You can probably instantly tell the advantage of these models compared to first and last touch. So much more of the story is told and so much less of the story is ignored. Paid search and direct are finally receiving some credit! Our next models consider whether paid search and direct are perhaps receiving too much credit from the linear and participation models.

Exploring U-shaped, J-shaped, and inverse J models

It's time to start advancing your understanding of attribution models into more advanced options: U-shaped, J-shaped, and inverse J. Each of these models is available in Adobe Analytics as long as you have a current or recent SKU of the product. To access them as of this writing, you have to be on Select, Prime, Ultimate, or Premium Complete SKUs of Adobe Analytics. Let's apply U-shaped, J-shaped, and inverse J models to the data in Table 12-2.

All of these models aim to continue the goals of linear and participation models — grant credit for the conversion to all involved channels — but to also prioritize the first and last touch channels more than those in the middle. We like to think of them as a mix between first touch, last touch, and linear models. Combining these models requires a little bit of math, but don't worry, you won't need your calculator!

>> **U-shaped starts by prioritizing both the first and last touches** — each receives 40 percent of the credit for the conversion. The remaining 20 percent is spread across all values in the middle, which are often referred to as *assisting interactions.*

>> **When it comes to the assisting interactions in a J-shaped model, the math is the same; 20 percent of credit is divided between all values in the middle. The remaining 80 percent is what makes the J-shaped model interesting.** Instead of evenly splitting it 40/40 between first and last touch, J-shaped prioritizes last touch by giving it 60 percent and saving the remaining 20 percent of credit for first touch. As you would expect, the result is a higher weight of credit towards last touch compared to anything else.

>> **If you take the math of J-shaped models and flip it, you know the math for inverse J:** 60 percent for first touch, 20 percent for last touch, and 20 percent for the assisting interactions in the middle. Inverse J puts more credit on the first touch.

Spend a minute and analyze the data in Table 12-3 to see how these three models are similar and different. We're again working with the watch example data from Table 12-1.

TABLE 12-3   Data Using U-Shaped and J-Shaped Models

Marketing Channel	Revenue (U-Shaped)	Revenue (J-Shaped)	Revenue (Inverse J)
Paid social	$20	$10	$30
Paid search	$3.33	$3.33	$3.33
Direct	$6.66	$6.66	$6.66
Email	$20	$30	$10

By definition, each of these models assumes that credit needs to be divided between at least three interactions: first, last, and assist. However, they all have some bylaws about how they handle just one or two interactions. All three give 100 percent credit if there is only one interaction. If there are two interactions, U-shaped gives 50 percent of credit to both. J-shaped gives 75 percent of credit to the last touch and 25 percent to the first touch. Inverse J reverses this with 25 percent to the last touch and 75 percent to the first touch.

The definition for all three of these models is easy to remember because the letters they are based on describe how touchpoints are prioritized:

>> **The letter U has a spike at the beginning and end**, therefore first and last touch are equally prioritized.

>> **The letter J has a spike at the end with a smaller point at the beginning**, therefore last touch is prioritized and first touch gets a little priority.

>> **Inverse J simply reverses that** by prioritizing first touch with last touch getting some extra credit — perhaps a better name would have been L-shaped!

The most important thing to note is how all three equally rank the assisting interactions in the middle. The values for paid search and direct in Table 12-3 are identical for all three models.

Using custom and time decay models

Now that you are comfortable with some of Adobe's more advanced attribution models it's time to customize! As analysts, we're naturally curious beings. That curiosity means we're never quite comfortable with decisions being made for us and, at times, we like to break the mold.

Adobe gives us the ability to do draw outside the lines and create a custom attribution model by using a concept called *starter-player-closer*. This concept is one we've already reviewed without giving it a name: defining the percentage of credit for first touch (starter), assisting interactions (player), and then last touch (closer). For example, U-shaped models give 40 percent credit to the starter and closer, and then 20 percent to the player(s).

In Adobe's custom model, you can manually define all three of these options based on your needs. We provide details on how to accomplish this later in the chapter.

The *time decay model* is perhaps the most complex model Adobe provides in Analysis Workspace today. Even the term *time decay* may cause you to shiver while you reminisce about high school biology class. Fear not, this is analytics, not biology — so we'll simplify things to make sure everything is clear and you aren't having nightmares about the periodic table again.

If science is your thing, you'll enjoy this explanation: The time decay model follows an exponential decay with a custom half-life parameter. Yikes! That already put us in a cold sweat. We prefer this explanation: The weight of each channel depends on the amount of time that passed between the touchpoint and the eventual conversion. In essence, the closer the interaction occurred to the conversion, the higher percentage of the credit the interaction receives. This model is most valuable for teams that run promotional campaigns for a predetermined number of days. These campaigns are often analyzed to emphasize channels that were interacted with most recently because the campaigns have a limited time to convince a prospect to become a customer. The only decision that you have is the half-life parameter. A good rule of thumb is to use your predetermined campaign length as the half-life parameter.

Defining best fit, algorithmic, and data-driven attribution

The last attribution model to discuss is one that has limited customers and a high amount of complexity, so we'll keep it short.

In Adobe Analytics, the model is called *best fit attribution.* In Google Analytics, it's called *data-driven attribution.* The concept is the same: a machine learning model is used to assign attribution values. Because machine learning employs algorithms, this model is often termed *algorithmic.* Every attribution vendor, Adobe included, touts their super-powered algorithms that proactively learn and deliver better results than any rules-based model could.

At the time of this writing, Adobe's algorithmic attribution model is accessible only in the Data Workbench product and it is not yet available in Analysis Workspace.

Operating Attribution IQ in Workspace

Now that you're an expert on a wealth of attribution models, it's time to apply those models to your data in Adobe Analytics using Adobe's attribution feature set called Attribution IQ. The three features of Workspace that have Attribution IQ influence are

>> Freeform tables

>> Calculated metrics

>> Attribution panel

Attribution IQ is especially powerful because it isn't focused on just advertising dimensions such as marketing channel or referrer. Instead, Adobe makes attribution modeling available to almost every dimension and metric in Analysis Workspace. Last touch attribution is Adobe's default for metrics based on any dimension. But you can modify that.

WARNING

A few metrics and dimensions are not accessible to Attribution IQ. Metrics such as unique visitors, visits, occurrences, and page views do not comply with Attribution IQ. For a complete list, head to Adobe's Attribution IQ FAQ in the knowledge base: `https://marketing.adobe.com/resources/help/en_US/analytics/analysis-workspace/attribution_faq.html`.

Before we walk through attribution models and their features, we have to mention that some of the models are SKU-dependent. You'll want to contact an administrator at your company to confirm which features you have access to. Access to Attribution IQ (and all features) is listed in Admin Console. Work with an admin to hover your cursor over Admin and then select Company Settings. From there, you'll see a link to View Feature Access Levels. Four features are tied to Attribution IQ, the three features listed above as well as the list of models that you have access to, as shown in Figure 12-1.

Applying Attribution IQ in freeform tables

To familiarize you with attribution, we start in an already familiar place: freeform tables. These are the most used visualizations in Workspace, so it's a good place to first use Attribution IQ. Adobe has incorporated freeform table attribution features in two subtly different methods — *modifying* and *comparing* a metric's attribution method. We provide a walkthrough of the attribution model comparison feature and identify how the experience is slightly different when you modify the attribution model instead.

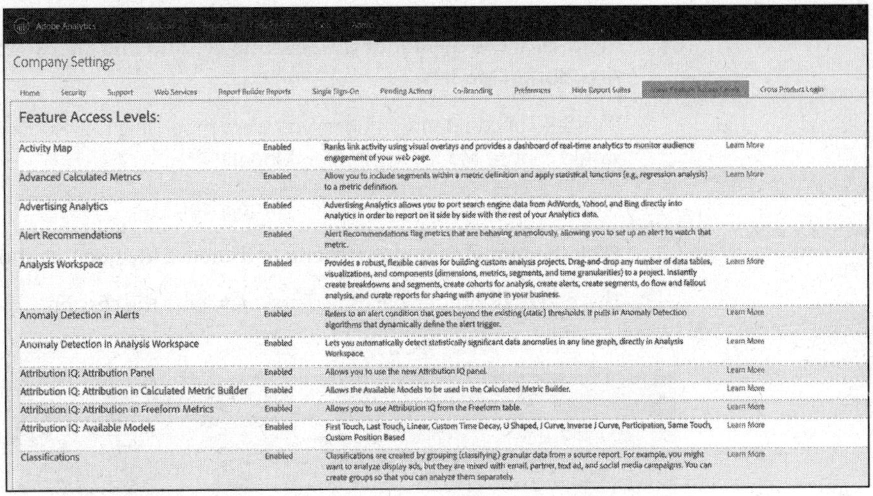

FIGURE 12-1:
A company has access to all features of Attribution IQ.

In the example, you use attribution to try to identify key pages on the website that are driving revenue:

1. **Open a new project in Analysis Workspace and add the page dimension. Add a second metric that isn't a calculated metric, such as revenue. Sort by revenue.**

   If your site has revenue, you'll see a table similar to the one in Figure 12-2, where all revenue is attributed to just a few order confirmation pages. Adobe uses a default attribution model of last touch, so you're seeing the most recent page where revenue was collected.

FIGURE 12-2:
A freeform table is shown with revenue attributed to just three pages.

2. **Right-click the header of the revenue column and choose to Compare Attribution Models.**

    If instead of comparing models you were modifying the model of revenue, you would choose Modify Attribution Model.

    A dialog appears with options for comparison.

3. **Click the Model drop-down menu and choose Inverse J, as shown in Figure 12-3.**

    This choice prioritizes pages accessed earlier in the session.

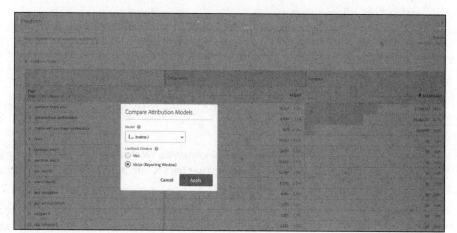

FIGURE 12-3:
The Model menu
with Inverse J
selected.

4. **Keep the Lookback Window option selected with the default, Visitor (Reporting Window), and then click Apply.**

REMEMBER

Because attribution handles changing dimensional values over time, you need to decide how much history you want to include in our analysis. A *lookback window* is the amount of historical data to include.

Adobe provides two options for lookback windows: visit and visitor (reporting window). In a visit lookback window , only one visit's worth of data is included. If you're analyzing how a dimension changes across multiple visits, select the visitor lookback window. The reason why reporting window is listed next to visitor is because Adobe isn't attributing your metrics to the full history of your visitors. Instead, only the data in the calendar timeframe, or reporting window, of your freeform table is included. Pages viewed before the start date set in the calendar are not included.

Your freeform table now has two new columns: Revenue (Inverse J | Visitor) and Percent Change (Revenue, Revenue).

If instead of comparing models you had chosen to modify your attribution model, you wouldn't have any new columns. Your revenue column would simply have changed to the inverse J model.

You can now easily identify the pages that helped drive that eventual purchase with a helpful Percent Change column that displays values with conditional formatting to more easily find outliers, as shown in Figure 12-4.

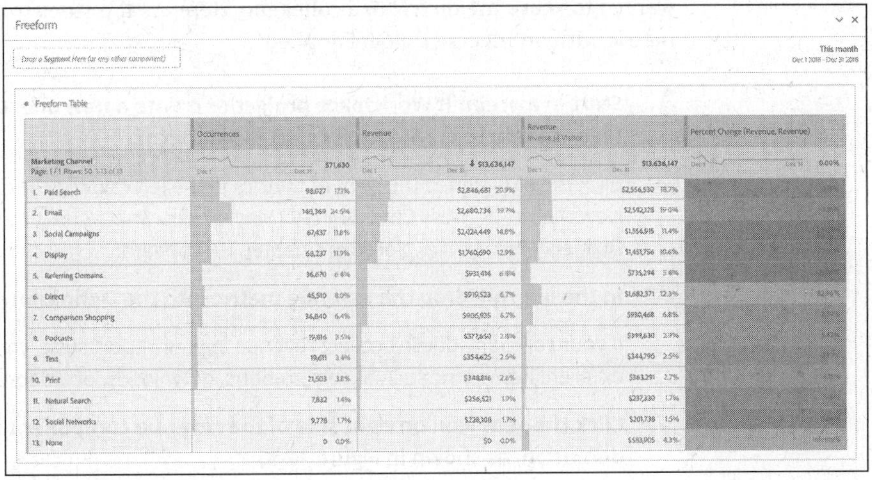

FIGURE 12-4:
The same metrics are applied to the marketing channel dimension.

5. **Change your dimension to marketing channel.**

   Because the attribution models are applied to the metrics, you can easily replace the page dimension with any other dimension.

The steps to taking advantage of Attribution IQ in a freeform table are simple and intuitive. We've found that the more comfortable you are with using these features in a freeform table, the more often you'll use them. Enjoy using these flexible capabilities! Next, it's time to graduate to using Attribution IQ with calculated metrics.

Creating calculated metrics with Attribution IQ

As we outline in Chapter 10, mastering calculated metrics is a must for analysts like you. And now that you also understand the value of Attribution IQ, we hope that you're as excited to merge the two technologies as we are to explain the steps to do so.

Calculated metrics powered by Attribution IQ can be as simple as saving a built-in metric with a different attribution model and as complex as your imagination allows! The simple example that you walk through will give you the tools to use both built-in and custom metrics.

Let's create the same metric we created in the freeform table, but using Calculated Metric Builder instead. This custom metric would be valuable if your goal is to make that metric accessible in visualizations other than a freeform table or if you wanted to share the metric to a colleague. Here are the steps to define the revenue metric with an inverse J model applied:

1. **Start in a prebuilt Workspace project or create a new one. Choose your favorite way to create a new calculated metric.**

   Click the plus sign to the right of Metrics in the left rail, choose Components ⇨ New Metric, or press Cmd+Shift+C (Mac) or Ctrl+Shift+C (PC). Calculated Metric Builder, which you explored in Chapter 10, appears.

2. **In the left rail, drop the revenue metric into the Definition drop zone.**

   If your company doesn't collect revenue in your report suite, consider using a different key metric such as registrations, downloads, or video views.

3. **Click the gear icon on right side of the revenue component in the definition, as shown in Figure 12-5.**

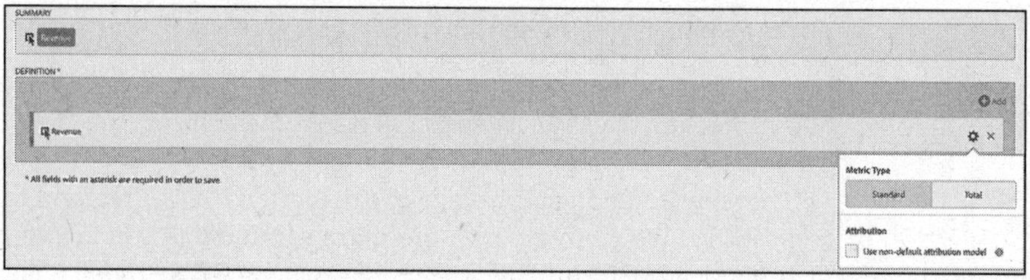

FIGURE 12-5:
The gear icon for revenue is clicked.

4. **Select the Use Non-Default Attribution Model check box.**

   If you've just completed the freeform table Attribution IQ instructions, the dialog box that appears will look familiar.

5. **Change Model to Inverse J, as shown in Figure 12-6.**

6. **Under Lookback Window, keep the setting at Visitor (Reporting Window), and click Apply.**

7. **Give your calculated metric a title and a description (see Figure 12-7) and, if you used a currency-based metric such as revenue, change Format to Currency, and add two decimal places.**

8. **Save your metric and use it anywhere in Workspace that accepts calculated metrics.**

After you learn to use the gear icon in Calculated Metric Builder, your analyses are instantly more valuable. Become more familiar with the feature by creating a calculated metric that divides two different metrics, each with non-default attribution models.

Comparing models using the attribution panel

The third and final method for taking advantage of the features of Attribution IQ is probably the easiest to use and get value from — the attribution panel.

The *attribution panel* was designed to help curious analysts like you compare and contrast different attribution models to more quickly identify the right model for the metric and dimension of your choosing. The attribution panel makes the process easy: Select a few options and you're instantly provided with a wealth of useful visualizations that help you make a more informed decision on attribution model choices.

Let's compare how our orders metric stacks up against J curve and inverse J. We've chosen these two because we feel confident that the first and last touch models are not inclusive enough for our complicated business. We also want to add a custom model that is based on a hunch that digital awareness campaigns for our brand aren't necessary due to our global branding. This custom model will focus strictly on players and closers. This should be fun!

Do the following:

1. **Open a Workspace project. Then click the top icon (Panels) in the left rail selector to open the list of panels. Drag the attribution panel to your project (see Figure 12-8).**

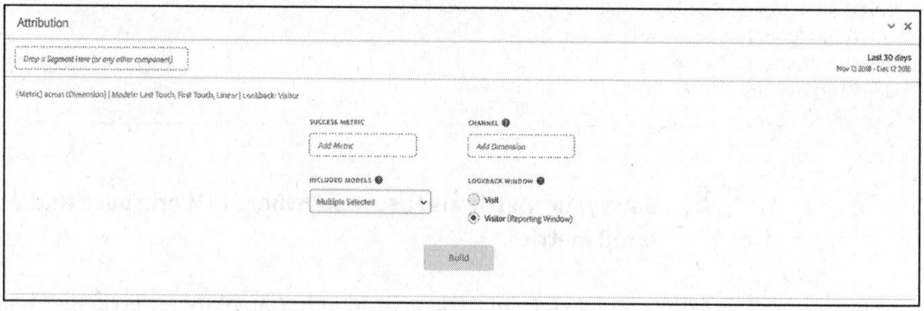

![A blank attribution panel in a new project]

FIGURE 12-8:
A blank attribution panel is shown in a new project.

The left rail selector is the thin column of three icons (Panels, Visualizations, and Components) to the left of the components in the left rail.

REMEMBER

2. **Click the third icon (Components) in the left rail selector. Drag Orders to the Success Metric slot in the attribution panel.**

Any metric that works with Attribution IQ can be applied to this visualization, so if your company doesn't have ecommerce, use your favorite key metric instead.

3. **Drag Marketing Channel to the Channel slot in the attribution panel slot.**

   The attribution panel can be used with any dimension that Attribution IQ supports — not just marketing channel. You could use campaign, internal search keyword, or even the page dimension here!

4. **In the Included Models drop-down menu, select the models that you'd like to compare.**

   We deselected the defaults — First Touch, Last Touch, and Linear — and selected J Curve and Inverse J, as shown in Figure 12-9.

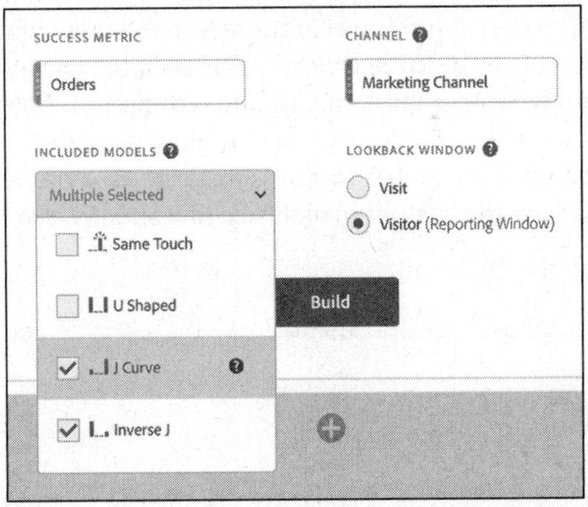

FIGURE 12-9: The attribution model selection process begins.

5. **From the Included Models drop-down menu, choose Custom. In the Custom Attribution dialog that appears, define a custom model with weights of 0/50/50 for Starter, Player, and Closer, respectively, as shown in Figure 12-10.**

   This custom model, shown in Figure 12-10, removes all credit from the first touch, provides 50 percent credit to the last touch, and splits the other 50 percent across all of the assisting channels. If any channels show a particularly low credit with this model, we might consider using that channel for an awareness campaign.

6. **Keep Lookback Window set to the default Visitor (Reporting Window), and then click the Build button.**

   Eight custom visualizations are built to help you learn more about how your selected attribution models affect credit for orders to individual marketing channels.

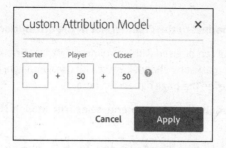

FIGURE 12-10:
The settings for
the custom
attribution model
are defined.

Figure 12-11 shows the top of the attribution panel results. The bar chart compares three versions of the orders metric (one for each selected attribution model), which are applied to the top 10 values of the selected dimension, which is marketing channel. Each cluster of three columns is associated with a different marketing channel. This powerful graph confirms our assumption about digital awareness campaigns — our custom model isn't the highest in only one channel: direct. Non-digital campaigns must be driving prospects to type our URL into their browser, which is why the custom model is so low and inverse J is so high for this channel.

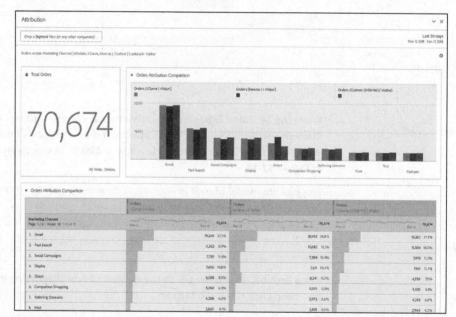

FIGURE 12-11:
Resulting
visualizations at
the top of the
attribution panel.

To the left of the bar chart is a summary visualization to provide you with context of the total number of orders during your time period. The freeform table at the bottom is live-linked to the bar chart to show a more data-heavy view of your metrics.

The next generated visualization is a Venn diagram titled Channel Overlap that shows the top three channels and how they overlap to drive your metric, as shown in Figure 12-12. This Venn diagram is also live-linked to the freeform table above it, so any three rows that you select in the table will be represented in Channel Overlap. To the right of the Venn diagram is a histogram that shows the number of touches visitors had to any channel. This information can be useful to better understand the optimal frequency when advertising to prospects. Chapter 13 provides a more thorough review of creating and customizing histograms and Venn diagrams.

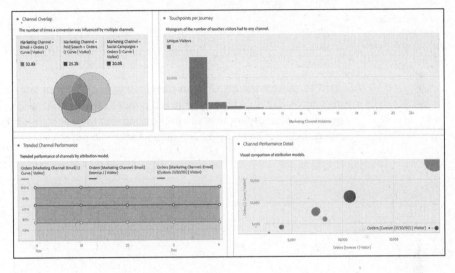

FIGURE 12-12: The second set of visualization results from an attribution panel.

The stacked area chart below the Venn diagram is titled Trended Channel Performance and is also live-linked to the freeform table above it. By default, the dimensional value with the highest number of orders is trended for each of your attribution models, though of course this changes as you select other rows in the freeform table. To the right is the Channel Performance Detail scatter chart, which plots each marketing channel based on the selected attribution model. This chart can help you quickly identify model and channel relationships because the plot is leaning more towards one of the models than the rest.

The final visualization, shown in Figure 12-13, is a visitor-based flow of data for marketing channels. You can use this visualization for an exploratory analysis of the order that visitors are traversing from one marketing channel to the next. Chapter 14 provides a deep dive into flow visualization.

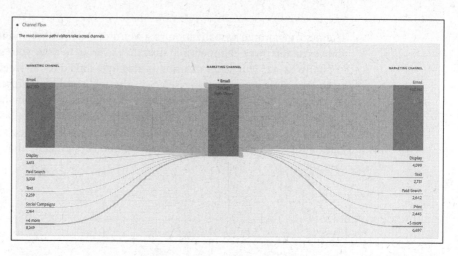

FIGURE 12-13:
The last visualization returned by the attribution panel.

Learn to master the attribution panel along with each of the Attribution IQ features, and you'll quickly find yourself a more capable analyst. Nothing is quite like the power of applying new attribution models to your data on the fly so you can answer questions you never considered asking before!

4

Visualizing Data to Reveal Golden Nuggets

IN THIS PART . . .

Visualize data patterns and trends with bar, line, area, and histogram charts.

Track drop-out points and identify user pathways to success events by using chart fallout and flow.

Organize and group data by cohorts to identify complex user patterns and trends.

Detect anomalies to identify significant positive and negative events.

IN THIS CHAPTER

» Maximizing the value of charts in Adobe Analytics

» Defining chart attributes

» Identifying trends with bar, line, donut, and histogram charts

» Using scatterplots to find hidden secrets across three metrics

» Deriving insights from Venn Diagrams

Chapter **13**

Creating Chart Visualizations for Data Storytelling

We've all heard the cliché "A picture is worth a thousand data tables." Well, the non-data science world has a slightly different version of that saying, but the concept is the same. Visualizations can concentrate a lot of words, yes, but also data.

Adobe Analytics has powerful and flexible tools for generating visualizations. In many cases, you can easily create a visualization from data in tables, such as line and area charts, bar and stacked bar charts, and the basic donut chart.

In other scenarios, you construct visualizations, specifically histograms and Venn diagrams, by piecing together data. You explore both scenarios — creating visualizations from existing data tables and building them from components — in this chapter.

Getting the Most from Charts in Adobe Analytics

Adobe Analytics makes it easy — and seamless — to generate charts from any table. In this section, we walk through how and when to use visualizations to illustrate and detect patterns and trends in data. You also discover how to invoke powerful features to customize donut charts, bar charts, and line charts.

We begin by reverse-engineering and experimenting with the built-in visualizations that come with template projects.

Getting visualization tips from templates

As noted, one effective pathway into exploring both the concepts and techniques for deploying effective visualizations is to study the charts that come with some of the template projects. Let's explore the charts that come with the Acquisition Web template to do just that.

You can follow these steps to generate, evaluate and explore options in that template. We also provide screenshots along the way so you can explore the charts and their settings right here in the online or print pages of this book:

1. **In Workspace choose Project ⇨ New.**

   The Templates dialog opens.

2. **Double-click Acquisition Web, as shown in Figure 13-1.**

   The Acquisition Web template opens with data in your Adobe Analytics configuration. (Your data will not match the data in the figure.)

3. **Scroll through the tables and charts for the Acquisition Web report in Workspace.**

Have a look at the way tables combine with visualizations in this template to provide an overview of a lot of data.

Dissecting a donut chart

The Acquisition Web template includes a donut chart. *Donut charts* are useful for one-dimensional comparison; they compare values, but without contextualization. For example, a donut chart comparing unique visitors in different browsers doesn't factor in the data's time period or how the data breaks down demographically or geographically.

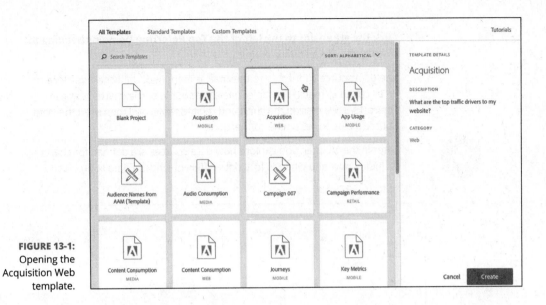

FIGURE 13-1:
Opening the
Acquisition Web
template.

The limited scope of donut charts is also their strength. They isolate a single metric, generally, and allow users to focus on an isolated slice of data. Maybe that's why the first chart in the Acquisition Web template is a donut chart. Let's take it apart, see what makes it tick, how to tweak it:

1. **With the Acquisition Web template open, examine the donut chart.**

   The donut chart displays Top Referring Domains, as shown in Figure 13-2. Note that a scroll bar appears when necessary so you can view all the legends associated with the chart.

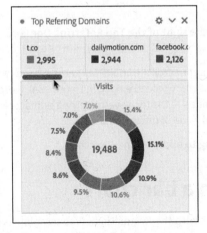

FIGURE 13-2:
Examining a
donut chart.

2. **Click the green dot to the left of the Top Referring Domains heading to display the Data Source dialog.**

   The data source connected to the chart is identified. Data chart dots are color-coded to match the table that is the source of the charted data. In Figure 13-3, we resized the chart and related table, and then used the Data Source dialog to reveal the connection.

   Later in the chapter, you explore how data sources are defined for charts, including how and when to lock data different kinds of data sources.

3. **Click the gear icon to the right of the Top Referring Domains heading to reveal options.**

   If we choose a smaller number for the Limit Max Items set, we can generate a chart that focuses on the more valuable data. In Figure 13-4, we're limiting the chart display to eight values — the top seven referring domains and an eighth value reflecting the total value of other domains.

4. **Click outside the dialog to apply the new settings.**

Breaking down a bar chart

The second chart that comes with the Acquisitions Web template is a bar chart titled Top Landing Pages. *Bar charts* have two dimensions (x and y). In this example, the y dimension displays the number of visits, and the x dimension displays the page.

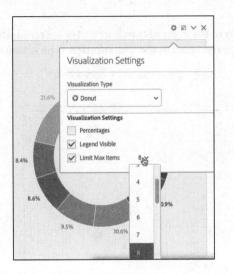

FIGURE 13-4:
Changing settings
to display a more
limited set of
values.

You can change the data shown in a chart, and you can change the way data is displayed by changing the chart type. Let's walk through both processes now:

1. **Find the Top Landing Pages bar chart in the top-right of the Acquisition Web template, shown in Figure 13-5.**

    By the way, as you did with the donut chart previously, you could restrict the number of values displayed by choosing a smaller number for the Limit Max Items value, which is also found in the Visualization Setting dialog that appears by clicking the gear icon in the top-right of the bar chart.

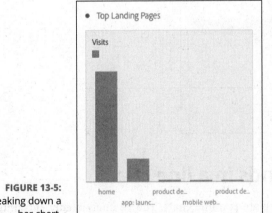

FIGURE 13-5:
Breaking down a
bar chart.

2. **Click the gear icon to the right of the chart's title — Top Landing Pages — and choose a different chart in the Visualization Type dialog that appears.**

   In Figure 13-6, we're changing the chart to a donut chart.

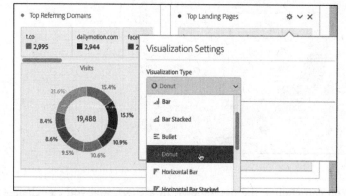

FIGURE 13-6:
Converting a bar chart to a donut chart.

3. **Experiment with other chart types.**

   If you're walking through this step-by-step with us, assign a horizontal bar chart style to this visualization, as shown in Figure 13-7. (The labels are more effective this way, don't you think?)

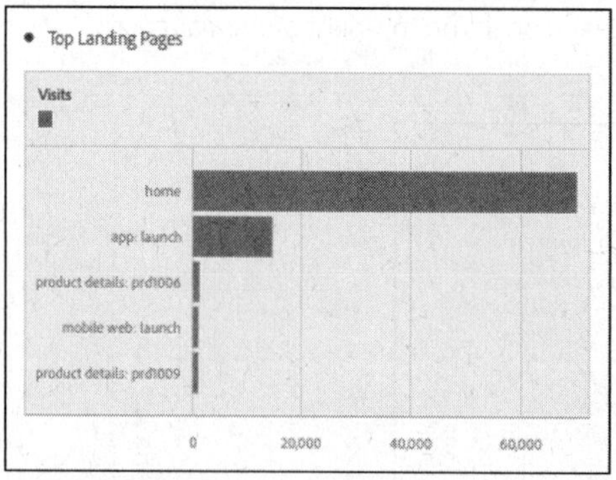

FIGURE 13-7:
Displaying data as a horizontal bar chart.

Looking at trends in a line chart

The third chart in the template is a line chart. You've undoubtedly encountered line graphs before (such as those that track rising and falling values of individual stocks or groups of stocks).

Line charts always have time as the x-axis. Whenever you're showing movement in a metric over time, you're using some form of line or time-series graph. A few new things are worth examining: This chart displays a y-axis (visits) and an x-axis (time). And it displays multiple values: visits, visits with a tracking code, and visits with a referrer.

The data source and settings for this chart are identified in the same way as the data source and settings for the simpler charts you've examined up to now. But because this visualization is more complex than the sample comparative charts you examined earlier, it has many more possible settings, as shown in Figure 13-8.

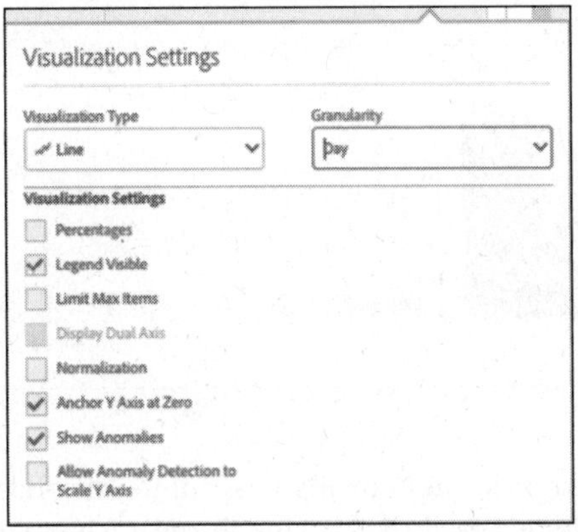

FIGURE 13-8: Defining display properties for a line chart.

Let's look at a few key options for the line chart:

>> The Granularity drop-down allows you to choose from a wide range of scales for the x-axis values, including day, hour, month, and year.

>> The Normalization check box forces metrics to equal proportions. This option has different implications depending on your data. We suggest that you use trial-and-error to see whether this option makes your data more accessible. You can preview the effect by toggling the check box on and off while observing the effect on your chart.

>> An option for enabling Anomaly Detection in the y-axis is available. You explore how to harness anomalies in Chapter 15 when you dive deeply into understanding and taking advantage of oddities to identify unknown and unexpected data patterns and divergences from patterns.

Sizing up data with stacked bar charts

The last chart in the Acquisition Web template gives you a great opportunity to explore stacking bar charts. As displayed, the chart titled Days Between Visits (scroll down to the bottom of the Workspace to find it) uses a simple bar chart to display three values (unique visitors; visitors with a tracking code; and visitors with a referrer).

Days between visits are displayed in the x-axis, and percentage breakdowns are displayed in the y-axis, as shown in Figure 13-9.

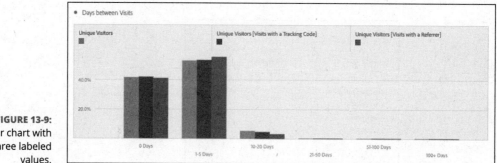

FIGURE 13-9: A bar chart with three labeled values.

For the data in the figures, it might be more useful to consolidate the values into stacked bars. We can do this easily by clicking the gear icon to display the Visualization Settings dialog and then choosing Bar Stacked from the Visualization Type drop-down menu, as shown in Figure 13-10. Note the stacked bar chart display changes even before we click outside the dialog.

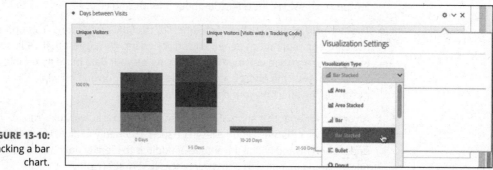

FIGURE 13-10: Stacking a bar chart.

The stacked bar chart more clearly identifies the large drop-off from people who have made a return visit within five days and visitors who are returning to the site in ten to twenty days.

Surveying multiple metrics with scatterplots

The Acquisition Web template doesn't include a scatterplot for us to dissect, but the Campaign Performance Retail template does. You can open this template as a new project in Workspace to examine the scatterplot there. (Refer to the beginning of this chapter and Figure 13-1 for steps to create a new project from a template.)

Or follow along with us here as we dissect that scatterplot to get a feel for when and how to use this flexible charting technique. The scatterplot in the template is shown in Figure 13-11.

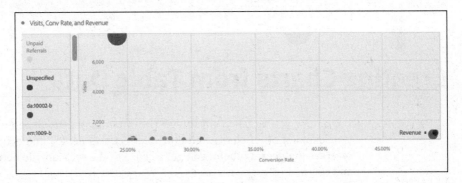

FIGURE 13-11:
A scatterplot.

REMEMBER

The data you see charted in the scatterplot in the Retail Campaign Performance template will be different than the data in the figure. It may be that your data doesn't have values for this chart.

The scatterplot illustrated in Figure 13-11 displays three values: visits (on the y-axis); conversion rate (on the x-axis); and revenue (indicated by the size of each data point). By presenting three different dimensions, this scatterplot provides a complex overview of the relationship between visits, conversion rate, and (yes, all important!) revenue for different paid (and unpaid) referral sources.

To see the data source for this chart — as with donut, line and bar charts — you can click the color-coordinated (and highly fashionable!) dot next to the chart title, and select the Show Data Source option. The source data is displayed as a table, as shown in Figure 13-12.

A table associated with a scatterplot chart requires at least two columns. The first column defines the x-axis, and the second column defines the y-axis. If a third column is available, the scatterplot chart uses it to determine the radius of the dot. In other words, columns 1, 2, and 3 map to X, Y, and dot radius, respectively.

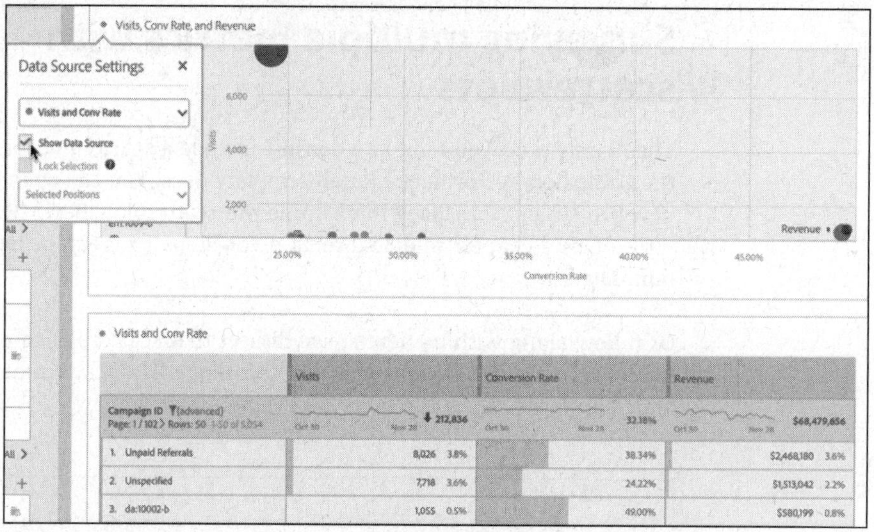

FIGURE 13-12:
Identifying and
examining source
data for a
scatterplot.

Creating Charts from Table Data

Up to now, you've taken advantage of two templates in Adobe Analytics to begin your exploration of charts and how to effectively deploy and configure them. By reverse-engineering them, you got a sense of the relationship between table data and charts.

Now let's flip the script, take it from the top, and walk through how table data gets turned into a chart.

Generating a chart from a row of data

Line, bar, and donut charts are generated and display data from freeform tables. You've seen that when you dissected charts in templates. In examining a scatter-plot, for example, you identified the source of the data by clicking the color-coded dot associated with the title of tables and charts. Good to know! That understanding will serve you well as you walk through an example of generating a chart from a data table.

To create a chart from scratch, we start with a table that displays the top twelve marketing channels in terms of orders, shown in Figure 13-13.

If you select a single row and click the Visualize icon, shown in Figure 13-14, the default result will be a line chart that tracks the data in the selected row over the timespan set in the Workspace calendar.

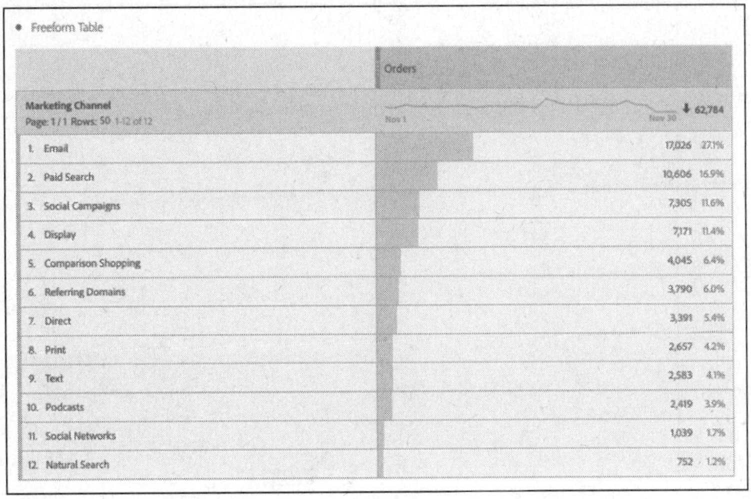

• Freeform Table

Marketing Channel Page: 1 / 1 Rows: 50 1-12 of 12	Orders Nov 1 – Nov 30 ⬇ 62,784	
1. Email	17,026	27.1%
2. Paid Search	10,606	16.9%
3. Social Campaigns	7,305	11.6%
4. Display	7,171	11.4%
5. Comparison Shopping	4,045	6.4%
6. Referring Domains	3,790	6.0%
7. Direct	3,391	5.4%
8. Print	2,657	4.2%
9. Text	2,583	4.1%
10. Podcasts	2,419	3.9%
11. Social Networks	1,039	1.7%
12. Natural Search	752	1.2%

FIGURE 13-13: A table with marketing channel as the dimension, and orders as the single metric.

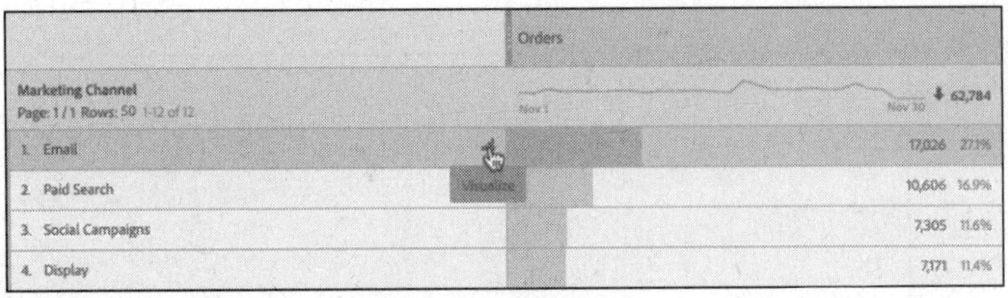

Marketing Channel Page: 1 / 1 Rows: 50 1-12 of 12	Orders Nov 1 – Nov 30 ⬇ 62,784	
1. Email	17,026	27.1%
2. Paid Search	10,606	16.9%
3. Social Campaigns	7,305	11.6%
4. Display	7,171	11.4%

FIGURE 13-14: Selecting a row of data to chart.

By default, the Show Anomalies setting is turned on, which accounts for the shaded areas above and below the line. You can tweak the display by clicking the gear icon and then turning off Anomalies in the Visualization Settings dialog that appears. Figure 13-15 shows a selected row charted in a line graph.

REMEMBER

Calendar settings can be edited by clicking the date range link at the top right of any project's workspace.

Generating a chart from multiple rows

If we use Shift+click to select multiple contiguous rows, or ⌘+click (Mac) or Ctrl+click (PC) to select noncontiguous rows, and then click the Visualize (gear) icon, the default result is a line chart with multiple lines, as shown in Figure 13-16.

In this example, it might be more effective to synthesize the data by displaying it as a stacked area chart, to focus on the peak in orders through all marketing channels mid-month, as shown in Figure 13-17. To do that, choose Area Stacked from the Visualization Type drop-down menu in the Visualization Settings dialog.

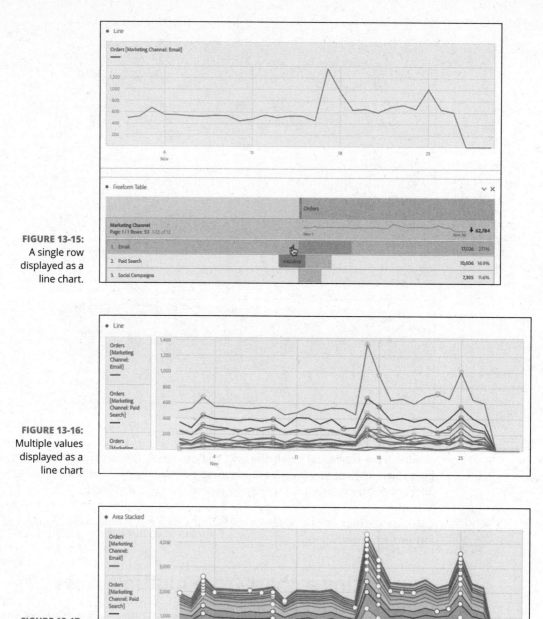

FIGURE 13-15:
A single row displayed as a line chart.

FIGURE 13-16:
Multiple values displayed as a line chart

FIGURE 13-17:
Displaying data as an area stacked chart.

Locking data displayed in a visualization

In the examples you just explored — generating a visualization from a single row and multiple rows of data — the data displayed in the chart is based on the content of the selected row.

That might sound like a tautology (restating the obvious): You select a row, graph it, and the graph displays the data in that row. But the point here is that the value in the selected row might change. In fact, why don't you find one of the tables that is the base for a visualization (perhaps from the preceding exercise) and click a different row in the table. Did you notice how the visualization is now focused on your newly selected row? This is made possible by Adobe's live linking feature, in which graph data is directly linked to the selection in the source table.

When you're using Workspace, live linking is valuable because it allows you to instantly visualize the data you're analyzing. However, we need to consider what happens to your graph if you save the project or change the timeframe. What data should appear?

Imagine you've created a line chart based on a table populated with a metric that focuses on leads by marketing channel. During that period, email was the top marketing channel. What if you changed the time period to the previous month, in which another marketing channel, such as paid search, moved into the top row of leads in this table? In that case, charts based on this table would display the *new* top-rated channel. What if you don't want that? What if, instead, you want to lock in email as the row of data that is charted?

To change the lock status for charted data, open the Data Source Settings dialog for the chart by clicking the colored dot to the left of the chart title. Select the Lock Selection option, shown in Figure 13-18, to lock the current value, not the row, to display in the chart. Note the lock icon that replaces the Data Source Settings dot. After you've locked a chart in this manner, the selected dimensional values no longer change — even if you change the time period or apply a segment to the table data source.

FIGURE 13-18:
Locking data for charting instead of rows.

Figure 13-18 also shows the drop-down menu that appears when you lock a selection. This menu provides the option to lock the chart to the item, dimensional value, position, or ranking in the table. In our example, it may be helpful to lock the item, so the chart always shows the selected item of email. However, it can also be helpful to lock based on the selected position, which would always chart the top-ranked marketing channel.

If you ever need to unlock a locked chart, you can do so by clicking that same colored dot to the left of the chart's title and deselecting the Lock Selection check box.

Building Histograms and Venn Diagrams

As mentioned, variations of line, bar, and donut charts are generated from and display data from freeform tables. The mental workflow here, if we can put it that way, is visualizing data that has already been essentially chewed up and digested in a table. (Ouch. Maybe that was an unfortunate metaphor, but you get the point.)

Venn diagrams and histograms are generated through a different mental workflow, and as such play an even more dynamic role than other charts in not just visualizing but also synthesizing data.

We show you what we mean by using a few examples in the following sections. But in terms of technical workflow, you do not generate histograms and Venn diagrams from existing data tables. You build them from scratch from components.

Organizing data with histograms

Histograms are a great way to visualize the distribution of key metrics. For example, if you want to identify visitor patterns to see what portion of visitors spend a lot of money at your company's site, you can drag the revenue metric into a histogram. You do that shortly, but first, the basics.

The histogram visualization can be added from the left visualization rail and dragged into any freeform panel, as shown in Figure 13-19.

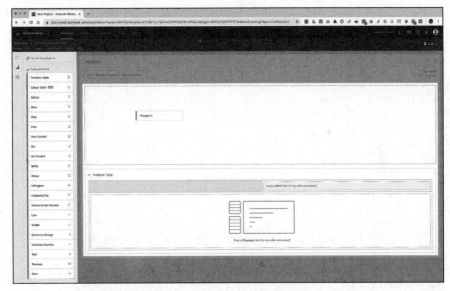

FIGURE 13-19: Generating a histogram from the left rail.

Or you can simply click the Histogram icon that is displayed when you create a new blank panel in Workspace, as shown in Figure 13-20.

When you drag a valid metric — one with sufficient and appropriate data from which a histogram can be generated — into the Add Metric box in the blank histogram, a blue Build button becomes operative. When you click that blue button, buckets are generated with evenly spaced value intervals.

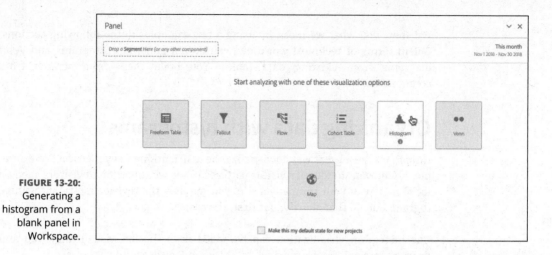

FIGURE 13-20: Generating a histogram from a blank panel in Workspace.

In Figure 13-21, we generated a histogram using the revenue metric. The result is a histogram with different revenue values (displayed on the x-axis), with corresponding numbers of unique visitors displayed on the y-axis. The x-axis displays spending ranging from $1 up to $25, spaced in $2 intervals.

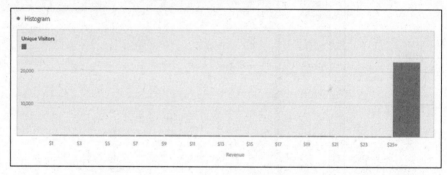

FIGURE 13-21: A histogram displaying revenue spent by different numbers of unique visitors.

As you can see in Figure 13-21, the default bucket size isn't a good fit for our data — hardly any of our sales are for less than $25.

We can change the starting bucket, the number of buckets, and the metric bucket size by clicking the gear icon to open the Visualization Settings dialog. As shown in figure 13-22, as we tweak the settings, the histogram display changes to something more useful for evaluating spending patterns.

Note that the Visualization Settings dialog provides options for counting the defined metric in Visitor (the default) and also Visit and Hit. In the example you're exploring here, it would be easy to toggle between visitors, visits, and hits to get a sense of how visitor activity patterns affect revenue.

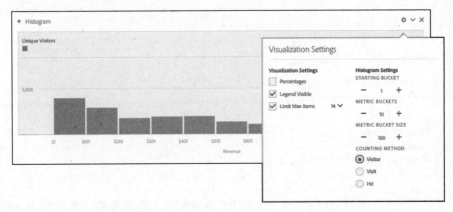

FIGURE 13-22:
Changing
visualization
settings for a
histogram.

You can turn a histogram into a freeform table. To do that, click the colored dot next to the histogram title and select Manage Data Sources ➪ Available Data Sources ➪ Show Data Source.

Deriving insights from Venn diagrams

Venn diagrams show overlap and intersection between datasets. In today's complex, global, highly integrated world, you see Venn diagrams employed in popular culture to explore how even very different events affect and intersect. Similarly, in the world of data analysis, Venn diagrams allow you to pull together a fluid and flexible set of metrics.

To generate a Venn diagram in a blank panel in Workspace, follow these steps:

1. **Double-click the Venn icon, which is displayed when you create a new blank panel in Workspace, as shown in Figure 13-23.**

   Alternately, you can select the Visualizations icon in the left rail and drag the Venn box into a report.

2. **Add up to three segments by dragging them into the Add Segment boxes.**

3. **Add a single metric by dragging it into the Add One Metric box.**

4. **When you have defined your segments and a metric, click the blue Build button.**

   A Venn chart is generated.

Let's explore this scenario: You're comparing visits from Apple devices and referred visits from Google by visitors in the United States.

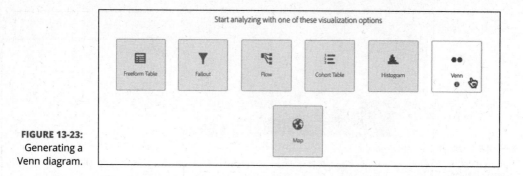

FIGURE 13-23:
Generating a
Venn diagram.

Figure 13-24 shows the segments and metrics you need to generate that Venn diagram. The three segments are Apple devices; referred from Google; and Country:United States. Revenue is the metric you'd like to compare in these three segments.

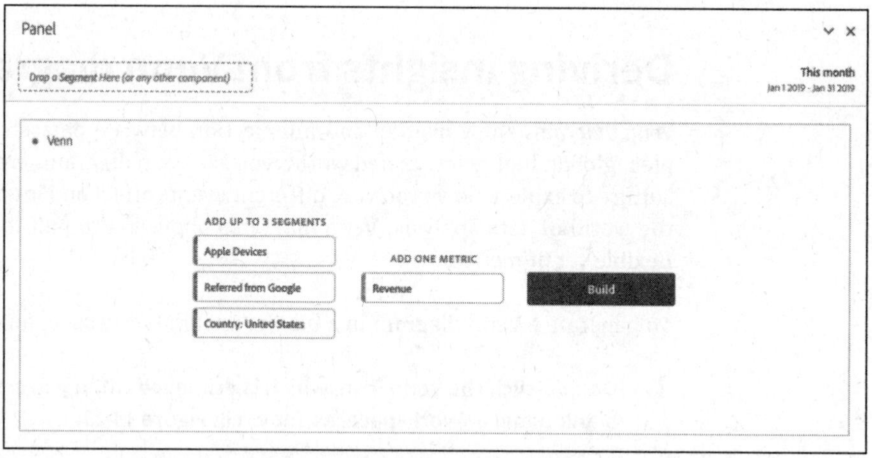

FIGURE 13-24:
A set of segments
and a metric for
generating a
Venn diagram.

Figure 13-25 shows the generated Venn diagram. At first glance, you can see that within this set of segmented data:

>> All Google-referred revenue is coming from the United States, as is almost all revenue from Apple devices.

>> Some revenue is generated from Apple devices referred from Google — there is some intersection here.

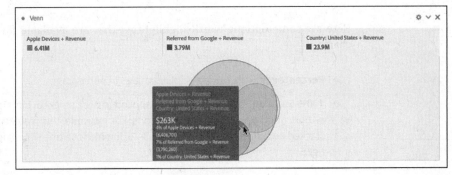

FIGURE 13-25:
Zooming in on an
intersection to
reveal detail data
in a Venn
diagram.

You can zoom in on this data more closely by hovering your cursor over any intersecting sections of the diagram. For example, by hovering your cursor over the intersection of Google referrals and Apple device, the data reveals the following:

>> Revenue from users of Apple devices that is referred also from Google constitutes 4 percent of revenue from Apple devices.

>> Revenue from users referred from Google who are on Apple devices makes up 7 percent of revenue referred from Google.

>> Of all revenue from the United States, 1 percent comes from users of Apple devices who were referred from Google.

As with a histogram, you can turn a Venn diagram into a freeform table. Simply click the colored dot next to the diagram title and select Manage Data Sources ⇨ Available Data Sources ⇨ Show Data Source.

Defining Chart Attributes in Detail

While surveying different types of visualizations and how to customize them, we've touched on many of the more widely applicable techniques for customizing chart displays. But there's more! We won't document every setting option, but some are worth identifying in more detail.

REMEMBER

Available visualization settings are contingent on the selected visualization type. That means not all setting options we are about to define can be applied to all visualizations. Some advanced settings appear only for specific visualizations, such as the histogram settings.

Here are some options worth highlighting that are available for many types of charts:

>> **Percentages:** This setting displays values in percentages.

>> **100% Stacked:** This setting can be applied to area stacked. bar stacked, or horizontal bar stacked visualizations. For example, this feature turns the stacked bar chart shown in Figure 13-26, left into the one shown in Figure 13-26, right.

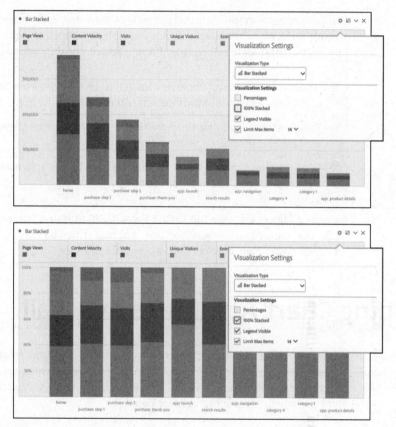

FIGURE 13-26:
A stacked bar chart without and with 100% Stacked enabled.

Turning on the 100% Stacked option changes the focus of the data picture from comparing categories to comparing the breakdown of segments within categories.

>> **Legend Visible:** This setting is enabled by default, but you can deselect it hide the filter details text for the Summary Number/Summary Change visualization.

- » **Limit Max Items:** This setting allows you to limit the number of items that a visualization displays.

- » **Anchor Y Axis at Zero**: If all the values plotted on the chart are considerably above zero, the chart default will make the bottom of the y-axis nonzero. That isolates the data values in relation to each other, but sometimes it is important to situate values in relation to zero. If you select this box, the y-axis will be forced to zero (and the chart will be redrawn).

- » **Display Dual Axis**: This option is available only if you have two metrics. It allows you to define one metric to display on the left y-axis and the other the right.

Legend labels are generated automatically. But sometimes they're too long, or not intuitive to an intended audience. To edit a legend label in a line chart, for example, do the following:

1. **Right-click one of the legend labels and choose Edit Label, as shown in Figure 13-27.**

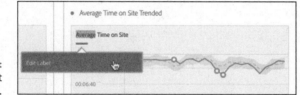

FIGURE 13-27: Editing a chart label.

2. **Enter the new label text or edit existing text.**

3. **Press Enter (PC) or Return (Mac), click outside the legend box, or click outside the new label box to save your changes.**

Visualization Beyond Data Charts

In this chapter, you focused on graphic visualizations of specific data. But you've undoubtedly noticed that we haven't touched on other options in the Visualizations left rail (or even a few of the visualizations that appear as options in a new blank panel).

In other chapters, you walk through other visualizations:

>> **Cohort tables:** Organizes data that shares common characteristics over a specified period. Cohort analysis is useful, for example, when you want to learn how a cohort engages over time with a product and identify trends. We describe cohort tables in Chapter 14.

>> **Fallout:** Visualizes where visitors leave (fall out) and continue through (fall through) a defined sequence of activity. You explore fallout and flow (the path a user takes through a site) visualization in Chapter 14.

>> **Heat map visualization:** You take a look at applying a heat map to your data using Activity Map in Chapter 16.

IN THIS CHAPTER

» Configuring and visualizing path
   analyses using flow and fallout

» Defining a cohort and setting up a
   cohort table

» Customizing your Workspace project
   for sharing

» Curating and sharing projects

Chapter **14**

Advanced Visualization

n Chapter 13, you examine the graphical side of visualization in Adobe Analytics: donut, line, and bar charts, scatter charts, and those ubiquitous Venn diagrams. Here, you go deeper into visualization. You discover the ways in which Adobe Analytics opens the door to tracking the activity of highly defined sets of users (cohorts) over time. And you learn how to analyze both exploratory (flow) and prescribed (fallout) path visualizations based on user behavior.

These features flex the muscles of Adobe Analytics, some in ways that are different than, or not available in, Google Analytics.

Finally, you customize a Workspace project to improve how you curate and share projects that are more accessible to a wide range of users.

Visualizing Flow Paths

Flow visualizations enable you to visually track the path through your website or app, starting from an entry point, or working backward from an exit point, or looking both ways from a defined value.

How, for example, are users getting to your success conversion point (placing an order, completing a survey, watching a video, and so on)? Or, starting from an entry point, what happens to users who enter your site from various marketing channels? Flow paths help identify where customers go before and after a specified nodal point, such as entry, a specific dimension, or exit.

And you can segment flow paths, trend flow paths, and even use a mixture of dimensions to further isolate the user's experience. In this section, you walk through how this works, and in the process explore how to get your money's worth out of flow visualizations in Analysis Workspace.

Defining flow paths

Flow paths are defined using *one* of the following three criteria. We emphasize *one* because you don't mix and match these criteria; you choose just one. Those criteria follow:

>> **Entry:** A flow visualization generated from an entry means that the first node, or column in your flow visualization, is the first value received by the visits or visitors that you are analyzing. Entry components must be dimensions. Because your analysis starts at the beginning, the visualization will allow you to analyze data only going forward in time. For example, you can start a flow visualization by analyzing the entry pages of your visitors. If you were to use the page dimension as your entry node, all values that have ever been the first value for a visitor would appear in that column.

>> **Dimensions or items:** If you choose this criteria, you can begin your exploratory flow analysis with either a dimensional value or a dimension. Your analysis can be more specific by starting with a dimensional value. For example, you may be interested in analyzing how users are getting to a specific blog post and where they're going next — an advantage of using a flow visualization based on an item. If you were to instead use the complete page dimension to spawn your analysis, every value of that dimension appears. Finally, dropping a dimension or dimensional item here allows you to analyze in both directions — forward and backward.

>> **Exit:** Exit components, like entry components, must be dimensions. When dimensions are used as exits, you're working backward from the last dimensional value captured by that dimension. Examples of dimensions that are commonly used exit components include page, marketing channel, and site section. Flow visualizations that are built using dimensions as exits are of particular value because you can look backward in time.

A good use case for exit path analysis is for a news or content site — the type of site whose core business is selling advertising. If you worked for this type of company, you would want to know the articles or content types driving visitors to exit the site. You could apply the flow visualization to an exit path to identify the pages, page types, article titles, or even article topics that are causing visitors to become bored with your site's content. This exit path analysis feature is rarely accessible to the flow visualizations in Google Analytics.

Creating a flow visualization

You've explored the value of flow visualizations. But you might be asking, how do I create a flow visualization? You're at the right place in the book for that. Follow these steps:

1. **In Workspace, create a blank panel and click Flow.**

If you're already working in a panel, perhaps with a segment or a custom timeframe applied, you can drag the flow visualization into your current panel by clicking the visualizations icon in the left rail selector, finding Flow, and dragging it over.

Unlike most of the graphic visualizations you explore in Chapter 13, flow visualizations don't start with existing freeform tables. Instead, you generate the data from scratch as you define the flow visualization.

REMEMBER

You can generate a blank panel in Workspace by clicking the + at the end of any existing panel, choosing Components ⇨ Insert Blank Panel from the Workspace navigation menu, or using the keyboard shortcut Alt+B . For more details, see the discussion on creating blank panels in Chapter 3.

2. **Examine the flow definition panel that appears, shown in Figure 14-1.**

You define the flow visualization by dragging components into one of the three boxes. You can customize the included date range by opening the calendar. Segments can be applied to flow visualizations only at the panel level; head to Chapter 9 for a review of this process.

REMEMBER

Calendar settings are defined by clicking the date range in the upper-right corner of a panel. See Chapter 3 for details.

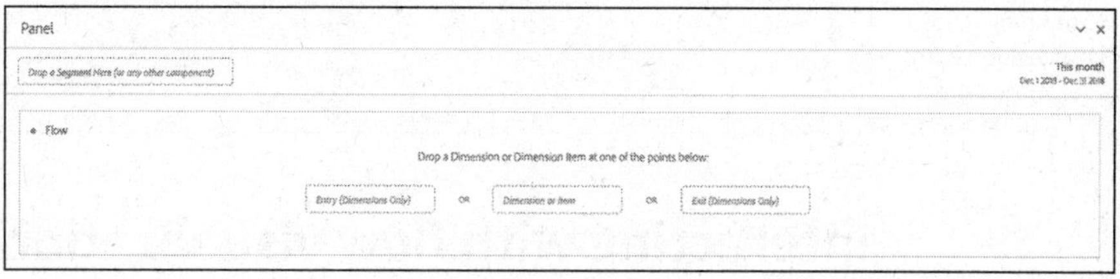

FIGURE 14-1:
Creating a flow visualization in a blank panel.

Panel			∨ ✕
Drop a Segment Here (or any other component)			This month Dec. 1 2018 - Dec. 31 2018

✛ Flow
Drop a Dimension or Dimension item at one of the points below:
Entry (Dimensions Only)   OR   Dimension or item   OR   Exit (Dimensions Only)

3. **Drag a dimension or dimensional item into the drop zone for one of the three available categories: Entry, Exit, or Dimensional item.**

   As you drag a single component into one of the drop zones, be sure you're sitting down (or at an ergonomically equivalent comfortable standing workstation) because a dramatic flow chart appears instantly. Figure 14-2 illustrates dragging the marketing channel dimension into the Entry box.

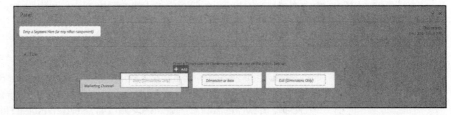

FIGURE 14-2: Defining a flow visualization by dragging a dimension into the Entry box.

4. **Examine the resulting flow visualization.**

   Of course, if you're following these steps with your own data, your results will look different than ours, which are shown in Figure 14-3. But note that paths in the diagram are proportional — those with more activity appear thicker.

Now that you have a feel for the process to create flow visualizations, it's time to learn how to interact with the dataset that is returned in the visualization.

FIGURE 14-3: Examining a flow visualization with a defined entry dimension.

Interacting with flow visualizations

As you've seen, the instant you drop an item into a flow visualization's drop zone, the data appears. The contents are defined by what you dragged into the drop zone. But that's just the beginning of the process. Let's examine more detailed ways you can create flow visualizations.

You can hover your cursor over different paths to identify the number of views of the highlighted path as well as the percentage of total path views that followed this path, as shown in Figure 14-4.

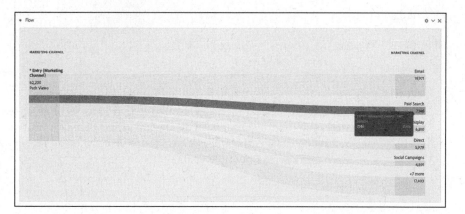

FIGURE 14-4:
Displaying data
for a path in a
flow visualization.

Because the goal of the flow visualization is to analyze a dimension's values over time, it's important to be able to explore values captured by Adobe after or before any item. Simply click any dimensional value in the visualization, and a new column appears to the right (if going forward in time) or to the left (if going backward in time). Figure 14-5 shows the results of clicking the item for email with subsequent items populated in the column on the right.

You can hover your cursor over any node to reveal details about the number and percentage of entries and exits and the top five links from the node you highlight. Figure 14-5, for example, shows a summary of the top five links from this point.

By default, each column displays only the top five values, and groups the remaining values into a single summary value labeled More. Figure 14-5 has +7 More because seven other dimensional items are grouped to make up an additional 17,403 paths.

Need to see the additional items that make up that last item? Then click the More node at the bottom of the diagram to display five more dimensional items. Keep clicking to add more rows. So far, we've only begun to explore the power of the flow visualization. Why do we say that? Because the flow diagram is interactive!

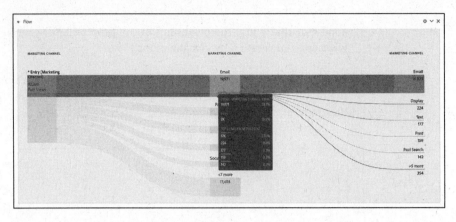

FIGURE 14-5:
Viewing a summary of entry data in a flow visualization.

You can use the gear (Settings) icon to display Flow Settings, shown in Figure 14-6. Here, you can toggle between displaying values based on Visit or Visitor. The Visit setting constrains the analysis to a single visit, whereas Visitor measures activity from users across multiple visits.

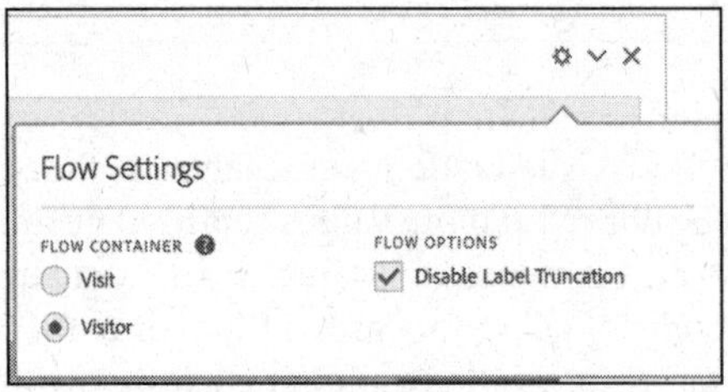

FIGURE 14-6:
Defining settings for a flow container.

You can also disable label truncation to display the full text for labels. (By default, labels are shortened to make the display less cluttered.)

To properly analyze the common paths of your customers, you need to do more than look forward or backward across your data. Even more powerful interactivity is available when you right-click a path to display the context menu shown in Figure 14-7.

Here are some options you can use to configure flow visualizations:

» **Focus on this node:** Changes the focus to the selected node. When you select this option, the focused node appears at the center of the Flow diagram.

» **Start Over:** Opens a new flow definition dialog. This option is significantly faster than deleting the entire flow visualization and dragging in a new one.

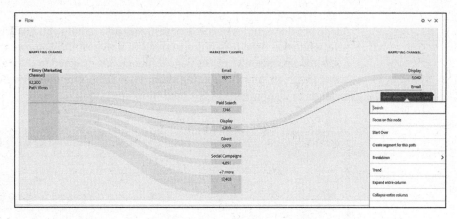

FIGURE 14-7:
A path is right-clicked in the flow visualization.

>> **Create Segment for This Path:** Opens Segment Builder, where you can access and edit a segment based on the path you've selected. You might use this option when you discover an interesting path so that you can apply the segment to other tables and visualizations or even share it to Experience Cloud for action. You explore building precise segments in Chapter 9.

>> **Breakdown:** Enables you to break down the path you've selected by available dimensions, metrics, segments, or time. Breakdowns help you more easily correlate unusual paths with the key dimensional values that drove them.

>> **Trend:** Creates a line chart that shows trended data. You might use this option if you discover a negative path and want to know whether the path is occurring more often or less often over time? And, of course, Adobe will run your trended path through Anomaly Detection algorithms to identify if any unexpected spikes or dips in your trend were statistically significant. To learn more about Anomaly Detection, head to Chapter 15.

>> **Expand Entire Column:** Clicks all visible nodes and connects them to the next column. By default, only clicked nodes are connected to the next column in the path. For example, if Figure 14-7, only the Display node was clicked, so only that value is connected to the next column of values. Right-clicking any node in the middle column and clicking the Expand Entire Column link will connect all five values in the middle column of Figure 14-7 (Email, Paid Search, Display, Direct, and Social Campaigns) to the next column.

>> **Collapse Entire Column:** Hides all nodes in the selected column. You might use this option when you need to remove a column from a path flow analysis.

The last feature of flow visualization to discuss is one of the most powerful — the capability to change the dimension you're analyzing in the middle of the path. You might want to change dimensions if you want to see how different marketing channels drove traffic to different pages, and how those pages led to different products.

Adobe provides guides in the flow visualization to help you understand what happens when you drop new dimensions into it. Figure 14-8 shows the experience in a flow visualization when the page dimension is dragged to the right of a flow that started with an entry marketing channel — the entire marketing channel column expands to display each of the next hits captured in Adobe.

FIGURE 14-8:
The page dimension is added to the right as the next dimension in the path.

In Adobe Analytics, you can easily replace dimensions with other dimensions too. Instead of adding a dimension to the right of your flow visualization, simply hover the new dimension on top of any column.

Analyzing Fallout Paths

Fallout visualizations show how visitors progress through (fall through) and leave (fall out of) a defined sequence of steps. Those of you coming from Google Analytics or a background in ecommerce analysis will know this feature as a funnel visualization.

Fallout visualizations (as they are called in Adobe Analytics) and funnel visualizations (as they are called in Google Analytics) aim to achieve the same goal — analyzing a prescribed set of steps that are defined by the analyst.

We use fallout visualizations to identify defined conversion success rates (for example, a purchase or registration) and associations and relationships between activities (such as reading a product warrantee and placing an order), as well as for more meta analytics of traffic flow, such as identifying how many people who search for an item actually purchase that item.

Here's another way to think about fallout paths. Flow allows you to explore and find paths you might not have thought of. Fallout paths allow you to dig into one specific path that you're very aware of.

Understanding fallout terms and concepts

Let's break down a few terms and concepts that will both help identify the value of fallout visualizations and prepare you to create them yourself.

First, typical fallout reports contain multiple steps so that you can see the number and percentage of users that fell through or fell out of the sequence.

These steps, which can be dimensional values, segments, or metrics, are called *touchpoints*. As you piece together a series of touchpoints, a fallout visualization displays conversion and fallout rates between each touchpoint in the sequence.

You can define a prescribed set of steps that you expect your visitors to be following, and then analyze which steps are the biggest barrier to completing the scenario. For example, you might expect that your visitors land on the home page, click to a product category page, enter the cart flow, and then make a purchase. Fallout helps identify which of these steps, if any, are losing the largest percentage of your visitors. As you might expect, Adobe makes the fallout visualization flexible, so virtually any scenario you can come up with will be supported.

Generating a fallout visualization

Now that you've been introduced to the role of fallout visualization and a few key concepts and terms, you're all set to create a fallout visualization. Here's how:

1. **Click the visualizations icon in the left rail selector and drag Fallout into the panel that you want to display the visualization.**

   Fallout visualizations can be dropped into blank panels or panels with pre-existing visualizations — the data in the fallout will be filtered based on any applied segments and the panel's calendar time period. Like flow visualizations, fallout visualizations are built on data that is not linked to an existing table. Therefore, your newly created fallout visualization won't have useful data; it will appear like the one in Figure 14-9. By default, all fallout visualizations begin with a row for All Visits. (We explain how you can hide this row later in the chapter.)

FIGURE 14-9:
A new fallout
visualization,
minus useful data
(yet), ready to be
configured.

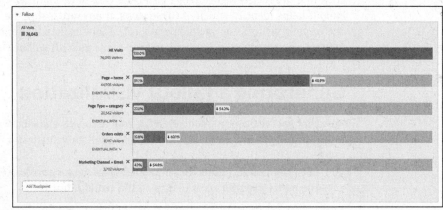

2. **Begin to add touchpoints by dragging dimensional values, segments or metrics into the Add Touchpoint box.**

   Typical touchpoints include a specific page, marketing channel, page type, key action, or segment. Like flow visualizations, a fallout can handle a mixture of dimensions, metrics, and segments. For example, Figure 14-10 shows four touchpoints after All Visits: Page = Home, Page Type = Category, Order Exists, and Marketing Channel = Email. Data is associated with the next visit's marketing channel (email), because a fallout is visitor-based by default. You can adjust Fallout to focus on a visit container instead of visitor if necessary.

FIGURE 14-10:
Four touchpoints
in a fallout
visualization.

3. **Drag a segment to the very top of the visualization, above the row of data associated with All Visits, as shown in Figure 14-11.**

   A new row is added to each individual touchpoint to represent the new segment. Figure 14-11 already shows one row for All Visits and a second for iOS; releasing the Android Devices segment would add a third row for each touchpoint. The value of this capability is you can compare the same path across different segments, identifying whether different groups of users are struggling with different parts of the journey.

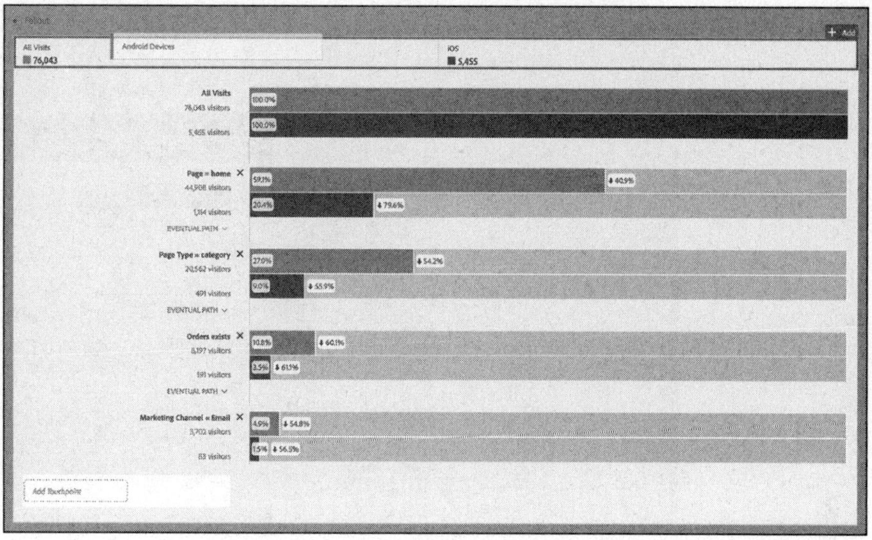

FIGURE 14-11:
The Android
Devices segment
is added to a
fallout's All Visits
and iOS
segments.

4. **To change settings, click the gear icon (Settings) for the fallout visualization, and make your selections in the Fallout Settings dialog that appears. Then click OK.**

   By default, the fallout container displays visitor data — your user's activity across visits. You can toggle to Visit to constrain the analysis to a single visit at a time. You can also hide the All Visits touchpoint by deselecting that option.

5. **Drag a new dimensional item on top of an existing touchpoint to expand the definition of that touchpoint.**

   You've now created a more complex definition of the touchpoint by adding a new dimensional item — doing so adds a logical OR operator to the dimensional items in the touchpoint. The number of dimensional items that you can use to define a touchpoint is unlimited.

   Figure 14-12 shows the interface as the App: Launch page is added to the Page = Home touchpoint, thereby creating a touchpoint that looks for Page = Home OR Page = App: Launch.

6. **Hover your cursor over the colorful side of each of the touchpoint's data in your new fallout. Now hover the cursor over the left side of each touchpoint to view each touchpoint's definition.**

   Note how hovering shows the Number of Visitors (or visits if you made that change in Step 4), Total Success %, and Touchpoint % for each touchpoint. Total Success % defines the percentage of traffic that started at the top of your fallout and made it to the touchpoint you're analyzing. Touchpoint % compares the current touchpoint to the previous one.

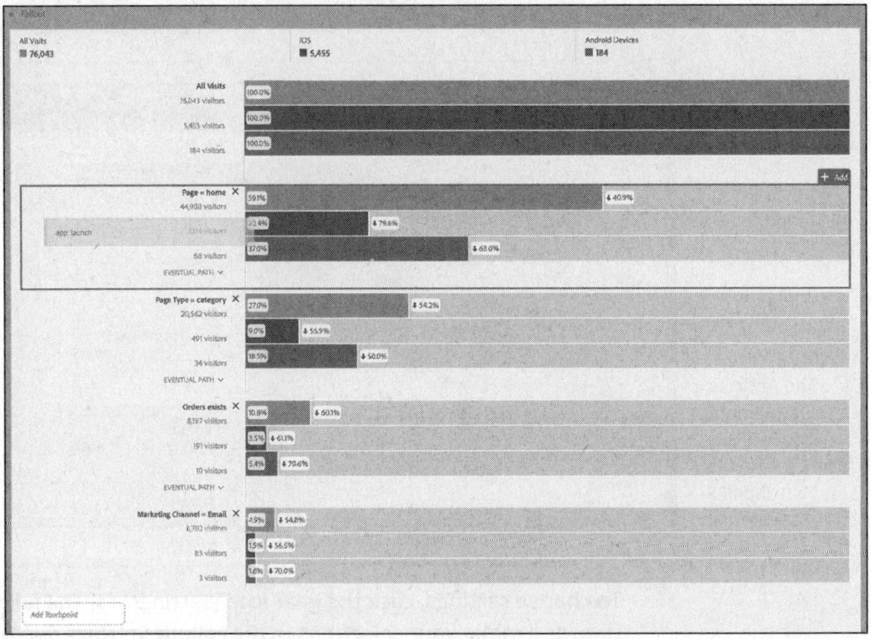

FIGURE 14-12:
A touchpoint is enhanced with a second dimensional item.

7. **Hover your cursor over the area to the left of the colorful data, locate the drop-down where Eventual Path is listed, and change the step to Next Hit.**

   This setting guarantees that the touchpoint is the very next action that occurs in your data, which is significantly more constricting. When you set a touchpoint to Eventual Path, the default, multiple actions and behaviors could be collected in Adobe Analytics between touchpoints. If your fallout container is set to Visitor, even unrelated visits can take place between touchpoints! Figure 14-13 shows the drop-down menu where the decision between Eventual Path and Next Hit takes place.

FIGURE 14-13:
A touchpoint is changed to be the next hit.

8. **Right-click any touchpoint's row of data.**

   The right-click context menu that appears is similar to the context menu when right-clicking the flow visualization. You can easily trend any (or all) touchpoints, segment any touchpoint, or break down the fallout or fallthrough. Adobe takes the fallout visualization from reporting to analysis — familiarize yourself with each of these options to become a fallout master!

The fallout visualization is one of Adobe's most interactive and flexible — the more comfortable you are with it, the more you'll find yourself using it. We've even used it to save time creating segments in Segment Builder! Just drop the necessary dimensions, metrics, and segments into a fallout, right-click, and click Create Segment from Touchpoint to create a prepopulated sequential segment!

Building Cohort Tables

Look up *cohort* in your favorite online dictionary, and you'll learn that a cohort is a group of people who share a set of similar demographic characteristics, such as fans who follow a band from venue to venue or a team of programmers who were hired at the same company under similar circumstances at about the same time. The term has its origins in the Latin word *cohort,* which refers to a military unit of men drawn from a common locale.

In data analytics, a *cohort* allows an analyst to zero in on a specific subset of people who have performed one action and then another. *Cohort analysis* involves a time factor to help you analyze how much time occurs between the first action — called the inclusion metric — and the second action — the return metric.

Cohort tables in Adobe Analytics can help you identify how much time usually passes between a visitor's first launch of an app and first purchase, for example. If you find an interesting cohort of users — those who made their first purchase within a week of their first app launch — Adobe makes it easy to create a segment of those users and analyze them further.

Understanding essential cohort table terminology

Before you walk through how to generate a cohort visualization and share an example, three terms are important to define:

>> **Granularity:** The level of timeframe specificity, which can be set to day, week, month, quarter, or year. Granularity is constrained by your calendar setting. So, for example, if your panel calendar is set for last month, it wouldn't make sense to set granularity to a time period longer than that (such as a quarter or a year).

Within the constraints of a calendar setting, a larger granularity setting will provide a much wider lens with which to examine cohort data. A shorter time period (such as a week) will zoom in on a precise segment of data.

>> **Inclusion criteria:** The conditions for inclusion in the cohort. In Workspace you must set a numeric constraint to the inclusion metric. For example, if the inclusion criteria is visits >= 1, only users who visited at least once during the time range of the cohort analysis will be included in the initial cohorts. Adobe enables you to add more than one metric to your inclusion criteria; there is no limit to the metrics that define your inclusion criteria. When you add multiple metrics, you apply a logical operator of either AND or OR to the metrics. A good use case for applying multiple metrics to your inclusion criteria is if you wanted to focus your cohort on visitors who have either registered for an account or logged in. Finally, Adobe also gives you the option to apply a segment to your inclusion criteria.

>> **Return criteria:** The conditions that define the return for your cohort. For example, if the return criteria is an order, only users who purchased after the period in which their inclusion activity placed them in the cohort will be represented as retained. Return criteria have the same requirements and options as the inclusion criteria — numeric constraints are required; multiple metrics can be applied; multiple metrics require logical operators; and segments can optionally be applied. A good example is focusing on visitors who have made more than two purchases on your site rather than just one.

>> **Cohort type:** The type of cohort, which by default focuses on retention — measuring how well your visitor cohorts return to complete your return criteria. The cohort type can be changed from retention to churn, which measures how your visitor cohorts fall out from your return criteria.

>> **Rolling calculations:** The calculation that defines the results. The Rolling Calculations option demands that visitors complete the return criteria in all consecutive returning time periods. An example will help make this crystal clear. If a visitor completes the return criteria three weeks after the inclusion period, a standard cohort table would include the visitor's data in two columns: Included and +3 Weeks. However, if the Rolling Calculation option is enabled for the cohort table, the visitor's data wouldn't be counted in the +3 Weeks column because the visitor didn't also complete the return criteria one week after inclusion and two weeks after inclusion. A different visitor would be included in the rolling calculation cohort table's +3 Weeks column if he also completed the return criteria one week after inclusion, two weeks after inclusion, and three weeks after inclusion. As you may have guessed, the rolling calculation is significantly more strict than the standard cohort calculation.

>> **Latency table:** The time that has elapsed before and after the inclusion event occurred. Latency tables are useful for analysis when the order of your inclusion and return criteria is less rigid. If it's possible for your return criteria to occur before your inclusion criteria, latency tables will help you identify how often and when this is occurring.

>> **Custom dimension cohort:** The dimension applied to the cohort. By default this is the time period, but you can change that to apply any dimension to the left column of the results. Custom dimension cohorts are useful if you're trying to analyze how cohort data is applied to different values of a dimension. For example, perhaps you're trying to analyze how often and how much time passes between an account registration and a purchase. Wouldn't it be interesting to differentiate this drop-off based on each of your different marketing channels? Set the custom dimension cohort to marketing channel and this analysis is possible!

With those terms noted, let's walk through how cohort visualizations are generated. In the process, you'll revisit these concepts.

Generating a cohort visualization

We've identified and defined key terms, so now you're ready to create a cohort table. Let's get down to detail!

To generate a cohort visualization, follow these steps:

1. **In Workspace, click Cohort Table from a blank panel.**

   Alternately, you can display visualizations in the left rail and drag the Cohort Table visualization into any panel. Similar to flow and fallout, cohort visualizations don't start with existing data tables. You create the data table from the cohort definition, which you do in the following steps. You can find the ABCs of creating blank panels in Chapter 3.

2. **Examine the Cohort Table definition box that appears, as shown in Figure 14-14.**

   Here you enter inclusion and return criteria, granularity, cohort type, and several advanced settings. You can also set the panel calendar to define a time range for your cohort table.

   Calendar settings are defined by clicking the date range in the upper-right corner of a panel. For more on calendar settings, see Chapter 3.

REMEMBER

3. **Drag the visits metric from the left rail to the Inclusion Criteria box for metrics.**

   Acceptable metrics can't include calculated metrics or revenue but can include other (non-calculated) metrics such as page views or orders, as well as custom metrics such as account registrations. Figure 14-15 shows a completed cohort table setup in which page views are defined as the inclusion metric.

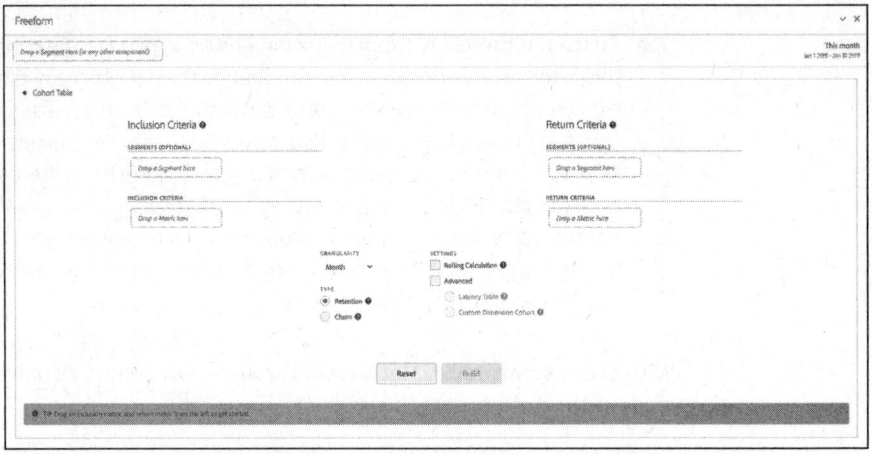

FIGURE 14-14:
Creating a cohort
table in a blank
visualization.

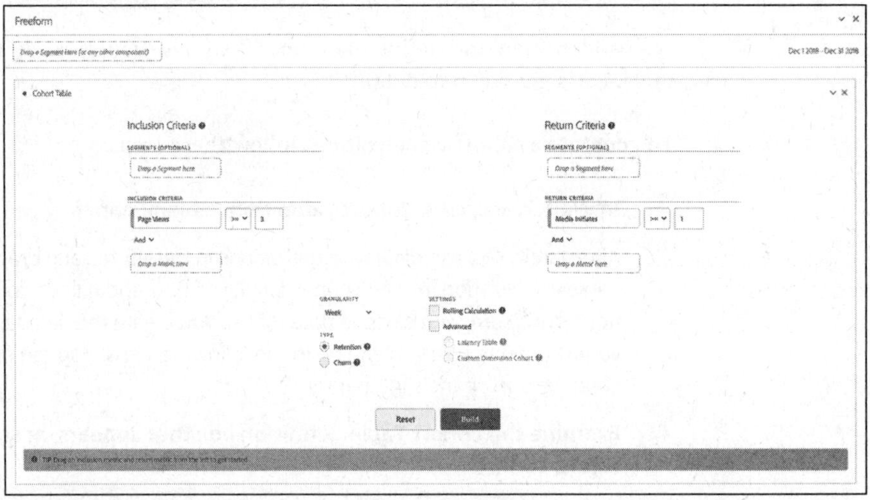

FIGURE 14-15:
A cohort table's
definition is
ready.

4. **Define the number of times your inclusion metric has to occur for your visitors to be included in the cohort.**

Choose a logical operator (greater than; greater than or equal to; equal to; less than; or less than or equal to) and enter a value in the blank box. Values can range from 1 (the default) to 9.

Why would you want to define a cohort with an inclusion metric that occurs more than once? Increasing the value (say from 1 to 3) further restricts the defined cohort.

5. **From the left rail, drag a different metric, such as media initiaties, for your return criteria.**

   If you were interested in using the same metric for your return criteria as you've already used for your inclusion criteria, you can save time by dragging and dropping metrics from your inclusion criteria to your return criteria.

6. **Define the number of times your return metrics must occur to define success for your cohort.**

   Like the inclusion criteria, return metrics require a logical operator and a value between 1 to 9.

7. **Set a granularity by using the Granularity drop-down list.**

   The Granularity menu defines the specificity of your cohort visualization: Day, Week, Month, Quarter, or Year. If you change the granularity to Week, the resulting visualization shows how many weeks pass between the inclusion and return metrics for your users.

   Figure 14-15 shows a cohort table for a time period of a week, with at least three page views as the inclusion metric and a return metric of at least a single media *initiate* (Adobe's term for a video view or audio listen). This cohort table focuses on visitors who have had at least three page views and, for those that initiate media, provides the amount of time that passes until their first media initiate.

8. **Examine the cohort type and optional settings.**

   The radio buttons for Type give you the option to change from a retention-focused cohort analysis to one that analyzes churn. The check boxes under Settings give you options for setting rolling calculations, latency tables, and custom dimension cohorts.

9. **Click Build to generate the cohort table.**

   The table in Figure 14-16 shows the results of the cohort table we built, illustrating how the relationship between visitors who viewed three pages and visitors who then initiated some media.

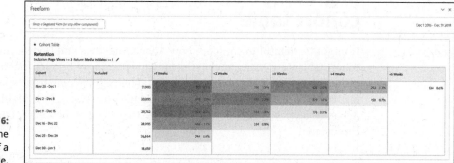

FIGURE 14-16: Examining the results of a cohort table.

The table is organized with rows of data that show each week within your panel calendar's time period. The first column, Included, displays the total number of visitors who were included in your cohort based on your inclusion criteria definition. In our example, this column shows the total number of visitors who saw three page views in each time period. For example, 21,903 visitors saw three page views the week of November 25–December 1; 20,895 visitors the following week, 20,762 the following week, and so on.

The remaining columns show the number and percentage of each row that completed the return criteria, as well as how much time passed for the return to occur. For example, 551 visitors (2.5 percent of the 21,903 visitors included in the cohort) returned with a media initiate in the week that followed November 25–December 1. 336 visitors in this cohort completed a media initiate two weeks later; 428 visitors three weeks later; and 292 visitors four weeks later.

Adobe Analytics uses color coding to make it easier to find cohorts with a significantly higher percentage of return metrics. Based on the data in Figure 14-16, you can see that the cohort of visitors with the quickest return to initiate media is the cohort that viewed three pages the week of November 25 and returned to the site within a week to initiate media. As analysts, we'd want to learn more about this cohort.

10. **Right-click the darkest cell in the cohort table and create a segment using the context menu that appears.**

Isn't it nice how this complex segment was pre-built for you? If you save the segment, you can apply it to any other visualization in Workspace and continue to learn more about that particular cohort of users.

Cohort tables in Workspace are complicated beasts — once tamed, however, they are incredibly useful visualizations. In addition to following the preceding instructions, we recommend playing with all the options, analyzing the results, and even creating segments to learn the details of the settings you've applied.

Migrating from Google Analytics' cohort table

It might be helpful to compare how Adobe Analytics and Google Analytics define cohort tables. For many of you, Google Analytics is your undergrad introduction to analytics. If you've worked with cohort tables in Google Analytics (as of this writing, cohort tables are a beta feature in Google Analytics), you might be coming to Adobe Analytics with some experiences that need to be deconstructed to avoid confusion.

Those differences can be summarized as follows:

» The only cohort type available in Google Analytics (at this writing) is acquisition date, which is the date a user first engaged your website.

» The available metrics in Google Analytics are constrained to goals, return visits, page views, and a few more. Plus, the include metric always has to be the same as the return metric. And unlike Workspace, there are no logical operators.

» Segments in Google Analytics can't be created based on the results of a cohort analysis. In contrast, Adobe enables you to right-click to create a segment.

» Segments can be applied directly to cohort analysis tables in Google Analytics. This feature makes it easier to differentiate cohorts based on segments you've defined. Segments in Adobe's cohort tables can be applied at only the panel level.

We've included a screenshot of the Google Analytics cohort table in Figure 14-17 for your reference.

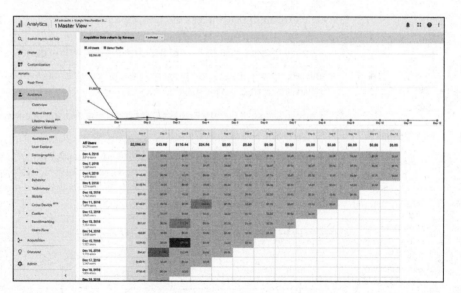

FIGURE 14-17:
The results of a cohort analysis in Google Analytics.

Customizing and Sharing Curated Projects

TMI!

That might be the subject line in an email after you invite colleagues, shareholders, clients, or executives to view a Workspace project. The solution? Curation.

By *curating a project*, you can restrict the set of dimensions, metrics, segments, and date ranges that you share with others. You can then share the curated project to others who may be overwhelmed by all the options.

A curated project is *not* a static report. The curated project, when shared with others who have access permission to Adobe Analytics, is fully functional in the sense that those who get it can apply breakdowns, add segments to panels, and in general interact with the project. But they will work with a smaller, constrained set of dimensions, metrics, segments, and date ranges that will simplify and focus their options.

Let's walk through the process of curating a project:

1. **Choose Project ⇨ Save As and give the project a new name.**

   By naming the project, you preserve the uncurated project while creating a new version that can be shared.

2. **Choose Share ⇨ Curate Project Data from the Workspace menu.**

   The Curated Components bar appears, as shown in Figure 14-18. By default, all metrics, dimensions, segments, and time ranges in your project's visualizations and tables are added to the list of curated components. The project in Figure 14-18 has visualizations with the page and page type dimensions.

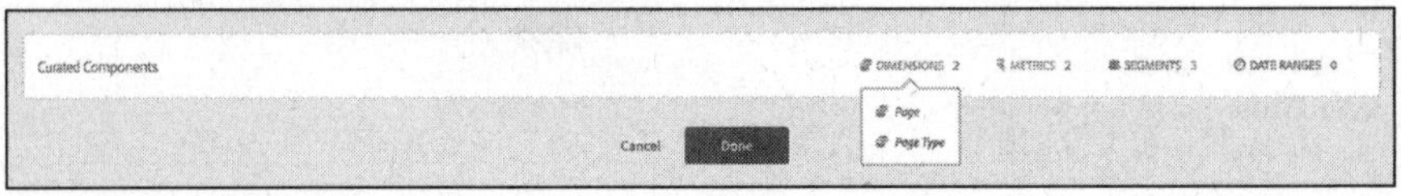

FIGURE 14-18:
The Curated Components bar is shown with two dimensions included.

3. **Drag new components into the Curated Components bar to give your end-users more access to interact with the visualizations.**

   You can choose any set of dimensions, metrics, segments, or date ranges. However, the point is to simplify the data options for recipients, so be prudent in adding components. Figure 14-19 shows a set of dimensions being added to the curated components list.

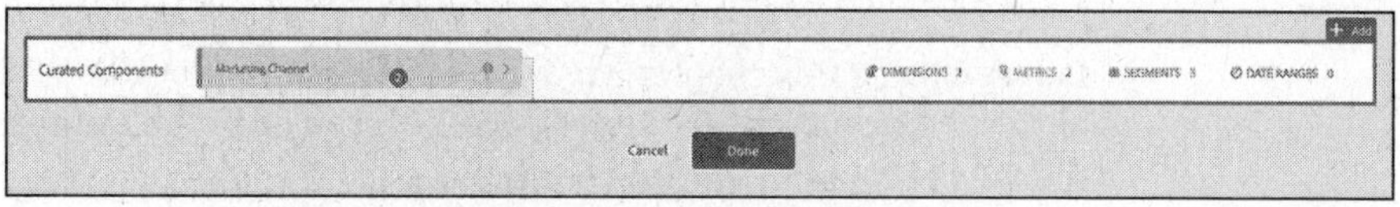

FIGURE 14-19: Adding two dimensions to a curated compo- nents set.

4. **Survey the entire set of any component by clicking it.**

   Items in italics are already included in visualizations in the project and there- fore can't be deleted. Items you added are displayed without italics and with an x so you can prune the set of components.

5. **After you finalize the constrained set of components, click Done.**

6. **Choose Project ⇨ Save from the Workspace menu to save the curated project.**

7. **Examine the changes to the left rail.**

   Only the metrics, dimensions, segments, and time ranges that you curated will be shown. However, if you click any of the Show All buttons in the left rail, you see a Show All Components option. That option is available to only the owner of the project and administrators.

To share the curated project, follow these steps:

1. **Choose Share ⇨ Share Project from the Workspace menu.**

   The Share Project dialog appears.

2. **Edit the name, description, and tags if necessary.**

3. **Click the down arrow next to Recipients and add recipients from the list of available people with access to the project.**

4. **In the Other Options section, select the Enable Any Available Additional Options check box.**

   These added options apply only to the defined list of recipients and won't apply if you add additional recipients later.

5. **Click the Share button.**

   Everyone you added to the Recipients list now has the project available to open in Workspace.

Changing Color Palettes

Before closing this chapter, we want to unleash your aesthetic side (who says data analysts have no sense of style?), and turn you on to the ability to change and customize the color scheme in your project.

Alternate color schemes apply to many elements in Workspace, including most visualizations. Particularly if you are presenting projects to a wider audience, a defined color palette can enhance the experience.

What does *not* change when you apply a new color palette? Alternate color palettes do not affect the following:

>> Summary change visualizations

>> Conditional formatting in freeform tables

>> Map visualizations

WARNING

Color palette support is not enabled for Internet Explorer 11.

To apply a custom color palette, follow these steps:

1. **From the Workspace menu, choose Project ⇨ Project Info & Settings.**

   The Project Info & Settings dialog appears.

2. **Click the down arrow next to Project Color Palette to display color palette options.**

   The set of predefined color palettes is shown in Figure 14-20.

3. **To define a custom set of colors, click Custom Palette.**

   A box appears where you can enter up to 16 comma-separated hexadecimal color values. We'll leave it to you to choose a set of appropriate web-friendly colors.

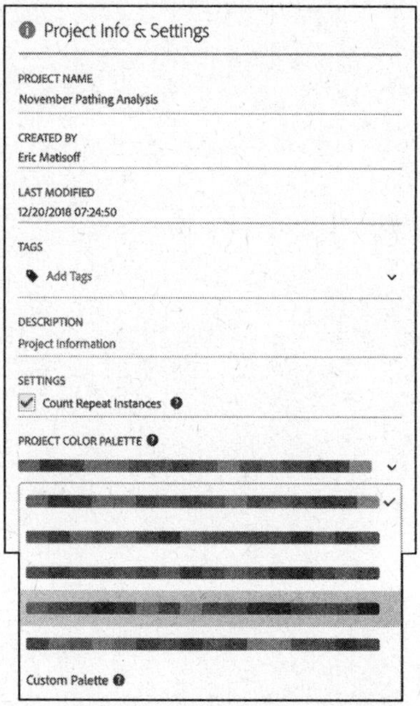

FIGURE 14-20:
Available color
palettes for
Workspace.

4. **Choose (or define) a color palette, and then click Save.**

   The new color palette is applied to your project.

Color palettes are a great finishing touch to your Workspace project. Many Adobe customers use it to apply their brand's official colors to their data visualizations. Others have a little more fun with it by applying colors that have to do with the time of year or type of analysis.

Chapter **15**

Leveraging Data Science to Identify Unknown Unknowns

Adobe has focused on incorporating human-driven, AI-assisted analyses in several features built into Analysis Workspace. Each feature uses a combination of data science, artificial intelligence, and machine learning to help you generate analyses and insights faster. All perform tasks that you could do on your own, but Adobe does it at scale to reduce your most mundane activities and increase your ability to find interesting and valuable data.

The three features you cover in this chapter are Anomaly Detection, Contribution Analysis, and Segment Comparison. Adobe has categorized these first two features, along with alerts, as part of Virtual Analyst. We find this branding to be appropriate because Virtual Analyst acts as an expert analyst who never leaves the office; the Virtual Analyst designates Adobe's machine learning-powered capabilities.

Detecting Anomalies

Anomalies — things that deviate from the norm or expected results — affect and play a key role in understanding all kinds of phenomena. And that applies to analyzing marketing data. Why does one product sell better than others through a specific marketing channel even though the products are similar? Why do people purchase more of a product on the first Tuesday of the month? And how can answering these mysteries open the door to more successful marketing?

Adobe Analytics provides powerful and intuitive tools for viewing and analyzing data anomalies contextually in Analysis Workspace. For example, Analysis Workspace's Anomaly Detection algorithm includes the following:

>> Support for hourly, weekly, and monthly granularity, in addition to the existing daily granularity

>> Awareness of seasonality (such as "Black Friday") and holidays

Let's walk through why Anomaly Detection is so important, why it works, and how it works. Then you zoom out a bit to look at how you can work with data that results from Anomaly Detection.

Using Anomaly Detection for KPIs

You start your exploration of Anomaly Detection by looking at how it helps you understand key performance indicator (KPI) metrics. For example, suppose your company sells bikes and accessories. Applying Anomaly Detection to a table or line chart might reveal the following:

>> Significant drops in average order value

>> A marked decline in landing page views

>> Spikes in low video bit-rates

>> Spikes in orders with low revenue

>> Spikes in video buffer events

>> Spikes or drops in trial registrations

Those are not unimportant events! And Anomaly Detection ferrets them out and shines a light on them, if we can mix metaphors for a moment.

But here we want to introduce another key factor in Anomaly Detection: using rules and formulas that take holidays and other significant calendar events into account. For example, a radical drop in orders, a marked decline in landing page views, or a spike in trial registration on the morning of December 25, in a country where most or many people celebrate Christmas, shouldn't set off alarm bells. Adobe's Anomaly Detection feature will set off alarm bells only if that radical drop, marked decline, or spike are statistically different — something the naked eye can't distinguish. Adobe Analytics has that covered, as you see when you walk through the basic algorithms behind Anomaly Detection shortly in this chapter.

WARNING

At this writing, Adobe Analytics Select and Adobe Analytics Foundation customers have access to only daily-granularity Anomaly Detection in Workspace. If you're unsure about whether you have access to additional features, check in with your administrator, who can find out by logging into the Adobe Analytics Admin Console and choosing Company Settings ⇨ View Feature Access Levels.

Understanding how Anomaly Detection works

Anomaly Detection provides a statistical method to determine if a given metric's change is statistically significant in relation to previous data. With Anomaly Detection, you're proactively informed of spikes or dips in your data that may not look like spikes or dips because, simply, you aren't as fast as a computer, let alone the slew of super-powered machines that are powering Adobe's algorithms. Anomaly Detection helps you to identify which fluctuations matter and which ones don't.

For example, imagine a business with a fairly simple weekly cadence — sales increase Monday through Thursday and decrease Friday through Sunday. Seems simple enough to recognize with the human eye? We agree. But how easy would it be to tell if this past Monday's sales increased more than normal — more than last week, last month, and last year?

Perhaps a good analyst like you would apply calculated metrics to identify this more quickly than other analysts, but you may not do that with every single analysis you perform. This is where Adobe's Anomaly Detection comes into play — every single metric you trend is automatically run through Adobe's algorithms to help you identify anomalies. The Adobe Analytics calculations that detect anomalies are super-fast and super-smart.

Understanding the logic and math behind Anomaly Detection

Adobe's put a lot of research into defining algorithms to detect anomalies. For some of us, that's all we need to know — we trust that solid logic and math are behind what us and isn't detected as an anomaly. If you're in the "just show me how to detect anomalies" mode, feel free to skip ahead to the next section. (We'll still be here with more explanation for how and why Anomaly Detection works.)

At some point in your relationship with Adobe Analytics, it's worth taking the time to walk through the math and logic behind how anomalies are identified. That peek under the hood will help you understand and appreciate the value, and validity, of what gets revealed.

Identifying statistical methods and rules behind Anomaly Detection

Anomaly Detection in Workspace uses a series of statistical techniques to determine whether an observation should be considered anomalous or not. Some of these techniques are complex, but others are basic and obvious.

An example of the latter: major holidays (such as the US holiday Thanksgiving) are factored into the Anomaly Detection equation. For example, if sales plummet during the afternoon of a major holiday, that's taken into account before Adobe Analytics sounds an alarm and misidentifies an anomaly.

Following is the complete list, as of this writing, of holidays that Adobe has applied to Anomaly Detection algorithms:

>> Memorial Day

>> Fourth of July

>> Thanksgiving

>> Black Friday

>> Cyber Monday

>> Christmas

>> Day before and after Christmas

>> Day of New Year's Eve

>> New Year's day

These holidays were selected based on extensive statistical analysis across many customer data points to identify holidays that mattered the most to the highest number of customers' trends. Although the list is certainly not exhaustive for all customers or business cycles, Adobe found that applying these holidays significantly improved the performance of the algorithm overall for nearly all customers' datasets.

A DEEPER LOOK AT ANOMALY DETECTION

Adobe's algorithms apply a time series model that incorporates an error, trend, seasonality (ETS) model for analysis. ETS is an application of exponential smoothing, an approach that data analysts have used since the 1950s to account for and contextualize spikes and dips in data. Over the past decades, that approach has continued to evolve. If you're interested in how smoothing models have been developed, you might dig into the book *Forecasting with Exponential Smoothing* by Rob Hyndman, Anne B. Koehle, Keith Ord, and Ralph D. Snyder. That book includes a section that explains the error, trend, seasonality (ETS) model that helps frame the complex math behind Anomaly Detection in Adobe Analytics.

Advanced Adobe customers often ask if the Anomaly Detection rules and algorithm can be adjusted. The short answer, unfortunately, is no. The rules for detecting — or filtering out — data that might indicate an anomaly are the result of substantial study by the folks at Adobe. These detection algorithms apply Anomaly Detection in a way that should be valuable for all companies. For example, if your company sells snowboards, skis, jet skis, and winter weather gear, you can't configure Adobe Analytics to discount dips in sales in July (in the northern hemisphere). You can build that type of seasonal variation into your reporting, but you can't customize Anomaly Detection for that task.

Adobe could have (and perhaps someday will) allow users to customize Anomaly Detection rules. At the same time, the fact that Anomaly Detection rules are currently fixed in Adobe Analytics highlights the reality that there will always be unique factors involved in data analysis that require critical thinking on the part of a human analyst.

Viewing anomalies in a date-based freeform table

We expect that you are now on the edge of your seat, waiting to learn how to apply Anomaly Detection to your Workspace projects. You can quickly access Anomaly Detection in Analysis Workspace in several ways. Often, we're already analyzing a set of trended data in a freeform table and would appreciate the automatic notification of anomalies. Follow these steps to view anomalies in a table that uses a date, such as day, hour, or month, as the lone dimension:

1. **Start with a freeform table in a panel with the timeframe set to last month.**

2. **Add a metric such as page views to the freeform table by dragging it to the first column header, which will automatically add day as your dimension.**

   The page views by day table in Figure 15-1 is a simple example, and one you've probably built dozens of times by now.

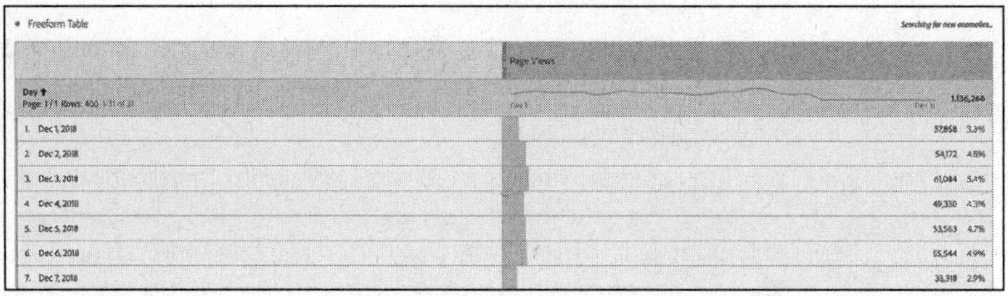

FIGURE 15-1:
A freeform table
on the hunt for
anomalies.

3. **In the freeform table, note the *Searching for New Anomalies* message that appears in the upper right.**

   Adobe Analytics is performing the computations you explored earlier in this chapter to track down and identify anomalies automatically.

   Within a few seconds, Adobe should complete its search for anomalies. Each row now automatically gets flagged with a triangle in the top-right corner if an anomaly has been detected.

4. **Hover your cursor over the triangle, as shown in Figure 15-2.**

   You see the extent to which the anomalous value differs from the expected value.

   Anomalous values are also represented visually in the cells of the table with a shaded green section indicating the gap between actual and expected values. In Figure 15-2, you can see that the shaded region in the first row ends significantly earlier than the vertical bar to the right of it, hence the anomaly's below-expected result shown in the details.

   Similarly, the shaded regions for December 18th and 19th extend beyond the vertical bar, representing an anomalous spike in the data.

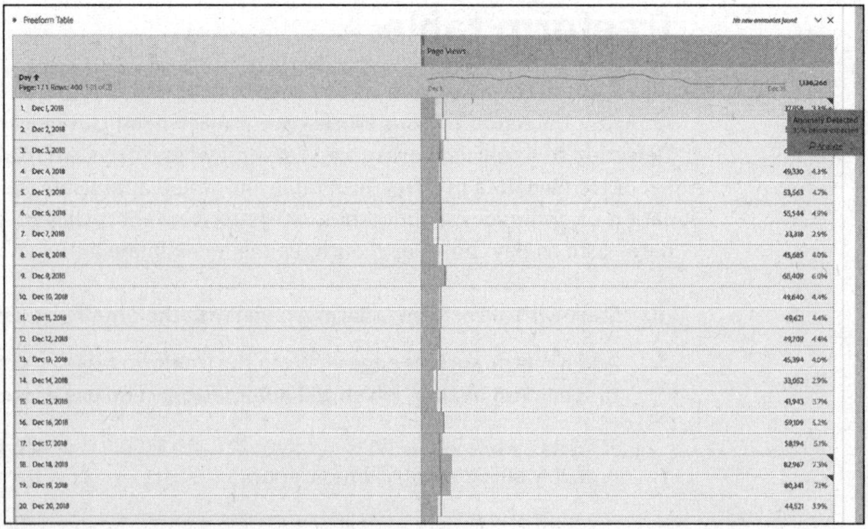

FIGURE 15-2:
The details of an
anomaly in a
freeform table
full of anomalies.

If these steps didn't result in any anomalies, don't blame us! It probably means that the metric you chose during the selected month doesn't have any anomalies — congrats on having steady data! However, no anomalies might also mean that you don't have access to Anomaly Detection. Try changing your date range and metric; if you still don't see anomalies, confirm with your administrator that you do have access to this feature.

Viewing anomalies without a date dimension via a trended line chart

As we've discussed earlier in this chapter, Anomaly Detection often kicks in automatically when you create a freeform table. But that's not always the case.

For example, if you create a freeform table using a dimension that is not a date (such as marketing channel, page type, or product), you won't see anomalies identified. But what if you *want* to see anomalies identified? For example, you might want to identify spikes in response to an email campaign even if your table is set up to compare different marketing channels.

To discover anomalies without a date dimension, follow these steps to learn how to create a trended line chart that has Anomaly Detection applied to it:

1. **Create a freeform table using a dimension that isn't a date (such as marketing channel) and any metric (such as page views).**

   Note how Adobe is not searching for anomalies because the dimension is not a date such as day or month.

2. **Hover your cursor over any dimension and click the Visualize button that appears, as shown in Figure 15-3.**

   After a few seconds of searching for anomalies, the line chart displays a shaded light green confidence band and a dotted line that indicates Adobe's forecast. Anomalies, if any, are shown as oversized data points on the trend line and will exist outside the green shaded region.

3. **To see more detail on any anomaly, hover your cursor over the anomalous data points.**

   The data point displays the anomaly's date, raw value, and percent difference from the expected value. If you see a link to analyze the anomaly, you also have access to trigger a Contribution Analysis. Don't click it just yet because your company may have limited access to this feature. Plus you wouldn't want to ruin the fun we have in store later in the chapter.

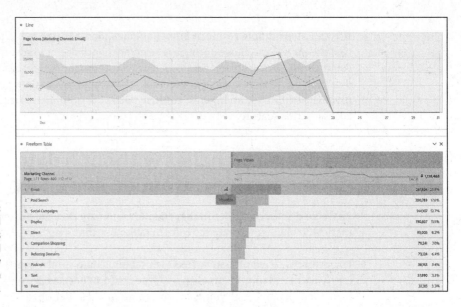

FIGURE 15-3:
The Email
channel is
trended and
anomaly
detection runs on
the line chart.

Adobe runs Anomaly Detection on every trended metric in Analysis Workspace. Did you just create a mega-powerful calculated metric with functions and apply multiple segments? Trend it and Anomaly Detection will be run. Did you just get 19 steps into a crazy flow path across multiple dimensions? Trend it and Anomaly Detection will be run. You'll soon be amazed at how often Adobe informs you of something you otherwise wouldn't have looked for — that's the magic of Anomaly Detection.

Turning off Anomaly Detection

We open this chapter with a discussion of the value of Anomaly Detection and have just successfully whet your appetite for the feature's ubiquity within Analysis Workspace. That is to say, Anomaly Detection is so built into Workspace that it occurs most of the time that you're working with data. But sometimes you don't want to display anomalies in your tables and line charts.

Why not detect anomalies? Well, Anomaly Detection is usually turned off strictly for visual purposes. We've been in meetings with executives who have a tendency to ask the wrong questions. If they see an oversized data point in our otherwise perfect Workspace project masterpiece, we'll have to spend 10 minutes explaining what it is, reassuring them that we've already looked into it, and reiterating that this isn't the purpose of this meeting anyhow. To avoid those rabbit holes, Adobe enables you to turn off Anomaly Detection in both charts and tables.

To turn off Anomaly Detection at the metric level in a freeform table, go to the Column settings by clicking the gear icon in the column header and then deselect Anomalies. This setting removes the triangles that appear for anomalies and the vertical bar that designates the expected value.

TIP

If you need to edit column settings for multiple metrics at a time, use keyboard shortcuts of Shift, ⌘, or Ctrl to select multiple column headers. Any changes that you make to the column settings will be applied to all selected columns.

To turn off Anomaly Detection in a chart, go to the chart's settings by clicking the gear icon in the top-right and then deselecting Show Anomalies. If the shading of the confidence band goes beyond the y-axis, select the Allow Anomaly Detection to Scale Y Axis option, which will increase the axis enough to make room for the metric's forecast.

Discovering Contribution Analysis

As you have learned, Anomaly Detection takes place automatically in Workspace in any table or line chart based on time. With this feature, you now know of anomalies that occurred within your data.

But the next question is why! Adobe Analytics provides a feature that leverages data science to isolate why an anomaly occurred. What event might have been a contributing factor? Did a particular browser affect the anomaly? Was the anomaly concentrated in a particular marketing channel? Adobe Analytics' Contribution Analysis will help track down the factors behind a detected anomaly.

WARNING

Contribution Analysis in Workspace is limited to Adobe Analytics customers based on your contract. Each Adobe customer has an allotted number of tokens in which the company can run a Contribution Analysis. Check with your administrator to learn how many tokens your company has access to before running a Contribution Analysis for training. This information can be obtained in the Admin Console by choosing Company Settings ⇨ View Feature Access Levels.

To implement Contribution Analysis, follow these steps:

1. **Hover your cursor over an anomaly in a trended table or line chart, and click Analyze in the pop-up that is displayed, as shown in a trended line chart Figure 15-4.**

   You can start Contribution Analysis from anomalies in a trended freeform table by hovering your cursor over the triangle that designates an anomaly and then clicking Analyze.

   The Contribution Analysis panel opens with some options to add or remove dimensions that are excluded.

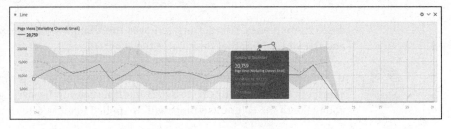

FIGURE 15-4:
Preparing to click Analyze from an anomaly in a line chart.

2. **Drag the dimensions you don't want analyzed by Contribution Analysis into the Excluded Dimensions box (see Figure 15-5).**

   By default, several dozen dimensions are automatically excluded from Contribution Analysis because they often show false positives or an incorrect result. The default list is useful, but we often add mobile-focused dimensions such as mobile DRM and mobile Java VM, which are rarely useful in our analyses.

TIP

Getting acclimated to Contribution Analysis requires some persistence. The first few times you run Contribution Analysis, you may get frustrated by obvious answers, false positives, or dimensions that you find useless. Don't get frustrated — keep honing your usage of the feature. With experience and trial and error, you will more quickly identify the dimensions to exclude. You can teach Adobe to remember excluded dimensions by dragging them into the Excluded Dimensions box and clicking the Set as Default button.

If you need to remove dimensions from the exclusion list, click the Dimensions button in the panel and deselect items by clicking the corresponding X.

FIGURE 15-5:
Adding dimensions to exclude from Contribution Analysis.

3. **Click the blue Run Contribution Analysis button.**

   A Contribution Analysis usually takes a half minute to two minutes to run, depending on the amount of data in your report suite.

4. **Examine the resulting visualizations.**

Let's review them together from top to bottom, left to right. Follow along in Figure 15-6 for a visual sample of Contribution Analysis results:

>> First you see a summary of the metric on which you've run a Contribution Analysis.

>> Next is a trend of your metric, with the date that you've run the Contribution Analysis highlighted with a darker green circle.

>> The first table is the most valuable result of the Contribution Analysis — Adobe's data-science-powered answer to the reason the anomaly occurred. The table lists dimensional items across all of your dimensions (except those you excluded, of course) along with a contribution score. The contribution score, a number between 0 and 1, is an expression of the significance of the dimensional item — the higher the score, the higher the significance. However, every item is statistically significant, so it's worth inspecting them all. The last two columns in this table display your metric and unique visitors for the Contribution Analysis.

This table is a fully functional freeform table, so we highly recommend breaking down the dimensional items, applying segments, and adding calculated metrics. If you do so, note that the contribution score will not be updated.

>> The last table in the results displays a list of segments that Adobe created based on clusters of the returned dimensional items. Think of these as pre-baked segments that Adobe created to help you get faster value from the results.

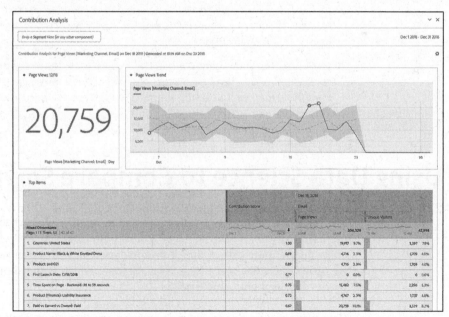

FIGURE 15-6: Contribution Analysis results.

GETTING THE MOST OUT OF CONTRIBUTION ANALYSIS

We've explored the nature of Contribution Analysis as applied to detected anomalies. And we've walked through how to configure Contribution Analysis to focus on specific dimensions that are most relevant to getting to the bottom of why sales slumped or spiked, why page views plummeted or peaked, or why revenue popped or dropped.

We have a few recommendations for new users of Contribution Analysis in Workspace:

- **Work with your administrator to ensure that you're getting the most out of your Contribution Analysis tokens.** As mentioned, your company has a limited number of tokens to run Contribution Analysis per month. However, if you run an analysis that is saved in a Workspace project, Adobe doesn't charge for a second token if you re-open a previously run Contribution Analysis.

- **Contribution Analysis is meant to decrease the time you spend manually dragging and dropping one dimension after another to see if it had any effect on the anomaly.** Don't fret that machine learning will soon be replacing your job! The Contribution Analysis feature is speeding your time to insights, not replacing you.

  If you find an anomaly, apply some of your preferred dimensions to analyze it — perhaps marketing channel, device type, and geolocation — and come up empty-handed, consider Contribution Analysis. The advantage of this feature is that it can help you identify dimensions at scale!

- **Don't just stop your analysis when the feature provides you with results.** The results of a Contribution Analysis tells only part of the story. It's up to you to break down the dimensions, apply the segments, and create new calculated metrics to tell a story with your data.

Using Data Science to Compare Segments

The third data-science-influenced feature in Analysis Workspace is called Segment Comparison. It's one of Adobe's most powerful features because it helps you easily differentiate two groups of visitors based on their behavior. In Chapter 13, we review the steps to create a Venn diagram, which is the simplest part of the results of a Segment Comparison.

Have you reviewed a Venn diagram recently and wondered about the following:

>> What are the metrics that differentiate my segments? For example, you might discover a correlation between your logged in visitor segment and views of blog articles.

>> What are the dimensions that differentiate my segments? For example, you might discover that iOS device types make up a significant portion of visitors who have converted.

>> What other segments can be applied to my segments to differentiate them? For example, you might see that visitors referred from paid search have a higher likelihood of being in the custom segment you created of first-time visitors who land on a product page.

If so, you've come to the right place! Those questions are the ones that Segment Comparison aims to answer, using machine learning every step of the way! First, we provide you with the steps to compare two segments that you've already created: iOS devices and purchasers. Then we dig into a few other examples of useful segment comparisons to try out.

Invoking Segment Comparison

To compare segments, follow these steps:

1. **Use the left rail selector to change the left rail's view to panels.**

2. **Drag the Segment Comparison panel into Workspace, as shown in Figure 15-7.**

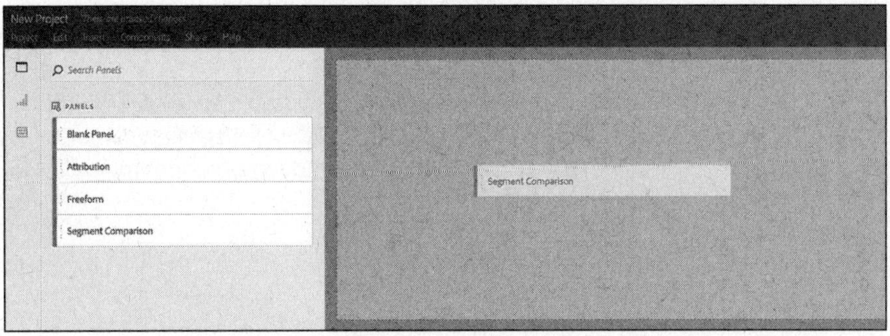

FIGURE 15-7: Dragging the Segment Comparison panel into workspace.

3. **Drag a segment into the Add a Segment area in the Segment Comparison panel, as shown in Figure 15-8.**

In addition to segments, you can also drag dimensions, dimensional items, metrics, and time ranges into the box. In our example, we drag a segment we've already created that focuses on iOS devices. If you'd like to create a segment in this workflow, hover your cursor over the Add a Segment box and click the plus sign that appears.

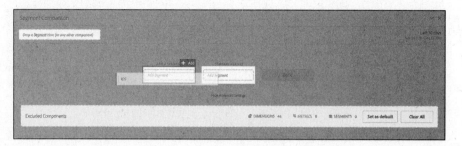

4. **Drag a second segment (or any other component) into the Compare Against box.**

   By default, Adobe includes a segment focused on Everyone Else, in case you merely want to compare this segment against its inverse. However, this results in a Venn diagram without any overlap. This can be useful, but for our example, we want to compare against a second segment.

   In Figure 15-9, we added a Purchasers segment to the Compare Against box. Based on the assumption that some visitors on iOS devices have made purchases, we can expect to see some overlap between the two segments.

5. **Click the Show Advanced link.**

   The box that appears should look familiar if you remember the Excluded Dimensions box for Contribution Analysis. As shown in Figure 15-9, you have the option to exclude dimensions, metrics, and segments from the analysis and results of your segment comparison. Just as in a Contribution Analysis, the reason to exclude dimensions is to avoid annoying results that may be accurate but aren't actionable. Because Segment Comparison also analyzes metrics and segments, they are added as options for exclusion.

6. **Click the blue Build button and examine the results that appear, often in less than a minute.**

As you can see in Figure 15-10, a wealth of visualizations are returned from Segment Comparison.

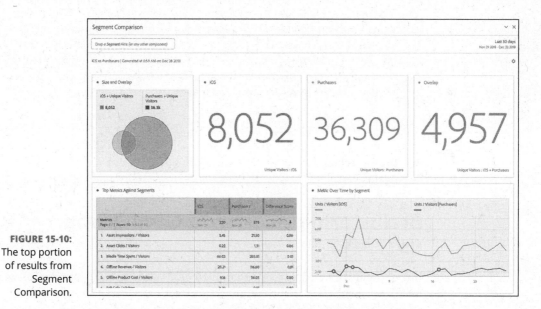

FIGURE 15-10: The top portion of results from Segment Comparison.

Let's review them from top to bottom, left to right:

>> The Size and Overlap visualization is a Venn diagram that you could have easily built based on your two segments and a metric of unique visitors. For an understanding of how to create and interact with this type of visualization, head to Chapter 13.

>> The next three summary visualizations show the count of unique visitors for each of your segments as well as the overlap between them. These summary visualizations can be a good reference as you perform your analysis.

>> The two visualizations in the second row of the results are *live-linked,* which means that when you click a value in the table on the left, the graph on the right is updated. The table on the left shows the top metrics that differentiate your two selected segments. A column for difference score sorts each of the metrics by their level of statistical significant, just like Contribution Analysis's contribution score. You'll be glad to see that Adobe runs Anomaly Detection on all metrics that are trended in the line chart on the right too! As you can see in the third row in the table in Figure 15-10, purchasers end up watching a significantly higher amount of media (an average of 285.81 seconds) than iOS visitors (an average of only 66.03 seconds).

>> The third row shows two more live-linked visualizations: a table on the left of the dimensional items that differentiates your two segments and a bar chart on the right that shows the stark difference when each of your two segments are applied to the dimensional items. A difference score is again applied to these visualizations.

>> The fourth and final row of your Segment Comparison results uses your own data to help you differentiate the segments you're comparing. Adobe analyzes all segments you have access to or have created so that it can provide a final list of differentiating segments. The freeform table live-links the differentiating segments to a Venn diagram on the right, which allows you to quickly find overlap between three different segments.

Adobe's Segment Comparison tool is a fantastic and fast way to learn more about your visitors. You'll be glad to hear that there is no limit to the number of times you or your company can use this tool, regardless of contract or SKU. If you don't have access to it, be sure to work with your administrator to understand why.

Brainstorming Segment Comparison use cases

If your brain isn't already working in high gear thinking creatively about how to use the Segment Comparison feature, let's give it a kickstart. Our first recommendation is to start with a segment of converters to your site.

As a reminder, someone who converts doesn't necessarily mean he or she has purchased. For websites and apps that don't sell anything, a conversion could mean a registration, a video view, or a threshold of unique views of content. Whatever your conversion, create a segment based on visitors who have accomplished it.

The most basic comparison to run is converters versus non-converters. At first, Segment Comparison will most likely tell you things you already know — your best marketing channels, micro-conversions that are leading indicators to success, or regions of the country that are more successful than others. Segment clustering in Segment Comparison's results may come in handy in use cases like these. Are there any unusual combinations of those dimensions that Adobe suggests reviewing? If Adobe provided you with any segments that are comprised of atypical dimension combinations, start your analysis there.

For those of you who do have a purchase funnel, consider creating segments for each of the key steps of the funnel — visitors who get to a product page but don't add to cart; visitors who add to cart but don't get to the checkout page; visitors who get to the checkout page but don't purchase; and visitors who purchase. Play around with each segment in Segment Comparison to learn more about what differentiates one segment from the other. Because you have unlimited access to the Segment Comparison tool, you might as well try it out!

Last, and certainly not least, try a mixture of marketing channel and account purchase status. For example, segment visitors who access your site via the most successful marketing channel and compare it to visitors who purchase. Then compare it to visitors who don't purchase.

Segment Comparison will often help you discover metrics, dimensions, and segments that differentiate segments that you hadn't thought to consider comparing before. Ideally, that newfound information will help drive your data curiosity.

Chapter **16**

Arming Yourself with Data from the Beyond

For the vast majority of this book, we focus on the features, capabilities, and advantages that Analysis Workspace brings to analysts like you. Adobe's browser-based application is one of the most flexible and powerful analysis tools in the industry, but sometimes you need other options, such as when you want to

» Integrate with other datasets

» Share data with constituents who aren't comfortable in Workspace

» Analyze data more visually through heat maps

In the pages that follow, we focus on each of these use cases and more. To work with data outside Adobe Analytics you still start in Workspace, but then you move from that application to Excel (or other spreadsheet applications), browser plug-ins, and data integrations. These are important tools in any analyst's toolbelt — for drawing on data outside Adobe Analytics, for sharing data with those outside the community of Adobe Analytics users, and for using tools (such as spreadsheets) outside Analytics to work with data.

Drawing Analysis outside Workspace

Analysis of Adobe data is not exclusive to Analysis Workspace. Over the years, Adobe has built several interfaces that support the data collected in Adobe Analytics as well as options for downloading and exporting this data. Whether your goal is integration or sharing your visualizations by using Excel or PDF, you have several options.

Exporting projects to CSV or PDF

One easy option for exporting data from a freeform table in Workspace is to highlight what you need and copy the data to the clipboard. Press Cmd+C (Mac) or Ctrl+C (PC) to copy all highlighted data in a freeform table to the clipboard. You can then paste the data in any application: Excel, a table in Word or PowerPoint . . . anywhere!

Another way to copy data from a freeform table is to right-click the area to the right of a table's name and click Copy to Clipboard, as shown in Figure 16-1.

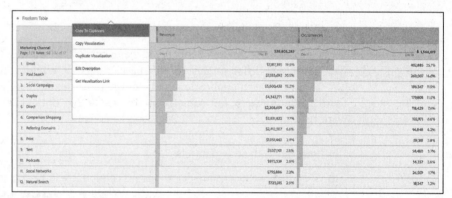

FIGURE 16-1:
Copying a freeform table to the clipboard.

Copying and pasting cells from a table in Workspace works well when you're sharing small sections of a project. But you can also export entire projects. Let's face it, as powerful as Workspace is, sometimes you want to massage data and perform calculations that require the complex capability to create equations in spreadsheet applications. Workspace projects can be exported easily to the ubiquitous and widely support CSV (comma separated values) format by choosing Project ⇨ Download CSV. CSV files can be opened in any spreadsheet application, including Microsoft Excel, Google Sheets, Numbers, or OpenOffice Calc.

Besides the ability to have all of your project's freeform tables exported into a single file, Adobe's CSV exports also include the data associated with your flow, fallout, and cohort table visualizations.

Sometimes you'll want to share reports widely, among an audience that doesn't want to wade through a Workspace report or even a spreadsheet. In this case, universally supported PDF is another option for export. You can export data to PDF from the same Projects menu, as shown in Figure 16-2.

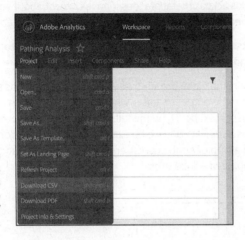

FIGURE 16-2:
The Projects menu provides access to download as CSV and PDF.

PDF data includes all visualizations exactly as they are shown in your browser before clicking Download. Therefore, carefully check how your data is presented *before* you export. For example, make sure that your visualizations and tables have the correct filters applied, that the correct number of rows is displayed, and that everything is properly formatted before exporting and downloading.

Sending projects from workspace to email

You can also use email to share Workspace projects. This feature in Workspace automatically provides options to export the project to PDF or CSV and attach that file to an email.

One big advantage to sharing a project through email is that the recipients can be inside or outside your organization — they don't need access to Workspace!

Here are the easy steps for sharing a report (either as a CSV or a PDF) via email:

1. **Open the project you want to send in Workspace.**

2. **Choose Share ⇨ Send File Now from the Workspace nav menu.**

   Or use the keyboard shortcut Alt+S. The Send File dialog appears.

3. **If necessary, edit, fill in, or update the Project Name, File Type, and Description fields.**

   Each of these fields acts as metadata (descriptive content about your project), which will be added to the exported file you are generating and emailing.

4. **In the Recipients text box, find the Adobe Analytics user(s) to whom you'd like to send your project.**

   You can also export the file to groups that your administrator has set up. If you want to send the output to a user whose email address isn't in Adobe, click in the Recipients text box, type the full email address, and press Enter. Figure 16-3 shows a project about to be exported to Dave (an Adobe user), Executive Staff (a group of Adobe users), and a couple of email addresses outside any grouping of Adobe users.

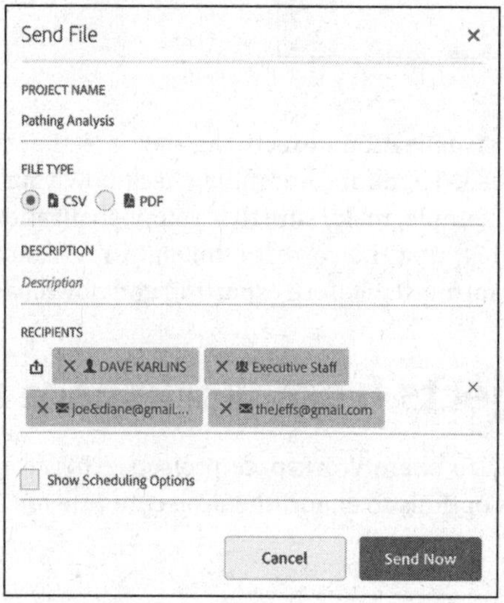

FIGURE 16-3: Getting ready to send a CSV export.

5. **(Optional) To schedule the export to be sent to your recipients on a regular basis:**

    a. Select the Show Scheduling Options check box.

    b. Select an option. Your scheduling choices are Starting On, Frequency, Frequency Detail, and Ending On.

> **TIP** Recipients can unsubscribe from your exports with a single click from any of the emails they receive.

6. **Click Send Now (or Send on Schedule, if you set up a schedule).**

As the number of people analyzing your Workspace projects grows, you'll be glad to have a wealth of ways to begin to disperse and share data from Adobe Analytics.

When you share projects, think about how you might want to prune and organize projects to focus on data most useful to a specific audience. Consider adding text visualization to describe the data on display. For example, as we discuss in Chapter 15, sometimes it's not helpful to spotlight anomalies such as seasonal upswings or dips in sales because it will distract your audience from focusing on more salient and defining trends. Also consider using Workspace's text visualization. The text visualization's rich text editor enables you to provide detailed contextual explanations as well as high-level executive summaries that outline key insights and recommendations.

Think, also, about optimal scheduling. Sending projects too frequently can overload your audience. But sending them too infrequently can result in trends that should have been distributed going unnoticed, preventing management or other teams from timely action. Be attuned to how your projects are being received and used, and adjust schedules accordingly.

The bottom line is this: the scheduling feature in Workspace allows you to bring a wider audience into the process of digesting and acting on data than just those who can navigate Analysis Workspace.

Creating alerts based on anomalies

One of our favorite ways to use automation to be aware of significant changes in our data is Adobe's Intelligent Alerts feature. Alerts can check data for abnormalities hourly, daily, weekly, or monthly by using either the same algorithms as Anomaly Detection or manual rules that you create. After you've set up Intelligent Alerts, Adobe can inform you by email or text message about any irregularities.

Before we go through the steps to create an alert, let's discuss some basic terminology that you'll encounter along the way. Adobe's Intelligent Alerts setup interface uses two different drop zones. Having multiple drop zones may seem unusual because Segment Builder and Calculated Metric Builder each require only one at a time, but it's easy to distinguish them because they are labeled.

When you start walking through the steps for defining an alert, you'll see a Metrics drop zone on top. You can drop any metric in Workspace into the Metrics drop zone: standard metrics, custom metrics, and even calculated metrics. If you add more than one metric to an alert, Adobe will trigger an alert if an anomaly is detected in any of the metrics.

The other drop zone you explore is labeled Filters. As you create your alert, you have the option to apply filters in this drop zone with a single dimension, multiple dimensions, a single segment, multiple segments, or any dimension-and-segment combination!

You also have to decide how metrics will be examined by Adobe. You do this in Adobe by defining an alert condition type, which must be set for all metrics in the drop zone. The first three alert condition types use Anomaly Detection algorithms. (If the mention of Anomaly Detection has you scratching your head, check out Chapter 15, where we define and deploy Anomaly Detection in detail.)

You can also define additional constraints so that alerts go off if the anomaly is above or below Adobe's predicted forecast. When you select one of these anomaly-based conditions, another drop-down list appears, requesting that you set a threshold. The higher the threshold, the less Adobe will alert you of an anomaly.

Workspace includes options for manually defining alert condition types. Don't worry about them. These options are less valuable than Adobe's algorithms for detecting anomalies, which have improved as Adobe Analytics has evolved. Have we *ever* defined manual alerts? Yes. For example, we've created alerts for when total page views or revenue drops to zero. If one of these events happen, we know something on the site is broken and needs to be fixed ASAP.

Following are the basic steps for creating an alert from scratch along with some additional context on creating them in your analysis workflow. Your Adobe Analytics contract might provide you only limited access to Intelligent Alerts, so work with your administrator if you don't see all of the options mentioned in the following steps:

1. **Start creating a new alert by choosing Components ⇨ New Alert from the nav menu in Analysis Workspace.**

   Or use the keyboard shortcut Shift+Cmd+A (Mac) or Shift+Ctrl+A (PC). The Alert Builder interface into view.

2. **If you're already partway through an analysis and want to create an alert based on data in a freeform table, select and then right-click the rows in which you'd like to create an alert, and choose Create Alert from Selection. Skip to Step 4.**

TIP

The drop zone for your alert is automatically populated — a huge time-saver that helps you skip Step 2 in this walkthrough.

3. **Drag a metric (such as Page Views) into the top drop zone for metrics.**

If you want to create a more complex alert, drag multiple metrics and even filters from the left rail to their corresponding drop zones. Remember: Metrics go in the top drop zone, and dimensions and segments go in the bottom.

You can add new rules to your alert by clicking the gear icon in the top-right of the drop zone and choosing Add Rule.

Both sections of this drop zone are automatically configured when you right-click rows from a freeform table to create an alert. (See Step 2.)

TIP

When you add or edit a component in the drop zone, the alert preview in the top-right is updated. This preview provides an approximation of the number of times the alert would have been recently triggered based on your current alert settings. The preview a great way to ensure that you're creating an alert that will trigger only when necessary — neither too much nor too little. Keep an eye on how the alert preview updates throughout the remainder of this process.

4. **Choose an alert condition type of Anomaly Exists for your metrics.**

The drop-down list that appears when you click Anomaly Exists is how you would create a manual rule type or a different anomaly-detection-powered alert.

5. **Examine the options for other thresholds by clicking the drop-down list to the right of the alert condition type, but eventually leave the threshold at the default 99%.**

Each metric has an alert preview incorporated in a green circle on the right side of each row. In Figure 16-4, you can see how the page views metric would have triggered once over the last 30 days. Adjusting the threshold of your metric higher or lower affects both alert previews.

6. **Define your time granularity.**

Time granularity is how often Adobe checks your rule(s). When you make changes to an alert's granularity, the alert preview adjusts because Adobe is searching a different time period for anomalies. By default, the granularity is set to daily, but you can adjust it by selecting Hourly, Weekly, or Monthly from the Time Granularity drop-down menu. (The menu is the third field from the top of the interface, after Title and Description.)

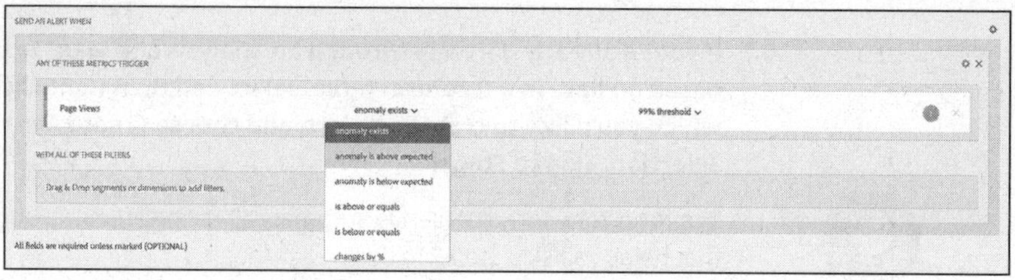

FIGURE 16-4:
The types of
conditions for a
metric trigger.

7. **Enter a title, a description, an expiration date, and your recipients in the fields at the top of the interface. Then click the blue Save button.**

We like to be explicit when setting a title and description so that we're properly informed if an alert is triggered. You can send alerts to yourself, other Adobe Analytics users, Adobe Analytics groups, or email addresses that you enter manually.

You can also set a mobile phone as a recipient. However, we limit alerts that trigger a text message to only the direst alerts. To enter a mobile phone number, type a plus sign, then your country code, and then the full phone number. For example, to send an alert to Jenny, an exec at Tommy Tutone's, we would enter +15558675309 in the Recipient field, and press Enter.

Tapping into Adobe data directly in Excel

Aside from Analysis Workspace, our favorite Adobe Analytics tool is Report Builder. This Excel plug-in for Windows taps directly into your report suite from the Excel interface. We could write several chapters on the subject if we had the room. Instead, we focus on the basics to get you started: installing the plug-in, logging in, and running your first report.

To install the plug-in, hover your cursor over Tools in the main Adobe menu and click Report Builder. Almost all Adobe Analytics contracts have some access to Report Builder. If you don't see it, speak to your administrator about getting access.

After you install the plug-in to Excel, a new section in the Add-Ins Ribbon will appear in the main Excel menu, as shown in Figure 16-5. Click Sign In from the Add-Ins menu to trigger the plug-in. Choose your method of login; Experience Cloud is the most likely choice.

The process for creating a report takes a few steps. Here are the highlights:

1. **After you've logged in, click the Create button from the Report Builder menu in Excel, listed under the Add-ins Ribbon.**

The plug-in takes a minute to initialize, and then the Request Wizard appears.

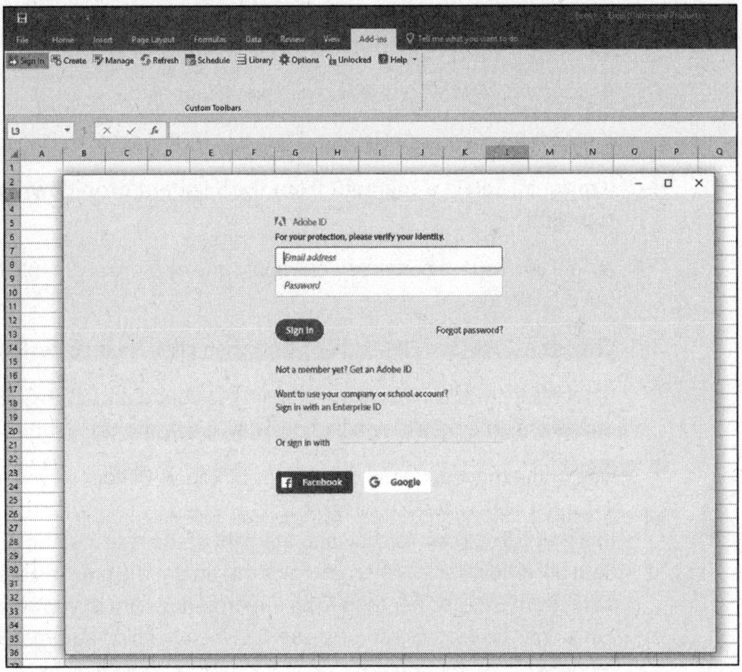

FIGURE 16-5:
The Experience
Cloud login
screen in Report
Builder.

2. **In the first drop-down menu, Report Suite, identify and select the report suite you want to report on.**

   Both standard report suites and virtual report suites are accessible here; the latter are listed with the term *virtual* in parentheses.

   Below your report suite selection is a list of radio buttons associated with the reports available to build.

3. **Click the plus sign next to Site Content to see its associated reports, and then click the Site Section radio button.**

   The taxonomy of this menu may seem alien — it's organized the same way as the menu in Adobe's older product, Reports & Analytics. Components are organized not as metrics versus dimensions but based on type. Click through each category to see what's listed. Here are the most important categories:

   - *Site content:* Page, site section, server, downloads, exits, custom links. Hierarchy is not listed because it is inaccessible in Report Builder.

   - *Paths:* Fallout and flow reports of page, site section, and any other custom props

   - *Campaigns:* Campaign tracking code

   - *Products:* Product and its classifications

- *Custom Conversion:* eVars and their classifications

- *Custom Traffic:* Props and their classifications

- *Marketing Channels:* First- and last-touch channel and channel detail

4. **(Optional) Select a segment from the Segment drop-down menu, in the top-right.**

As in a Workspace panel, you can apply one or more segments to a Report Builder request.

5. **Choose a date (see Figure 16-6), and then click Next to design your request.**

If necessary, you can apply a granularity to your data, which is similar to applying a time breakdown by hour, day, week, month, quarter, or year.

TIP

One of the most powerful capabilities of Report Builder is how well-integrated it is into Excel. One such integration is enabled by the red arrow icon pointing to a green Excel cell, as shown to the right of the report suite, segment, and date drop-down lists. When you click this arrow, the plug-in asks you to use a value from Excel rather than from the drop-down list. If you're talented at Excel functions, this feature can be powerful when building automated, cross-tabular reports.

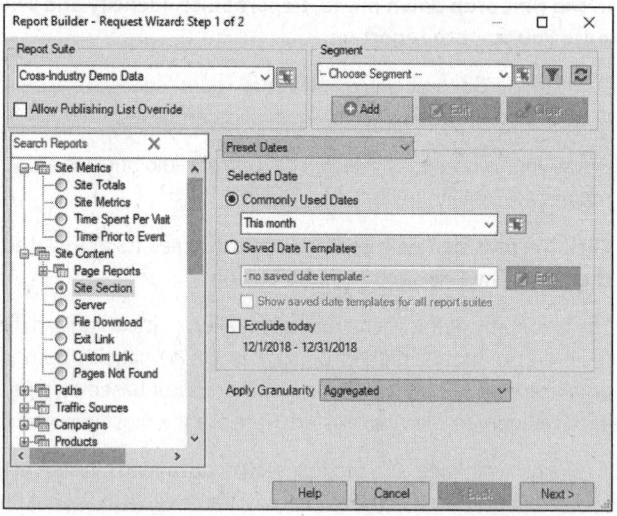

FIGURE 16-6:
The first step in the Request Wizard is complete.

6. **Drag a metric (such as Page Views) from the left column, which lists your metrics and dimensions, to the Metrics drop zone on the right.**

You can drag multiple metrics to the Metrics drop zone. The area in the bottom-right displays a preview of your request as you build it.

7. **Click the Dimensions tab, at the top of the left column.**

This is where you can apply dimensional breakdowns to your report.

8. **Click the button with the red arrow to the right of the Select 1 Cell text box.**

A dialog box appears so you can assign a location in Excel where the data will be output.

9. **Click any blank cell in Excel, and then click the button with the red arrow again to return to the second step in the Request Wizard, as shown in Figure 16-7.**

Your request is now ready to submit, but more options are available. For example, you can click the Top 1-10 link to extract more or fewer rows to Excel. If you're feeling adventurous, click the Custom Layout radio button at the top to create a custom layout — not for the faint of heart but intuitive enough for you to do after some practice.

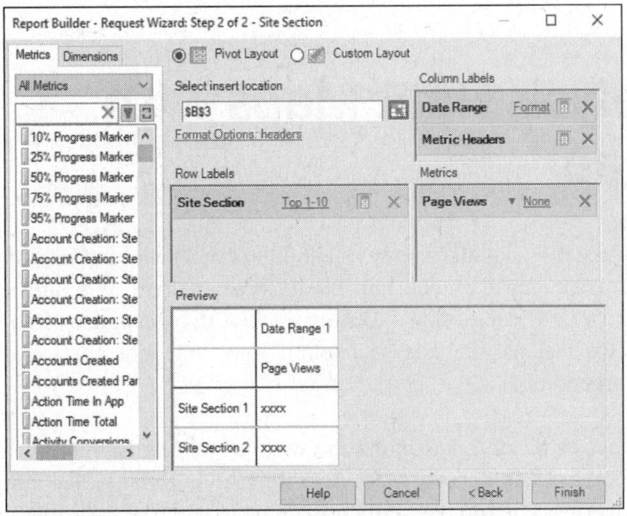

FIGURE 16-7:
The second step
of the Request
Wizard.

10. **Click Finish and wait for your data to return.**

The data usually returns in a few seconds to a few minutes, depending on the amount of data you've requested. For example, Figure 16-8 shows the total number of page views per site section for December.

We hope Adobe's Report Builder tool has you grinning at the possibilities. We see it used for deep analyses that require months and months of granular data integrated with other non-Adobe datasets in Excel. This advanced analysis often

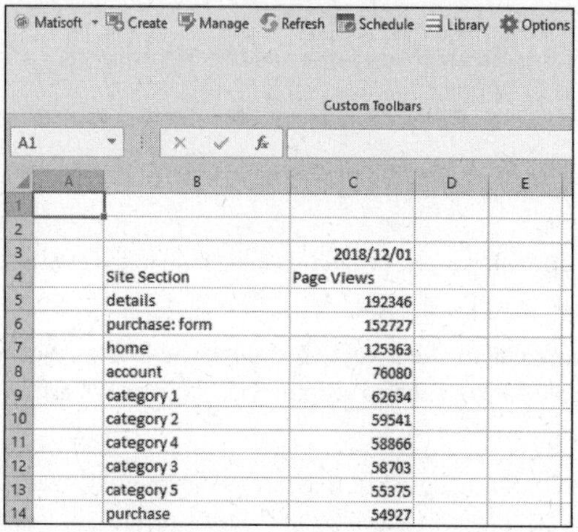

	A	B	C	D	E
1					
2					
3			2018/12/01		
4		Site Section	Page Views		
5		details	192346		
6		purchase: form	152727		
7		home	125363		
8		account	76080		
9		category 1	62634		
10		category 2	59541		
11		category 4	58866		
12		category 3	58703		
13		category 5	55375		
14		purchase	54927		

FIGURE 16-8: A simple Report Builder request is returned to Excel.

requires some of Microsoft's most powerful statistical and logical functions to drive automated visualizations and analysis. As you begin to feel the need to automate and integrate, don't forget to consider using Report Builder.

Visual Analysis Heat Maps with Activity Map

Let's face it — not all of your stakeholders will be as excited about freeform tables and scatter charts as you are. Plenty of managers, VPs, and execs just want to know "what the data says." Unfortunately, that response often contends with the need we feel as analysts to explain how the data got us to the result we're recommending.

To convey a bit of this explanation without talking segments and calculated metrics, you can use Activity Map. Activity Map is a visual heat map in your browser that overlays the top elements on any page with data. Simply install the plug-in, browse to your company website, and fire up the plug-in for a nice visual representation of your data.

The visuals generated by Activity Map can be useful in meetings where recommendations need to be accompanied by or backed up with graphic representations of data. However, it's best to create screen captures of Activity Map and put them in a slideshow rather than futz around configuring an Activity Map on the fly while trying to make a compelling presentation.

REMEMBER

Activity Map populates four dimensions in Analysis Workspace by default: Activity Map link, region, link by region, and page. Head to Chapter 6 for a thorough review of these dimensions.

To install the plug-in, hover your cursor over Tools in the main Adobe navigation menu and choose Activity Map. If you don't see this link, you may want to speak to your administrator to gain access to the Activity Map feature. Click the blue Download Activity Map button, which downloads the plug-in and prompts you to install it. Adobe supports recent versions of all major browsers: Internet Explorer, Firefox, Chrome, and Safari.

After you've installed the plug-in, browse to your company's website and find the Adobe Analytics logo icon in your browser's toolbar. This icon is associated with Activity Map. Click the icon to log in, most likely with the Experience Cloud login option, and you'll be ready to heat map!

In Figure 16-9, you can see some sample data for the adobe.com website with the Activity Map overlay applied. A dialog with five buttons appears, acting as your remote control for the data.

FIGURE 16-9:
Sample data on adobe.com shown in Activity Map.

The five buttons focus on the following:

>> **Standard versus Live data:** Standard data is similar to the data you've been analyzing in Workspace this book — fully processed data from metrics captured in a specific report time frame. Live data is real-time data that appears in Activity Map for analysis in less than five minutes! Live data

certainly is exciting to watch during major events such as ad campaigns, product launches, and Super Bowl commercials (if your company can afford them).

>> **Metrics:** The majority of your metrics — even calculated metrics — are accessible in standard mode. The only metric available in live mode is link clicks.

>> **Segments:** In standard mode, one or multiple segments can be applied at the same time in Activity Map, just like in Workspace and Report Builder. Unfortunately, one major disadvantage to live data is that it can't be segmented.

>> **Bubbles versus Gradient:** These options are for visualizing your data overlays. We like them both. Figure 16-9 displays gradients.

>> **Date range:** This calendar is similar to the one in Analysis Workspace.

Although Activity Map is mostly self-explanatory, we want to mention a few other details before moving on:

>> You can drag the plug-in's remote control box if it's in your way.

>> Hover your cursor over the eye icon at the top-right of the remote-control box to display Toggle Page Details. Click it to see a table summary of all data points on the current page — rank, link, region, visibility, and the selected metric.

>> Click the gear (Settings) icon to select a different report suite or customize the heat map as you see fit.

Integrating within Adobe Products

As the saying goes, "The more you analyze, the more data you'll crave." Well, that isn't a saying, but maybe it will be now! It's in this vein that we discuss several ways in which data from other products, Adobe and non-Adobe, is shared with Adobe Analytics for a more complete analysis experience. As long as your company owns the product that you want to integrate, the data-sharing features are available at no additional cost. If any of the integrations listed in this section are not set up, talk to your administrator to make that happen today.

The following integrations provide additional context as you analyze as well as Workspace access to the users of these other products. Yes, that's right — soon you'll be teaching users of other products how to use Analysis Workspace!

Each of these integrations is built into Adobe Experience Cloud, so you and your administrator will have a limited amount of work to do if they aren't already set up. Several integrations are bidirectional — data goes to and from Adobe Analytics. For the others, data goes only to Adobe Analytics. Let's dig in!

Dissecting Adobe Audience Manager audiences in Workspace

The next three integrations require access to other Adobe Experience Cloud products. One of the most useful integrations across Adobe products is *Audience Analytics,* which is the integration of Audience Manager and Adobe Analytics. Audience Manager, Adobe's data management platform, is used to integrate multiple datasets and make them available for action.

Integrated datasets can include first-party data (from Adobe Analytics or your customer relationship management system), second-party data (from business partner relationships in which another company is sharing data with yours), and third-party data (from data providers such as Acxiom and Bombora to enhance the profile of your unknown visitors with demographic and psychographic traits).

If those buzzwords and definitions are a little too intense for you, let's consider an example audience that you'd be able to create in Audience Manager: 25-to-34-year-old women who live in the Chicago metro area, have platinum credit cards, and are in the market for a car. Let's dissect each of these traits before considering how that data is shared from Audience Manager to Adobe Analytics:

>> 25-to-34-year-old women: This data could be populated based on a third-party data provider such as Acxiom.

>> Who live in the Chicago metro area: This data could come from your Adobe Analytics report suite's geolocation data (which we describe in Chapter 6).

>> Have platinum credit cards: This data would potentially come from a second-party data source — maybe your company has a relationship with American Express in which data is shared with Audience Manager.

>> Are in the market for a car: This data could come from psychographic data from another third-party data provider.

Regardless of the data source, the important thing to consider here is that any audience that you define in Audience Manager becomes available as a segment that you can apply to your website or app behavioral data in Adobe Analytics for further analysis. The Audience Analytics integration bridges the divide between the datasets that Audience Manager organizes and the powerful visualization and analysis toolset of Analysis Workspace. This integration enables one new dimension in Adobe Analytics called *audiences name.* If you don't see Audience Manager but you know your company owns and uses it, work with your administrator to enable the integration.

Figure 16-10 shows some of the visualizations you can create with the new dimension. Because the audiences name dimension is fully integrated into your dataset, you can use the dimension to create any visualization in Workspace.

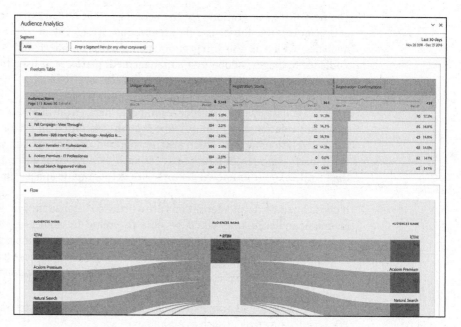

FIGURE 16-10:
A few visualizations based on Audience Analytics data.

Technically, this integration is bidirectional, going from Audience Manager to Analytics and vice versa, because of the segment sharing capability that we discuss in Chapter 9. You can easily create an audience in Audience Manager based on multiple datasets, share it with Analytics for analysis, enrich it with additional metrics and dimensions, and then share it back with Audience Manager for highly targeted advertising and personalization. Adobe considers this process to be a virtuous cycle focused on segmenting, analyzing, enriching, and taking action.

Integrating your tests and personalization

The next integration that we highly recommend is *Analytics for Target,* which integrates the data from Target, Adobe's AI-powered solution for testing and targeting, into Adobe Analytics for deep analysis in Workspace. Analytics for Target is often to referred to colloquially as *A4T*, which you may have heard at the company water cooler. This Target integration also ensures that segments and metrics from Analytics are available in Target, making the feature a tight, bidirectional integration between the solutions.

Adobe has big plans for expanding the scope of this integration soon. In the meantime, we highly recommend taking advantage of the ability to analyze your tests by using metrics and segments from Analytics — it's a huge time-saver and gives your friends who spend all day in Target the ability to analyze further in Workspace. This integration requires only that your company has access to both Analytics and Target, plus a small amount of setup.

Capturing email metrics in Workspace

The third and final integration of another Adobe solution with Adobe Analytics is with *Adobe Campaign,* a marketing automation and email/mobile service platform that focuses on highly customized workflows to drive emails, mobile notifications, and direct mail messages to your known customers. Campaign's *KPI Sharing* integration with Analytics extracts data from Campaign and pushes it into Analytics. The integrated dimensions focus on delivery and campaign labels, whereas the metrics include clicks, opens, bounces, and more. For a complete list, head to Adobe's knowledge base on the subject at `https://helpx.adobe.com/campaign/standard/integrating/using/campaign-dimensions-and-metrics-in-analytics.html`.

Adobe has also built an integration from Analytics to Campaign called *Triggers.* This feature allows you to send personalized emails to your customers as a reaction to specific behaviors tracked on your website by Adobe Analytics. When KPI Sharing is combined with Triggers, a bidirectional integration is created that empowers you to analyze your Campaign data in more detail as well as spark conversation with your customers based on action or inaction. A certain SKU and contract is required to enable these integrations, so work with the administrators of Campaign and Analytics at your company to understand what is possible.

Integrating beyond Individual Products

Adobe Analytics also has a wealth of pre-baked integration points that aren't 1-to-1 — product A integrating with product B. These integration options allow you to import data from non-Adobe data sources or even opt in to a feature that integrates data across more than one hundred Adobe customers.

Analyzing ad data in Adobe

The first integration to discuss is one of our favorites. *Ad Analytics* is focused on importing data from the three top paid search engines — Google, Yahoo, and Bing — into Adobe Analytics. This integration goes in only one direction, from the search engines into Adobe; no data is sent from Adobe to the search engines.

Metrics such as impressions, clicks, cost, average position, and quality score are automatically imported into Adobe Analytics. Imported dimensions include keyword, network, ad, account, campaign, placement, and ad group. If you're unfamiliar with these, check out the thorough review in the Adobe knowledge base at `https://marketing.adobe.com/resources/help/en_US/analytics/advertising/overview.html`.

Besides the fact that this data integration finally brings together advertising and behavioral data in one interface, we love Ad Analytics because Workspace includes a pre-built template for analysis. Note that the template, shown partially in Figure 16-11, works only after you complete the integration with your paid search engines.

The Ad Analytics feature doesn't require access to any other Adobe products but your company must have a current Analytics SKU. If you don't see data associated with this integration in your report suite, work with your administrator to understand whether an update to your report suite's setup or contract is required.

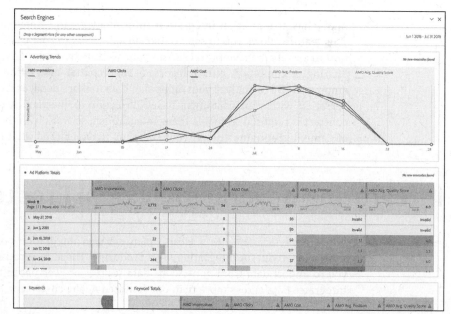

FIGURE 16-11:
The search engines template is shown for use with ad analytics.

Accessing the scale of Experience Cloud

Imagine if your data wasn't constrained to just a single browser on a single device. Most people have several Wi-Fi or cellular-enabled devices that could potentially browse your company's website or app. If each device looks like a different visitor, as is the default in Adobe Analytics, there is no way to truly analyze the full journey of a customer or prospect.

A few years ago, Adobe released Device Co-op so that its customers in North America could access a lower (more detailed) level of granularity in their data: from visitors to people. This feature empowers brands that use Experience Cloud to opt in, at no additional cost, and share generic data about their consumers to other companies in the co-op without violating security or privacy concerns. The reason for doing this? Cross-device analysis! As an Adobe Analytics customer, you can complete a few minimal technical updates to your implementation and quickly gain access to a new metric — people. The people metric helps you understand not just the total number of devices that perform certain actions and behaviors on your site, like the visitors metric does, but the total number of people across devices.

Let's consider how the feature works for companies. Suppose that two Fortune 500 companies, Matisoft and KarlinsCorp, have both joined Device Co-op. You're a loyal customer of Matisoft and have logged in to their website and app on five different devices. Upon login, a hashed/encrypted version of your login ID is sent to Adobe's Device Co-op. Matisoft then has a link between all five devices based on that encrypted ID and can consolidate dimensional values across those devices as a single person by using the people metric.

You then decide to research KarlinsCorp. You browse the KarlinsCorp website on your laptop and mobile phone, without logging in on either device. Because KarlinsCorp is also a part of the Device Co-op, your two devices appear as a single person in Analysis Workspace.

If your company isn't taking part of Device Co-op, they should reconsider. The feature requires some basic setup, a no-fee contract, and a potential update to your privacy policy. Speaking of privacy, Adobe shares only *one* thing from brands to other brands in the co-op — the fact that devices are linked. Data about the person's behavior, location, and even the brand that linked the devices is not shared.

In addition to Adobe Analytics, several other products in Experience Cloud get value from Device Co-op too. Plus, Adobe has hinted at a game-changing analytics feature that would take advantage of Device Co-op called Customer Journey

Analytics. This feature applies device linkage data to more than just the people metric; Customer Journey Analytics injects people-based analysis everywhere in Analysis Workspace. Segmentation, flow, fallout, and more would be accessible at a new, even higher level of granularity — the person. The entire industry is looking forward to this capability and we fully expect Adobe to make a huge splash when Customer Journey Analytics is released.

Connecting data into Adobe Analytics today

Adobe has created several relationships with technical and marketing products over the years. These relationships often result in an opportunity to import and export data by using either the Data Connectors feature (for older integrations) or Experience Cloud Exchange (for newer integrations). One favorite example of an Exchange integration is with Dun & Bradstreet. Dun & Bradstreet curates one of the world's largest commercial databases used to anonymously identify B2B prospects who are visiting your digital property. Importing this data into Adobe Analytics provides an account-based view of your behavioral data that couldn't otherwise be obtained unless the prospects registered and identified the company they work for. Another Exchange integration that we love integrates data from DialogTech, a call center vendor that dynamically inserts toll-free numbers to your website or app, so that behavior that occurs on the phone can be tied to online actions.

These integrations often require a bit of JavaScript, some login/password sharing across companies, and plenty of QA (quality assurance). The Data Connectors and Experience Cloud Exchange features span a variety of marketing and ad technologies, from ad servers to survey companies to search engine optimization platforms. The complete list of categories, as organized in the Data Connectors listing in Adobe Analytics, is shown in Figure 16-12.

To see a complete list of the integrations offered in the Exchange, head to www.adobeexchange.com/experiencecloud.html.

In addition to pre-built integrations with external platforms, Adobe Analytics data can be integrated by using API and FTP. API (application programming interface) is one of the most common ways to push additional data into Adobe Analytics. Adobe can receive bulk data imports through FTP (File Transfer Protocol) by using a feature called Data Sources. Both options require significant custom coding and implementation to work. If you're considering going down this road, work with a seasoned consultant to ensure that everything is set up properly.

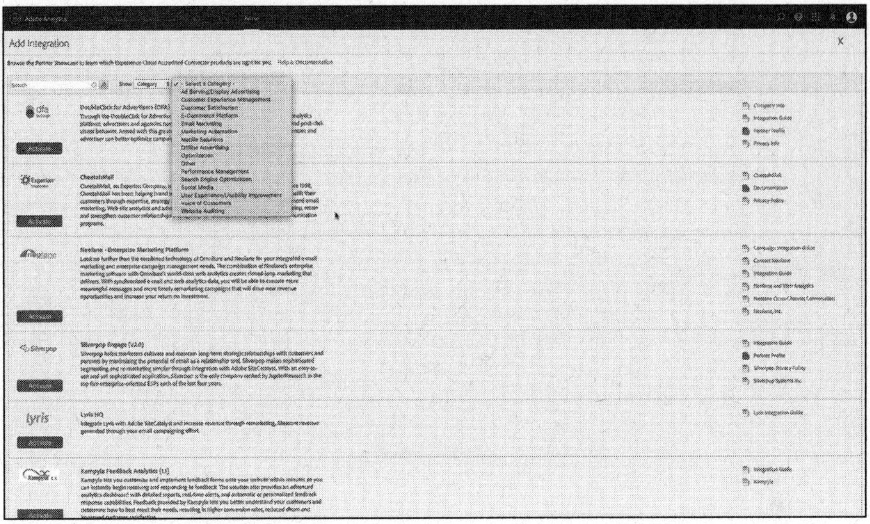

FIGURE 16-12:
The landing page
for creating and
editing Data
Connectors.

Incorporating any dataset in the future

If you haven't been keeping up with Adobe's latest innovations and brand names, Adobe Experience Platform is Adobe's complete revision of how their products work together and access external datasets. The Experience Platform sits on top of Microsoft Azure and allows for each of the Experience Cloud solutions to access the same dataset. Integration is no longer needed because the data is the same whether you're analyzing it in Workspace, personalizing it in Target, or triggering emails in Campaign.

Importing non-Adobe data into Adobe Experience Platform is the other key integration opportunity. Even if you're using non-Adobe technology for some of your digital business, it can be integrated with Adobe data and analyzed in Analysis Workspace. And you'll soon be able to import offline data into Experience Platform too, so that company data that is collected in-store or offline can be calculated, analyzed, and segmented. As of this writing, Adobe Experience Platform is not available, but we expect it to become available later in 2019. Get excited!

5
The Part of Tens

IN THIS PART . . .

Access ten handy recipies for custom-defined segments to track successes and failures in your web presence.

Explore our top ten list of Adobe Analytics resources ranging from essential to fun.

Chapter **17**

Top Ten Custom Segments

Key to making yourself at home in and productive with Adobe Analytics is curating a set of customized segments that you can deploy to zero in on essential elements of site activity.

Your set of customized segments will depend on your environment and the type of analysis you're making. In this chapter, we provide ten of our favorite custom segments. We think you'll find these helpful in their own right, and we hope that they stimulate ideas for custom segments unique to your needs.

As a bonus, our list of top ten custom segments includes how–to instructions for creating them, so consider this a chance to review and build your skills.

As you browse through the top ten custom segments we've curated for you, note that we provide more specific detailed instructions for the first example — identifying purchasers — and focus more on the specific steps for particular segments in the following examples. If you need a refresher on creating segments, start with the first example here. For a deeper excursion into segments, see Chapter 9.

Identifying Purchasers

We start our top-ten set of custom segments by defining a custom segment almost anyone can use: Who's buying stuff?

It's super-valuable in all kinds of reporting to be able to analyze this segment of visitors. After all, these are your success stories, and the easier it is to highlight them in tables, the more you can harvest and exploit data that facilitates *more* sales.

Let's conceptualize our objective before we hit Segment Builder: We want to identify *visitors* for whom an *order exists*. With that criteria clearly in focus, you can define a custom segment to look at data for purchasers by following these steps:

1. **If the Segments component isn't displayed in the left rail, click Components in the left rail selector, as shown in Figure 17-1.**

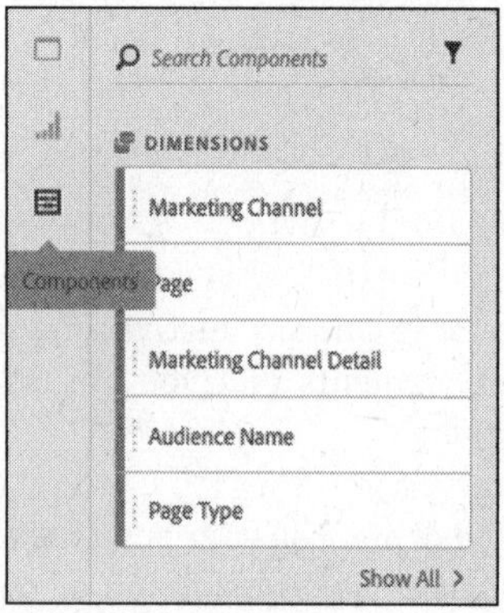

FIGURE 17-1:
Displaying
components.

2. **Launch Segment Builder by clicking the Create Segment (+) icon as shown in Figure 17-2.**

   The Segment Builder panel opens.

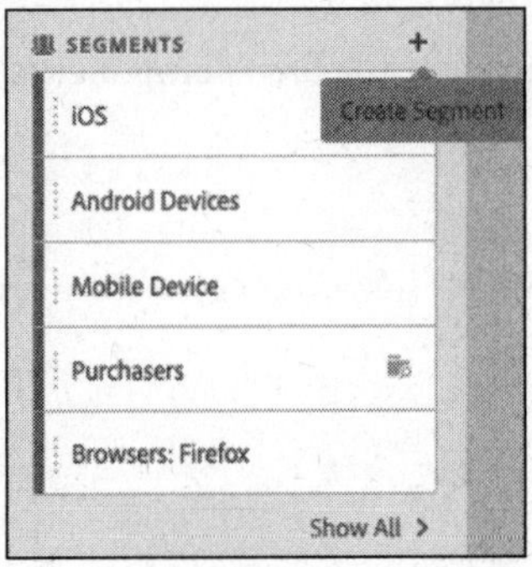

FIGURE 17-2:
Launching
Segment Builder.

3. **Enter a title, a description, and tags for this custom segment, as shown in Figure 17-3.**

    The title is required. The description will remind you and clue in colleagues as to what this custom segment does. Tags will make it easier for you and your colleagues to find this segment later.

FIGURE 17-3:
Titling, describing,
and tagging a
custom segment.

4. **In the Definition section of the Segment Builder, choose Visitor from the Show drop-down list, as shown in Figure 17-4.**

    We select this container type because we're focusing on showing data for visitors who make purchases.

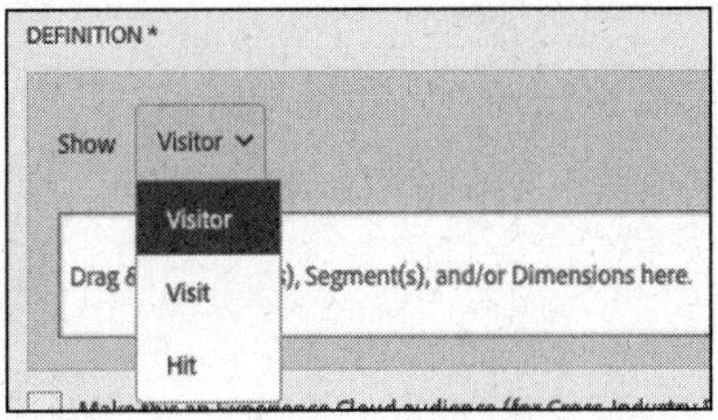

FIGURE 17-4:
Selecting Visitor
from the Show
options in
Segment Builder.

5. **Search for the orders metric using the Search Components box in the left rail, as shown in Figure 17-5.**

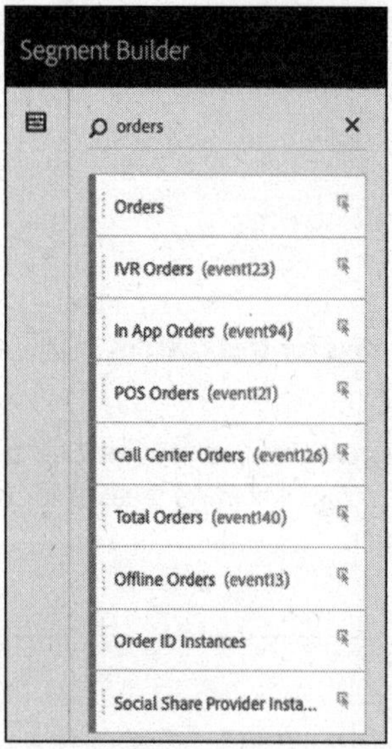

Segment Builder

🔍 orders ✕

Orders	
IVR Orders (event123)	
In App Orders (event94)	
POS Orders (event121)	
Call Center Orders (event126)	
Total Orders (event140)	
Offline Orders (event13)	
Order ID Instances	
Social Share Provider Insta...	

FIGURE 17-5: Locating the orders metric.

6. **Drag orders into the Segment drop zone, as shown in Figure 17-6.**

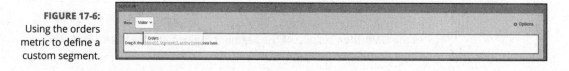

FIGURE 17-6: Using the orders metric to define a custom segment.

7. **Choose Exists from the local operator drop-down list, as shown in Figure 17-7.**

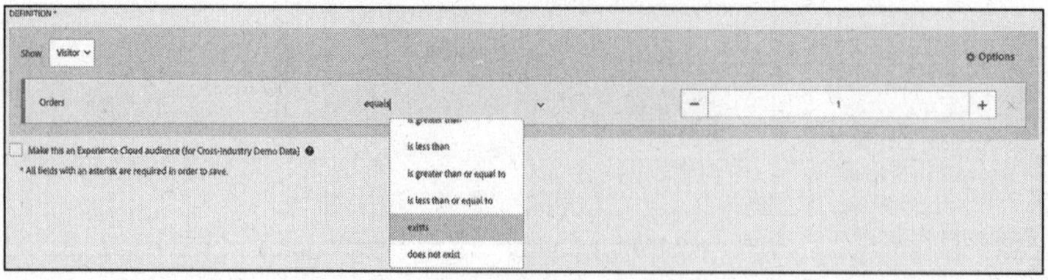

FIGURE 17-7: Defining Exists as the criteria for segmenting purchasing visitors.

8. **With the custom segment defined and titled, click Save.**

You can now apply this segment to any panel, any table, and most visualizations. In Figure 17-8, the custom segment has been applied to a table of various metrics measuring search engine sources.

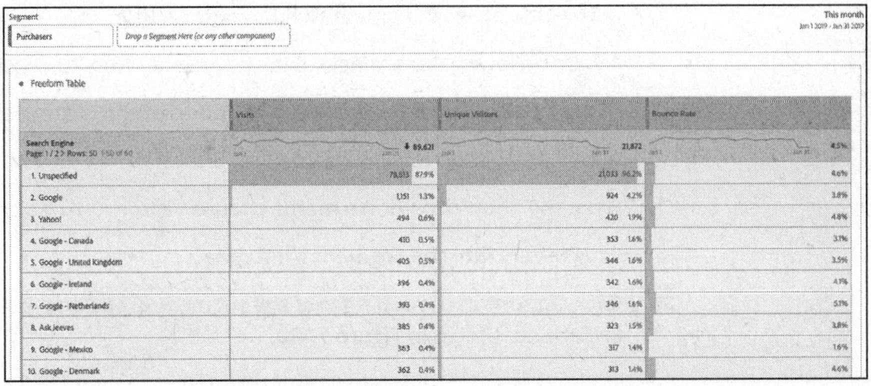

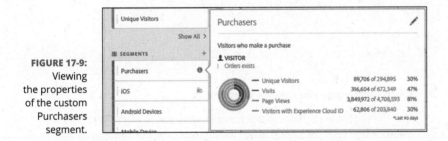

FIGURE 17-8:
Applying the custom segment.

9. **To quickly view the properties of the custom segment, click the *i* icon, as shown in Figure 17-9.**

The properties appear in the top half of the dialog that opens. If you need to edit the custom segment, click the pencil icon.

FIGURE 17-9:
Viewing the properties of the custom Purchasers segment.

Defining a Non-Purchasers Segment

Our first top-ten custom segment identified purchasers. Next, you create a segment to isolate and identify visitors who do not purchase anything.

For this example, we won't step through the process of defining custom segments in general in the same level of detail that we did in the first custom segment. If you need more detailed assistance in defining custom segments, jump back to the first section of this chapter. (For a full-fledged exploration of segments, see Chapter 9.)

Here, we jump right into Segment Builder, and follow these steps to define a non-purchasers segment:

1. **In the Title area of Segment Builder, enter a title.**

   If you're following our example to the letter, enter Non-Purchasers.

2. **In the Description area, enter a description of the custom segment.**

   We entered *Visitors who did not purchase products.*

3. **From the Show drop-down menu, choose Visitor.**

4. **Drag orders into the Segment drop zone.**

5. **Click Options in the top-right of the segment drop zone and choose Exclude, as shown in Figure 17-10.**

   A pink highlight surrounds the segment's Definition drop zone.

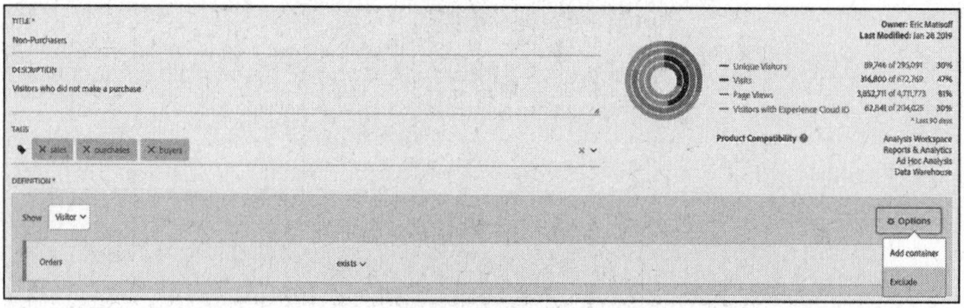

FIGURE 17-10:
Defining a custom segment for visitors who do not make a purchase.

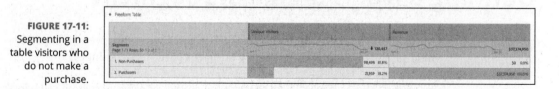

6. **Click Save to save the custom segment.**

   You can apply the segment in any panel or table and in most visualizations. When you or your colleagues hover your cursor over the info icon for this segment, you'll see the segment definition, shown in Figure 17-11.

FIGURE 17-11:
Segmenting in a table visitors who do not make a purchase.

Isolating Single-Page Visitors

"One and done" sometimes refers to star basketball players who put in an obligatory year in college before signing with the NBA. Data analysts, on the other hand, sometimes have to bucket visitors who hit one page and are gone. We find identifying these "one and done" users useful, for example, when analyzing marketing campaigns. What can we identify as a shortcoming in advertising that brought a visitor to our property but wasn't effective enough to get the visitor to view more than one page? We can ask questions about the landing page, campaign name, device type, geolocation, time of day, and more to help optimize our ad budget to limit the number of single-page visitors that we have in the future.

Let's create a custom segment to isolate single-page visitors now.

If you've come directly to this custom segment but need detailed direction to define custom segments, jump back to the first section of this chapter (or, for a full-fledged exploration of segments, see Chapter 9).

Follow these steps to create a custom segment that buckets single-page visitors:

1. **In the Title area of Segment Builder, enter a title.**

   We typed *Single Page Visitors*.

2. **In the Description area, enter a description of the custom segment.**

   We typed *Visitors who only went to one page.*

3. **In the Show drop-down menu, choose Visitor.**

4. **Click the gear (Options) icon on the right and choose Add Container, as shown in Figure 17-12. Then add a second container.**

FIGURE 17-12: Adding a container in Segment Builder.

5. **Change the first container type to Visit, as shown in Figure 17-13.**

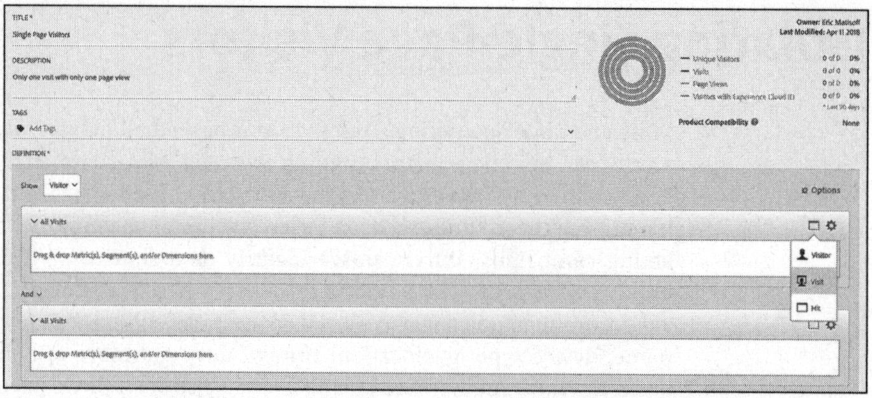

FIGURE 17-13:
Changing a
container setting
to Visit.

6. **Change the second container type to Visitor. Then click the gear icon to the right of the second container and choose Exclude, as shown in Figure 17-14.**

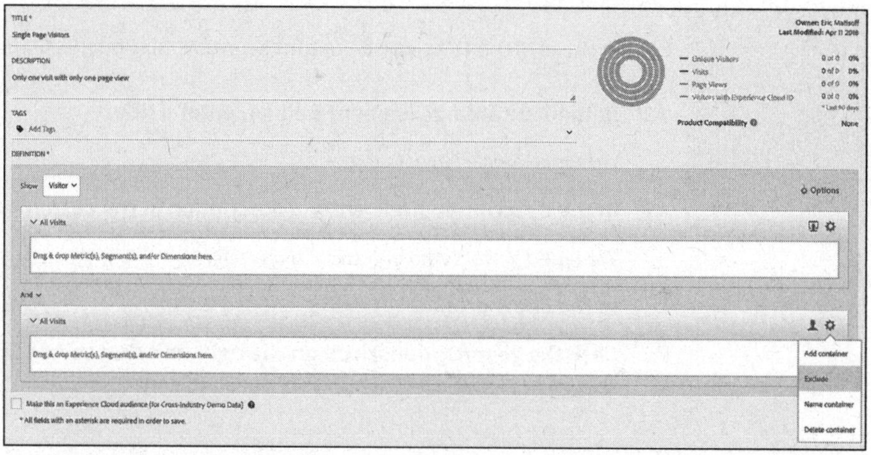

FIGURE 17-14:
Setting the
second container
to an Exclude.

7. **Drag the visit number dimension and then the single-page visits dimension into the first container.**

8. **Drag the visit number dimension into the second container.**

9. **Set the values to each of the three dimensions in your segment definition.**

   In Figure 17-15 we defined Visit Number equal to 1; Single Page Visits equal to Enabled; and Visit Number greater than 1.

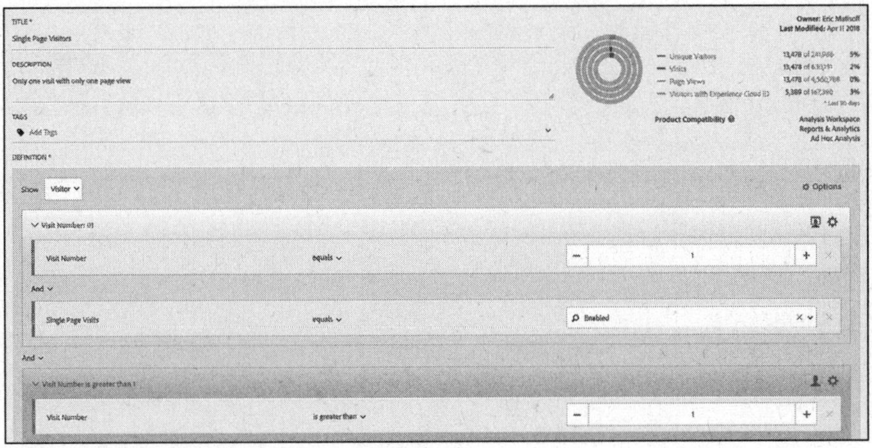

FIGURE 17-15:
The complete definition for a custom single-page visitors segment.

10. **Click Save to save the custom segment.**

You can apply the segment in any panel.

Identifying Single-Visit, Multi-Page Visitors

Now that you're getting more comfortable with the process of creating complex segments, we're going to simplify our instructions even more. We start with the complete definition and then point out any difficult or complex steps along the way.

Here's a segment for identifying visitors who access multiple pages on your site but have visited the site only once. You might find this segment handy when you need to further analyze the success of an ad campaign that has a better bounce rate than expected but isn't creating the type of stickiness that would drive multiple return visits.

For step-by-step instructions on defining custom segments, jump back to the first section of this chapter.

The definition for this segment is almost identical to the preceding segment, single-page visitors. The only difference, as shown in Figure 17-16, is that you set the logical operator for the single-page visits dimension in the first container to Does Not Equal instead of Equals.

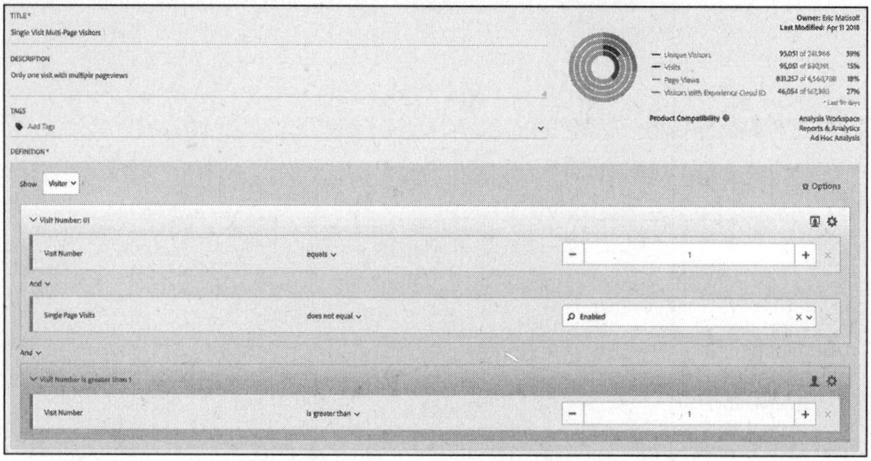

FIGURE 17-16:
The complete definition for a single-visit, multi-page visitors segment.

Bucketing SEO to Internal Search

Here again, we won't describe the entire process of defining custom segments with the level of detail we did for the first few custom segments in this chapter. If you need detailed assistance in defining custom segments, jump back to the first section of this chapter.

Analysts have been trying to identify proxies for natural search keywords ever since Google removed access to them from analytics platforms. One of our favorite ways to solve for the missing data is to analyze internal search term data as a proxy. If a visitor arrives at your site by a natural search and then performs an internal search on your site, chances are good that the keywords are related. We like to use this segment to analyze internal search terms and entry pages to identify opportunities for improved analysis.

Because the internal searches metric is non-standard, your visit-based segment might look slightly different than ours, which is shown in Figure 17-17. The key ingredients remain the same: Marketing Channel Equals Natural Search; and a second container that limits your internal search metric to the second hit in a visit. The hit depth dimension ensures that the internal search occurs immediately after the initial landing page view.

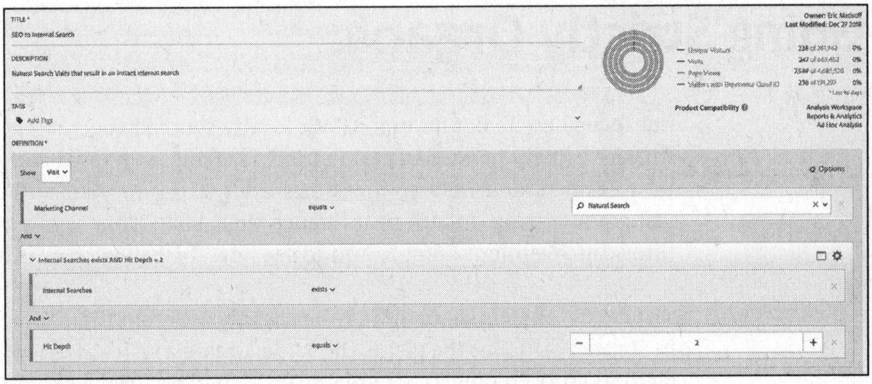

FIGURE 17-17:
The complete definition for this SEO to internal search segment.

Segmenting Pre-Purchase Activity

The next custom segment will help you better understand what happens before a purchaser enters the purchase/cart flow. The insights you derive from this segment will help you better understand the types of activities that often result in purchases.

In this custom segment, you need to know how your website/app and the implementation are set up to define the purchase flow. Find the dimensional value or metric that defines the beginning of the checkout process and set that to the first step in your visit-based container. The second complexity occurs after you've dragged in Orders to the Segment drop zone and changed to a sequential segment by adjusting the logic operator to Then. To focus your analysis on the action before your segment's definition, adjust the sequence type from the default Include Everyone to Only Before Sequence, as shown in Figure 17-18.

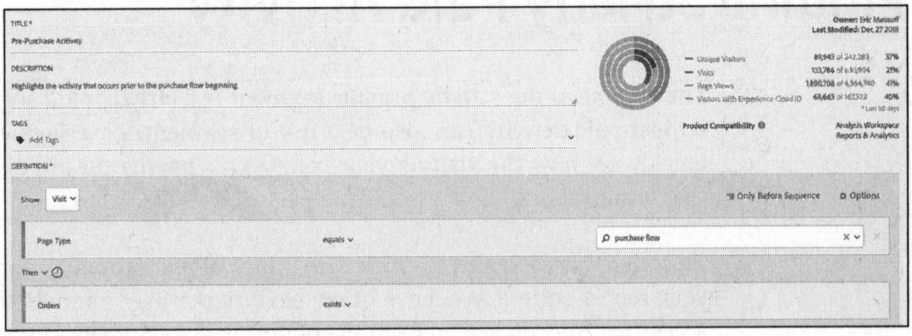

FIGURE 17-18:
The complete definition for this pre-purchase activity segment.

Going Strictly Organic

Our focus here is not on non-GMO, locally sourced vegetables, but on identifying website activity generated from strictly organic, non-paid sources. It can be useful to understand how your visitors are getting to your site naturally, without using advertising dollars to influence their visit. This segment is a great one to throw into Segment Comparison to see how the behavior is different from others.

The details of your segment may be slightly different than ours, which you can see in Figure 17-19. But the gist is the same. Create a visit-based segment that focuses on marketing channels that are unpaid — and be sure to set an Or logical operator between them.

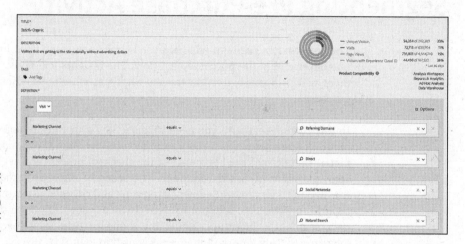

Finding Strictly Paid Activity

The inverse to the strictly organic segment is a strictly paid segment. Zooming in on just paid activity can also be a useful segment for a Segment Comparison to quickly see how the visitors your company is paying for are different from those that occur naturally.

This visit-based segment, with the Or logical operator again, may be different in your report suite if you have other paid marketing channels that we don't have access to. You can see an example of defining a segment for strictly paid activity in Figure 17-20.

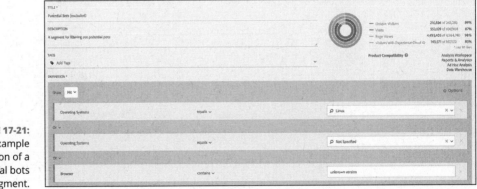

FIGURE 17-20:
An example definition of a strictly paid segment.

Filtering Out Potential Bots

If Shakespeare were writing today, instead of "out damn'd spot," Lady Macbeth might have the said "Out damn'd bot!" Okay, maybe not. But for a data analysts, identifying and removing bots from traffic data is essential to working with valid data. With that in mind, here's a recipe for a custom segment that can isolate potential bots.

The definition of this potential bots segment was provided by Adobe based on significant research into bot activity. Weeding out unknown operating systems or browsers and Linux servers allows you remove a significant amount of bot traffic from report suites. The only advanced concept is to make sure you have applied an exclusion to the entire segment by clicking Options, Exclude in the Segment drop zone. Defining all three criteria as exclusions will shade the entire drop zone red, as shown in Figure 17-21.

FIGURE 17-21:
An example definition of a potential bots segment.

Identifying Checkout Fallout

In Chapter 14, we explore the value of visualizing flow (the pathway to a success event) and fallout (points where visitors drop out of the path to a success event).

Here, we provide a blueprint for creating a custom segment to assist in identifying checkout fallout, specifically visitors who access the checkout page but don't convert. Here we are identifying activity where the visitor got all the way to the checkout page but didn't click the Buy button.

We've found this segment, shown in Figure 17-22, useful for identifying common causes for cart abandonment. Plus, it's a fantastic segment to share to the rest of Experience Cloud to remarket and try to reignite the purchase process for these visitors.

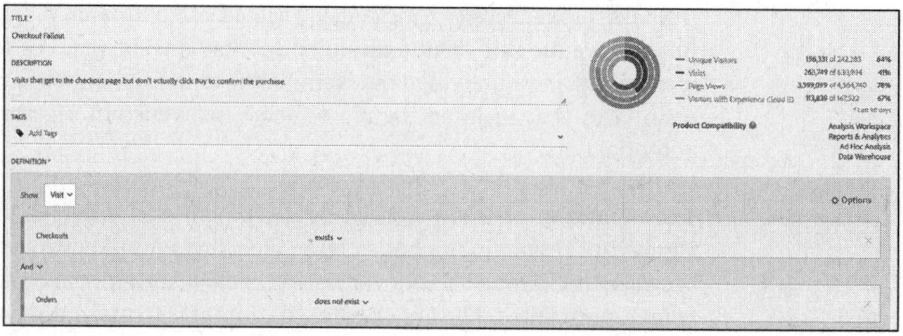

FIGURE 17-22: Defining a segment for visitors who begin to checkout but don't purchase.

IN THIS CHAPTER

» Checking out Adobe's *Analytics Implementation Guide*

» Understanding why you need a measurement plan

» Using data governance

» Setting up your web analytics solution design

» Listening in on the Digital Analytics Power Hour

» Getting insights from analytics agencies

» Going to conferences, conferences, conferences

» Joining the Adobe Experience League

» Learning the latest from the Adobe Analytics YouTube channel

» Hacking the bracket with Adobe Analytics

Chapter **18**

Top Ten Analytics Resources

Where do you go for resources to expand your command of Adobe Analytics beyond this book? In this chapter, we compile a set of our favorites. Some are official Adobe sites, with real-time updated documentation. Others are more generic resources for data analytics. And at least one of them is in here mainly for those who, to quote Sheryl Crow, "want to have a little fun."

Checking Out Adobe's *Analytics Implementation Guide*

You might be too young to remember, but people used to buy software apps from stores, and the apps came with a book documenting how to use the app. Adobe's *Analytics Implementation Guide* plays that role. This soup-to-nuts set of resources from Adobe provides a macro guide and a micro guide to the tasks you need to complete to implement Analytics. Go to `https://helpx.adobe.com/analytics/kb/analytics-standard-implementation-guide.html`.

Much of the material in the *Analytics Implementation Guide* is presented as downloadable PDFs. Those PDFs are supplemented with a wide range of video tutorials, as shown in Figure 18-1.

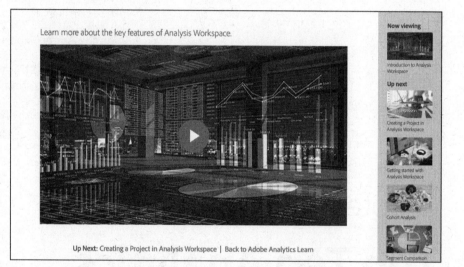

FIGURE 18-1:
The first in a series of video tutorials from Adobe introduces key features of Analytics Workspace.

To provide a menu of sorts as to what you 'll find in the *Implementation Guide*, we've curated a set of key topics. We suggest that you visit the site, bookmark it, and note available white papers, documentation, and videos. You'll want to keep this site handy as you engage in deeper levels of Adobe Analytics.

Topics include the following:

>> **Discovery and requirements:** How to define your analytics goals and gather requirements for the implementation, starting with developing and documenting an objective understanding of the website and its business goals. During this phase, your consultant or partner gathers measurement requirements.

TIP

What Adobe calls "gather[ing] measurement requirements" is synonymous with what are often called creating a business requirements document (BRD). This document maps the goals of a website or app to the overall business goal of the enterprise, and suggests industry best practices.

>> **Installation and provisioning:** How to set up Adobe Analytics and get an email with login credentials.

>> **Configuration and implementation:** What you need to have in place before launching Analytics, including documenting a solution design reference document and a tech spec. The solution design reference document contains an overview of the website data layer, launch elements/rules, and Adobe Analytics variables. The tech spec is detailed documentation on how to implement each component of the solutions and how to validate them.

>> **Post implementation:** In this phase of unrolling Analytics, you work with a consultant or partner to identify data accessible through Adobe Analytics, and brainstorm how to use that data to optimize your digital business. This phase also includes enabling various time-saving features of Adobe Analytics, such as Report Scheduler, Workspace, and Microsoft Report Builder. (Report Builder is a Windows-only plug-in.)

>> **Implementation resources:** Here you find links to three comprehensive additional resources and documentation for Adobe Analytics. Those resources follow:

- The *Analytics Implementation Guide* (a downloadable PDF)
- Analytics Implementation Training (training resources for your team)
- Analytics Video Learning (a library of helpful videos)

Understanding Why You Need a Measurement Plan

We emphasize measurement plans in this top-ten list because they are the foundation on which successful analytics frameworks are built. The article "How to Create a Measurement Plan and Why You Really Need One" is a useful discussion of measurement plans. And, as the title implies, it also provides specific tools for building a measurement plan. Read it at www.freshegg.co.uk/blog/analytics/performance-measurement/how-to-create-a-measurement-plan-and-why-you-really-need-one.

Those tools include a nicely formatted and thoughtfully designed Excel spreadsheet that serves as a template (and model) for a measurement plan, including creating an integrated strategy with a website measurement plan based on identified goals. Figure 18-2 shows the template spreadsheet that comes with the article, as hosted at the UK-based freshegg site (thus the British spelling of *Organisation*).

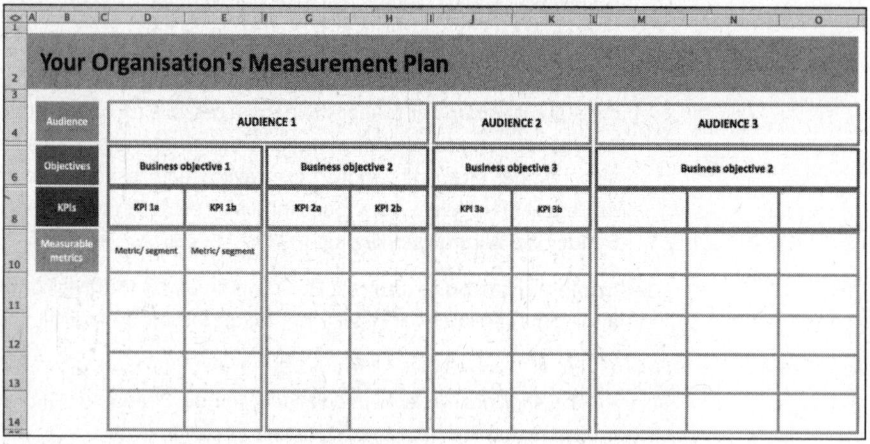

FIGURE 18-2:
A model and a template spreadsheet for a measurement plan and an evaluation plan.

Using Data Governance

The article "Data Governance: The Key to Building Consistent, Outstanding Digital Experiences," by Eric, identifies the conundrum that "more often than not, marketers have more data than they know what to do with — and that just might be their biggest problem." The article draws on real-world experiences at Southwest

Airlines and Zebra Technologies Corporation (which acquired Motorola) — as shown in Figure 18-3. Read the article at `https://theblog.adobe.com/data-governance-key-building-consistent-outstanding-digital-experiences/`.

The article and case study provide a concise argument for the following themes that run throughout this book:

>> Keep analytics at the center of your data governance

>> Invest in products, definition, and processes

>> Train your team for success

>> Pay the price for better digital experiences

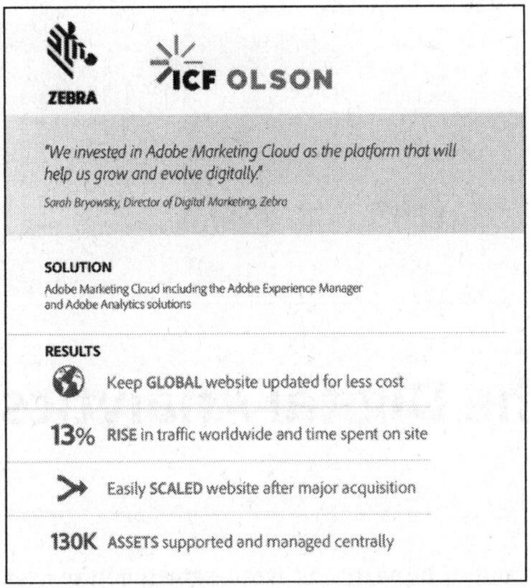

FIGURE 18-3: A summary of implementing Adobe Analytics to manage integrating acquisitions and rescaling their online presence.

Setting Up a Web Analytics Solution Design

A *solution design or solution design reference (SDR)* connects the business requirements and goals defined in a measurement plan with the technical requirements necessary to successfully deploy analytics technology. The article "7 Steps to Set

Up Your Web Analytics Solution Design" identifies and walks through seven strategic steps to developing an effective solution design to protect the integrity of your web analytics implementation. See the article at www.observepoint.com/blog/7-steps-solution-design-data-governance/.

Also at this link is access to a half-hour webinar featuring Jason Call, senior data analytic expert at ObservePoint, as shown in Figure 18-4.

FIGURE 18-4: A high-level exploration of SDR concepts.

Listening In on the Digital Analytics Power Hour

One of the most thorough, honest, and irreverent mediums for staying on top of the industry is via podcast. The three hosts of the Digital Analytics Power Hour — Michael Helbling, Tim Wilson, and Moe Kiss — provide their explicit feelings on a wide variety of analytics topics. The hosts often invite other people in the industry to ensure that multiple opinions are represented and new technologies and ways of thought are discussed. Figure 18-5 provides the podcast's raison d'etre, as shown on the podcast website (https://analyticshour.io).

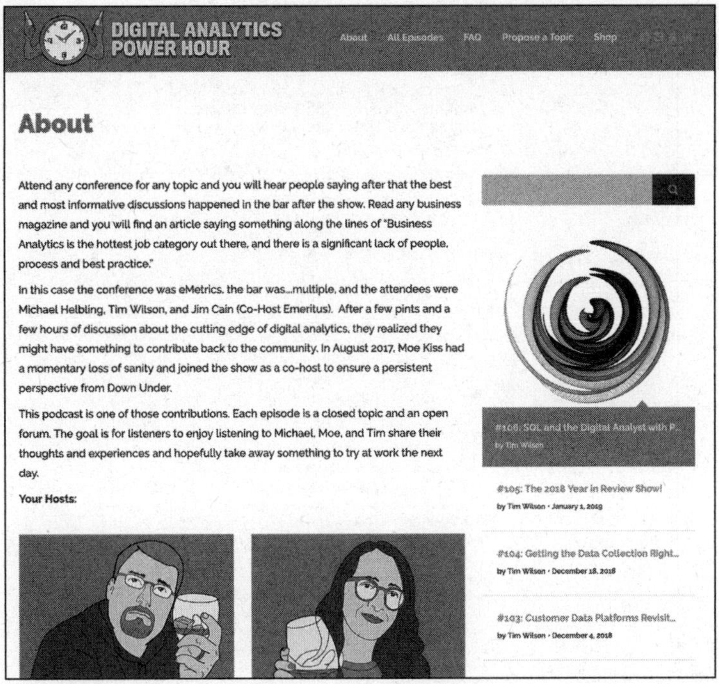

FIGURE 18-5:
About the DAPH
podcast.

Getting Insights from Analytics Agencies

The analytics agency world is chock full of smart and successful consultants. We couldn't possibly link to all of their content, but we do want to call out a few resources that are especially valuable to the growing Adobe Analytics analyst.

The team at 33 Sticks shares a unique set of insights and experiences working with customers to implement digital analytics. Check out the blog articles and 33 Tangents podcasts episodes (`https://33sticks.com/category/blog/`), shown in Figure 18-6. The content addresses a wide range of topics from digital analytics to business and technology to remote work.

The masters at Analytics Demystified have been writing content about Adobe Analytics for more than 10 years. We highly recommend spending some time on their blog (`https://analyticsdemystified.com/blog/`) to learn about real-world applications of Adobe technology and how-to's. Adam Greco's content is especially valuable to both new and seasoned analysts.

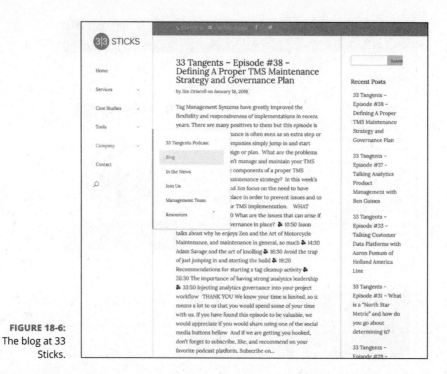

FIGURE 18-6:
The blog at 33
Sticks.

Attending Conferences, Conferences, Conferences

Analytics enthusiasts are a tight-knit group of people who love to share and learn from each other. There is no better way to learn more about analytics, Adobe, and data industry trends than by attending and networking at analytics conferences. Some of our favorite industry events include the following:

>> **Adobe SUMMIT:** Adobe's annual multiday conferences in Las Vegas, Nevada and London are worth every penny. These can't-miss events are the preferred way for thousands of digital marketers and analysts to learn about Adobe's vision, new features, and best practices. The thousands of attendees include successful business leaders, celebrities, and a who's-who of the analytics industry — new friends and selfies encouraged! The home page for the 2019 SUMMIT conference in Las Vegas is shown in Figure 18-7. Visit https://summit.adobe.com.

>> **Adobe Insider Tour:** In addition to SUMMIT, Adobe hit the road for the first time in 2017 and the feedback has been impressively positive. These fun, free, half-day events bring members of the Adobe Analytics product team to cities around the world (from Chicago and Dallas to London and Sydney) to spread

tips and tricks with Adobe solutions, provide a glimpse into the Adobe roadmap, and give Adobe partners and customers the chance to present. If the tour is coming to your city, you'll be glad you took the time to enjoy the festivities. Sign up as an Adobe Insider to be informed of upcoming events at `https://adobe.ly/aainsider`.

>> **DA Hub and Measure Camp:** Two of our favorite vendor-agnostic events are known as unconferences. An *unconference* aims to avoid the large keynotes, huge breakout sessions, and generic conversations that some larger conferences are known for. Instead, the unconference focuses on small *huddles* — group conversations — and a more tight-knit group of attendees. Attendees of these unconferences are a highly loyal group that you will want to meet and discuss analytics with. Information about the upcoming DA Hub can be accessed at `www.digitalanalyticshub.com` and regional Measure Camp information can be found at `https://measurecamp.org/`.

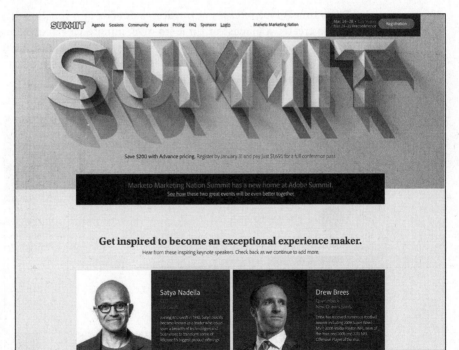

FIGURE 18-7: The 2019 SUMMIT conference home page.

Joining the Adobe Experience League

Adobe's Experience League (`http://experienceleague.adobe.com`) is a repository of valuable information about Adobe Experience Cloud products. On this site,

Adobe provides videos, tutorials, and a community forum. If you log in with your Adobe ID, you'll receive a tailored experience based on content you've previously viewed and the features you use in Adobe products.

Learning the Latest from the Adobe Analytics YouTube channel

The Adobe Analytics YouTube channel (https://adobe.ly/aayoutube) is one of the best ways to stay on top of new features and the latest best practices. The Adobe product team manages the content here, and you may even recognize the name of one of the common presenters — one of your two favorite analytics authors, Eric Matisoff!

Every time Adobe releases new features or adds new functionality to old features, Adobe creates a playlist of three-to-five-minute videos explaining the changes. Over 10,000 subscribers regularly watch the 180+ videos that are to-the-point and easily accessible thanks to the well-organized YouTube playlists that Adobe has created. See Figure 18-8. Subscribe today!

FIGURE 18-8: Comparing more than one segment in a report.

Hacking the Bracket with Adobe Analytics

In Chapter 1 you see how much we enjoy drawing on sports to understand and apply analytics. The fun, interactive site Hack the Bracket (`http://explore adobe.com/hack-the-bracket/`) draws on data processed by Adobe Analytics to predict the outcome of NCAA basketball championship matchups. The campaign web page is shown in Figure 18-9.

FIGURE 18-9:
Playing Hack the
Bracket with
Adobe Analytics.

Sound like fun? Try it! Of course, Adobe does not make any warranties about the completeness, reliability, and accuracy of the predictions, and any action you take on the predictions provided is strictly at your own risk.

Index

Q

quarter of year, 142
query string parameters,
   127–128, 130

R

referrer dimensions, 121–123
registrations, 104
regular expressions, 229
reloads, counting, 97
Report Builder plug-in
   creating reports with, 328–332
   description of, 46
   virtual report suites and, 188
report suites, 41–44, 176, 221
   curating via, 188–189
   identifying, 187–188
   redefining visits with context-
      aware sessions, 189–190
   removing bot traffic in, 357
   reporting on with Report
      Builder, 329
reports
   building with freeform tables
   data, sorting and filtering,
      75–78
   dimensions, 68–72
   metrics, 73–74
   overview, 67
   Segment drop zone, 78–80
   templates, 81–85
   difference between analysis
      and, 10–11
   difference between report
      suites and, 41
Reports and Analytics
   interface, 47
responsive design, 14
return frequency dimension,
   146–147
return metric, 291
revenue per visit metric, 196
Rolling Calculations option, 292

rows of data
   creating charts from multiple,
      267–269
   creating charts from single,
      266–267
Rule Builder, automating
   classifications with,
   228–234
rule set, 230

S

scatter charts, 253
scatterplots, 265–266
scheduling feature, 325
SDK (software development kit),
   14–15
SDR (solution design reference),
   17, 112, 363–364
search engine marketing
   (SEM), 126
search engine optimization
   (SEO), 126
search engines
   Bing, 338
   data from, 128–130
   Google
      analyzing internal search
         term data as proxy, 354
      importing data for Ad
         Analytics from, 338
   natural, 130
   overview, 126–127
   paid search dimension, 128
   paid search visits, detecting,
      127–128
   search keyword analysis, 130
   visits from, 99
   Yahoo, importing data for Ad
      Analytics from, 338
search keyword analysis, 130
searches metric, 99
seasonal variation, 307
second metric, 73–74
Segment Builder, 181

adding segment containers in,
   351–352
creating alerts and, 326
defining custom segments
   with, 346–349
Segment Comparison, 54,
   314–319
   cases for using, 318–319
   comparing segments with,
      315–318
   identifying organic website
      activity with, 356
segment containers
   adding in Segment Builder,
      351–352
   for calculated metrics, 203–204
   distinguishing
      factoring in calendars,
         180–181
      hit-based, 178–179
      visit-based, 179–180
      visitor-based, 180
   identifying, 177–178
   setting, 181–187
      describing and categorizing,
         183–184
      in freeform tables, 185
      sharing between users and
         Adobe solutions, 185–187
Segment drop zone, 78–80
Segment Overlap, 24
segments, 175–190
   adding to panels, 60
   applying classifications to, 218
   applying to filters for
      alerts, 326
   applying to flow visualizations,
      281, 285
   approved, 184
   calculated metrics and,
      194–195
   comparing with Segment
      Comparison, 315–318
   for creating derived metrics,
      204–206

About the Authors

David Karlins analyzes, writes about, teaches, and implements evolving developments in digital communication design and technology. His forty books on digital graphic and interactive design include *HTML5 and CSS3 For Dummies* and *Building Websites All-in-One For Dummies* (co-author).

Eric Matisoff, global evangelist for analytics and data science at Adobe, conveys the vision of Adobe Experience Cloud in meeting rooms and on conference stages. He has been an Adobe Analytics analyst, consultant, and trainer since 2007, but this is his first book. Eric currently lives in New York City with his wife and son, with a daughter on the way!

Dedications

To all our readers, thanks and stay in touch.

— David Karlins

To my incredible wife and son, Heidi and Nolan — I love them more than all the eVars in all the world.

— Eric Matisoff

Authors' Acknowledgments

Thanks to the universe of friends, colleagues, and cohorts who have shared insights into communication design over the years; to Eric Matisoff for his indefatigable enthusiasm and expertise; to our agent, Margot Hutchinson, who convinced me to embark on this adventure; and to Steven Hayes at Wiley who reached out to us with this exciting project.

— David Karlins

I have to start by thanking my incredible and incredibly supportive family. Thank you Heidi, Nolan, baby Matisoff, Mom, Dad, Jeff, Lauren, and Tatiana. Big thanks to Greg Papania too for sharing your writing experience with me. I love you all!

Next goes a huge thanks to my great Adobe family. Thanks to Ben Gaines — without you we wouldn't have Workspace and we would have a significantly less useful and accurate book. Thanks to Jeff Allen for introducing me to the good folks at Wiley for the opportunity to write this. And a big thanks to my awesome manager, Marc Eaman, and also to Jen Lasser, Workspace product manager extraordinaire.

Thanks to Dave Karlins, my co-author in crime. I had a blast writing this with you — thanks for all the great advice and support along the way.

Finally, thanks to Margot Hutchinson, our agent, and Steven Hayes at Wiley. I truly appreciate your help and support to make this project happen!

— Eric Matisoff

Publisher's Acknowledgments

Executive Editor: Steve Hayes
Project Editor: Susan Pink
Copy Editor: Susan Pink
Technical Editor: Ben Gaines

Editorial Assistant: Matt Lowe
Sr. Editorial Assistant: Cherie Case
Production Editor: Vasanth Koilraj
Cover Image: © alphaspirit/Shutterstock